Words Their Way

Word Study for Phonics, Vocabulary, and Spelling Instruction

Second Edition

Donald R. Bear
University of Nevada, Reno

Marcia Invernizzi
University of Virginia

Shane Templeton
University of Nevada, Reno

Francine Johnston
University of North Carolina at Greensboro

Merrill
an imprint of Prentice Hall

Upper Saddle River, New Jersey   Columbus, Ohio

Library of Congress Cataloging-in-Publication Data

Words their way : word study for phonics, vocabulary, and spelling
    instruction / Donald R. Bear . . . [et al.].—2nd ed.
        p.   cm.
    Includes bibliographical references and index.
    ISBN 0-13-021339-X
    1. Word recognition.   2. Reading—Phonetic method.   3. English
language—Orthography and spelling.   I. Bear, Donald R.
LB1050.44.B43   2000
372.46′2—dc21   99-31421
                                                                              CIP

Cover Photo: Anthony Magnacca
Editor: Bradley J. Potthoff
Developmental Editor: Hope Madden
Editorial Assistant: Mary Evangelista
Production Editor: Mary M. Irvin
Production Management and Editorial Supervision: Larry Goldberg,
    Carlisle Publishers Services
Design Coordinator: Diane C. Lorenzo
Cover Design: Rod Harris
Text Design: Carlisle Communications, Ltd.
Illustrations: Francine Johnston
Production Manager: Pamela D. Bennett
Director of Marketing: Kevin Flanagan
Marketing Manager: Meghan Shepherd
Marketing Coordinator: Krista Groshong

This book was set in Palatino by Carlisle Communications, Ltd. and was printed and
bound by Courier/Kendallville. The cover was printed by Phoenix Color Corp.

Printed in the United States of America

Photo credits: Donald R. Bear, pp. 1, 24, 91, 138, 172, 210, 220, 278. Virginia Coffey, p. 58.
Marcia Invernizzi, p. 249. Anthony Magnacca/Merrill, pp. 6, 12, 31, 47, 83, 111, 182, 242.

10 9 8 7 6 5 4 3

ISBN: 0-13-021339-X

Prentice-Hall International (UK) Limited, *London*
Prentice-Hall of Australia Pty. Limited, *Sydney*
Prentice-Hall of Canada, Inc., *Toronto*
Prentice-Hall Hispanoamericana, S. A., *Mexico*
Prentice-Hall of India Private Limited, *New Delhi*
Prentice-Hall of Japan, Inc., *Tokyo*
Prentice-Hall (Singapore) Pte. Ltd., *Singapore*
Editora Prentice-Hall do Brasil, Ltda., *Rio de Janeiro*

This book is dedicated to our families and friends.

Donald R. Bear
Marcia Invernizzi
Shane Templeton
Francine Johnston

About the Authors

Donald Bear (right)

Donald Bear is director of the E. L. Cord Foundation Center for Learning and Literacy at the University of Nevada, Reno. As a preschool, third grade, and fourth grade teacher, he extends his experience by working in the center with children who have difficulties learning to read and write. Reading Buddies is a literacy program that takes word study and literacy practices used in the center and translates them into schoolwide tutoring programs. He and his colleagues conduct word study workshops and consult with many school districts to develop their literacy programs. Donald can be reached through www.unr.edu/cll or www.surf.to/wordstudy.

Shane Templeton (left)

Shane Templeton is foundation professor of curriculum and instruction at the University of Nevada, Reno, where he is program coordinator for literacy studies and teaches undergraduate and graduate reading/language arts courses. He has taught first and second grades, and English at the secondary level. His research focuses on the development of orthographic knowledge. He has written several books on the teaching and learning of reading and the language arts and is a member of the usage panel of the American Heritage Dictionary. Shane can be contacted through www.unr.edu/cll.

Marcia Invernizzi (left)

Marcia Invernizzi is an associate professor of reading education at the Curry School of Education at the University of Virginia. Marcia is also the director of the McGuffey Reading Center, where she teaches the clinical practica in reading diagnosis and remedial reading. Formerly an English and reading teacher, Marcia continues to extend her experience through her work with Book Buddies, Virginia's early intervention reading initiative, and the Center for the Improvement of Early Reading Achievement (CIERA). Contact Marcia through www.ciera.org.

Francine Johnston (right)

Francine Johnston is a former elementary teacher who learned about word study during her graduate work at the University of Virginia. She is now an assistant professor of literacy education at the University of North Carolina at Greensboro, where she also works with classroom teachers as a consultant and researcher. She is currently investigating the changing beliefs and practices teachers bring to phonics and spelling instruction.

PREFACE

Words Their Way: Word Study for Phonics, Vocabulary, and Spelling Instruction provides a practical way to study words with students. Based on the research on invented and developmental spelling, the framework of this text is keyed to the five stages of spelling or orthographic development. Ordered in this developmental format, *Words Their Way* complements the use of any existing phonics, spelling, and vocabulary curricula.

TEXT ORGANIZATION

The organization of the text and of each chapter is straightforward. The first three chapters present an overview of how words are learned, a discussion of development, and methods for assessment and for getting started. Chapter 4 outlines fundamental practices in word sorting and makes a clear presentation of how to organize word study in a classroom curriculum.

The remainder of the text, Chapters 5 through 9, focuses on particular stages of literacy development. A description of each stage and word study appropriate for that stage is followed by a series of games and activities that best complements the stage of development. The organization of this text should facilitate using it in some different ways. To explore the nature of word study and the type of classroom organization and environment that enhances implementation of word study, we suggest you begin reading this text at the beginning—with Chapter 1. If, on the other hand, you want to jump right in and explore word study activities with your students, we recommend that you skim Chapters 4 through 9, look for activities related to the developmental levels of your students, and examine a few closely. Then try one or two out with a small group of students.

As you look more carefully through activities designed for more advanced readers, you may find yourselves and your students getting as involved as we did. The more you learn about words—what they mean, how they are structured, and how they are used—the more your interest is piqued and the more you can demonstrate just how fascinating words are in their meaning, history, usage, and connotation.

TEXT FEATURES

One of the unique features of this text is the description of more than 300 word study activities. These activities are set up to follow literacy development from emergent to more advanced. Often presented in a game-like format, these activities are actually minilessons that draw upon what students concurrently are learning in developmental reading and writing. In each activity, students examine words and their patterns and reflect on how words are organized, how they are spelled, and what they mean. We have included activities that are especially interesting to students and can easily be integrated into the many contexts in which reading and writing activities occur.

Throughout the activity sections in this text, we have labeled some activities with a generic 📖 symbol to indicate that they can be adapted to any other developmental level. For example, the game Concentration is easy to adapt for students' developmental levels by changing the words and patterns students examine.

NEW IN THIS EDITION

We hope you will be pleased to see a more explicit scope and sequence of word study instruction for each developmental stage. Word sorts receive greater emphasis as a regular part of classroom instruction.

The discussion of classroom organization in Chapter 4 has been expanded to include more ideas for organizing instruction. The processes of sorting words and using word study notebooks are described in more detail. In this second edition, the last two stages, the syllables and affixes stage and the derivational relations stage, are placed in separate chapters (Chapters 8 and 9), with greater attention given to each stage.

We have added more games, assessments, word lists, and sorts. The appendix contains all of the reproducible materials in one place. It begins with the various assessment materials that were presented in Chapter 3. The pictures for sorting, game templates, sorts, and word lists are also conveniently collected in the appendix. A detailed contents can be found on page 287.

These word lists are used in small-group, partner, and individual sorts as well as with the games and activities included in Chapters 4 through 9. The sorts are presented developmentally by features. Pick and choose words from the many word lists to make sorts and to use in games.

A section containing developmentally appropriate activities concludes Chapters 5 through 9. These sections are tabbed in blue for easy location.

An instructional video to accompany *Words Their Way* presents classrooms in action to show how teachers use our approach and activities to organize their classrooms for study and to conduct word study lessons. Individuals may purchase this video (ISBN 0-13-022183-x) through their local bookstore or directly from the publisher at 1-800-374-1200. College instructors who adopt *Words Their Way* for their classes may request a complimentary copy of the video from their Prentice Hall representative.

ACKNOWLEDGMENTS

Words Their Way: Word Study for Phonics, Vocabulary, and Spelling Instruction is a community undertaking. Many of the activities are credited to our students and colleagues. Edmund Henderson, our mentor at the University of Virginia's McGuffey Reading Center, was the first person to show us a number of these activities. Surely, many of these activities go back to Ed's training with Russell Stauffer at the University of Delaware. Many of the activities and ideas for word sorts come from our own experiences with university students and classroom teachers. We appreciate all of this collaboration to create a rich word study resource for you.

In addition, we gratefully acknowledge those colleagues and peers whose reviews throughout the developmental process helped us refine our work. They are Anne Hall, University of South Florida; Patricia P. Kelly, Virginia Tech; Beverly Otto, Northeastern Illinois University; Mary C. Shake, University of Kentucky; Terry Piper, Memorial University of Newfoundland; Ruth Beeker, University of Arizona; Edward W. Holmes,

Towson State University; Eilene K. Glasgow, Pacific Lutheran University; and Melba M. Hutsell, St. Mary's University. We are grateful to the reviewers of this second edition for their helpful comments and suggestions. Phyllis Y. Coulter, Eastern Mennonite University; R. Malt Joshi, Oklahoma State University; Marilyn McKinney, University of Nevada at Las Vegas; and I. LaVerne Raine, Texas A&M University–Commerce. We also thank our colleagues and our students at the University of Nevada, Reno; the University of Virginia; and the University of North Carolina at Greensboro. We offer you our sincere appreciation.

Through valuable feedback from many teachers about the first edition we have learned more about words and how children learn about word study. Through your sharing, ideas, and questions you have helped us to present word study ideas and materials that teachers use in their teaching.

Wishing you great success in your word study, we are

Sincerely yours,

Donald R. Bear
Marcia Invernizzi
Shane Templeton
Francine Johnston

CONTENTS

ACTIVITIES

CHAPTER 7

Activities for Students in the Within Word Pattern Stage   198

CHAPTER 8

Activities for Students in the Syllables and Affixes Stage   229

CHAPTER 1

Why Word Study?

Literacy is like a braid of interwoven threads. The braid begins with the intertwining threads of oral language and stories as shown in Figure 1-1. As children experiment with putting ideas on paper, a writing thread is intertwined as well. As they move into reading, the threads of literacy begin to bond. Students' growing knowledge of spelling or **orthography**—the correct sequences of letters in the writing system—strengthens that bonding. The size of the threads and the braid itself become thicker as orthographic knowledge grows.

During the primary years, word knowledge is fundamentally **aural**. From the oral language that surrounds them—world experiences and stories—children develop a rich speaking vocabulary. As children have opportunities to talk about and to categorize their everyday experiences, they begin to elaborate what they know and to expand their oral vocabulary. As they observe parents, siblings, and caregivers writing for many purposes, they begin to experiment with pen and paper, gradually coming to understand the forms and functions

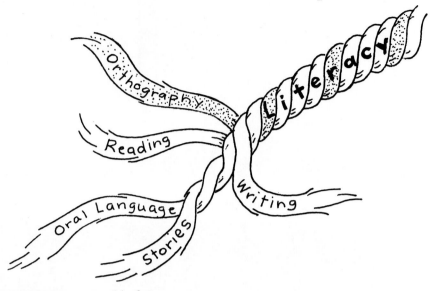

FIGURE 1-1 Braid of Literacy

of written language. The first written words students learn are usually their own names, followed by those of significant others. Words like *Mom, cat, dog,* and *I love you* represent people, animals, and ideas dear to their lives.

As students mature as readers and writers, they learn vocabulary from written language that they have not heard in their aural language. Print becomes a critical medium for conceptual development. Whenever purposeful reading, writing, listening, and speaking take place, words are learned along the way. Even more words are acquired when they are explicitly examined to discover the orthographic relationships among words—their sounds, their spelling patterns, and their meanings.

The aim of this book is to demonstrate how an exploration of orthographic knowledge can lead to the lengthening and strengthening of the literacy braid. To do this, teachers must know a good deal about the way in which these threads join together to create this bond so that they can direct children's attention to "words their way."

There are similarities in the ways learners of all ages expand their knowledge of the world. It seems that humans have a natural interest to find order, to compare and contrast, and to pay attention to what remains the same despite minor variations. Infants learn to recognize Daddy as the same Daddy with or without glasses, with or without a hat or whiskers. Auto mechanics learn to recognize carburetors despite changes in size or manufacturer. Through such daily interactions, individuals categorize their surroundings. Students expand their vocabularies by comparing one concept with another. Gradually, the number of concepts they analyze increases, but the process is still one of comparing and contrasting.

Word study occurs in hands-on activities that mimic basic cognitive learning processes: comparing and contrasting categories of word features and discovering similarities and differences within and between categories. For example, students often misspell words that end with the /k/ sound, spelling the word *snake* as SNACK or even SNACKE. By sorting words that end in *ck* and *ke* into two groups by sound as the student is doing in Figure 1-2, students discover the invariant pattern that goes with each (*ck* only follows a short vowel). The system is laid bare when words are sorted into categories.

FIGURE 1-2   Student Sorting Words by Sound

During word study, words and pictures are sorted in routines which require children to examine, discriminate, and make critical judgments about speech sounds, word structures, spelling patterns, and meanings. The activities presented in this book build on what students do on their own. Just as *Math Their Way* (Baretta-Lorton, 1968) used concrete manipulatives to illustrate principles of combining and separation, so *Words Their Way* uses concrete pictures and words to illustrate principles of similarity and difference.

WHY IS WORD STUDY IMPORTANT?

Letter-sound correspondences, phonics, spelling patterns, high-frequency word recognition, decoding strategies, word use and meanings—these and many other word skills are what written word knowledge is all about. Becoming fully literate is absolutely dependent on fast, accurate recognition of words in texts, and fast, accurate production of words in writing so that readers and writers can focus their attention on making meaning. Designing a word study program that explicitly teaches necessary skills and, at the same time, engages children's interest and motivation to learn about how words work, is clearly one of the most important aspects of a literacy program. Indeed, how to teach children these basics in an effective manner has sparked controversy among educators for nearly a century.

Phonics, spelling, and vocabulary programs are often characterized by (1) explicit skill instruction, (2) a systematic scope and sequence, and (3) repeated practice. Unfortunately, much of the repeated practice consists of rote drill, and children have little opportunity to manipulate word concepts or apply critical thinking skills. Children do need explicit skill instruction within a systematic curriculum. However, as William James (1958) said, "Teaching is not telling." Children need hands-on opportunities to manipulate word features in a way that allows them to generalize beyond isolated, individual examples to entire groups of words that work the same way.

Getting good at word recognition, spelling, and vocabulary is not just a matter of memorizing isolated rules and definitions. The best way to develop fast, accurate perception of word features is to engage in meaningful reading and writing, and to have multiple opportunities to examine those same words out of context, in isolation, in all their glory. The most effective instruction in phonics, spelling, and vocabulary, links word study to the texts being read, provides a systematic scope and sequence of word-level skills, and provides multiple opportunities for hands-on practice. In a sense, word study teaches students how to look at words as they read and write. This word study is well worth the 10 to 15 minutes of time daily.

What Is the Purpose of Word Study?

The purpose of word study is twofold. First, through active exploration, word study teaches students to examine words to discover the regularities, patterns, and rules of English orthography needed to read and spell. This knowledge is conceptual in nature and reflects what students understand about the general nature of the English spelling system. Second, word study increases specific knowledge of words—the spelling and meaning of individual words.

General knowledge is what readers and writers access when they encounter a new word, when they don't know how to spell a word, or if they don't know a specific word's meaning. The better their knowledge of the system, the better they are at decoding an unfamiliar word, inventing a correct spelling, or guessing a word's meaning. For example, if you have knowledge of short vowels and consonant blends, you would have no trouble attempting the word *crash* even if you have never seen it or written it before; its spelling is unambiguous, like so many single-syllable short vowel words. Knowledge of how words similar in spelling are related in meaning, such as *compete* and *competition*, allows readers to access the meaning of a word like *competitor* even if it's the first time they've seen it. Of course there are additional clues offered by context that also increase the chances of reading and understanding a word correctly.

But to become fully literate, students also need specific knowledge about individual words. Knowledge about the English spelling system will allow them to get in the right ballpark. The word *rain,* for example, might be spelled RANE, RAIN, or RAYNE—all are orthographically and phonetically plausible. But only specific knowledge will allow the student to remember the correct spelling. The relationship between specific knowledge and knowledge of the system is reciprocal. Each supports the other. Ehri (1992) expressed it like this:

> What students store in memory about specific words' spellings is regulated in part by what they know about the general system. Learners who lack this knowledge are left with rote memorization which takes longer and is more easily forgotten. Similarly, what students learn about the orthographic system evolves in part from the accumulation of experiences with specific word spellings. (p. 308)

The purpose of word study is to examine words in order to reveal consistencies within the written language system and to help students master the recognition, spelling, and meaning of specific words.

THE BASIS FOR WORD STUDY

Word study has evolved from decades of research in developmental aspects of word knowledge with children and adults (Henderson, 1990; Henderson & Beers, 1980; Templeton & Bear, 1992). This line of research has documented the convergence of spelling errors in clusters that reflect children's confusion over certain recurring orthographic principles. These clusters have been described in relationship to the types of er-

ALPHABET ----------► PATTERN ------------► MEANING

FIGURE 1-3   Three Layers of English Orthography

rors noted, specifically: (1) errors dealing with the alphabetic match of letters and sound (BAD for *bed*), (2) errors dealing with letter patterns (SNAIK for *snake*), and (3) errors dealing with words related in meaning (INVUTATION for *invitation*). The same clusters of error types have been studied in children with learning disabilities, children with dyslexia, and adults of low literacy (Viise, 1996; Worthy & Invernizzi, 1989). Research into the linguistic logic underlying children's spelling as they progress in literacy forms the basis for the scope and sequence of word study instruction.

Word study also comes from what researchers have learned about the structure of written words. Developmental spelling researchers have examined the three layers of English orthography (Figure 1-3) in relation to developmental progressions from alphabet to pattern to meaning. Each layer provides information, and in mature readers and writers, there is interaction among the layers.

Alphabet

The English spelling system is **alphabetic** because it represents the relationship between letters and sounds. This relationship is usually read in a left-to-right fashion. In the word *sat*, it is clear that each sound is represented by a single letter. The /s/, /a/, and /t/ sounds are blended together to come up with the word *sat*. In the word *chin*, three sounds are heard, even though there are four letters. This is because the first two letters, *ch*, function like a single letter, representing a single sound. So, letters can be matched—sometimes singly, sometimes in pairs—to sounds from left to right to come up with words. This is the alphabetic principle in English spelling, the first layer of information, at work.

Pattern

What about words like *cape, bead,* and *light*? If these words were spelled with single letters, they would look something like CAP, BED, and LIT; but of course these spellings already represent other words. There is another level of information that overlays the alphabetic layer. It is obvious that English does not have a single sound for each letter under all conditions. Single sounds are sometimes spelled with more than one letter or are affected by other letters that don't stand for any sounds themselves. If you look beyond single letter-sound matchups and search for **patterns** that guide the grouping of letters, however, you will find more consistency than you may have expected.

Take for example the *ape* in *cape*. The final-e "makes" the preceding vowel letter, *a*, stand for a "long" or tense-vowel sound. The *e* does not stand for a sound itself, but it plays a very important role. The *ape* group of letters follows a pattern that can be described this way: When you have a vowel, a consonant, and a silent-e in a single syllable, this letter grouping forms a pattern that usually will function to indicate a long vowel. This pattern is referred to as the consonant–vowel–consonant–silent-e (CVCe) pattern.

Another example is *bead*. Quite often, a CVVC pattern in a single syllable means that the word has a long vowel sound—the second vowel letter is silent but serves to indicate that the first vowel letter is long. CVCe and CVVC patterns very often represent long vowel spellings.

The notion of pattern makes the alphabetic layer more understandable as well. In the CVC pattern (*sat, chin*), regardless of how many consonant letters are on either side of the single vowel, the fact that there is but one vowel letter in that pattern means it will usually stand for a "short" vowel sound. As you learn more about words, your brain comes to operate in terms of these patterns rather than in terms of any specific letters. In the case of spelling, your brain can be much more efficient if you come to understand how these patterns work.

Syllables follow spelling patterns, too. These patterns are described with the same V and C symbols. Let's consider two of the most common syllable patterns. First, there is the VCCV pattern. *Robber* is a VCCV pattern (this refers to the vowel and consonant of the first syllable and the consonant and vowel of the second syllable). In this pattern, the first vowel is usually short. Knowledge of this pattern can help students figure out an unknown word in reading, and it can help them with the correct spelling of an uncertain word when they're writing. If a student is puzzling over whether *robber* has one *b* or two (because only a single /b/ sound is heard) and if the student is aware of the VCCV pattern, he or she could make a very good guess and write down two *b*s. Second, there is the VCV syllable pattern, as in *radar, begin,* and *limit.* Most of the time this pattern signals that the first vowel is long, but as in the case of *limit,* the first vowel can, on occasion, be short. Still, this pattern is an important one as we'll see later on. In short, knowledge about patterns within single syllables, and syllable patterns within words, will be of considerable value to students in both their reading and their spelling.

Meaning

Overarching both alphabet and pattern in sophistication is the layer of **meaning.** Groups of letters can represent meaning directly, and when students learn this, they will be much less puzzled by unusual spellings. Examples of these units or groups of letters are prefixes, suffixes, and Greek and Latin roots.

Word study must be combined with a lot of literature reading.

As one example of how meaning functions in the spelling system, think of the prefix *re.* Whether it is pronounced "ree" as in *rethink* or "ruh" as in *remove,* its spelling stays the same because it directly represents meaning. Why is *composition* not spelled COM-PUSITION? Because it is related in meaning to *compose.* The spelling in the related words *compose* and *composition* stays the same even though the sound that the letter *o* represents changes. Likewise, the letter sequence *photo* in *photograph, photographer,* and *photographic* signals family relationships among these words—despite the changes in the vowel sound in the second syllable.

By building connections between meaning parts and their derivations, students enlarge their vocabulary. As you'll see, this powerful interaction of spelling and meaning opens up a whole new frontier in exploring and learning about words.

In summary, students invent and discover these basic principles of spelling—alphabet, pattern, and meaning—when they read good stories, when they write purposefully, and when they are guided by knowledgeable teachers in word study activities. This word study should give children the experiences they need to progress through these layers of information:

- Children need hands-on experience comparing and contrasting words by sound so that they can categorize similar sounds and associate them consistently with letters and letter combinations. This is the heart of the alphabetic principle. For example, words spelled with short-e (*bed, leg, net, neck, mess*) are compared to words spelled with short-i (*sit, list, pick, tip, with*).
- Children need hands-on experience comparing and contrasting words by consistent spelling patterns associated with categories of sound. They need opportunities to recognize these patterns in other words they encounter in text. For example, words spelled with *ay* (*play, day, tray, way*) are compared to words spelled with *ai* (*wait, rain, chain, maid*).
- Children need hands-on experience categorizing words by meaning, use, and parts of speech. By grouping words together by broad categories of meaning, children see that words with similar meanings are often spelled the same, despite changes in pronunciation. *Admiration* is spelled with an *i* because it comes from the word *admire.*

WORD STUDY IS DEVELOPMENTAL

Word study is not a "one size fits all" program of instruction. One of the most unique qualities of word study is the critical role of differentiating instruction for different levels of word knowledge. Research over more than 20 years has established how children learn the specific features of words as well as the order in which they learn them. Knowledgeable educators have come to know that word study instruction must match the needs of the child. This construct, called **instructional level,** is a powerful delimiter of what may be learned. Simply put, educators must teach to where a child "is at." To do otherwise results in frustration or boredom and little learning in either case. Just as in learning to play the piano, students must work through Book A, then Book B, and so on, learning to read and spell is a gradual and cumulative process. Word study begins with finding out what each child knows about the cumulative aspects of English spelling.

One of the easiest ways to know what children need to learn is to look at the way they spell words. Children's spellings provide a direct window into how they think the system works. By interpreting what children do when they spell, educators can target a student's "zone of proximal development" (Vygotsky, 1962) and plan word study that the student is conceptually ready to master. Further, by applying basic principles of child development, educators have learned how to engage children in learning about word features in a child-centered, developmentally appropriate way.

What Are the Stages of Word Knowledge?

Developmental spelling research describes children's growing knowledge of words as a series of chronologically ordered stages. The stages are differentiated by the kinds of cues used by the child when encountering words and by specific featural knowledge of how the English spelling system works. In *Words Their Way*, we use the word *stage* as a metaphor to inform instruction. In reality, children grow in conceptual knowledge of the three general layers of information, and of specific word features. Children move hierarchically from easier one-to-one correspondences between letters and sounds, to more difficult, abstract relationships between letter patterns and sounds, to even more sophisticated relationships between meaning units as they relate to sound and pattern. Stages are marked by broad, qualitative shifts in the types of spelling errors children commit as well as behavioral changes in their reading and writing (Invernizzi, Abouzeid, & Gill, 1994).

There is remarkable consistency between the stages of spelling development and the stages of reading acquisition described in this book, as well as the developmental benchmarks described by other researchers such as Ehri (1997), Frith (1985), and Juel (1991). There is converging evidence that reading and spelling are integrally related, especially in the earliest stages. Stages of word knowledge are described briefly in the following paragraphs and summarized in Figure 1-4. The synchrony of spelling and writing will be elaborated further in Chapter 2.

During the **emergent** stage, reading and writing may be undertaken in earnest by the child but it will be recognized by adults as more pretend than real. Children may write with scribbles, letter-like forms, or random letters that have no phonetic relationship with the words they confidently believe they are writing. These children may call out the name of a favorite fast-food restaurant when they recognize its logo or identify a friend's name because it starts with a *T*, but they are not systematic in their use of any particular cue. During the emergent stage, children do not have letter-sound correspondences, and lack an understanding of the alphabetic principle, or it is only beginning to emerge. Ehri (1997) designated this as the "prealphabetic phase," and children's use of logos led Frith (1985) to name it the "logographic stage." Juel (1991) used the term "selective-cue" to describe how children select nonalphabetic visual cues like the two *o*s in *look* to remember a word.

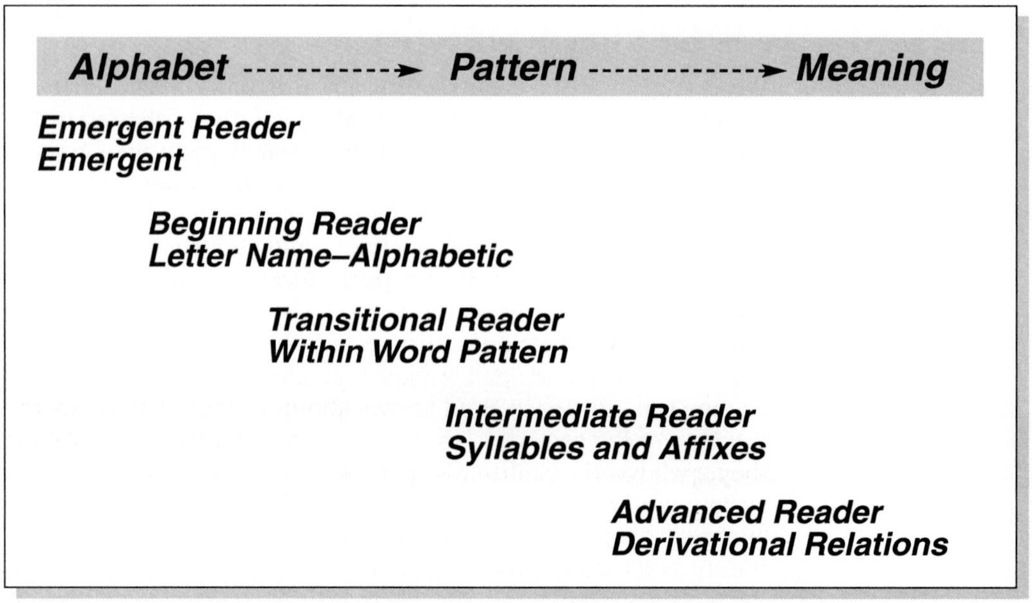

Alphabet ----------▶ **Pattern** ------------▶ **Meaning**

Emergent Reader
Emergent

  Beginning Reader
  Letter Name–Alphabetic

    Transitional Reader
    Within Word Pattern

      Intermediate Reader
      Syllables and Affixes

        Advanced Reader
        Derivational Relations

FIGURE 1-4   Reading Stages and Stages of Word Knowledge

The understanding of the alphabetic nature of the English language is a major hurdle for readers and spellers. The child who writes *light* as LT has made a quantum conceptual leap, having grasped that there are systematic matches between sounds and letters that must be made when writing. This early **letter name–alphabetic** speller is a **beginning reader** who has moved from pretend reading to real reading. Just as early attempts to spell words are limited, so too, beginning readers initially have limited knowledge of letter-sounds as they identify words by phonetic cues. Ehri (1997) described these readers and writers as being in the "partial alphabetic" phase. The kinds of reading errors children make during this phase offer insights into what they understand about print. Using the context as well as partial consonant cues, a child reading about good things to eat might substitute *candy* or even *cookie* for *cake* in the sentence "The cake was very good to eat." Readers in this stage require much support in the form of predictable, memorable texts.

As readers and writers acquire fuller knowledge of letter-sounds in the later part of the letter name–alphabetic stage they will include, but often confuse, vowels in the words they write. Reading errors will reflect those same confusions. Children who spell BAD for *bed* may make similar vowel errors when they read *hid* as HAD in "I hid the last cookie." These students resemble Ehri's "full alphabetic" readers who begin to use the entire letter string to decode and store sight words. The reading of letter name–alphabetic spellers is often disfluent and word by word (Bear, 1992). If such spellers are asked to read silently, the best they can do is to whisper. Readers in this stage continue to benefit from repeated readings of predictable texts, but also from the reading of text with many phonetically regular words. "Decodable" text supports the development of decoding strategies and the acquisition of sight words (Juel & Roper-Schneider, 1985).

Transitional readers and spellers move into the **within word pattern** spelling stage where single letter-sound units are consolidated into patterns or larger chunks, and other spelling regularities are internalized. Longitudinal research on spelling development has identified the progressive order in which children appear to use these larger chunks. After automating basic letter-sounds in the **onset** position (initial consonants, consonant blends, and consonant digraphs), children focus on the vowel and what follows (Ganske, 1994; Invernizzi, 1985, 1992; Viise, 1996). Short vowel **rimes** are learned first along with consonant blends in the context of simple word families or **phonograms** such as *h-at, ch-at,* or *fl-at*. These chunks come quite easily, probably as a result of their frequency in one-syllable words. Once the rime unit is solidified as a chunk, children appear to "use but confuse" the various long vowel markers of English (Invernizzi, 1992). Other stage models of reading acquisition also describe a fourth stage in which readers use progressively higher order units of word structures to read and spell (Chall, 1983; Frith, 1985; Gibson, 1965). Ehri (1997) called this the "consolidated alphabetic" phase in which children's reading is supported by familiarity with frequently occurring letter pattern units.

Transitional readers can read independently and, for the first time, silently (Bear, 1982; Henderson, 1990). Transitional readers and spellers have a sizable sight word vocabulary and can read fluently at their instructional level (Zutell & Rasinski, 1989). Writing and reading speeds increase significantly between the letter name–alphabetic stage and the transitional, within word pattern stages (Bear, 1992; Invernizzi, 1992).

Two additional stages of word knowledge characterize **intermediate** and **advanced** readers: **syllables and affixes** and **derivational relations.** These independent readers will struggle with issues such as how to pronounce the name of the main character in *Caddie Woodlawn* (sometimes calling her "Cadie"), or the meanings of words that they have no trouble decoding such as *insufferable*. When they spell, they will struggle with when to double at the juncture of two syllables (is it *robbin* or *robin*?) and the spellings of words such as ACOMODATE for *accommodate*. Stage models of early reading acquisition lump these stages of reading together in the "automatic stage" (Gough & Hillinger, 1980).

There is considerable consistency between spelling achievement and reading achievement through the fifth grade (Zutell & Rasinski, 1989). Morris and Perney (1984) found that first graders' invented spellings were a better predictor of end-of-grade reading than a standardized reading readiness test. A recent study by Sawyer et al. (1997) reported that a child's score on a developmental spelling inventory (Ganske, 1994) was the most powerful predictor of decoding. Developmental spelling predicted word decoding better than curricular experience, phoneme segmentation, and phoneme manipulation. Moreover, the spelling inventory identified the exact word elements children had mastered, and those currently under negotiation. Thus, ascertaining levels of development in spelling and reading has enormous potential for guiding instruction.

Word knowledge has a central role in a balanced language arts program, linking reading and writing as shown in Figure 1-5. Word knowledge accumulates as students develop orthographic understandings at the alphabetic level, the pattern level, and the meaning level in overarching layers of complexity. All that students know about phonics, word recognition, spelling, vocabulary, and even word usage (syntax) are part of their word knowledge.

How Do I Know Where to Begin?

Students acquire word knowledge through implicit learning that takes place as they read and write, and through explicit instruction orchestrated by the teacher. The teacher decides what to teach and when to teach it by considering each child. An informed, developmental interpretation of children's efforts as they read and write shows which words they can read and spell, and of those, which they might learn more about. There is more to pacing instruction than plugging students into an arbitrary sequence of spelling features. Instructional pacing must be synonymous with instructional placing—fitting the features of words to be taught to the students' understanding of what is to be learned.

How do teachers know where to begin word study? They find out the extent of students' word knowledge: how words sound, how words are spelled, what words mean, and how they are used. A good deal of what students know about the orthography is revealed in their invented spellings. Research on invented spelling has shown that students learn the features of English orthography in a common progression. According to

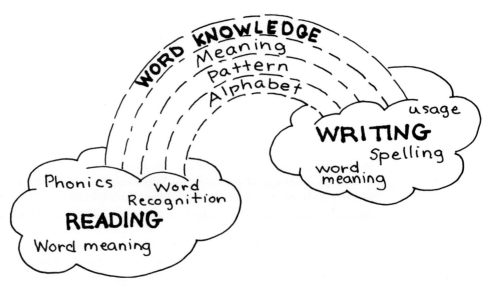

FIGURE 1-5   Word Knowledge Links Reading and Writing

Henderson (1990), teachers can use spelling assessments, like the ones discussed in Chapter 3, to select the content of instruction in word recognition, alphabet study, phonics, vocabulary, and spelling.

WORDS THEIR WAY

To help students explore and learn about words their way, instruction must be sensitive to two fundamental tenets:

1. Students' learning of spelling and vocabulary is based on their developmental or instructional level.
2. Students' learning is based on the way they are naturally inclined to learn, on their natural course of conceptual learning.

Honoring these two tenets almost guarantees that students will learn their way—building from what is known about words to what is new. Rather than a variety of rote memorization activities designed only to ensure repeated exposure, the teaching tasks suggested in this text encourage active exploration and examination of word features that are within a child's stage of literacy development. Word study is active, and by making judgments about words and sorting words according to similar features, students devise their own rules for how the features work. The simple act of making judgments about words this way helps students learn the relationships among alphabet, pattern, and meaning. Meaningful practice helps students internalize word features and become automatic in using what they have learned.

Now that we have looked at the nature of words and the spelling system that represents them in print, it is time to examine the nature of these stages of developmental spelling knowledge and the reading and writing characteristics of each stage.

Words and the Development of Orthographic Knowledge

As you learned in Chapter 1, there are three layers of information in English spelling:

1. **Alphabetic**, in which individual letters match up to individual sounds following a left-to-right sequence
2. **Pattern,** in which groups of letters function as a single pattern or unit to represent sounds
3. **Meaning,** in which groups of letters represent directly the meaning units underlying words

Developmentally, students progress in their strategies and awareness of these layers from alphabet to pattern to meaning.

This chapter explores students' development of orthographic knowledge in terms of these layers of information. Teachers can observe the development of these three layers of information in their students' spelling, particularly in their invented spellings. Notably, the order in which students come to understand and apply a knowledge of these different layers of information parallels the order in which the information appeared historically in the spelling system (Templeton, 1976, 1992). Students' knowledge of these layers of the orthography underlies their ability to read words efficiently and effectively as well as to write most words with little conscious effort. It is this broader level that we will consider first in this chapter—the overall interaction among word knowledge, reading, and writing, described as the synchrony model of literacy development. Then we will look more closely at each of the developmental stages.

THE SYNCHRONY OF LITERACY DEVELOPMENT

Developmental spelling theory suggests that invented spelling is a window into a child's knowledge of how written words work and can be used to guide instruction (Invernizzi, Abouzeid, & Gill, 1994). Specific kinds of spelling errors at particular stages of orthographic knowledge reflect a progressive differentiation of word elements which determine how words are read and written. Insight into these conceptual understandings helps teachers direct children's efforts as they learn to read and spell.

The scope and sequence of word study is based on this developmental foundation. When teachers do word study with students, they are addressing learning needs in all areas of literacy because development in one area relates to development in other areas. This harmony in the timing of development has been described as the **synchrony of reading, writing, and spelling development** (Bear, 1991b; Bear & Templeton, 1998). This means that development in one area is observed along with advances in other areas. All three advance in stage-like progressions which share important conceptual dimensions.

An understanding of these dimensions is crucial for effective literacy instruction. Figure 2-1 presents an integrated model of how reading, writing, and spelling progress together, in synchrony. This chart is similar to ones teachers might use to discuss children's development in parent-teacher conferences. We discuss this figure in conjunction with sharing the student's writing with parents, and showing them a collection of books that illustrate instructional level reading materials arranged by the **developmental levels** in the figure. This figure shows parents where their children are along the developmental continuum and across reading, writing, and spelling. The actual behaviors presented are ones that the parents can relate to in their children.

Word study activities in this text are organized around this model. If you can identify your students by the stages of reading, writing, and spelling, you will know which chapters contain the activities most relevant to your students' development. Figure 2-2 is an elaboration of Figure 1-4. Figure 2-2 presents an approximate grade and age range for the matching stages of reading and spelling.

HOW ORTHOGRAPHIC KNOWLEDGE DEVELOPS: STAGES OF SPELLING DEVELOPMENT

Because word study is based on stages of spelling, the word study activities presented in this book are arranged by stages of spelling. The principles of word study and the organization of word study in the classroom are discussed in depth in Chapter 4. Chapters 5 through 9 are devoted to instruction based on these stages. Knowing the stage of spelling of each of your students will determine your choices of appropriate word study

Reading and Writing Stages:

Emergent	Beginning			Transitional			Intermediate			Advanced		
Early Middle Late	Early	Middle	Late	Early	Middle	Late	Early	Middle	Late	Early	Middle	Late

Pretend read

Beginning: Read aloud, word-by-word, fingerpoint reading

Transitional: Approaching fluency, some expression in oral reading

Intermediate: Reads fluently with expression. Develops a variety of reading styles. Vocabulary grows with experience, reading, and writing.

Pretend write

Beginning: Word-by-word writing, may write a few words or lines

Transitional: Approaching fluency, more organization, several paragraphs

Intermediate: Writes fluently with expression and voice. Experiences different writing styles and genres. Writing shows personal problem solving and reflection.

Spelling Stages:

Emergent—>	Letter Name—Alphabetic—>	Within Word Pattern—>	Syllables and Affixes—>	Derivational Relations—>
CHAPTER 5	CHAPTER 6	CHAPTER 7	CHAPTER 8	CHAPTER 9

Examples:

bed	b bd	bad		_bed_			
ship	s sp	sep shep		_ship_			
float	f ft	fot flot flott		flowt floaut flote _float_			
train	t trn	jran tan chran tran		teran traen trane _train_			
cattle	c kd	catl	cadol	catel catol	cattel	_cattle_	
cellar	s slr	salr	celr	saler celer	seler	celler seller _cellar_	
pleasure	p pjr	plasr	plager	plejer pleser plesher		pleser plesher plesour plesure _pleasure_	
confident						confedent confiednet confedent confident _confident_	
opposition						opasishan oppasishion oposision opositian opposition _opposition_	

From *The Synchrony of Literacy Development: A Guide to Instruction*, Bear, 1998.

FIGURE 2-1 The Synchrony of Literacy Development

Alphabet ----------> **Pattern** ------------> **Meaning**

Emergent Stage
Pre-K to middle of 1
Chapter 5
Emergent

    Beginning Stage
    K to middle of 2
    Chapter 6
    Letter Name–Alphabetic

        Transitional Stage
        Grade 1 to middle of 4
        Chapter 7
        Within Word Pattern

            Intermediate Stage
            Grades 3 to 8
            Chapter 8
            Syllables and Affixes

                Advanced Stage
                Grades 5 to 12
                Chapter 9
                Derivational Relations

Key:
Reading Stage
Grade range
Instructional chapter
Spelling Stage

FIGURE 2-2   Reading and Spelling Stages, Grades, and Corresponding Instructional Chapters

activities. This chapter presents an overview of these stages which, as shown in Figure 2-2, guides you to the instructional chapters arranged by stages.

The idea of stages is used to describe particular scenarios of students' orthographic development. Over the past 20 years we have established criteria to determine which stage of development students are in, and have worked with many, many teachers in using the guidelines discussed in this chapter and the procedures described in Chapter 3.

By conducting regular spelling assessments, perhaps three times a year, you can track your students' progress and development. (This assessment procedure is discussed in Chapter 3.) An important prerequisite, however, is to know something about the stages of spelling development.

Levels of Learning

For each stage, students' orthographic knowledge is defined by three functional levels (Invernizzi, Abouzeid, & Gill, 1994):

1. What students do correctly—an independent or easy level
2. What students "use but confuse"—students experiment; where instruction is most useful
3. What is absent in students' spelling—spelling concepts are too advanced; instruction for what is absent is frustrating

In the following discussion of each stage, a table is presented which describes spelling development according to these three functional levels. To determine what orthographic features and patterns to explore with each child, we focus on what they use but confuse because this is where instruction will be of most benefit to a student. In Vygotskian terms, the level of awareness where students use but confuse is their "zone of proximal development" (Vygotsky, 1962). By studying the stages of spelling development, it becomes obvious what sequence the study of orthographic features should take.

History of Stages of Spelling

Edmund Henderson described six stages of spelling in 1981, but he began to study children's spelling with his students over a decade earlier. First at the University of Delaware and later at the University of Virginia, Henderson examined the specific spelling features children used to spell when they wrote. He and his colleagues found that children's spelling errors were not random and that they evolved over time (Henderson, Estes, & Stonecash, 1972). About the same time, in Boston, Carol Chomsky (1971) and Charles Read (1971, 1975) were also looking at preschoolers' invented spellings. There was a natural match in interests when Read and Henderson discovered each other. The discovery of Read's work in the linguistic arena helped Henderson and his students make sense of the spellings they had been collecting. Henderson and Read explored and identified the common errors students make as they learn more about the orthography. Subsequently, these patterns in spelling development have been observed across many groups of students, from preschoolers (Templeton & Spivey, 1980) through adults (Bear, Truex, & Barone, 1989; Worthy & Viise, 1993), as well as across socioeconomic levels, dialects, and other alphabetic languages (Beers & Henderson, 1977; Ehri, 1993; C. Gill, 1980; Shen, 1996; Stever, 1980; Temple, 1978). In addition, the analysis of children's spelling has subsequently been explored by a number of other researchers (Richgels, 1995; Treiman, 1985; Wilde, 1991).

By 1974, Henderson had formulated stages of spelling and orthographic knowledge. Ever since then, he and his students have refined these stages and have reworked the labels to reflect their changing understanding of the stages and to represent most appropriately what occurs at each level. The following names of the stages are descriptive of students' spelling behavior and make it easier to remember the basic strategies that students use to spell:

Stages of Spelling
Emergent
Letter name–alphabetic
Within word pattern
Syllables and affixes
Derivational relations

Stage I: Emergent Spelling

The **emergent** period of literacy development is a period of prereading and pretend writing. In emergent reading, children pretend to read by rehearsing familiar storybooks and by reciting well-known poems and jingles by heart. Likewise, emergent readers pretend to write. They may scribble or write in letter-like forms with all the seriousness and vigor of a stenographer. Their spelling may range from random marks to legitimate letters bearing no relationship to sound. Because of this lack of correspondence to sound, however, this stage of developmental orthographic knowledge is decidedly prephonetic. The characteristics of this stage are presented in Table 2-1.

Emergent writing, like scribbles, does not meet the usual requirement that a written text have a direct correspondence to spoken language and that it be "rereadable." Although there is great power to a picture, writing is different from a picture. Writing is based on oral language and the thoughts that can be talked about.

Emergent spelling may be divided into a series of steps or landmarks. At the beginning of this stage, students produce large scribbles which are basically drawings. The movement may be circular, and children may tell a story while they draw. At the earliest points in this stage, there are no designs that look like letters, and the writing is not much different from a drawing. The marks are merely scribbles on the page. As you can see in Figures 2-3A and B, the child has drawn large circles and called it writing. There is little order to the direction in the writing; it goes up, down, and around, willy-nilly.

Gradually, especially when they are sitting next to other children who write letters, children begin to use letters and something that looks like script. And about the time they are able to draw "tadpoles" for people (see Figure 2-3C), they acquire the convention of **directionality** (left to right in English).

Throughout this stage, children begin to learn letters, and particularly the letters in their own names. The writing by Carly, presented in Figure 2-4, is characteristic of a child in the middle of the emergent stage of spelling. When asked to spell a series of words, she spelled the words by using the letters she knew best—the letters in her name. She is beginning to use letters to represent words, but there is no sound-symbol correspondence between what she writes and the sounds of the word. Many emergent spelling children develop a special relationship with the letters in their names as one of their first forays into the alphabet. Upon entering preschool, Lee noticed that other children had names that used some of the same letters in her name. Perplexed and somewhat annoyed, she pointed to the letters that were also in her name. "Does everyone else have an *e* too?" she asked. Children in the emergent stage also begin to see the letters in their names in environmental print. Walking around the grocery store, Lee pointed to the box

---

TABLE 2-1 Characteristics of Emergent Spelling*

	What Students Do Correctly	What They Use but Confuse	What Is Absent
Early Emergent	• Write on the page • Hold the writing implement	• Drawing and scribbling for writing	• Sound-symbol correspondence • Directionality
Middle Emergent	• Horizontal movement across page • Clear distinction between writing and drawing • Lines and dots for writing • Letter-like forms	• Letters, numbers, and letter-like forms • Writing may wrap from right to left at the end of a line	• Sound-symbol correspondence
Late Emergent V for *elevator* D for *down*	• Consistent directionality • Some letter-sound match	• Substitutions of letters which sound, feel, and look alike: B/p, D/b	• Complete sound-symbol correspondence • Consistent spacing between words

*Characteristics of emergent spelling are discussed in depth in Chapter 5.

of Cheer detergent and said, "Look Mommy, there's my name." At the ages of 3 and 4, whenever Lee saw a word with two *es* in it, she said it was her name.

Gradually, and as children are encouraged to write and draw their stories, they begin to write down prominent phonetic features—especially the initial consonants—of a word or two. Toward the end of emergent spelling, children even start to memorize some words and write them over and over again; words like *no, Mom,* and *love* top the list.

Children in the emergent spelling stage begin to recognize the most basic visual characteristics of written text (that writing moves from left to right, top to bottom) and that the writing is somehow related to what they say. Throughout most of the emergent stage, children do not know about letter-sound correspondences; at best, they may make a few letter-sound matches. The ability to make a few letter-sound matches is evident in Figure 2-3D where *Jasmin* is spelled JMOE. The movement from this stage to the next stage hinges on learning the alphabetic principle: letters represent sound, and words can be segmented into sounds.

Heavy-handed phonics lessons that are not based on the student's developmental level can be destructive and work against children's growth in literacy. Such programs may expect all students to memorize, recognize, and produce the initial sounds of words before children are ready to do anything with this information.

The most teachers need to do with phonics during the emergent stage is to teach children to recognize and write the letters of the alphabet and to play with the sounds in words. When emergent children are exposed to directed instruction that is developmentally appropriate, their writing reflects this influence—and this signals the beginning of the end of the emergent stage of spelling. With a fairly stable knowledge of the alphabet, children analyze sounds in words. You will see in Chapter 5 that toward the end of the emergent stage, students are introduced to picture sorts in which they categorize words by beginning consonants or rhyming sounds.

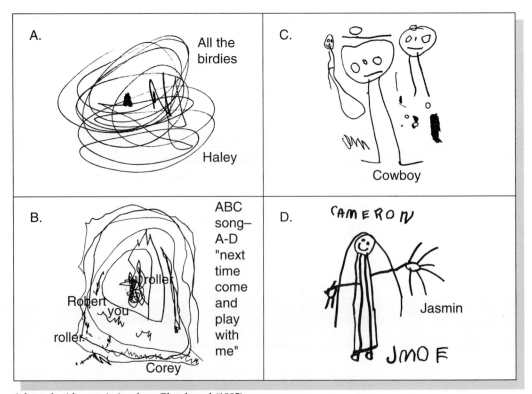

Adapted with permission from Bloodgood (1995).

FIGURE 2-3   Early Emergent Writing

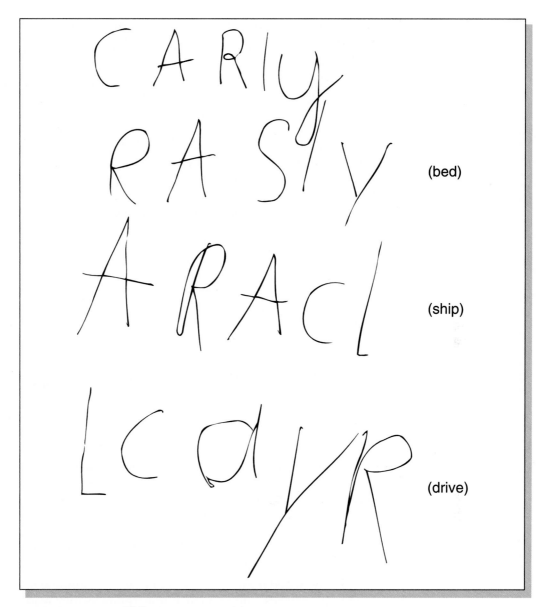

FIGURE 2-4 Middle Emergent Writing

Stage II: Letter Name–Alphabetic Spelling

The next stage of literacy development includes the beginning of conventional reading and writing. Children begin to read predictable pattern books, rhymes, and jingles. The familiar language patterns of these materials support students as they try to finger point to words as they match their speech to print. Their beginning writing is slow and disfluent as they work word by word and sound by sound to match letter names to the sounds they are trying to write. Because the beginning readers use the literal names of the letters with the alphabetic principle when they spell, they are called **letter name–alphabetic** spellers (Read, 1975). Letter name–alphabetic spellers spell in a linear, sound-by-sound fashion, just as they read and write. During the early part of this stage, students first spell beginning sounds in syllables and then the first and last sounds. By the middle of this stage, students begin to use a vowel in each syllable, and then begin to spell short vowel patterns conventionally.

Early Letter Name–Alphabetic Spelling

Students in the early part of the letter name–alphabetic stage are beginning readers. They can finger point to words accurately as they read, and they have begun to learn some sight words. Their choice of reading materials is limited to simple pattern stories and brief individual dictations recorded by their teachers. The characteristics of this early letter name–alphabetic stage of spelling development are summarized in Table 2-2.

Students who are early in the letter name–alphabetic stage apply the alphabetic principle primarily to consonants. Often, students spell the first sound and then the last sound of single-syllable words. For example, *bake* may be spelled B or BK. The middle elements of syllables, the vowels, are usually omitted. Modern psycholinguistic research has shown that consonants are the "noise" and vowels the "music" of language (Crystal, 1987). Spellers in the early part of the letter name–alphabetic stage attend to the noise and use the alphabetic principle to find letter names in the alphabet to spell the most prominent features in words—the consonants. Sometimes, strong vowels draw students' attention; for example, the long vowel at the beginning of *ice* may lead the child to spell *ice* as I or IS.

When students use the alphabetic principle, they find matches between letters and the spoken word by how the sound is made or articulated in the mouth. For example, students may substitute a /b/ sound for a /p/ sound because they are made in the same way except for one feature—in making the /p/ sound, air comes out of the mouth in an explosive way, whereas with the /b/ sound, there is no accompanying explosion of air.

When spelling *drip*, many children substitute a *j* for the consonant blend *dr* and spell *drip* as JP. Try saying *jip* and *drip* and notice how the *dr* and *j* feel similar in the mouth. A less obvious example is the substitution of an *f* for a *v* to spell *drive* as DF. Like the /dr/ and /j/ sounds, the /f/ and /v/ sounds are made in pretty much the same way. Given that *f* is a much more familiar letter, students choose it to represent the /v/ sound. A bit of linguistic analysis on your part will show you how similar the sounds are. Choosing an *f* for a *v* is a logical mistake given the limited experience of the student in this stage of development. (A student's relative experience will influence choice; for example, a child named Virginia would perhaps learn the /v/ sound first and, as a result, begin *face* with a *v*.)

Middle and Late Letter Name–Alphabetic Spelling

The general picture for reading throughout the letter name–alphabetic stage is one of *disfluency*. As is discussed in more detail in Chapter 6, beginning readers read aloud when they read to themselves, and they often fingerpoint as they read. In addition, they read in a word-by-word fashion without expression. A variety of support techniques and materials—dictations, pattern books, and rhyme—are used so that these beginners can use their memory and understanding of the rhythm of language for support as they read through simple texts.

What is unique about the middle and late part of this stage is that vowels and stressed syllables are represented (see Table 2-2). For example, to spell the word *baker*, children in the middle part of the letter name–alphabetic stage use the letter name of this long vowel and spell *baker* as BAKR. During this stage, students begin to see the differences between consonants and vowels, and there is substantial growth in how they use short vowels. As you will see in the word study activities in Chapter 6, students study short vowel patterns before they study long vowels. Attention is not directed to the silent vowels of long vowel patterns (as in *beat* and *rate*), until students can spell short vowels and words like *bet* and *rat* easily.

Late letter name–alphabetic spellers continue to use a phonetic spelling strategy in which they focus on the letter-sound matches. For example, early letter name–alphabetic spellers spell a difficult word like *caught* as CT or KT. In the middle of the letter name–alphabetic stage, students insert a vowel and often spell *caught* as COT. To ask students

TABLE 2-2 Characteristics of Letter Name–Alphabetic Spelling*			
	What Students Do Correctly	**What They Use but Confuse**	**What Is Absent**
Early Letter Name–Alphabetic B, BD for *bed* S, SHP for *ship* Y for *when* L, LP, for *lump* U for *you* R for *are* FT for *float*	• Represent most salient sounds, usually beginning consonants • Directionality • Most letters of the alphabet • Clear letter-sound correspondences • Partial spelling of consonant blends and digraphs	• Letters based on point of articulation: J, JRF for *drive* • Often long vowels by letter name	• Consistency in beginning and end of syllables • Some spacing between words • Vowels in syllables
Middle Letter Name–Alphabetic BAD for *bed* SEP or SHP for *ship* FOT for *float* LOP for *lump*	• Most beginning and ending consonants • Clear letter-sound correspondences • Frequently occurring short vowel words	• Substitutions of letter name closest in point of articulation for short vowels • Some consonant blends and digraphs	• Preconsonantal nasals: LOP for *lump*
Late Letter Name–Alphabetic *lump* spelled correctly FLOT for *float* BAKR for *baker* PLAS for *place* BRIT for *bright*	• All of the above plus: • Regular short vowel patterns • Most consonant blends and digraphs • Preconsonantal nasals • Some common long vowel words: *time, name*	• Substitutions of common patterns for low-frequency short vowels: COT for *caught*	• Most long vowel markers or silent vowels • Vowels in unstressed syllables

*Characteristics of letter name–alphabetic spelling are discussed in depth in Chapter 6.

to focus on *aught*—a difficult and infrequent visual pattern—is an overload. This vowel will be spelled correctly later on after some of the easier long vowel patterns are learned. By the middle of the letter name–alphabetic stage, spellers have learned that syllables have vowels. They begin to understand the closed syllable, the consonant-vowel-consonant (CVC) unit. They will not necessarily know these terms, but they do show evidence of their implicit knowledge through their invented spellings. Over the course of the letter name–alphabetic stage, students make the match between short vowel sounds and the standard or correct spelling. With plenty of reading, they also learn the odd spellings of high-frequency words like *was* and *come*. By the end of this stage, they are able to represent most initial consonant digraphs and blends correctly.

One of the hallmarks of a student who is moving from the letter name–alphabetic stage to the next stage, within word pattern spelling, is the correct spelling of inwords with *m*s or *n*s like *bump* or *bunch*. *N*s and *m*s are referred to as **nasals.** They are made by air passing through the nasal passage. In a word like *jump* the nasal is called **preconsonantal** because it occurs in front of another consonant. Henderson recognized that the correct spelling of the preconsonantal nasal was a reliable and important event (see Table 2-2).

Stage III: Within Word Pattern Spelling

This third stage of spelling development occurs in synchrony with the transitional stages of reading and writing. As described in Figure 2-1, transitional learners approach fluency in both reading and writing. Their reading changes from word by word to phrasal reading fluency. With easy, independent-level material, students stop fingerpointing. When they read to themselves, they usually read silently. From the beginning to the end of the transitional stage, students move from needing support materials and techniques to being able to pick up many different texts and reading them independently—from the Sunday comics to easy chapter books such as *Freckle Juice* (Blume), *Superfudge* (Blume), and *Ramona the Pest* (Cleary). Likewise, students write more quickly and with greater fluency. In spelling, transitional readers move away from the literal application of letter names to include patterns or chunks of letter sequences that relate to sound and meaning. As the name of this stage indicates, **within word pattern** spellers take a closer look at the vowel within syllables, and they begin to examine long vowel patterns (Henderson, 1990). Knowledge of within word patterns affords greater efficiency and speed in reading, writing, and spelling. As can be seen in Table 2-3, the within word pattern stage begins when students can correctly spell most single-syllable short vowel words. They also spell consonant blends and digraphs correctly and can read low-frequency short vowel words which they cannot spell.

The transitional stage can be a fragile period in a child's literacy development. With adequate time spent reading materials at independent and instructional levels, students take off with fluency and motivation on a positive trajectory. Without such practice, however, or if too much time is spent struggling with materials that are too difficult, students' growth at this stage is stunted, and they lose motivation.

At this point in their reading and writing development, students begin to think more abstractly. They begin to talk about what a story has meant to them, and the discussions of texts move easily beyond generalities and summaries (Barone, 1990). As they examine orthography, within word pattern spellers show a similar level of abstraction in their thinking. They begin to work with the more abstract patterns of long vowels. In the letter name–alphabetic stage, a student's strategy is a linear one; each letter stands for a sound, and for the most part, there is a one-to-one correspondence between sounds and letters. During the within word pattern stage, the code is expanded to include patterns for long vowels, like the CVVC pattern (*nail, beak*), the CVCe pattern (*name, time*), and the CVV pattern (*hay, tie*).

In the within word pattern stage, students also develop a sense that patterns do not always have to be consistent with sound, as in *have, come,* and *some,* which do not fit the long vowel pattern. With changes in the ability to reflect and to use abstract patterns, students also begin to think more about their spoken vocabulary. They can play with words in meaning sorts in the same way that they may arrange baseball cards. To foster this analysis, students keep lists of words arranged by topic. In this way, their interest in vocabulary is easily expanded upon in the next stage of spelling development where the spelling-meaning connection is explored.

The focus for instruction is on what students are using but confusing at that moment, so teachers involve students in exploring long vowel patterns. Children in this stage have a sight reading vocabulary of probably 200 to 400 words and can work with word sorts. An important new feature during this stage is that students develop **word study notebooks** (see Chapter 7) in which they enter groups of words that they have sorted or have found to follow particular patterns. Students begin with one vowel and spend some time examining the various patterns of that long vowel. Next, they examine similar patterns in another long vowel. Comparisons are made across the two long vowel patterns—for example, the CVCe patterns in *name* and *line.* After these comparisons, students examine some of the special patterns for the vowel being studied, as in *climb* and *kind* when they study the long-i. Throughout the word study, students record these categorizations in word study notebooks.

Students learn to read and spell words they see frequently and whose patterns they can understand (Beck & McKeown, 1991). During the within word pattern

TABLE 2-3   Characteristics of Within Word Pattern Spelling*

	What Students Do Correctly	What They Use but Confuse	What Is Absent
Early Within Word Pattern FLOTE for *float* PLAIS for *place* BRIET for *bright* TABL for *table*	• Initial and final consonants • Consonant blends and digraphs • Regular short vowel patterns and preconsonantal nasals • Good accuracy on *r*-influenced single-syllable short vowel words: *fur, bird* • Some infrequently used short vowels and frequently used long vowel words: *like, see*	• Long vowel markers: SNAIK for *snake*, FELE for *feel*	• Consonant doubling: SHOPING for *shopping*, CAREES for *carries* • Vowels in unaccented syllables
Middle Within Word Pattern SPOLE for *spoil* DRIEV for *drive*	• All of the above plus: • Slightly more than half of the long vowel words in single-syllable words: *hike, nail*	• Long vowel markers: NITE for *night* • Consonant patterns: SMOCK for *smoke* • Inventive substitutions in frequent, unstressed syllable patterns: TEACHAUR for *teacher* • *ed* and other common inflections: MARCHT for *marched*, BATID for *batted*	
Late Within Word Pattern CHUED for *chewed*	• All of the above plus: • Single-syllable long vowel words • May know some common Latin suffixes: *inspection*	• Low-frequency long vowel words: HIEGHT for *height* • *ed* and other common inflections • Common Latin suffixes are spelled phonetically: ATENSHUN for *attention*	• Consonant doubling • e-drop: AMAZEING for *amazing*

*Characteristics of within word pattern spelling are discussed in depth in Chapter 7.

stage, there is overlapping cognitive growth in written responses, writing fluency, and problem solving. Within word pattern spellers work with the orthography and with the writing system at a more abstract level than the letter name–alphabetic spellers. The study of common single-syllable patterns is the focus throughout the within word pattern stage. Students are not ready to study two-syllable word patterns unless they clearly and easily understand the differences between long and short vowel patterns.

Throughout the derivational relations stage, students study the spelling-meaning connection.

Stage IV: Syllables and Affixes

The synchrony of literacy development is also evident in the growth to the **syllables and affixes** stage and the intermediate stages of reading and writing. If you refer back to Figure 2-1, you can see that intermediate learners read fluently. Their word recognition is automatic, and because of this, their minds are free to think as rapidly as they can read. This period of literacy development is generally accompanied by the ability to think abstractly. Intermediate writers are also fluent writers. The content of their writing displays complex analysis and interpretation. As noted in Table 2-4, in spelling, these readers grapple with meaning units such as prefixes and suffixes. Intermediate readers negotiate the conventions of preserving pattern-to-sound relationships at the place where syllables meet. Accordingly, this stage of orthographic development is called syllables and affixes.

Intermediate readers read most texts with good accuracy and a good reading rate, both orally and silently. For these students, success in reading and understanding is related to familiarity and experience with the topic being discussed. Students in the intermediate stage acquire, through plenty of practice, a repertoire of reading styles. The same is true for writing.

The syllables and affixes stage represents a new point in word analysis when students consider where syllables meet at their **juncture.** In the previous stages, students examined single-syllable words and patterns. In this stage, they examine polysyllabic words and patterns. The analysis of multisyllabic words is more complicated, for there is more than one perceptual unit to consider. For example, a two-syllable word like *dungeon* may be divided into *dun* and *geon.* For easy words, and especially where the text gives plenty of contextual clues, this analysis is done at an unconscious or tacit level. The analysis of unfamiliar multisyllabic words will call on students to divide words into syllables and then see how the syllables fit together.

TABLE 2-4	Characteristics of Syllables and Affixes Spelling*		
	What Students Do Correctly	**What They Use but Confuse**	**What Is Absent**
Early Syllables and Affixes SHOPING for *shopping* CATEL for *cattle* KEPER or KEPPER for *keeper*	• Initial and final consonants • Consonant blends and digraphs • Short vowel patterns • Most long vowel patterns • *ed* and most inflections	• Consonant doubling: HOPING for *hopping* • Long vowel patterns in accented syllables: PERAIDING or PERADDING for *parading* • Reduced vowel in unaccented syllables: CIRCUL for *circle* • Doubling and e-drop: AMAZZING for *amazing*	• Occasional deletion of middle syllables: CONFDENT for *confident*
Middle Syllables and Affixes SELLER for *cellar* DAMIGE for *damage* FORTUNET for *fortunate*	• All of the above plus: • Consonant doubling: *shopping, cattle* • Double and e-drop: *stopping, amazing*	• Syllables that receive less stress: HOCKY for *hockey*, FAVER for *favor* • Spell sounds at syllable junctures like single-syllable words: PUNCHUR for *puncture*, ATTENSHUN for *attention*	• Assimilated prefixes: ILEGAL for *illegal* • Root constancies in derivationally related pairs: CONDEM for *condemn*
Late Syllables and Affixes CONFEDENT for *confident*	• All of the above plus: • Long vowel patterns in accented syllables: *compose/composition* • Double and e-drop (except where overlaps with assimilated prefixes)	• Some suffixes and prefixes: ATTENSION for *attention*, PERTEND for *pretend* • Vowel alternation in derivationally related pairs: COMPUSITION for *composition* • Consonant alternations in derivationally related pairs: SPACIAL for *spatial*	

*Characteristics of syllables and affixes spelling are discussed in depth in Chapter 8.

Word study in this stage begins with the consonant-doubling principle. A frequently occurring word like *stopped* may require very little processing time; recognition of this frequent word may be close to automatic. However, a word like *clopped* may call for slightly more analysis. Beyond consonant doubling for suffixes (*ed* and *ing*), students examine consonant doubling in words like *settle, success,* and *occasion*. When students understand why some consonants are doubled, they begin to think about and study the meaning of prefixes.

It is often at this time that teachers and students study plurals where the link between syntax and spelling is also obvious. They examine the various spelling changes for the plural as in *funnies,* and *foxes*. Toward the middle of this stage, students come to see the convention of *tion* and *sion* as affixes for changing verbs into nouns. They also study other syntactic and semantic affixes like *er, or, ian,* and more.

As word study proceeds in this stage, the examination of accent or stress becomes a more central interest, and the meaning connection is made with numerous language systems. For example, notice how a change in accent can affect the syntactic and semantic function of the word *contract*:

> You signed the contract for a year.
> He may contract the disease.

Beginning in the syllables and affixes stage, and throughout the derivational relations stage, students study the **spelling-meaning connection** (Templeton, 1983). As you will see briefly in the discussion to follow, and in depth, in Chapters 8 and 9, students learn about English spelling at the same time that they study to enrich their vocabularies.

During these two stages, students' reading and speaking vocabularies grow along with their concept development. The research in upper level word study and development has highlighted the importance of reading in vocabulary development (Templeton, 1976). From adolescence on, except perhaps for slang, most of the new vocabulary students learn comes from reading. The meaning connection is central to this stage, and new vocabulary reflects the new subject areas which students explore (Templeton, 1992).

Stage V: Derivational Relations

The **derivational relations** stage corresponds to the advanced stage of reading and writing. Advanced readers have a broader experience base which allows them to choose among a variety of reading styles to suit the text and their purposes for reading. The same picture is evidenced in writing development. With purpose and practice, students develop and master a variety of writing styles, and they spell most words correctly (see Table 2-5). Advanced readers encounter the advanced vocabulary of Greek and Latin origin. This stage of orthographic knowledge is known as derivational relations because this is when students examine how words share common derivations and related roots and bases. They discover that the meaning and spelling of parts of words remain constant across different words (Henderson & Templeton, 1986; Templeton, 1983).

After the common prefixes and suffixes are examined, students begin to examine the meaning of bases and roots and the classical origin of polysyllabic words or the study of derivational morphology. For example, it is not a big jump from seeing what *trans* means from exemplars like *transportation, transport, transplant,* and *transmit* to looking deeper at some of the basic English bases like *ten* in *tennis, tendency, tenet, tenant, pretend,* and so on. Throughout this stage they learn about the history of words and their derivations. With plenty of reading, writing, and word study their vocabularies continue to grow and branch out into specialized areas of study and interest.

In word study, teachers show students how to consider both the spelling of a word and its meaning. Students begin to see how spelling tells them about meaning and how pronunciation can blur meaning. A student who misspells *competition* as COMPOTITION may see the correct spelling more easily by going back to a base or root, as in *compete* where the long vowel gives a clear clue to spelling. When a student spells *composition* as COMPUSITION, the spelling can be clarified by referring to the long-o in the related word *compose*.

The aim of word study in this stage is to teach students how to examine words for their related histories. One of the exciting aspects about word study sessions at these advanced stages is that teachers do not always know the meaning connections themselves, and so there is a freshness that comes with the word study explorations. Here, word study is managed with the assumption that together students and teachers can explore the histories of words and that words are interesting. Word study sessions throughout these stages can begin with this basic question: Did you find any interesting words in your reading? And so, together the group is off exploring, studying the words students

TABLE 2-5 **Characteristics of Derivational Relations Spelling***			
	What Students Do Correctly	**What They Use but Confuse**	**What Is Absent**
Early Derivational Relations OPPISITION for *opposition*	• Spell most words correctly • Most vowel and consonant alternations	• Unaccented or *schwa* sounds misspelled: BENAFIT for *benefit* • Some silent consonants: CONDEM for *condemn* • Some consonant doubling: AMMUSEMENT for *amusement* • Some suffixes and prefixes: APPEARENCE for *appearance*, PERTEND for *pretend* • Some vowel alternation in derivationally related pairs: COMPUSITION for *composition*	• Silent letters related to derivation: TERADACTIL for *pterodactyl*
Middle Derivational Relations	• Spell most words correctly • Common Latin suffixes: *attention*	• Some silent letters: EMFASIZE for *emphasize*, INDITEMENT for *indictment*	• Same as above • Some reduced vowels: PROHABITION for *prohibition*
Late Derivational Relations	• Spell most words correctly	• Assimilated prefixes: ACOMODATE for *accommodate* • Unfamiliar derived forms, Greek & Latin forms, and foreign borrowings	• Some uncommon roots: EXHILERATE for *exhilarate*

*Characteristics of derivational relations spelling are discussed in depth in Chapter 9.

bring to the session. Teachers show their students that they themselves are excited by what can be learned about words, language, and ideas. The word study activities in Chapter 9 are ordered in terms of development, but there is some flexibility in the exact order in which the affixes and roots are studied.

Sometimes the words that students examine are familiar but fascinating in their histories, and as the students study words, a new dimension is added to their vocabularies. As an example, a student brought the word *panacea* to the group because its meaning was unclear to her. What was fascinating was how the word study came around to a simple word—*company*. The students and the teacher could see that both words had *pan* in them, and over the course of the session, students began to wonder if *pan* represented the same meaning in both words. Subsequently, they found out that there are four different meanings of *pan*. *Company* can literally mean "to break bread with," because *com* means "with," and *pan* in this word means "bread." At the beginning of this word study session, no one knew that *company* would be studied or that such a charming word story would appear.

The history of the English language has many wonderful stories to tell. It takes on more importance during the derivational relations stage, as students learn the meanings behind the vocabularies in specialized areas of study.

THE HISTORY OF ENGLISH SPELLING AND CHILDREN'S LEARNING OF ENGLISH SPELLING: SOME INTRIGUING PARALLELS

We have been referring to the role of the history of English as it has impacted the development of the spelling system. Students develop knowledge of the system in a manner that parallels this historical development. We hope you might be intrigued just enough to explore the historical foundation further and to involve your students as well. The parallels between historical development and individual development are important for two reasons: First, this comparison serves to emphasize the complexity that learners must negotiate; second, the comparison helps teachers appreciate the wonderful and instructive terrain that they can explore with their students.

The English language began about A.D. 450 when the Angles, Jutes, and Saxons—three tribes that lived in northern Europe—invaded the British Isles. These invaders were a primitive lot, known to practice human sacrifice. The invaders, however, brought the beginnings of the English language with them—what is now referred to as Old English—as well as the name by which the later English nation would be called, *Angleland.* Eventually the invaders settled down to more peaceful activities, primarily farming and raising livestock. Much of their language included words that had to do with these pursuits (words such as *sheep, dirt, tree,* and *earth*), and many of their words would come to constitute the most frequently used words in the English language today. In fact, all of the 100 most frequent words in Contemporary English come from Old English.

Around A.D. 600, St. Augustine arrived in Britain, and with him came Christianity and many Latin words associated with the church. Monasteries were established, eventually becoming cultural and intellectual centers. Because of this influence, English became the first of the European languages to be written down. Britain became the center of learning in Europe, providing a multitude of books for the rest of the continent. Throughout the seventh and eighth centuries, Anglo-Saxon England rose to cultural heights unmatched in Europe.

Another invasion was to interrupt this development, however. In the late eighth century, the Vikings landed and began a process of conquest that lasted well into the following century. Their arrival brought a large segment of Danish vocabulary into English (for example, *want, skill, raise*). Their conquests were eventually halted by Alfred the Great, a legendary figure in English history. Among other things, Alfred encouraged the translation of books into English and instituted a widespread literacy campaign.

By the end of the first millennium, the English language had grown over the course of some 500 years in its vocabulary, its structure, and its capacity to express meaning. It was the language of the intellect in medieval Europe. Yet another invasion, this time from the northwest of France, brought radical changes to the English language, and English as a written language practically disappeared for almost 200 years. In 1066, William the Conqueror invaded and brought the Norman French language with him. This is the point from which most scholars date the beginning of Middle English.

Norman French was used at court and in legal affairs. For years after the invasion, however, there was little intermingling with English. But with the passing of time, Old English and Norman French came together, and by the early 1200s, what is now called Middle English began to appear. The French legacy remains in the English spoken today: some 40% of Modern English is from French (for example, *nourish, commence, interrogate*). By the 1300s the demand for books increased because of the increased availability of paper. With the introduction of the printing press in England in 1476, the market was even greater. About the same time, the Renaissance brought a rediscovery of the classical languages, Greek and Latin. Many new words would soon be created from Greek and Latin word elements, which lent themselves to combination (as we'll see in Chapter 9). This was particularly useful because the "voyages of discovery" of the late fifteenth and sixteenth centuries introduced so many new objects and ideas that needed to be named.

Spelling, however, had become a topsy-turvy affair. It had been fairly standard by the time of the Norman invasion, but the influx of French began to change that. The professional scribes, and later the printers, had quite a degree of flexibility in how they spelled words. It would not be until the middle of the 1700s—the period of English now called Modern English—that spelling would finally be standardized. This would be the result of the publication of Samuel Johnson's *Dictionary of the English Language* in 1755.

Before we leave Middle English, however, we should note an important phenomenon that would have implications for the way we spell English today and for children's learning of conventional English spelling. This phenomenon is called the great vowel shift. Although it would take a great deal of space to explain why it occurred, we can look at its effects more easily: In a nutshell, the long and short vowel sounds that a letter represented in Middle English changed by the time Modern English began (around 1500). In Middle English, for example, the long and short sounds for the letter *e* were /ā/ and /ĕ/ ; the long and short sounds for the letter *i* were /ē/ and /ĭ/ . One of the effects of the great vowel shift was to change the long vowel sound of these letters to the present-day /ē/ for the letter *e* and /ī/ for the letter *i*; the short vowel sounds of these letters, however, stayed as they were in Middle English. (Later, in Chapter 6, we will examine children's invented spellings during the letter name–alphabetic phase of development, and we will see that at some point they match up long and short vowel sounds very much as they were matched in Middle English.)

Scholars divide Modern English into two periods: Early Modern English (1500–1700) and Contemporary English (1700–present). Because of the Renaissance, Greek and Latin came to influence English; this continued even more intensively during Early Modern English. New words were created from Greek and Latin elements, and many other existing words came to be respelled to reflect what scholars believed were their historical roots in Latin and Greek. For example, *dette* was respelled *debt* (related to Latin "debitum"); *sithe/sythe* was respelled *scythe* (the *c* was inserted to reflect the Latin "cisorium" meaning "to cut"). The rich language heritage of Early Modern English was used to its fullest extent in the writings of Shakespeare in the later sixteenth and early seventeenth centuries; indeed, these writings have profoundly influenced the nature and the vocabulary of English. During the time of Shakespeare's life the English language grew at an incredible rate, more so than at any time before or since. It was also during this time that the first spelling books appeared, and they helped to contribute to the standardization of English spelling that was for the most part completed by the time of Johnson's dictionary in the middle of the eighteenth century.

In this brief overview, we have left out a number of fascinating bits of information about the evolution of English spelling over the last 1,500 years. Nonetheless, we hope it will help you appreciate the implications of the parallel between the sequence in which students learn about English spelling and the historical development of English spelling: Once children know what "words" are, they expect that spelling represents sounds in a straightforward left-to-right manner, just like it was done in Old English. Somewhat later, they learn the more complex vowel patterns that came into English with the French language after the Norman invasion. Henderson (1990) compared the spelling strategies of letter name–alphabetic children to those of the Anglo-Saxons: Both follow an alphabetic strategy. Templeton (1976) described how children in the middle letter name–alphabetic stage categorize long and short vowels the way these vowels were categorized in Early Middle English, before the great vowel shift. Moreover, letter name–alphabetic children learn first the conventional spelling of short vowels. Historically, it is interesting that the spellings of many short vowel words in Modern English are older than the spellings of similar long vowel patterns. For example, *pet* is easier for children to spell and came into English spelling earlier than *piece*; *bet* is easier for children to spell and came in earlier than *beat.* (Actually, we can go even farther back. Many of the CVC patterns have their origins in the Indo-European language, the mother of over half of the world's languages, including English and almost all of the European languages.)

During the within word pattern stage, students' growth in orthographic knowledge reflects the influence of French during Middle English. During the fifteenth century when scribes experimented with the spelling of different long vowels, they borrowed the *ai* from twelfth-century French, as in *plain* and *saint;* and *ea* was used to spell the vowel in words like *deal, meal, meat, reason,* and *ease* to distinguish the vowel sound in these words from the short-e. By the seventeenth century, however, the original sound that *ea* represented was pronounced the same way as present-day short-e. (Modern French preserves the sound differences in *ai* and short-e, as in the spelling of *raison* and *aisle.*) Other examples in which spelling has stabilized but the pronunciation changed include the spelling-pronunciation mismatch in words such as *bread, earth, great,* and *heart* (Scragg, 1974). English has also used the French grapheme *ie* in *piece, brief,* and *relief* with the same effect.

Later still, students learn about the ways in which spelling represents meaning most directly, despite changes in pronunciation, as in the consistent spelling of the element *jud* in the words *judge, prejudice,* and *adjudicate.* Cummings (1988) referred to this as the "semantic demand" on the spelling system, and observed that, historically, "the rise of the semantic demand . . . *is repeated in microcosm* [italics added] in the development of any individual's writing and reading skills" (p. 14). Learners come to understand the role and influence of the many Greek and Latin words and word elements that became a part of the spelling system during the Renaissance and into the sixteenth and seventeenth centuries.

Words—their structure and how students learn about them—are of tremendous significance in literacy development. These first two chapters have established why this is so. In the following chapters you will learn how to determine where your students are developmentally and how to organize your instruction to address most effectively the features of words they will need to explore.

CHAPTER 3

Getting Started: The Assessment of Orthographic Development

Teaching is about understanding: students developing new understandings of life and literacy; teachers understanding their students. This chapter is about understanding students through an assessment process that begins with observation. At the beginning of the school year, or whenever a new child enters the class, teachers need to know what the instructional goals should be for each student. Teachers assess students' knowledge to plan an effective program of word study which helps students learn to read and write. So, how do teachers learn about students' literacy development? Particularly, how do teachers learn about students' orthographic knowledge—the knowledge they have about the writing system? Teachers learn about students' orthographic knowledge and development by reading and writing with them, and through informal spelling inventories.

This chapter presents a method to assess students' orthographic knowledge and to determine a stage of spelling development for each student. You can base your plan for word study instruction on your assessments of students' spelling and orthographic knowledge. This assessment process will also allow you to monitor students' growth periodically throughout the year.

SPELLING-BY-STAGE ASSESSMENT: THREE STEPS

Consider the following writing sample to learn about this kindergartner's literacy development. Sarah called this her first restaurant review. Although it appears to be a menu, she posted it on the wall the way she had seen reviews posted in restaurants.

1 CRS KAM SAS	(First course, clam sauce)
2 CRS FESH	(Second course, fish)
3 CRS SAGATE	(Third course, spaghetti)
4 CRS PUSH POPS	(Fourth course, Push Pops)

This writing tells a lot about Sarah: She sees a practical use for writing, she has written quite a long and complete message, and she enjoys writing and displaying her work. She has a good grasp of how to compose a list, and she is beginning to understand menu planning. Her spelling shows what she knows about the orthography and what she is using but confusing. Based on this information, it is possible to make some preliminary statements about the type of word study that would be beneficial.

As for Sarah's orthographic knowledge, this sample shows that she has learned many consonants and that she is experimenting with short vowels. The substitutions are entirely predictable given the research on spelling development (Bear & Templeton, 1998; Templeton & Bear, 1992a; Templeton & Morris, 1999; Zutell, 1994). Other than in the word *course,* she has placed a vowel in each syllable. The deletion of the vowel in CRS is due to the semivocalic nature of the *r*. In this example, the letter *r* represents the /r/ and the vowel sound. According to the sequence of development presented in the previous chapter, Sarah is in the letter name–alphabetic stage of spelling.

This chapter offers various guides to follow to determine a stage of spelling development for each student. The instructional chapters, 5 through 9, provide detailed discussions of the orthographic features to look for in each stage of development, as well as a series of word study activities to use with students in each stage. For Sarah, the activities presented in Chapter 6 for students in the letter name–alphabetic stage will be most useful.

There are three steps in this assessment process:

Step 1. Collect a spelling sample that includes several invented spellings.
Step 2. Analyze the spelling sample for stage of development and orthographic knowledge.
Step 3. Monitor growth and plan instruction.

The spelling sample in Figure 3-1 is the kind of raw data used to determine a spelling stage. In the next section we will take you through the steps of conducting a spelling-by-stage assessment.

The information in Box 3-1 presents some practical guidelines to use as you conduct your assessments. Consider these points so that you will be sensitive to factors that may inhibit students in their spelling.

1. *Collect a Spelling Sample.* To determine stages of spelling, the first step in the assessment process is to document the way students spell. Students' spelling can be collected from daily writing, or you can administer one of the spelling inventories described in this chapter. You will want to look at students' spelling across several samples—journal entries, first drafts of stories and reports, as well as spelling inventories. Compare the spellings from the inventories to spellings from students' writing to make sure students are performing at a similar level in both types of writing.

Sharon
1. bed   11. spole   spoil
2. ship   12. serveng   serving
3. when   13. chued   chewed
4. lump   14. cairies   carries
5. float   15. marched
6. train   16. shower
7. place   17. catel   cattle
8. drive   18. faver   favor
9. bright   19. ripan   ripen
10. shoping   shopping   20. celer   cellar

Late Within Word Pattern   11/20

FIGURE 3-1   Sample of a Student's Spelling Paper

The spelling inventories presented in this text are quick and easy to administer. The information they provide will indicate what your students know about words, and help you plan instruction in your class. These lists have been specially designed to obtain a significant number of invented spellings, a sample large enough to determine a spelling stage. As a teacher just learning to administer the inventory, analyze development, and plan instruction, you may prefer to start by assessing one small group of students before trying to assess the whole class.

By analyzing what students use but confuse, you will know where to focus instruction. So be sure to collect a sizable sample of invented spellings. The spelling inventories are especially useful when students' writings do not contain invented spellings. This is particularly true when students limit their word choices to words they know how to spell or use other sources such as word walls for correct spellings.

2. Analyze the Sample for Spelling Stage and Orthographic Knowledge.   The second part of the assessment process is to analyze students' work to determine a level of spelling development. With a little practice, you will be able to look at students' spelling inventories and determine a stage of spelling for each student. At first, though, you will look at each invented spelling to see what students were using but confusing. Later in this chapter, you will learn about some tools that will make it easier to analyze students' spelling.

3. Monitor Growth and Plan Instruction.   The last part of the assessment process is focused on using this information to monitor students' growth and to plan and organize instruction. Upon completing the spelling-by-stage assessment, you will find that your students are spread across a range of stages, and it will be necessary to organize small groups. This assessment process will steer you to the developmentally appropriate word study activities presented in Chapters 5 through 9.

IMPLEMENTING THE SPELLING-BY-STAGE ASSESSMENT

Inventories used for spelling-by-stage assessment are not tests or part of students' grades. Teachers administer these inventories three times over the school year (e.g., September, January, and May) to check students' progress and to plan word study according to

BOX 3-1 *Five Guidelines for Assessment*

There are a few guidelines to keep in mind as you think about assessment and organizing instruction for word study in the classroom.

1. *Work from a developmental model.*

Use the developmental model in Figure 2-1 by reading from top to bottom across the literacy behaviors of reading, spelling, and writing. Look for corroborating evidence to place students' achievement somewhere along the developmental continuum. This model helps to generate expectations for students' development using an integrated literacy approach. For example, a student's reading behaviors should be in synchrony with the range of writing behaviors.

2. *Use informal assessments as you teach.*

Instead of relying on standardized tests and test results reported in grade levels, use informal assessments and observe students' literacy behaviors in your daily teaching. After watching students participate in word sorts and writing workshops, you can determine what students are learning about the orthography. By observing while teaching, you can gather information and, based on the developmental model presented in Chapter 2, make sense of what students do in their spelling and word recognition.

Teachers observe a variety of behaviors. Consider these examples:

- Teachers learn about students through their oral reading fluency and expression.
- Teachers learn about students at the beginning of the year with learning and literacy interviews, writing samples, and reader response activities.
- Throughout the year, teachers learn about students by talking with them and by trying to solve problems together. These problems can be part of less verbal situations such as working puzzles or playing checkers, or highly verbal situations such as Guided Reading-Thinking Activities (GRTAs; Bear & Barone, 1998; Templeton, 1997).

3. *Welcome surprises for what they say about individual children.*

The expectations you develop by using the model illustrated in Figure 2-1 may or may not be seen in a student's performance. Expectations are one thing; what students can do and what they want to show may not match expectations based on the developmental model. The mismatches observed between reading, writing, and spelling development are most interesting and informative, and they need to be examined carefully.

Some students are out of synchrony in their development. This is true for the notoriously bad speller who is a capable reader. When there is indeed a mismatch between reading and spelling, you can help a student improve his or her spelling and obtain a developmental synchrony by pinpointing the stage of spelling development, and then by providing developmentally rich instruction that addresses the student's needs. Using these assessments and the developmental model, you can develop individual educational plans for students and plan for small-group instruction accordingly.

4. *Do not assess students at their frustration levels.*

This is a common mistake. The **frustration level** is the level at which students are very far from being correct in their work, and where even your assistance would not be sufficient for them to learn. Although there may be times when you dip into students' frustration level, this is no place to collect meaningful information about development. You should take a commonsense approach here: How well does anyone do when under extreme pressure to perform, and, in this case, when the speller knows that he or she is not doing well? And how realistic a reflection of proficiency is this performance anyway? Part of the frustration a student experiences comes from not having the structural and cognitive background to support a reasonable guess. Students' frustration work can put you off the developmental track, for so often work performed at the frustration level contains a fair amount of "spitting at the page," where students spell by plugging in letters.

5. *Start with what students can do and track progress over time.*

In the diagnostic process, focus on what students' errors reflect about what they know. For example, a student who spells *feet* as FETE has moved beyond the simple linear approach to spelling; otherwise the student would have spelled *feet* as FET.

The assessment must be conducted on a schedule that is helpful. Assess informally throughout the year to track progress and help explain students' development to the next teacher. To most successfully assess your students' development and progress you should conduct informal spelling assessments three times over a school year.

development. Most teachers use the same list throughout the year. However, as students progress, you may want to use a more advanced spelling inventory to examine how students spell more challenging words. These spelling-by-stage assessments create student profiles and can be included in students' portfolios.

The following discussion of the spelling inventories includes many examples for you to consider. Specific directions for administering the inventories, and the error and feature guides are compiled in the appendix. You will also find the following spelling inventories in the appendix:

Elementary Spelling Inventories

1. Elementary qualitative spelling inventory A—*bed, ship, when*
2. Elementary qualitative spelling inventory B—*net, trip, crime*
3. Primary qualitative spelling inventory—*tan, pet, dig*
4. Intermediate qualitative spelling inventory—*speck, switch, throat*
5. McGuffey Graded Qualitative Spelling Inventory, Grades 1–8

Upper Level and Content-Specific Spelling Inventories

6. Upper level qualitative spelling inventory—*confusion, pleasure, resident*
7. Content area spelling inventory in biology
8. Content area spelling inventory in geometry
9. Content area spelling inventory in U.S. history

The sixth inventory is a developmental spelling inventory for middle school and high school. The first word (*confusion*) is the easiest word to spell, and *camouflage* is the most difficult word. Spelling inventories in the content areas—biology, geometry, and U.S. history—are presented next. These inventories provide the teacher with a sense of students' development and knowledge of the content-related terms.

When you are first learning how to determine a spelling stage for students, you will want to use the guides that accompany several of these inventories. With practice, you will be able to look over a student's paper and quickly determine where the student is developmentally. It can be extremely helpful for teachers to review each others' assessments. To ensure independent ratings, both raters should record their assessments on separate class rosters, or on the back of the paper.

Spelling stages can be further refined by dividing them into thirds: early, middle, and late. The gradations within each stage make the assessment of orthographic knowledge more precise than just a stage designation. The three gradations within each stage make it possible to resolve scoring differences between raters. For example, a teacher who says that a student is in the late letter name–alphabetic stage is quite close to a teacher who has determined that the student is an early within word pattern stage speller. In the section on organizing instruction (step 3 of the assessment process), which appears later in this chapter, the gradations make it easier to group students for instruction.

The developmental scale presented in Figure 3-2 shows these gradations. For example, the within word pattern stage is divided into thirds: early within word pattern, middle within word pattern, and late within word pattern. The 15-point scale presented beside these stage gradations is used when a numerical score for the stages of spelling is needed. For example, numerical scores come in handy when you want to examine growth in classrooms and tutoring programs. With computer software such as Microsoft Excel, it is easy to show statistically what students' growth in orthographic knowledge has been.

The spelling-by-stage assessment has been used for over 18 years by classroom teachers. With some training, such as the training provided in this chapter, teachers' spelling-by-stage assessments are reliable. In several studies, these assessments have been highly correlated with scores on standardized spelling tests. In one study, teachers who were involved in a 1½-hour training session learned to make spelling-by-stage assessments with good accuracy. Interrater reliabilities are usually quite high (> .90), and the correlation between the spelling-by-stage assessments and the number of words spelled correctly is equally high.

Spelling-by-Stage Assessment Scale

Gradation	Stage	Numerical Scale
Early	Emergent	1
Middle	Emergent	2
Late	Emergent	3
Early	Letter Name–Alphabetic	4
Middle	Letter Name–Alphabetic	5
Late	Letter Name–Alphabetic	6
Early	Within Word Pattern	7
Middle	Within Word Pattern	8
Late	Within Word Pattern	9
Early	Syllables and Affixes	10
Middle	Syllables and Affixes	11
Late	Syllables and Affixes	12
Early	Derivational Relations	13
Middle	Derivational Relations	14
Late	Derivational Relations	15

Adapted from Bear (1988).

FIGURE 3-2   Stages of Spelling Development for Spelling-by-Stage Assessment

More so than the number of words spelled correctly, the spelling-by-stage analysis leads to a developmental assessment which guides word study instruction (Bear, 1992). If you are interested in finding a grade level for students in Grades 1 through 8, you may want to use the McGuffey Qualitative Spelling Inventory (Schlagal, 1992) presented in the appendix. These words are drawn from frequency lists for grade levels, and were selected qualitatively for the features they ask students to consider.

Where Do Inventories Come From?

Throughout the course of our work with Edmund Henderson at the McGuffey Reading Center, we learned to develop effective spelling inventories. The words we used in our assessments were chosen *to reflect high frequency spelling features or patterns.* For example, a word like *train* will show which students use the alphabetic principle characteristic of the letter name–alphabetic stage (TRAN), compared to students who use but confuse long vowel patterns typical of the within word pattern stage (TRANE).

As part of research studies, many of Henderson's students developed shorter lists. Darrell Morris developed a variety of short lists, as well as a spelling inventory which covers the range from emergent spelling through within word pattern spelling (Morris, Nelson, & Perney, 1986). With a point system to score the inventory, they found that the spelling score predicted achievement at the end of first grade with greater power than a standardized reading measure. In his dissertation on beginning reading, Bear developed a spelling list that scaled words from easiest to hardest. Arranging the words from easiest to hardest made it possible to limit the number of words that students had to spell. After collecting thousands of samples, Bear developed error guides that matched the developmental sequence from late in the emergent stage to well into the derivational relations stage (Bear, 1992; Bear, Templeton, & Warner, 1991).

The feature guides presented in the appendix are an extenuation of the dissertations of Kathy Ganske (1994) and Neva Viise (1992). They developed spelling inventories which classified students' errors in a hierarchy of orthographic features that represent spelling development at each stage.

In the classroom, these spelling inventories have been used to obtain a general picture of students' development. Although the lists presented in the appendix do not test for all spelling features, the words do cover the crucial orthographic features for each stage of spelling. This makes it possible to analyze the words students spelled to determine a spelling stage.

The words in the first four elementary spelling inventories and the upper level inventory are arranged from easiest to hardest. In the first elementary list, *bed* has been the easiest word, and *emphasize* has been the most difficult word for students to spell correctly. The same ordering has been used in the development of the upper level spelling inventory. In a study of 456 middle school students, 95% spelled *inspection* correctly, and only 19% spelled *emphasize* correctly. The words in these lists cover a wide range of features and levels of difficulty.

Elementary Spelling Inventories

The elementary spelling inventories presented in the appendix are used through sixth grade. By April, kindergartners can take the inventory, and by October, every first grader can attempt the first 10 words. Certainly by second grade, all students can participate. Given its extensive use and its broad applicability from Grades K–6, the first elementary spelling inventory in the appendix, beginning with the words *bed, ship,* and *when,* is given the greatest attention in this chapter. The same inventory can be used several times during the year as long as these words are not taught directly or assigned in spelling tests. There are three additional inventories to use as alternate forms.

How to Administer the Spelling Inventories

These spelling inventories are as easy as any spelling test to administer and should take no more than 15 minutes to complete. One of the nice things about most of the inventories is that they can be discontinued after students miss five words in a row. The spelling lists and the basic directions for administering the inventories are presented with each inventory in the appendix. These lists can be reproduced and used by teachers to create a school profile and to help track students' progress over several years.

Create a Relaxed Atmosphere

Students need to know why the spelling inventory is being administered; they need to be encouraged to relax and do the best they can. It is easier to create a relaxed environment working in small groups, especially for kindergarten and first grade students. Students in second grade and up are usually comfortable at spelling and can take the inventory quickly and easily as a whole class. Sometimes children are particularly uptight about taking what they see as a test. Therefore, it is important to emphasize to students that their work will help you be a better teacher, and that this is not a test that will be part of a grade. Be direct in an explanation for having them spell the words:

> Your work spelling these words will help me be a better teacher. Your work will help me understand how you are learning to read and write and how I can help you learn.

Teachers often tell students that as long as they try their best in spelling these words, they will earn an A for the assignment. Once these things are explained, most students are able to give the spelling a good effort.

When a student is extremely frustrated and upset, ask the student to spell the word to you: "You've worked hard writing and spelling. I'll be glad to do the writing if you will spell to me. I'll be your secretary by writing down what you spell." Most students welcome this invitation. Some students approach all writing tasks with some trepidation.

When a student has a death grip on the pencil, it is best to back away and look elsewhere for spelling information. In contrast to the death grip, some students write so lightly or so tiny that their writing cannot be read. This is another sign that it is time to ease the pressure the student is feeling.

Ask students to write the words down the page in no more than two columns. (Invariably, a few younger students write from left to right.) After the initial instructions, say each word twice. It is common practice to say the word in a sentence. Sentences are provided for the first elementary list and the upper level spelling inventory. However, for most words, saying the word in a sentence is time consuming and may even be distracting. There are a few words for which the context of a sentence will be helpful. For example, *cellar* is used in a sentence to differentiate it from *seller.*

Occasionally, after spelling an entire list, and if there is time, students are asked to place a star by the words which they think they may not have spelled correctly, and to take a second try at the words they starred. Throughout this reexamination, students show their willingness to reflect on their work. These notations and successive attempts are additional indicators of the depth of students' orthographic knowledge.

Lower elementary students sometimes copy from each other when they are uncomfortable spelling. It is easier to see if a student is copying when the inventory is administered in small groups. Students can be asked not to copy or look onto another paper. You can conduct lessons like the one described in Box 3-2 to show students how to spell words they are not sure they know how to spell. Since there will be many opportunities to collect corroborating information, there is no reason to be upset when primary children copy. If it is clear that a student has copied, make a note to this effect after collecting the papers.

Can You Read Students' Handwriting?

After collecting the papers, or while walking around the room, teachers should look for words they cannot read. Without making students feel that something is wrong, it is appropriate to ask them to read the letters in the words that cannot be deciphered: "I am having a little trouble reading some letters. Can you tell me the letters in this word?" Students who write in cursive and whose writing is difficult to read can be asked to print. There will only be a few papers that should cause much difficulty in this regard.

How Many Words Do Students Spell?

As noted in the directions of the elementary spelling inventory, teachers look at students' papers after each set of five words. Once familiar with analyzing spelling, teachers can walk around the room and scan the papers after each set of words to see whether or not to continue. The spelling can stop as soon as a spelling stage can be determined. For example, you will know if a student is an emergent speller after just five words. Play it on the safe side and discontinue the spelling when there is enough information. The administration of the inventory can be spread over a few days; for those who need to continue, subsequent sets are administered in groups on another day.

A similar provision for discontinuing the assessment is noted in the upper level spelling inventory. We have found that a sufficient number of words has been collected when a student misses five out of the first eight words. By walking around the room, teachers can see if there are several students who have missed this many words. If so, on subsequent days, teachers can move students to small groups and use the elementary inventory with those who had so much difficulty with the upper level list.

Analyzing Students' Papers

We have developed a checklist, error guides, and feature guides to help you analyze students' spelling. The forms you need are contained in the appendix. The analysis begins when you score students' papers, but then the focus is on a qualitative analysis. In this

BOX 3-2

Spelling the Best We Can: A Lesson to Encourage Invented Spelling

Students have to be comfortable spelling words they may not know how to spell. The ability to spell is important to their writing. A hesitant writer who labors over spelling words will lose the reward of expressing new ideas. Students who are willing to risk being wrong by inventing their spelling have an easier time getting their ideas down.

To help students feel more comfortable writing, before the spelling assessments, conduct a few lessons either in small groups or with the whole class. The theme of this lesson is "How to spell the best we can." Lessons like the one to follow can be conducted over several days. Each aspect of the lesson should be repeated a few times.

A Discussion to Encourage Invented Spelling

"We're going to do a lot of writing this year. We will write nearly every day. Sometimes our writing will be drawings and pictures. We will also write stories and write about what we see and do. When we write, there are times when we do not know how to spell a word. This is part of learning: If we already knew how to spell all words, we wouldn't need to learn. When we want to write a word, and we don't know how to spell it, what might we do?"

Student responses usually include:

Ask the teacher.
Ask someone.
Look it up.
Skip it.

At this point you could tell your students, "Write down all the sounds you hear and feel when you say the word. Write down all the sounds and go on. We can work on the spelling together later, but for now, get your ideas down."

A second part of this lesson is to spell a few words together:

"Who has a word they want to spell? What is a tough word you don't know how to spell?"
A child may offer, "Ninja turtle."
"That's a great one. Can we keep to the second word, *turtle*?"
Assuming that they agree, ask them to say the word *turtle*.

"Turtle."
Begin then to examine the orthographic features: "What's the first letter at the beginning of *turtle*? Say the word again, and then tell me."
"Turtle. T."
Write down a *T*. Then ask a few students what the next sounds are that they "hear and feel."

After a few minutes, you may generate several spellings of turtle: TL, TRTL, TERDL, and TERTUL.

Finally, talk about what to do if the student can only figure out one or two sounds in a word. "Start with the sound at the beginning. Write the first letter and then draw a line." Here, you would write *T* with a line: T_____.

Occasionally, a child will be hypercritical about another student's attempt: "That's not the right way to spell it!" You cannot tolerate someone being criticized for earnest effort. Be careful to handle this criticism firmly. You may say: "The important thing is that you have written your word down, and that you can reread what you have written." Then direct the group's attention back to the board: "On the board here, there are four spellings of *turtle*. They all could be correct." Remind students that they are learning, and that there will be times when they don't know how to spell a word and that it is OK to spell the best they can. "We do learn over the years, and you will see your writing improve the more you write. At the end of the year, you will be surprised to see how much more you can write."

One lesson to discuss spelling will not suffice, so plan to conduct similar lessons over a 2-week period. There are three points to keep in mind:

- Model for students—show them how to spell words they do not know how to spell.
- Conduct writing workshop lessons on what to do when an author does not know how to spell a word.
- Have students reread their writing to be sure that they can reread what they have written.

qualitative analysis, you look at students' papers to see what they know as well as what they don't know.

The **checklist** is an easy first step. Through a series of questions, you can check the student's progress through the stages. As you can see in the sample in Figure 3-3, the **error guide** classifies specific spelling errors and shows along the developmental continuum at the top what stage the student is in. Use the **feature analysis** like the one in Figure 3-4 to see a listing of orthographic patterns the student has shown in the spelling. You will have a score for the total number of features students know across the entire developmental array.

With some practice, you can determine what stage a child is in without using these forms, if you wish. Using the forms provided in the appendix, you can see that there are four steps in a qualitative analysis of students' spelling:

1. What orthographic features do students know?

    Use the checklist and feature guides found in the appendix. See Figure 3-4 for an example of a feature guide. On the error guides, look at what words and features students spelled correctly.

2. What do students use but confuse?

    A collection of typical misspellings can be found in the error guides in the appendix.

3. What stage of spelling are students in?

    Consider gradations within the stage: early, middle, or late.

4. What are the focuses of word study instruction for the different developmental levels in the class?

    Choose and develop phonics, spelling, and vocabulary activities. Refer to the sequence chart at the end of Chapter 4. For specific sequences for each stage, refer to the sequence of contrasts at the beginning of the activities chapters, Chapters 6 through 9.

To locate the best activities for your students, start with the error or feature guides to determine a spelling stage, and then turn to the appropriate chapters and use the activity titles to discern the features that are being examined.

It takes some practice to gain confidence and speed analyzing the papers with the error guide. This is because the teacher is looking for a general stage designation and then a gradation within the stage. But, teachers have become accurate in their analyses with an hour or two of practice. With one pack of class papers, a teacher can see the differences in students based on the developmental scheme presented in this book. The analysis of a class of 28 students takes 40 minutes, and will vary from 20 to 60 minutes depending upon how advanced the spelling is and how comfortable the teacher is in determining a stage of spelling for each student.

When working with a pack of student papers, keep the following materials in sight so that you have a guide for thinking about the spelling: an error or a feature guide, and a list of stages in Figure 3-2 or the developmental chart in Figure 2-1. The stage of spelling that you determine for students can be recorded directly on the students' papers if you are using the error guide, or on the feature guide.

How Many Words Did Each Student Spell Correctly?

Before determining a stage of development, take a moment to correct the papers by writing the word beside each error. Date each paper for future reference, and then count the errors and report the ratio of correct to total. For example, if a student spelled 20 words and spelled 16 words correctly, write 16/20.

Error Guide for Elementary Spelling Inventory 1

Student's Name: *David* Teacher: *Cooper* Grade: *2* Date: *9/8*

Number spelled correctly: **1**
Number of words attempted: **10**

Features	Consonants Initial Final		Short Vowels		Digraphs and Blends	Long Vowel Patterns		Other Vowel Patterns	Syllable Junctures, Consonant Doubling, Inflected Endings, Prefixes Suffixes			Bases and Roots		
SPELLING STAGES	EMERGENT		LETTER NAME—ALPHABETIC			WITHIN WORD PATTERN			SYLLABLES AND AFFIXES			DERIVATIONAL RELATIONS		
	MIDDLE	LATE	EARLY	MIDDLE	LATE	EARLY	MIDDLE	LATE	EARLY	MIDDLE	LATE	EARLY	MIDDLE	LATE
1 bed	b	bd	bad	*bed* (circled)										
2 ship	s	sp shp	*sep* (circled)	shep	<u>ship</u>									
3 when	w	yn wn	*wan* (circled)	whan	<u>when</u>									
4 lump	l	lp lmp	*lop* (circled)	lomp	<u>lump</u>									
5 float	f	ft vt flt	fot	*flot* (circled)	flott	flowt	floaut	flote <u>float</u>						
6 train	j	t trn	jran	chran tan *tran* (circled)	teran	traen	trane	<u>train</u>						
7 place	p	ps pls	pas pas	palac *plas* (circled)	plac	pase	plais	plase <u>place</u>						
8 drive	d	j jrv drf	drv griv	jriv *driv* (circled)		jrive	drieve	draive <u>drive</u>						
9 bright	b	bt brt	bit	*brit* (circled)		bite	brite	briete <u>bright</u>						
10 shopping	s	sp spg shp	sapg	sopn	shapng	shopn	shopin	*sopen* (circled)	sopin	shopin	shoping <u>shopping</u>			

Middle Letter Name—Alphabetic

FIGURE 3-3 David's Spelling Marked on an Error Guide

Feature Analysis for Elementary Spelling Inventory 1

Student's Name: **Carol** Teacher: **Price** Grade: **1** Date: **9/4** Total Points: **9**

	EMERGENT LATE	LETTER NAME–ALPHABETIC EARLY MIDDLE LATE		WITHIN WORD PATTERN EARLY MIDDLE LATE		SYLLABLES AND AFFIXES EARLY MIDDLE LATE	DERIVATIONAL RELATIONS EARLY		
	Consonants Initial Final 2/2 6/6	Short Vowels 5	Digraphs and Blends 13	Long Vowel Patterns 5	Other Vowel Patterns 6	Syllable Junctures, Consonant Doubling, Inflected Endings, Prefixes Suffixes 24	Bases and Roots 5	Word	Points /66
1 bed	b ✓ d ✓	e						bed	2
2 ship	p ✓	i	sh					ship	1
3 when	n ✓	e	wh					when	1
4 lump	l ✓	u	mp					lump	1
5 float	t ✓		fl	oa				float	1
6 train	n ✓		tr	ai				train	1
7 place			pl	a-e				place	0
8 drive	v ✓		dr	i-e				drive	2
9 bright			br	igh				bright	0
10 shopping		o	sh			pp ing		shopping	0

Carol's Spelling: bd, sp, trn, lop, fot, chrn, ps, drv, bit, sp

FIGURE 3–4 Carol's Spelling Marked on a Feature Guide

How to score reversals.   Reversals present a small problem. Reversals should be noted, but in the qualitative analysis they should be seen as the letters they were meant to represent. For example, *bed* with the *b* written backwards or *ship* with the *p* written backwards should be counted as correct. These letter reversals occur with decreasing frequency through the letter name–alphabetic stage. By the within word pattern stage, reversals are rare. Notes about students' reversals can be made on students' profiles in their portfolios and planning guides, when it is a problem of extreme frequency or when they occur with regularity in the within word pattern stage, the time when reversals would normally cease to appear.

Relationship between number of words spelled correctly and stages of spelling.   The correlation between the number of words spelled correctly and teachers' spelling-by-stage assessments has been reported to be quite high. In fact, this correlation between stages and the number of words spelled correctly led us to think that the spelling-by-stage assessment would be useful and reliable. In several research studies, the number of words spelled correctly and the stage assessment are highly related to standardized reading achievement measures at all levels, from kindergarten through postsecondary levels (Bear, 1992).

On the first spelling inventory, students who spell words 1–5 (*bed* through *when*) correctly are usually considered to be at least at the end of the letter name–alphabetic stage, and may be in the within word pattern stage, particularly if they are experimenting with long vowel patterns. Students who spell words 1–10 correctly, or nearly so, are in the beginning of the syllables and affixes stage. Lastly, students who spell most of the words from 1–20 correctly are in the derivational relations stage. These ranges can be summarized as follows:

Ranges of Development Based on Number of Words Spelled Correctly

Number of Words Spelled Correctly	Range of Development
0	Emergent—Letter Name–Alphabetic
1–5	Letter Name–Alphabetic—Within Word Pattern
5–10	Within Word Pattern—Syllables and Affixes
10–25	Syllables and Affixes—Derivational Relations

This range is broad, and a qualitative assessment is much more helpful in planning word study activities.

Boundaries between stages.   Even though the words are arranged by difficulty, students' growth is gradual. They do not move absolutely from one stage to another, abandoning all vestiges of the previous stage. Therefore, it is helpful to think of the boundaries between stages of development as fuzzy. Because of this fuzziness, there are students who spell *ship* as SIP and spell *float* correctly. However, there are not many students who spell *ship* as SEP and still spell *float* correctly.

Counting the number of words spelled correctly is easy, and is a starting point, but more qualitative information than the number of errors is needed to determine a stage of spelling development or to plan word study activities. Therefore, teachers who are new to qualitative spelling-by-stage assessments should use the error and feature guides to determine stages of orthographic knowledge for their students.

Qualitative Checklist

Through a series of 20 questions, the checklist takes you through the progression of orthographic features that students learn. With the checklist presented in the appendix, you can look at student writing samples as well as inventories and see what features are used correctly all of the time, often, or not at all. Through this checklist, you will be able to locate a student's spelling stage from emergent through derivational relations. The checklist is an excellent first step in analyzing students' spelling. This form can be used three times over the school year to document students' progress.

Error Guides

The error guides in the appendix present the most common errors observed for each word. The errors are arranged in terms of sophistication, and they are classified under the stage they represent. There is a spelling progression for each word. For example, the growth in errors for *beaches* can be seen from B, BS, BCS, BCHS, to BEECHES.

Refer back to Figure 3-3 for an example of an error guide. The spelling sample recorded onto the error guide shows how a spelling stage can be identified by looking at the configuration of circles. This spelling sample was collected by the classroom teacher of a second grader in September. It is clear that the student, David, included a vowel in each major syllable, and that he was experimenting with short vowels. Although he spelled *bed* correctly, he spelled *when* as WAN. As is discussed in detail in Chapter 6, it is natural for students to experiment with short vowels in this way. In addition, David had learned to spell a few consonant blends and digraphs, but probably not most of them. His teacher looked at his spelling and determined that David was in the middle of the letter name–alphabetic stage of spelling. David's development is a little less advanced than we would want for a beginning second grader, and it may be that he would benefit from some individual tutoring. To plan word study instruction for this student, refer to the sequence of word study activities presented at the end of Chapter 4, as well as the word study activities in the activities section of Chapter 6.

You will find five other spelling samples in Box 3-3 to analyze and compare to our assessments.

Feature Guides

The words in these spelling inventories are designed to "catch fish" by showing students' knowledge over a number of key spelling features that have been shown to relate to specific strategies during the different spelling stages. Feature guides have been created to help teachers understand students' development by orthographic feature. The feature guide in the appendix can be reproduced for each student. The features a student represented correctly are checked in this form. An additional point is added if the entire word is correct. Not every feature, however, is scored, and some words are keyed to specific features that are evident at a specific spelling stage.

You will see at the top of this feature guide a progression of features from initial consonants in the emergent stage, to bases and roots in the derivational relations spelling stage. Total the number of points under each feature, and across for each word. Look down each feature column to determine the needs of individual students.

Refer back to Figure 3-4 for an example of a feature guide in which each word the student spelled was scored by features present. For example, the student scored two points for including the *b* and the *d* in *bed*. By marking the features students have used in spelling, you can see what orthographic features they have mastered. The progression across the top shows the point where instruction should begin as implied by the developmental stage theory. In Figure 3-4, you would start instruction where the child shows a solid knowledge (in this case, initial consonants) and then move on to short vowel word families.

Finding Students on the Developmental Continuum

Each stage is divided into thirds: early, middle, or late. With the error and feature guides, it is evident what features students have mastered and which ones they are still working to master. The question then is this: Where does each student fit along the developmental continuum? A student who appears to have worked through most of the features

BOX 3-3	*Check Your Assessment with Ours*

If you do not have a class to work with, or you want to see a broad spectrum of responses, please take a look at the five students' spelling below.

Our spelling analyses have been printed at the bottom of the samples. Were you close to our assessments? Was there an agreement of stages? If you are off on more than one or two cases, try again. One mental anchor is that within word pat-tern students have mastered simple short vowel patterns, and they experiment with different long vowel spellings. If you have divided the stages into thirds, you may find that our assessments may not be as different from yours as they first appear. Chapters 5 through 9 include many fur-ther samples to consider.

Examples of Students' Spelling in September

	Greg	Jean	Reba	Alan	Mitch
Grade	First	First	Second	Third	Third
bed	BD	bed	bed	bed	bed
ship	SP	SEP	ship	ship	ship
when	WN	WHAN	when	when	when
lump	L	LOP	lump	lump	lump
float	F	FLOT	FLOTE	FLOTE	float
train		TRAN	TRANE	train	train
place		PLAC	PLAIS	place	place
drive		DRIV	drive	drive	drive
bright		BRIT	BRITE	BRIGT	bright
shopping		SOPNG	SHOPEN	SHOPING	shopping
spoil			SPOAL	SPOALE	spoil
serving			serving	SERVEING	serving
chewed			CHUD	CHOUED	chewed
carries			CARES	CARRES	carries
marched			MARCD	marched	marched
shower				SHOUER	shower
cattle				CATTEL	cattle
favor				FAVIR	favor
ripen				ripen	ripen
cellar				SELLER	CELLER

Spelling-by-Stage Assessment
Greg—early letter name–alphabetic
Jean—middle letter name–alphabetic
Reba—middle within word pattern
Alan—late within word pattern
Mitch—At least in the middle of the syllables and affixes. Another five words would be helpful.

relevant to a stage is probably at the end of the stage (e.g., late letter name–alphabetic). Conversely, if a student is beginning to use the key elements of a stage, but still has some remnants from the previous stage, it can be said that the student is in an early point in that new stage (early letter name–alphabetic).

You do not need to make the discrimination within stages too weighty a decision. When it comes to planning instruction, you will take a step backwards, choosing word study activities at a slightly easier level than the stage determination may have indi-cated. It is important to take this step backwards because students need to learn how to sort words and to play the word study games, and clearly, it is easier to teach students how to sort when they can read the words easily. One of the fundamental principles of word study described in Chapter 4 is to take a step backwards when planning instruction, and so the determination of a stage for students is tempered by this practice.

The McGuffey Spelling Inventory

There are times when teachers want to use a longer and more detailed spelling list. For example, a teacher may want to obtain a full inventory of the students' knowledge of short vowels or consonant blends and digraphs. The first four inventories for the elementary grades do not attempt to measure each feature in depth. A more complete list of spelling words can be found in the McGuffey Qualitative Inventory of Word Knowledge (Schlagal, 1992) presented in the appendix. The testing on the McGuffey inventory is stopped when students miss more than 40% on a list. This test is useful for conducting individual testing, and for obtaining grade-level information. The spelling begins with the grade level that corresponds to the student's performance in reading.

This inventory spans Grades 1 through 8. Instructional spelling levels are found when a student scores between 40% and 90% on a list (Morris, Blanton, Blanton, & Perney, 1995; Morris, Nelson, & Perney, 1986). The words in these lists present plenty of opportunities to observe a student's spelling of a variety of features. Consider what patterns the students know and what they are using but confusing. As you look over students' spelling, consider the order in which the students' spelling is growing. You can refer to the sequence of development described in Chapter 2 to see where the students are developmentally. For example, students who show a high level of correctness in spelling the single-syllable words on the third grade list may begin to show the edge of their learning in spelling the many two-syllable words on the fourth grade list. Speaking developmentally, students in the syllables and affixes stage will make spelling errors that demonstrate that they are experimenting with how syllables combine—for example, spelling *fossil* as FOSSEL, and *capture* as CAPCHUR.

For most elementary classes, students' spelling on any of these inventories will show you what you need to know to plan word study instruction. Later in this chapter, you will learn how to use these results to organize groups for instruction.

Upper Level and Content-Specific Spelling Inventories

The upper level qualitative spelling inventory is used in middle school through post-secondary classrooms. The words in this list were chosen because they help identify, more specifically than the elementary inventory, what students in the syllables and affixes and derivational relations stages are doing in their spelling. These words are arranged in order of difficulty, and the directions presented with the inventory suggest that the teacher stop giving the inventory to students who have missed five out of the first eight words. Students who score at this level are usually in the within word pattern stage. On a subsequent day, the teacher can pick up with the test in small groups. For the students who missed many of the first words, the teacher should move back to the elementary list.

Students' spelling on this upper level list shows how they make "the meaning connection" with the orthography (Templeton, 1983). Students in these final stages of spelling learn to preserve meaning in spite of changes in sound. For example, in pronunciation, the second vowel in *reside* changes from a long-i to a **schwa** sound in *resident*. In spite of this sound change, the spelling remains the same and is a cue to meaning.

This upper level inventory has been used in studies to relate spelling development and reading development in seventh and eighth graders and high school students (Bear, Templeton, & Warner, 1991). In addition, this list has been used to help assess students at the university level who are having reading difficulties as well as to assess students for general equivalency diploma (GED) programs.

Spelling inventories guide teachers in determining students' developmental level.

The content-specific spelling inventories in the appendix have been developed with secondary teachers who want to assess students' general orthographic knowledge as well as their knowledge of the content-specific vocabulary.

Upper Level Spelling Inventory

The upper level error guide in the appendix presents errors from students in the within word pattern, syllables and affixes, and derivational relations stages. The errors found in most students' spelling are probably listed here. As teachers circle the errors, they find that the errors fall fairly evenly in a column down the page. Errors that are not listed on this page are written beside the closest invented spelling.

Students in the within word pattern stage and even in the syllables and affixes stage omit syllables in the middle of words. It seems that for these students there can occasionally be an overload, and the middle syllables are forgotten (PROPARTY for *prosperity*, CORSPOND for *correspond*). Their misspellings of the suffixes are often phonetic renderings uncommon in English (SHUN for *tion*). Students in the within word pattern stage also tend to overuse long vowel patterns (DECORATORE for *decorator*, ENDIGHTMENT for *indictment*).

Students in the syllables and affixes stage begin to spell common suffixes correctly. Toward the end of this stage, they begin to also spell less common word endings correctly (the *ate* in *fortunate*, the *or* in *decorator*, the *ious* in *hilarious*). These students also become more accurate in spelling words in which the consonants are doubled (*commotion*, *propellant*).

During the derivational relations stage, students make the meaning connection with classical roots and stems, and they spell the less common words correctly. This upper level spelling inventory includes several difficult and infrequent orthographic patterns. For example, students who spell *indictment*, *adjourn*, and *camouflage* correctly demonstrate quite a sophisticated knowledge of English orthography.

An example of a marked upper level guide is presented in Figure 3-5. Although Marshall's spelling errors cover the range of the last two spelling stages, it was determined that he was in the late part of the syllables and affixes stage. He has learned many of the more difficult affixes, and is learning when some words are spelled with double consonants. He spelled *opposition* correctly and omitted the double consonants when he spelled SUCESSION for *succession*, CORESPOND for *correspond*, and PROPELENT for *propellant*.

Content Area Spelling Inventories

Several content-specific spelling inventories have been developed (McIntosh & Bear, 1993). These content area inventories give teachers an indication as to how well students will be able to read printed materials related to the content areas, and, at the same time, provide some insight into the students' conceptual background knowledge and vocabulary.

Students who score well on the content-specific inventories tend to do better in these classes than students who are unable to spell many of the content words correctly. It may be that the student who has a difficult time spelling the content words also has a difficult time reading the texts (Bear, Templeton, & Warner, 1991). A relationship between students' orthographic knowledge (as evidenced in word recognition and spelling) and reading achievement has been observed throughout the developmental sequence from emergent through advanced stages of reading and writing (Bear & Templeton, 1998; Templeton & Bear, 1992b).

The premise underlying the content area spelling assessments is that when students' orthographic knowledge is strong, their reading is easier and more fluent. For example, isn't it possible that the students who spell *oxygen* correctly are more capable readers than students who spell it as OXIGIN? Their ideas are no brighter, but their verbal proficiencies allow them to read with greater ease than the student who has a difficult time spelling and reading the key vocabulary.

The words teachers select for content area inventories are often the key vocabulary words for the course. The words in the content spelling inventories can also function as a prompt in the same way that a structured overview, a No Book Directed Reading-Thinking Activity (DRTA); (Bear & McIntosh, 1990; Gill & Bear, 1988), a web, or a cluster help students to think about the topic they are studying. Teaching students these words in isolation, in rote vocabulary exercises, is not the direction to take. Instead, teachers can help students make meaning connections between what they know and what they are trying to learn (Templeton, 1992).

Teachers start to examine this meaning connection with students by asking them to star the words on the list that are familiar: "Put a star if you know the meaning of a word, no matter how you spelled the word." Students who spell accurately star more words. This record of familiarity with the subject can be a reference to track students' vocabulary growth in the particular content area.

Finally, before collecting students' papers, some teachers take a moment at the overhead projector to ask students to think about how words are related to the content area. Together, the teacher and the students brainstorm a list of related words. For example, if *geology* were a word on an inventory, students could work together to find other words that have *geo* in them. Similarly, some teachers ask students to sort the words in the content inventory into related groups. The meaning relations are at the heart of word study in the content areas. The spelling and meaning connection is discussed in more detail in Chapters 8 and 9. As papers are collected, teachers may reiterate that students' work will help them determine what to teach and will not be a part of their grades.

The U.S. history inventory presented in the appendix is accompanied by a developmental error guide that will also give teachers a clearer sense of students' spelling development.

Error Guide for Elementary Spelling Inventory 1

Directions: Circle student's spelling attempts below. If a spelling is not listed, write it in where it belongs on the developmental continuum. Circle the spelling stage that summarizes the student's development.

Student's Name __Marshall__   Teacher __Gardner__   Period __6__   Grade __Sr.__   Date __9/22__

Number spelled correctly: __7__
Number of words attempted: __22__

STAGES:

SYLLABLES AND AFFIXES / DERIVATIONAL RELATIONS

	WITHIN WORD PATTERN		SYLLABLES AND AFFIXES			DERIVATIONAL RELATIONS	
	MIDDLE	LATE	EARLY	MIDDLE	LATE	EARLY	MIDDLE	LATE

Late Syllables and Affixes

1. confusion – confushon confution confusion confution confussion confution **confusion**
2. pleasure – plasr plager plejer pleser plesher plesour plesure pleasur **pleasure**
3. resident – resatin reserdent resudint resedent reseadent **resident** resadent
4. puncture – pucshr pungchr puncur puncker punksher punchure puncure punture puncsure **puncture**
5. confidence – confadents confedents confadence confedense confedence **confidince** confidense **confidence**
6. fortunate – forhnat frehnit foohinit forchenut fochininte *fortunet* fortunate **fortunate**
7. decorator – dector decrater decorater decarator decrator decorate decorater decorater **decorator**
8. opposition – opasion opasishan opozcison opasitian opposion oposition opposision oposition **opposition**
9. prosperity – proparty propary property prosperaty prosparaty **prosparity** prosperaty **prosperity**
10. succession – sucesion sucksession sucession succsession **succession** succesion **succession**
11. emphasize – infaside infacize ephacise emphasize emfisize imfasize emphisize **emphasize**
12. correspond – corspond corispond corospond **correspond** corrospond
13. commotion – comoushown comoshion comosion camotion cumotion comocion comossion comotion **commotion**
14. propellant – porpelent proplent porpelont **propelont** propelentt propelent propellent **propellant**
15. hilarious – halaris halerace halaryous hollarries halarios hollarous halarious hallarious hularious helariaus halarous **hilarious** hilerious helarious **hilarious**
16. criticize – critise crisize critize critasise critize critasise critaize **criticize** critiçize criticise **criticize**
17. indictment – enditment inditment enditement endightment **inditement** endightment indightment indicment **indictment**
18. reversible – reversbell reversabul reversobol **reversabel** reverseable **reversable** revercible reversabile reversable **reversible**
19. category – cadagoure kadacorey cadacory catagery cadigore catagore catigoury catigory catorgory catigorie **catagory** category **category**
20. adjourn – *ajurn* agern ajurn ajorne ajurn adgorn adjorn adjourne adjorn **adjourn** adjourn **adjourn**
21. excerpt – exherpt exhert exherpt exsort exerp ecsert exsert exert **camophloge** exsurpt exserpt **excerpt**
22. camouflage – camaflag camoflosh comoflodge camaphlauge camouflague camaflauge *camaphloge* camoflauge camoflage camaflouge camoflage **camouflage**

STAGES:

	WITHIN WORD PATTERN	SYLLABLES AND AFFIXES			DERIVATIONAL RELATIONS	
	MIDDLE LATE	EARLY MIDDLE LATE			EARLY MIDDLE LATE	

FIGURE 3–5 Marshall's Spelling Marked on an Upper Level Error Guide

In part, the relationship between literacy achievement and achievement in content classes is strong because the ways in which students are tested are dependent upon their literacy proficiency. Because literacy is counted on heavily to communicate ideas in school, and because content instruction is textbook oriented, students who have difficulty with these spelling tests often have problems earning good grades. Because they cannot read well, they are denied access to ideas. Teachers help these students who have difficulty with the text by finding materials on the topics that they can read with fair ease.

Consider a few of the spellings of three children who took the biology spelling inventory:

Word	Brian	Samantha	Teresa
allergy	ALLERGEEY	ALERGIE	*allergy*
antigen	ANTIJUN	ANTIGENE	*antigen*
immunity	IMUNTY	IMMUENTY	*immunity*
carcinogen	CARSOMAGEN	CARSINAGEN	CARCINIGEN
vaccine	VACINE	*vaccine*	*vaccine*

Brian is in the within word pattern stage. When he comes to a word at his frustration level, he drops a middle syllable—a common pattern when students try to spell polysyllabic words at a frustration level. Samantha has spelled one word correctly, and has made a meaning connection in her spelling of *antigen*. Teresa is in the derivational relations stage and will most likely find her texts easy to read. The teacher will need to find support materials for Brian, because his text is probably too difficult for him.

In summary, the content spelling inventory is used to assess literacy achievement and the vocabulary knowledge students bring to their content studies. Students who are way off in their invented spellings of these content words are likely to have trouble reading the textbook. In word study activities, teachers help students grow in both their conceptual and orthographic development by studying the meaning connection.

Spelling Among Students Who Speak Other Languages

To obtain a complete understanding of the word knowledge among students for whom English is a second language, teachers study how students approach literacy in their first language. A spelling inventory in the child's spoken language can be administered. An excellent spelling inventory for Spanish has been developed by Tom Estes at the University of Virginia (Estes, 1998).

The Influence of Spanish on Spelling in English

It is important to study how students' pronunciation and knowledge of Spanish are used when they spell in English. A variety of substitutions can be traced to the influence of students' knowledge of Spanish on the students' spelling. For example, because there is no *th* in Spanish, students who are more familiar with Spanish may spell *the* as DA. The same is true for the *sh* consonant digraph, and so a word like *ship* may be spelled CHAP because the CH and the A are as close as Spanish can offer to the *sh* and the short-i sound.

The silent *h* in Spanish can be spelled with a *J*, and so *hit* may be spelled JET. Short-i is a bit confusing for Spanish speaking students, and the short-i may be spelled with an *e*. The correspondence between the English short-o sound, as in *pop*, is represented with an *a*, which seems close to the strong *a* vowel in Spanish; *hot* could be spelled JAT.

The impact of a student's knowledge of spoken Spanish on English spelling can be seen in this spelling sample from Rosa, a second grader:

1. bed	bed	**11.** spoil	SPOYO
2. ship	SHEP	**12.** serving	SORVEN
3. when	WAN	**13.** chewed	SHOD
4. lump	LAMP	**14.** carries	CARES
5. float	FLOWT	**15.** marched	MARSH
6. train	TRAYN	**16.** shower	SHOWAR
7. place	PLEAYS	**17.** cattle	CADOTO
8. drive	TRAYV	**18.** favor	FAYVR
9. bright	BRAYT	**19.** ripen	RAYPN
10. shopping	SHAPEN	**20.** cellar	SALLAR

Several of Rosa's spellings follow the logical substitutions that are seen in English speaking children in the letter name–alphabetic stage, that is, SHEP for *ship*, WAN for *when*. Many of her spelling errors make a good deal of sense in relation to her knowledge of Spanish. For example, given that there is no short-u in Spanish, her substitution of LAMP for *lump* makes sense given the way "a" is pronounced in Spanish, as in the *a* in "father" and "gracias." The AY in three of her spellings shows Rosa trying to find a spelling for the long-i. The long-i is really two vowels (a diphthong), and the Y, pronounced as a long-e in Spanish, is used to spell the second half of the long-i. In *spoil* as SPOYO Rosa seems to be using the /y/ sound as in *yes* to help spell /oil/. We find the substitution of SH for the *ch* in *chewed* as further evidence that Rosa is learning English spelling. Because there is no /sh/ sound, it is very common for children to spell *shoes* as CHOES; the *ch* is close to the /sh/ in pronunciation. In this misspelling, Rosa may have overgeneralized what she knew about *sh* in English.

As this spelling sample illustrates, students' invented spellings in other languages are not wrong, but are logical and "interestingly correct." Through understanding children's other languages, teachers understand students' literacy development in English.

WORD STUDY GROUPS

Once it is clear what stages of development students are in, teachers begin to think about organizing instruction. In this section, we discuss grouping students for word study instruction through the **developmental classroom profiles.** These profiles are pictures of students' orthographic knowledge and provide a starting point for planning instruction.

Why Group?

Many teachers who group for guided reading also conduct guided word study in three and sometimes four small groups. Classroom organization charts like those presented later in this chapter, help teachers think of literacy groups. Many elementary teachers now divide classroom activity into three types of work: (1) **circle work** with the teacher (e.g., guided word study groups); (2) **seat work,** in which students work in groups, pairs, or individually on activities and projects; and (3) **center work,** in which students work individually or with a partner in centers or stations set up around the room. At any given time, the class is divided into thirds with approximately the same number of students involved in each of the three types of activities. This format is discussed at length in Chapter 4.

Guided instruction with the teacher is a special time for discussion and word study at a table or on the floor (Henderson, 1981; Templeton, 1997). Teachers keep coming back to this configuration; it seems that it is easier to manage three groups than two, four, or five.

Recent trends in literacy instruction have discouraged some teachers from developing word study groups based on development. Indeed, there are many reasons to be suspicious of homogeneous or ability grouping because often the low groups receive inferior instruction (Stanovich, 1986). However, it can also be argued that students benefit from developmentally appropriate instruction, and that this type of instruction is difficult to achieve when students are heterogeneously grouped for word study.

Clearly, it is a mistake to use ability grouping as the sole way to group students. Throughout the day, there must be a broad mixing of students across ability groups so that talents and ideas can be shared. Experience has shown that when students study a particular orthographic feature, it is best if they are in groups with others who are ready to benefit from guided word study; these groups create proximal learning partners for word study. For example, it is difficult to study long vowel patterns when some of the students in the group are in the letter name–alphabetic stage and still working on short vowel patterns. As the developmental model has shown, students in the within word pattern stage use but confuse long vowel patterns, and they benefit most from examination of this feature.

In addition to the homogeneous groups that work with the teacher in circle or small-group sessions, and the word-sorting partners in word study centers, there are times when students work together in word study workshops or even whole-class word study sessions. While students work on different sorts and with different words, they can work side by side during word study sessions. This is a good time for teachers to observe students sorting, and for students to show each other how they sort. After students sort, they are asked to explain their sorts to someone else before putting them away.

Classroom Profiles

We suggest two ways to create class profiles of your students' stages of spelling and their progress: the **spelling-by-stage classroom organization chart** and the **classroom composite.** The blank spelling-by-stage chart and the feature classroom composite form in the appendix can be used to sketch out word study groups. It is a simple matter to fill in the developmental charts.

Spelling-by-Stage Classroom Organization Chart

In the spelling-by-stage chart, students' papers are reviewed, and their names are recorded underneath the correct gradation within a spelling stage. These charts are a good place to see the class at a glance. Once students' names are entered, teachers begin to look for groupings by thirds. Is there a natural break? You can see some ways to organize word study instruction in the examples presented here. Three classroom profiles are presented in Figure 3-6. The first profile is of a first grade class. This class has many emergent spellers. Four groups were suggested for this class at this point in the school year. In the third and sixth grade examples, the teachers have drawn circles to create groups across spelling stages. The teacher in the sixth grade classroom could consider running two groups at the upper levels, and at times, combine them as one group. The three children in the letter name–alphabetic stage will need special attention because they are significantly behind for being in sixth grade. Ideally, these students will have additional instruction in a tutoring program to review and practice activities that are appropriate for students in the letter name–alphabetic spelling stage.

Figure 3-7 presents two classroom charts which show the guided reading and word study groups in a multigraded classroom in September and May (Bear & Barone, 1989). The groups have stayed remarkably the same except that everyone is further up the scale; graphically, everyone has shifted to the right. Again, you will notice that the groups do not follow stages strictly. There are some children in the within word pattern stage working with children in the syllables and affixes stage. Especially in September, teachers are careful to take a step backwards, so this group would begin with long vowel pattern study. Similarly, in the next group, someone in the middle of the within word pattern stage is working with someone in the middle of the letter name–alphabetic stage. Some of the word study group placement decisions are based on social and psychological factors related to self-esteem, leadership, and behavior dynamics.

There was a fair spread in developmental levels in this multiaged primary classroom. Beginning in the third grade, in some schools, there is less of a spread in students'

First Grade Spelling-by-Stage Classroom Organization Chart

SPELLING STAGES	EMERGENT			LETTER NAME–ALPHABETIC			WITHIN WORD PATTERN			SYLLABLES AND AFFIXES			DERIVATIONAL RELATIONS		
	EARLY	MIDDLE	LATE	EARLY	MIDDLE	LATE	EARLY	MIDDLE	LATE	EARLY	MIDDLE	LATE	EARLY	MIDDLE	LATE

EMERGENT EARLY: Gerald, Doug, Danielle, Jon, Jennifer — 5; Jona, Adam, Caritha, Rayhe — 6
EMERGENT MIDDLE: Buck, Felicia, Brad, Shawn, Luis — 7
EMERGENT LATE: Tammy, Kristy, Brandon, JJ
LETTER NAME–ALPHABETIC EARLY: Milo, Jennifer
LETTER NAME–ALPHABETIC MIDDLE: Brandi, Matthew, Jerrilynn — 5

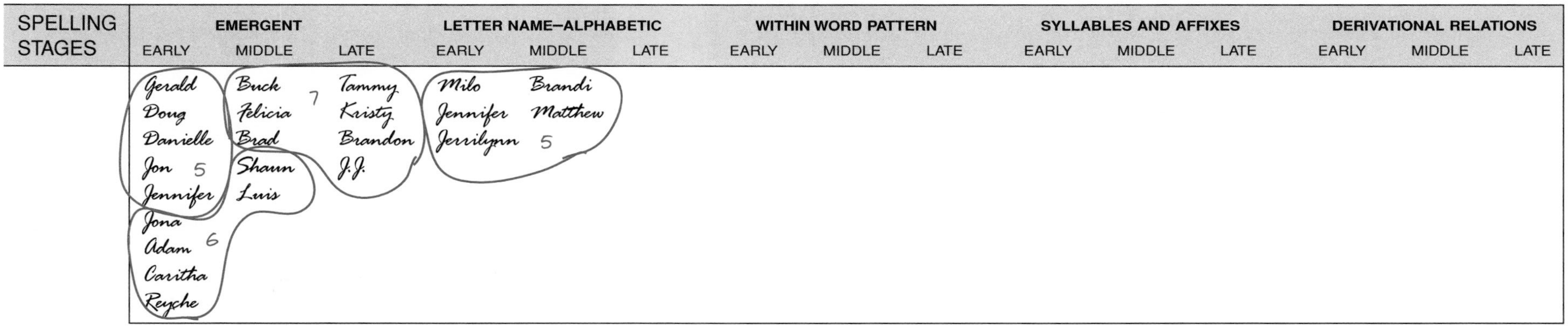

Third Grade Spelling-by-Stage Classroom Organization Chart

SPELLING STAGES	EMERGENT			LETTER NAME–ALPHABETIC			WITHIN WORD PATTERN			SYLLABLES AND AFFIXES			DERIVATIONAL RELATIONS		
	EARLY	MIDDLE	LATE	EARLY	MIDDLE	LATE	EARLY	MIDDLE	LATE	EARLY	MIDDLE	LATE	EARLY	MIDDLE	LATE

LETTER NAME–ALPHABETIC EARLY: Kyle — 6
LETTER NAME–ALPHABETIC MIDDLE: Tiffany, Jason, Chris, Ken, Aaron, Juan, Jean; Sabrine, Cody
WITHIN WORD PATTERN EARLY: Joanne — 7
WITHIN WORD PATTERN MIDDLE: Nancy, Grace -->, Amy
WITHIN WORD PATTERN LATE: Jill, Rachel
SYLLABLES AND AFFIXES EARLY: Lisa — 5
SYLLABLES AND AFFIXES MIDDLE: Joe

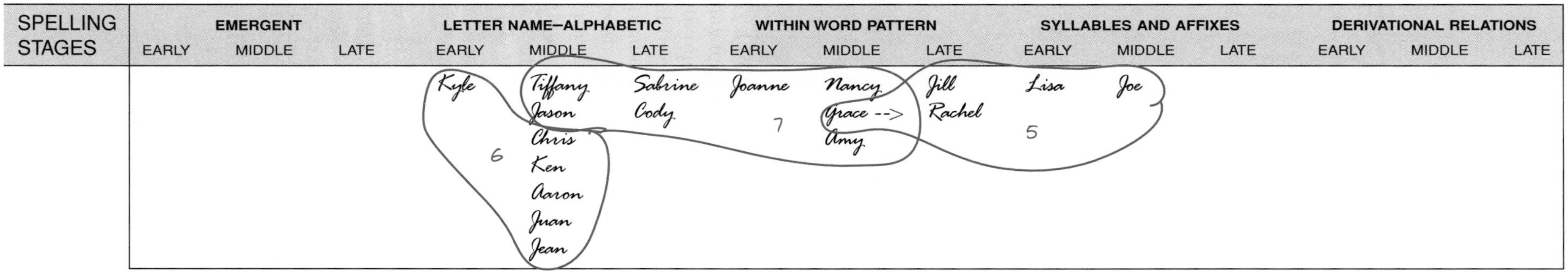

Sixth Grade Spelling-by-Stage Classroom Organization Chart

SPELLING STAGES	EMERGENT			LETTER NAME–ALPHABETIC			WITHIN WORD PATTERN			SYLLABLES AND AFFIXES			DERIVATIONAL RELATIONS		
	EARLY	MIDDLE	LATE	EARLY	MIDDLE	LATE	EARLY	MIDDLE	LATE	EARLY	MIDDLE	LATE	EARLY	MIDDLE	LATE

LETTER NAME–ALPHABETIC EARLY: Victoria, Juan — 3; Mike
WITHIN WORD PATTERN MIDDLE: Jon, Elizabeth--> Nicole
SYLLABLES AND AFFIXES EARLY: <-- Arcelia — 9
SYLLABLES AND AFFIXES MIDDLE: Phong, Ray, Scott, Don, <-- Rashid
SYLLABLES AND AFFIXES LATE: Sean, Maro, Christa, Jonna 6, Heather, Esther
DERIVATIONAL RELATIONS EARLY: Steve, Sheri — 11; Desiree, Eric, Mary — 5

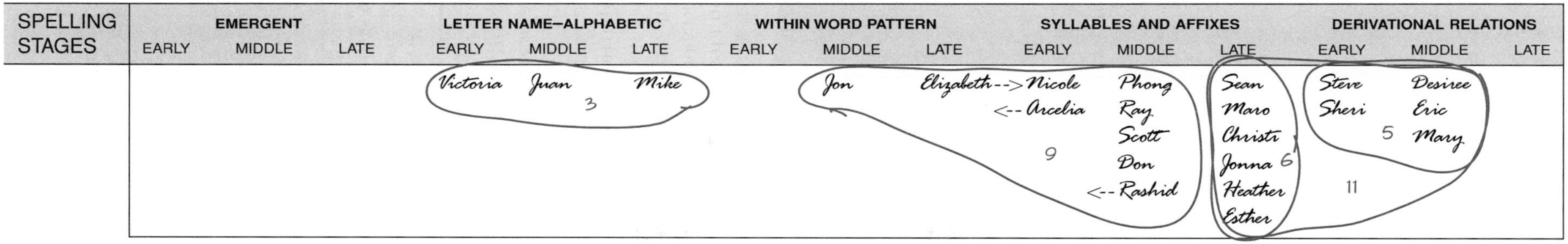

FIGURE 3-6   Examples of Spelling-by-Stage Classroom Organization Charts

Spelling-by-Stage Classroom Charts for September

SPELLING STAGES	EMERGENT			LETTER NAME–ALPHABETIC			WITHIN WORD PATTERN			SYLLABLES AND AFFIXES			DERIVATIONAL RELATIONS		
	EARLY	MIDDLE	LATE	EARLY	MIDDLE	LATE	EARLY	MIDDLE	LATE	EARLY	MIDDLE	LATE	EARLY	MIDDLE	LATE
	Jed	Casey Jamie	Sarah	Mary Gerald Loren	Michael	Jesse Eldon	Nicole Elder	Lucas		Sam J.R.	Jess Imran Lyn Chris	Matthew Ryan Anna Amir	Amanda Jacob			

Spelling-by-Stage Classroom Charts for May

SPELLING STAGES	EMERGENT			LETTER NAME–ALPHABETIC			WITHIN WORD PATTERN			SYLLABLES AND AFFIXES			DERIVATIONAL RELATIONS		
	EARLY	MIDDLE	LATE	EARLY	MIDDLE	LATE	EARLY	MIDDLE	LATE	EARLY	MIDDLE	LATE	EARLY	MIDDLE	LATE
				Jamie Casey	Loren		Sarah	Lyn Nicole Michael Lucas Gerald Jed	Sam	Jesse Eldon	Ryan Jess Chris Elder Mary	Amanda Matthew Imran Anna	Jacob		

Adapted from Bear & Barone (1989).

FIGURE 3-7 Spelling-by-Stage Classroom Charts in a First to Third Grade Multiaged Classroom

development. Such was the case for the third grade class in November profiled in Figure 3-8. The majority of the students were centered around the beginning of the syllables and affixes stage. In part, to make for a manageable setting, as noted by the arrows in the figure, two children were moved into the first group and two children worked in the third group.

Classroom Composite Organization Chart for the Feature Analyses

The analysis by feature is easily transferred to the classroom composite form in the appendix. Looking at this class composite, you gain a sense of your group as a whole and how to form small instructional groups. *Highlight children who are making more than one error on a particular feature.* For example, a child who gets all but one of the short vowels correct has a good understanding of short vowels; this would be a good place to begin word study instruction. However, children who only get two or three of the short vowels need a lot of work on that feature. Keep moving back in feature until you find an independent level where they are very accurate. If students are new to word study activities with you, the independent level would be a good place to start instruction. It is clear in the class composite in Figure 3-9 that most of the students were in the syllables and affixes stage of development. Another group of students would begin word study by looking at single-syllable word patterns for long vowels and less frequent short vowel patterns. One child would begin with short vowel word study.

Some word study groups are quite similar in development, and it is fine to conduct the same activity with two groups. Smaller groups of 8 to 10 students make it easier for them to listen to each other, and for you to observe how they sort. There are also students at each end of the developmental continuum who, in terms of word study and orthographic development, are outliers. It can be helpful to include these children in the closest developmental group, and work with them on separate activities but within the group. For example, when the group is sorting, the teacher may ask these students to work with a different pack of words, or to work with a partner. In addition, the teacher should look for other ways to get more practice to these students through individual tutoring and work with a literacy specialist.

Groups are fluid, and if a student is challenged to frustration, or if a student is not challenged by the activities, then groups should be reorganized. There are many literacy activities in which students are not grouped by developmental level, as in partner reading, writing workshops, science, social studies, and the many small-group projects related to units of study.

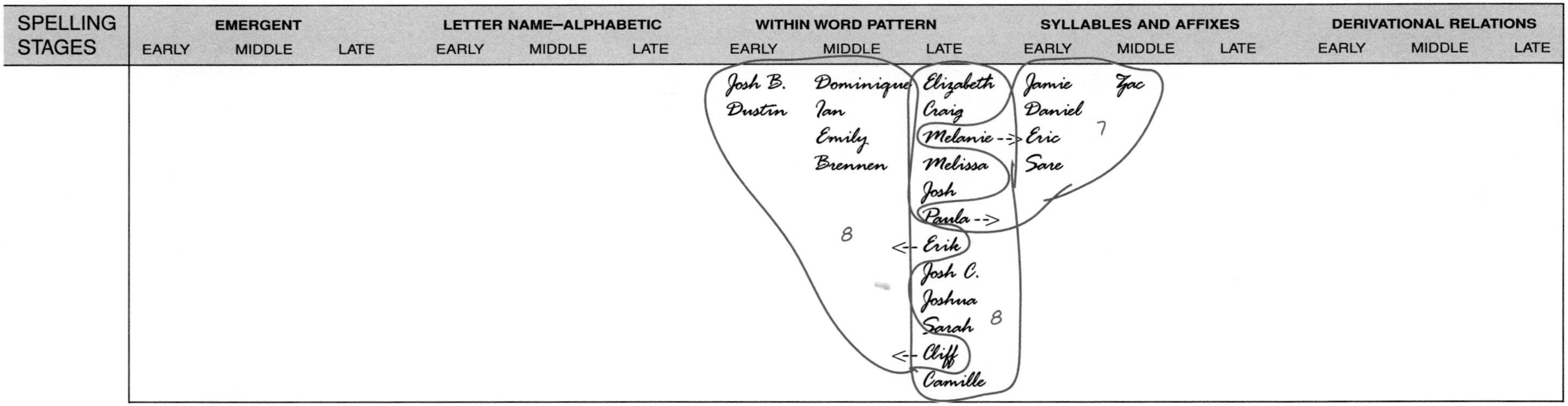

SPELLING STAGES	EMERGENT			LETTER NAME–ALPHABETIC			WITHIN WORD PATTERN			SYLLABLES AND AFFIXES			DERIVATIONAL RELATIONS		
	EARLY	MIDDLE	LATE	EARLY	MIDDLE	LATE	EARLY	MIDDLE	LATE	EARLY	MIDDLE	LATE	EARLY	MIDDLE	LATE
							Josh B. Dustin	Dominique Ian Emily Brennen 8	Elizabeth Craig Melanie –> Melissa Josh Paula –> <– Erik Josh C. Joshua Sarah 8 <– Cliff Camille	Jamie Daniel Eric Sare	Tye 7				

FIGURE 3-8 Spelling-by-Stage Assessment in a Third Grade Classroom, Late in November

Teacher Freedman School Kridel Elementary Grade 5 Date September

		EMERGENT LATE		LETTER NAME–ALPHABETIC EARLY MIDDLE LATE		WITHIN WORD PATTERN EARLY MIDDLE LATE		SYLLABLES AND AFFIXES EARLY MIDDLE LATE	DERIVATIONAL RELATIONS EARLY
Students' Names Points	Total Initial	Consonants Final		Short Vowels	Digraphs and Blends	Long Vowel Patterns	Other Vowel Patterns	Syllable Junctures, Consonant Doubling, Inflected Endings, Prefixes Suffixes	Bases and Roots
Possible points	67	3	6	5	13	5	6	24	5
1 Stephanie Lovel	65	3	6	5	13	5	6	23	4
2 Andi Warren	64	3	6	4	13	5	6	22	5
3 Henry Washington	63	3	6	5	12	5	6	22	4
4 Molly Maltes	59	3	6	5	13	5	6	19	2
5 Jasmine Rogers	58	3	6	5	13	5	6	18	2
6 Maria Hernandez	58	3	6	5	13	5	6	18	2
7 Mike Metton	58	3	6	5	12	5	6	19	2
8 Lee Stephens	58	3	6	5	13	5	6	17	3
9 Beth Hall	55	3	6	5	13	5	5	17	1
10 Gabriel Sargent	53	3	6	5	13	5	6	13	2
11 Yamal Mitris	53	3	6	5	13	5	5	14	2
12 John Mortensen	50	3	6	5	13	4	4	14	1
13 Elizabeth Stanton	50	3	6	5	13	4	5	13	1
14 Maria Herrera	50	3	6	5	12	5	5	14	0
15 Patty Leiker	50	3	6	5	13	5	6	12	0
16 Sarah Hamilton	44	2	6	5	12	5	4	10	0
17 Jared Wards	44	3	6	4	12	4	6	9	0
18 William Letes	43	3	6	5	13	4	2	10	0
19 Steve Willmes	43	3	6	4	12	4	3	9	2
20 Anna Leckey	42	3	6	5	12	3	4	9	0
21 Nicole Wooster	41	3	5	5	12	3	3	10	0
22 Robert Herbert	35	3	6	5	12	1	2	6	0
23 Celia Chambers	18	3	5	3	4	0	1	2	0
Students ≥ 2		0	0	1	1	4	8	22	20

Missed ≥ 2

FIGURE 3-9 Example of Classroom Composite for Elementary Spelling Inventory 1 Feature Guide

CHAPTER 4

Organizing for Word Study: Principles and Practices

O nce you have ascertained the developmental level of each of your students, you are ready to organize your classroom for word study. In earlier chapters, you learned that children acquire specific orthographic features in a hierarchical order: first, basic letter-sound correspondences; second, the patterns associated with long and short vowel sounds; third, word structures associated with syllables and affixes; and finally, Greek and Latin roots and stems that appear in derivational families. The scope and sequence of word study skills is based on developmental spelling research and mirrors this evolution. Word study instruction is aimed where each child "is at" in the developmental process of growth and change. Pinpointing the developmental level of every child in your classroom is the first step toward organizing for word study instruction. Instruction is then planned to target your students' **zone of proximal development** (Vygotsky, 1962).

THE ROLE OF WORD SORTING

Word study is a method for calling attention to word elements. As children progress in literacy, they learn how to look at words differently. At first, emergent and beginning readers learn to pay attention to initial sounds. Once beginning sounds are automated, they learn to look further. By the time they become transitional readers, reading their first *Frog and Toad* (Lobel) books, they are ready to look at vowel patterns. Later, as children read words of more than one syllable, they learn to look for syllables and affixes. When mature readers come to a word they don't know, they look for familiar roots and stems. Picture sorts and word sorts are designed to help students learn how and where to look at words.

Word study is an active process in which students categorize words and pictures to reveal essential differences and similarities among words. The word sort in Figure 4-1, for example, is designed to help students discover that the final *tch* pattern is associated with short vowels, whereas *ch* is associated with long vowels. *Rich* and *much* are "oddballs" which do not fit the pattern. Word-sorting activities provide opportunities for students to make logical decisions about word elements including sound, pattern, meaning, and use. Repeated practice categorizing words by particular features helps students identify and understand invariance or constancy in the orthography. Progress in the students' understanding of orthographic invariance is related to reading, writing, vocabulary, and spelling development. This is why we say that there is a synchrony among reading, writing, and spelling development (Bear, 1991b).

The sorts discussed in this chapter are phonics, spelling, or vocabulary activities that use categorization to reveal generalizations about words. The chapter begins by describing different kinds of sorting activities. Then 10 principles of word study are presented to help teachers gauge the integrity of their word study program. Some word study activities are easier than others, and teachers must find a balance in the difficulty of the activities they present. Through several examples and general scheduling outlines, ways to organize word study classrooms at several developmental levels are presented. Through the course of this chapter, you will read about how several veteran teachers organize their classrooms. We will address some issues such as editing expectations and grading before ending with a general outline for choosing features of study.

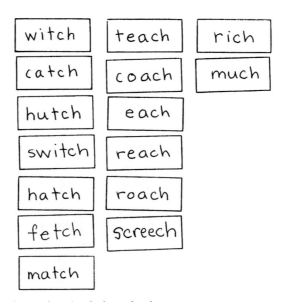

FIGURE 4-1   Word Sort by Final *ch* and *tch* Patterns

TYPES OF SORTS

There are two basic sorts: **picture sorts** and **word sorts.** Each serves a different purpose.

Picture Sorts

Picture sorts are for teaching children to categorize sounds and to associate sound segments with letters and spelling patterns. Picture sorts can be used to develop **phonological awareness,** the ability to identify and categorize various speech sounds like rhyme and alliteration. Picture sorts can also be used to teach **phonics,** the consistent relationship between letters and sounds. At different points in development, pictures are sorted by initial sounds, consonant blends or digraphs, rhyming families, or vowel sounds. Picture sorts call attention to the sound segments under study, and help students learn the letters that represent them.

Picture sorting is particularly suited for students in the emergent, letter name–alphabetic, and early within word pattern stages of spelling development who do not have extensive reading vocabularies. These are the students who are focused on the alphabetic principle or the basic single-syllable patterns of English orthography. Picture sorts may be used with English as a second language (ESL) students who are struggling with unfamiliar sounds or vocabulary. However, picture sorts are not particularly useful for native speakers of English at the level of syllables and affixes or derivational relations.

The basic premise of all sorting tasks in a word study approach is to compare and contrast word elements, separating or categorizing the examples that go together from those that don't. Picture sorts, such as the one shown in Figure 4-2, are first modeled by teachers as they work with students who share similar word study needs. Working as a group, children are given a collection of picture cards to sort into contrasting categories. They say the names of the pictures as they place them in the groups under the teacher's direction. At the end of this guided activity, students work independently to sort similar sets of pictures into the same categories.

Picture sorting differs from commercial phonics programs in four important ways. First, picture sorting works from the known to the unknown; the names of the pictures can already be pronounced. As children sort through a stack of picture cards,

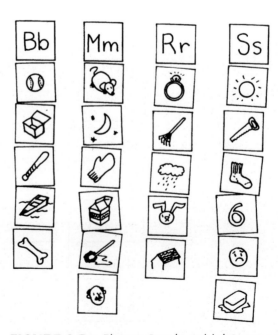

FIGURE 4-2   Picture Sort by Initial Consonant Sounds

they pronounce the name of each picture and concentrate on analyzing the sounds within each word. This is not possible if students cannot name the words in the first place. Unfortunately, this is too often the case with unknown words in commercial phonics programs.

A second way in which picture sorting differs from packaged phonics programs is that picture sorting is analytic, whereas most phonics programs are synthetic. Rather than building up from the phoneme to the word in a synthetic approach, picture sorting begins with the whole and then examines its parts. In learning about vowel sounds, for example, the whole word is first pronounced—"cat." Only then is the initial consonant peeled off from the "at." Through this analytic approach, picture-sorting tasks work first with **onsets** (beginning consonant elements) and **rimes** (phonograms), before working down to the level of individual **phonemes.** Research in phonemic awareness suggests that individual phonemes are abstract and that analysis of onsets and rimes provides a more accessible, intermediary stepping stone to the more difficult level of phoneme (Goswami, 1990; Treiman, 1991). Through picture sorts, students learn to analyze speech sounds into their constituent parts.

A third way in which picture sorts differ from most phonics programs is that picture sorting does not involve rote memorization, isolated sound drills, or overreliance on poorly understood rules. Sorting tasks are conducted so that students determine similarities and differences among target features as they utilize higher level critical thinking skills to make categorical judgments. When students make categorical decisions about whether the middle vowel sound in *cat* sounds more like the medial vowel sound in *map* or *top*, independent analysis and judgment are required. Students make decisions for themselves.

Efficiency is a fourth reason why picture sorts are more effective than most commercial phonics programs. Picture sorting doubles or triples the number of examples children study, and they study them in a shorter amount of time. Workbooks may have only three to five examples per page, and most of these exercises ask children to fill in the blank or color their choices from the answers provided. It takes an average first grader 10 to 20 minutes to complete such a workbook activity, time that could be better spent reading. In contrast, sorting a stack of 20 to 30 picture cards takes just a few minutes. Compare the number of examples in Figure 4-3 to see the differences.

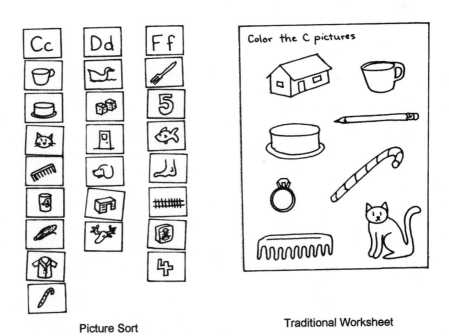

Picture Sort   Traditional Worksheet

FIGURE 4-3 Picture Sorting Offers More Practice Than Traditional Worksheets

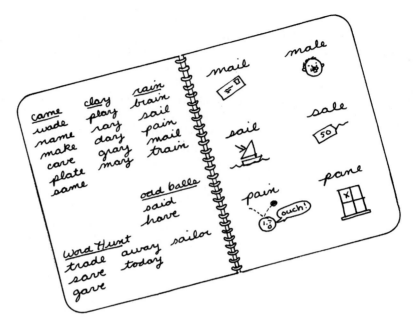

FIGURE 4–4   Word Study Notebook

Although picture sorts are used mainly for sound, they can also be used to teach word meanings through **concept sorts.** Picture sorts are particularly useful for students learning English as a second language. Pictures of a dog, a cat, a duck, and so on can all be grouped to make an animal category. These can be contrasted with pictures of a flower, a tree, a cornfield, a pumpkin, and so on—all examples of plants. English vocabulary is expanded as students sort pictures into conceptual groupings and repeat the names of each picture and the category to which it belongs.

Word Sorts

Word sorts are like picture sorts except that printed **word cards** are used. Since learning to spell involves making associations between the spelling of words and their pronunciations, it is important that children know and can already pronounce most of the words to be sorted. Because children are sorting known words, their sorts help them to discover the orthographic patterns that represent certain sounds and meanings. These understandings are then extended to the reading and spelling of new words.

Word sorting is useful for all students who have a functional sight word vocabulary. Letter name–alphabetic spellers sort their words into groups that share the same beginning sounds, by **phonograms** or word families (*jump, lump, stump* vs. *lamp, stamp, camp*), and by meaning. Students in the within word pattern stage sort their words into groups by vowel patterns (*wait, train, mail, pain* vs. *plate, take, blame*). Within word pattern spellers hear the sounds and see the consistency in the way vowel sounds are spelled. Syllables and affixes spellers benefit from sorting words into groups by syllable stress or syllable structure. Spellers learning derivational relations sort words by similarities in **roots** and **stems** such as the *spect* in *spectator, spectacle, inspect,* and *spectacular* versus the *port* in *transport, import, portable,* and *port-o-john.*

Like the picture-sorting routine, the word sort is first introduced by the teacher. Following the demonstration and discussion, children are guided in sorting written words in contrasting categories and are directed toward correctness as necessary. After this guided practice, children sort independently. These sorts might later be written into columns in word study notebooks, such as the one shown in Figure 4-4.

Let's walk through a series of word sorts that would be appropriate for a group of within word pattern spellers. This example will help make the concept of word sorting come to light. These students sort to examine long vowels. In this example, they are learning long-e spelling patterns.

In conducting vowel pattern word sorts, students first sort by **sound** and then by **pattern.** Students begin by sorting a deck of word cards into two piles by sound: long vowel sounds and short vowel sounds. The categories would look like this:

Short-e	Long-e
men	cheap
shed	priest
head	clean
deaf	niece
thread	need
best	thief
	creep

In the second step, students sort each column of words by orthographic patterns. There are three columns for long vowels and two for short vowels:

CVC	CVVC	ea	ie	ee
men	head	cheap	priest	need
shed	thread	clean	niece	creep
best			thief	

These sorting tasks can be challenging for children who, in the past, have looked at words by sound or isolated rule alone. They may have heard the rule, "When two vowels go walking, the first one does the talking." As you can see from the preceding example, this rule doesn't always work. While *ee* is a very consistent pattern for long-e, *ea* has two vowel sounds. Rules with many exceptions are disheartening and teach children nothing. Learning about English spelling requires students to consider both sound and pattern simultaneously to discover consistencies in the orthography. This requires both reflection and continued practice. The goal is for students to sort by sound and pattern simultaneously, automatically, and accurately.

Variations of Sorts

Variations of picture sorts and word sorts can serve different instructional purposes. Teaching explicitly through direct instruction, encouraging student hypothesis testing, connecting word study to reading and writing, building speed and automaticity—all are important instructional goals, and for each, there is a sort. Closed sorts, open sorts, word hunts, writing sorts, repeated sorts, and speed sorts will be described in relation to their instructional purpose.

Teacher-Directed Word Sorts

Most of the word sort tasks described in this book are teacher-directed or **closed sorts.** In closed sorts, teachers define the categories and model the sorting procedure (Gillet & Kita, 1978). For example, in a beginning-sound phonics sort, the teacher isolates the beginning sound to be taught and explicitly connects it to the letter that represents it using a **key word** to designate the categories. The teacher models the categorization of additional beginning sounds, then gradually releases the task to the students' control as they replicate the process. As they work, teachers and students discuss the characteristics of each sort. Then there are many opportunities for students to practice sorting independently. This practice is carefully monitored and corrective feedback is provided.

Student-Centered Sorts

Student-centered or **open sorts** are particularly useful after students are already accustomed to sorting and are quite adept at finding commonalties among words. In open sorts, students create their own categories with the set of words. These sorts are more diagnostic in nature because they reveal what students know about examining the orthography when they work independently. Open sorts provide an opportunity for students to test their own hypotheses and they often come up with unexpected ways to organize words. For example, when given the words shown in Figure 4-1, some students sort by the final patterns (*tch* or *ch*), others sort by the vowel sounds (long and short), and others sort by rhyming words. Some of the most productive discussions about the orthography come when students explain why they sorted the way they did in an open sort. As students become sorting pros, they begin to anticipate teacher-directed closed sorts.

Connecting Sorts to Reading and Writing

Concept Sorts

Sorting pictures or words by concepts or meaning is one of the very best ways to link vocabulary instruction to what your students already know and to expand their conceptual understanding of essential reading vocabulary. **Concept sorts** are appropriate for all ages and stages of word knowledge and should be used regularly in the content areas. Mathematical terms, science concepts, social studies vocabulary words—all can be sorted into conceptual categories for greater understanding.

Concept sorts can be conducted as both open and closed sorts. Open concept sorts are perfect for assessing background knowledge before embarking on a new unit of study. A new science unit on matter, for example, might begin by having children categorize the following words into groups that go together: *steam, wood, air, ice cube, rain, metal, glue, paint, plastic, smoke, milk,* and *fog*. A discussion of the reasons behind their conceptual groupings is most revealing! As the unit progresses, closed concept sorts can be used for teaching essential concepts and terminology. Having children categorize other examples under the key words *solid, liquid,* and *gas* will help them sort out the essential characteristics for each state of matter. Information about reptiles and amphibians as well as examples of each might be sorted as shown here:

┌──── Amphibians ────┐		┌──── Reptiles ────┐	
usually lay eggs in water	frogs	usually lay eggs on land	turtles
three-stage life cycle	toads	two-stage life cycle	snakes
moist skin, no scales	salamanders	dry scaly skin	alligators
	newts		chameleons
			iguanas

The creative possibilities for concept sorts are endless. They can be used as advanced organizers for anticipating new reading. Concepts sorts can be revisited and refined after reading, and they can be used to organize ideas before writing. Concepts sorts are even useful for teaching grammar. Words can be sorted by parts of speech.

Guess My Category

When children are comfortable with sorts, you can introduce any new area of study with a collection of objects, words, or pictures with an activity called Guess My Category. In this sort you do not label or describe the categories in advance. Rather, it will be the job of your students to decide how the things in each category are alike. You begin by sorting two or three pictures or words into each group. When you pick up the next picture or word, invite someone to guess where it will go. Continue doing this until all the pictures or words have been sorted. Try to keep the children who have caught on to the attributes of interest from telling the others until the end. Playing Guess My Category stimulates creative thinking. You might give small groups of students sets of words or pictures that might be grouped in a variety of ways. Ask each group to come up with their own categories working together. Allow them to have a miscellaneous group for those things that do not fit the categories they establish. After the groups are finished working, let them visit each others' sorts and try to guess the categories that were used. Guess My Category items can later be placed in centers or stations where students may work together to form different groupings. Emergent to beginning readers can dictate to an aide, parent volunteer, or older student their reason for putting together the objects as they did, or they can compose their reason using invented spelling.

Word Hunts

Students don't automatically make the connection between spelling words and reading words, even though they are almost the same thing (Ehri, 1997). Word hunts help students make this connection. In **word hunts,** students hunt through their reading and writing for words that are further examples of the sound, pattern, or meaning unit they are studying.

Teachers can model word hunting with a portion of text copied onto chart paper, or they use copies of text on overhead transparencies. Working line by line, teachers demonstrate how to locate words that fit the categories under study. After this teacher demonstration, students return to texts they are reading and writing, and they hunt for other words that contain the same features. These words are then added to the columns in the word study notebook under the corresponding key word.

Here is an example of a word hunt by a small group of students in Mrs. Fitzgerald's third grade class during a unit on folktales (see Figure 4-5). After working with long-o and short-o in word study, they found and charted these lists from *The Three Billy Goats Gruff* (Galdone, 1973):

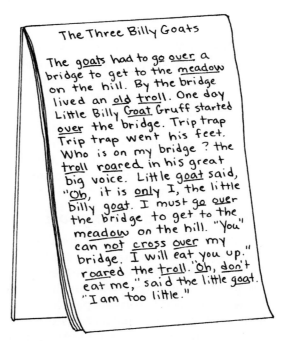

FIGURE 4-5   Word Hunt With Story Retelling

Long	Short	?
oh	not	voice
goat	gobble	who
go	cross	too
meadow	got	roared
don't	on	
over		
troll		
old		

After this sound sort, students sorted these words by orthographic patterns and organized them in their word study notebooks:

Groaned and *goat* were added to the *oa* column.
Home was added to the *o*-consonant-*e* column.
Troll and *old* were added to the *o*-consonant-consonant column.
Meadow was added to the *ow* column.
A new pattern of open, single, long-o spellings was discovered with *so, going,* and *over.*

This word hunt added more examples for the students to consider, and new categories were created.

Word hunts connect word study to other literacy contexts and can also extend the reach to more difficult vocabulary. One child sorted one-syllable *a* words into three columns, by vowel sound and long vowel patterns.

Short-a	Long-a	
cat	drain	snake
lap	maid	lake
chat	tail	plate
relax	**explain**	**escape**

After sorting the one-syllable words into groups by vowel sound and pattern, the student returned to the book she was reading to find other examples to add. The words in bold print were added to her columns. Through a simple word hunt, this student was able to generalize the consistency in the pattern-to-sound representation within one-syllable words to two-syllable words! Word hunts provide a step up in word power.

When conducting word hunts with emergent to beginning readers, teachers should have children scan texts that they have already read before *and* that are guaranteed to have the phonics features they are searching for in them. Several companies publish little books for emergent readers that contain recurring phonics elements. *Ready Readers*® by Modern Curriculum Press, and the **phonics readers** published by Creative Teaching Materials are two examples of simple little books organized around specific phonics features that repeat in the text. Although such text may not be the heart of your reading program, they offer children a chance to put into practice what they are learning about words and to see many words at the same time that work the same way.

Buddy Sorts and Writing Sorts

In addition to closed sorts and open sorts, there are buddy sorts and writing sorts. A **buddy sort** should be done after students have had a chance to practice a sort several times and can be done with a partner. A key word is laid down for each category. One partner calls out a word without showing it and the other points to the key word it would follow. Buddy sorts are particularly useful for students who could use some time attending less to the visual patterns and more to the sounds because they do not see the word they are asked to sort. Buddy sorts provide a useful study activity to prepare for a spelling test.

Writing sorts are a variation of both closed sorts and buddy sorts. In writing sorts, a key word is written down first for each column. Then words are called out by the teacher or a partner, and students write the word in the proper category using the key word as a model for spelling. Writing sorts provide an important link to writing and reading, especially when combined with word hunts. Writing sorts are also an instructionally sound way to construct spelling tests for the early grades.

Building Automaticity

Repeated Individual Sorts

To become fluent readers, students must achieve fast, accurate recognition of words in context. The words they encounter in context are made out of the very same sounds, patterns, and meaning units they examine out of context, in word study. One of the very best ways to build accuracy and automaticity in word recognition is to build fast, accurate recognition of these units. To meet that goal, it is necessary to have students do a given picture or word sort more than one time. Repeated individual sorts are designed for just that—repeated sorting. Just as repeated reading of familiar texts builds fluency, repeated individual sorts provide a student with the necessary practice to build automaticity.

Speed Sorts

Once students have become accurate with a particular sort, **speed sorts** are motivating and develop fluency. *Speed sorting* is no different than ordinary word or picture sorting except that students try to complete the task quickly. It helps to have a stopwatch on hand to actually time the sort. The students try to beat their previous times, and this helps them build automaticity in the categorization of particular orthographic features. Students can be paired with other students to time each other, and they learn to chart their progress.

All of these sorts differ quite a bit from traditional spelling instruction. Sorting activities give students plenty of practice and experience manipulating and categorizing words by sound, pattern, and meaning until they can sort quickly and accurately.

TEN PRINCIPLES OF WORD STUDY INSTRUCTION

A number of basic principles guide the kind of word study described in *Words Their Way*. These principles set word study apart from many other approaches to the teaching of phonics, spelling, or vocabulary. The 10 guiding principles are summarized in Figure 4-6, and discussed in detail in the following paragraphs.

1. *Look for what students use but confuse.* Students cannot learn things they do not already know something about. This is the underlying principle of Vygotsky's zone of proximal development and the motivating force behind the spelling-by-stage assessment described in Chapter 3. By classifying invented spellings developmentally, a zone of proximal development may be identified and instruction can be planned to address features the students are "using but confusing" instead of those they totally neglect (Invernizzi, Abouzeid, & Gill, 1994). Figure 4-7 displays a writing sample of a child who is experimenting with vowel patterns in words such as CHIAN for *chin* and CREM for *cream*. She is putting an extra vowel in a word that doesn't need it and leaves it out where it is needed. As was discussed in Chapter 2, using but confusing is a signal that students are close to learning something new about the orthography. Take your cue from the students, not the curriculum. Teachers look to see what features are consistently present and correct, to determine what aspects of English orthography the students already

1. Look for what students use but confuse.

2. A step backward is a step forward.

3. Use words students can read.

4. Compare words "that do" with words "that don't."

5. Sort by sight and sound.

6. Begin with obvious contrasts first.

7. Don't hide exceptions.

8. Avoid rules.

9. Work for automaticity.

10. Return to meaningful texts.

FIGURE 4-6   Principles of Word Study

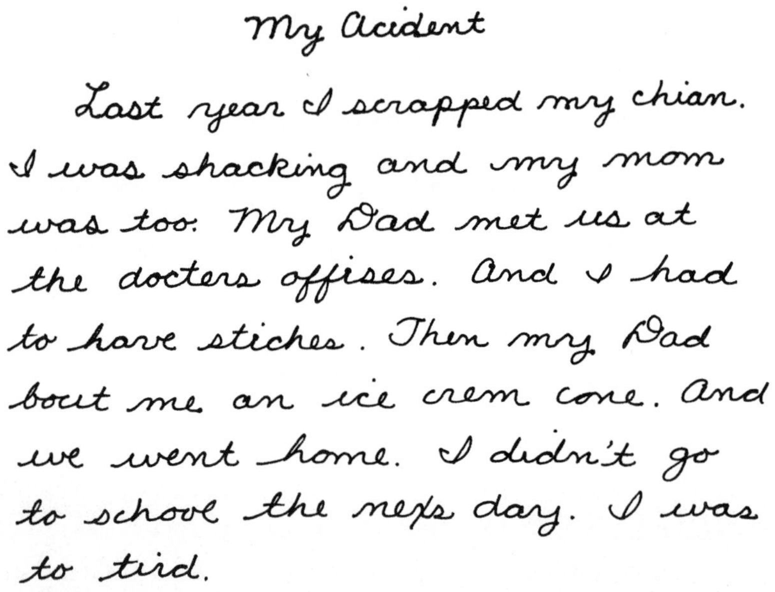

My Accident

Last year I scrapped my chian. I was shacking and my mom was too. My Dad met us at the docters offises. And I had to have stiches. Then my Dad bout me an ice crem cone. And we went home. I didn't go to school the nexs day. I was to tird.

FIGURE 4-7   Writing Sample With Examples of Using but Confusing

know. By looking for features that are used inconsistently, teachers determine those aspects of the orthography currently under negotiation. These are the features to target.

2. *A step backward is a step forward.* Once you have identified students' stages of developmental word knowledge and the orthographic features under negotiation, take a step backward and build a firm foundation. Then, in setting up your categories, contrast something new with something that is already known. If, for example, you are beginning to introduce a new sound or pattern, be sure to present it in contrast to a familiar sound or pattern. It is important to begin word study activities where the students will experience success. For example, students in the within word pattern stage who are ready to examine long vowel patterns begin by sorting words by short vowel sounds, which are familiar, and long vowel sounds, which are being introduced for the first time. Then they move quickly to sorting by pattern. A step backward is the first step forward in word study instruction.

3. *Use words students can read.* Since learning to spell involves achieving a match between the spoken language and the orthography, your students should examine words that they can readily pronounce. Dialect does not alter the importance of this basic principle of word study. Whether one says "hog" or "hawg", it is still spelled *hog*. The consistency is in the orthography, and it is your job as the teacher to make those consistencies explicit. It is easier to look across words for consistency of pattern when the words are easy for students to pronounce. Known words come from any and all sources that the children can read: from **language experience** stories, from recent readings, from poems, and even from old spelling books collecting dust on the shelf. As much as possible choose words to sort that students can read out of context.

4. *Compare words "that do" with words "that don't."* In order to learn what a Chesapeake Bay retriever looks like, you have to see a poodle or a bulldog, not another Chesapeake Bay retriever. What something *is* is also defined by what it is *not*; contrasts are essential to students building categories. Students' spelling errors suggest what contrasts will help them sort out their confusions. For example, a student who is spelling *stopping* as STOPING will benefit from a sort in which words with double consonants before adding *ing* are contrasted with those that don't as in Figure 4-8.

5. *Sort by sound and sight.* Students examine words by how they sound and how they are spelled. Both sound and visual pattern are integrated into students' orthographic knowledge. Too often, students focus on visual patterns at the expense of how words are alike in sound. The following sort illustrates the way students move from a **sound sort** to visual **pattern sort.** First, students sorted by the differences in sound between hard-g and soft-g. Then students subdivided the sound sort by orthographic patterns. See what you can discover from this sort.

First Sort by Sound of G		**Second Sort by Pattern**		
Soft	Hard	dge	ge	g
edge	bag	edge	cage	bag
cage	twig	ridge	huge	twig
huge	slug	judge	stage	slug
ridge	flag	badge	page	flag
judge	drug	lodge		drug
stage	leg			leg
badge				
page				
lodge				

To establish categories, select a **key word** or picture that will label the category clearly. Students read both the key word (or picture) and the new word (or picture) each time a new example is categorized. When the sort is done, have students read down each column of words (or pictures) and explicitly state what sound they have in common. Finally, be sure to have students verbalize what letter or spelling patterns represent that sound. To sort by sight and by sound, students say it, sort it, then say it again.

6. *Begin with obvious contrasts first.* Whenever students begin the study of a new feature, teachers choose key words or pictures that are distinctive. For example, when students first examine initial consonants, teachers do not begin by contrasting *M* with *N*. They share too many features to be distinct to the novice. They are both nasals, and they are visually similar as well. Better to begin by contrasting *M* with something totally different at first—*S* for example—then work toward finer distinctions as these categorizations become quite automatic. Move from general, gross discriminations to more specific ones.

Likewise, be wary of two-syllable words for beginners, even if only picture cards are used. *Banana* may start with a *b*, but the first *n* is stressed or pronounced the loudest, and some beginners will be confused.

FIGURE 4-8   Doubling Sort: Comparing Words "That Do"
With Words "That Don't"

7. *Don't hide exceptions.* Exceptions arise when students make generalizations. Don't hide these exceptions. By placing so-called irregular words in a miscellaneous or **oddball** category, new categories of consistency frequently emerge. For example, in looking at long vowel patterns, students find these exceptions: *give, have,* and *love;* yet it is no coincidence that they all have a *v.* They form a small but consistent pattern of their own. True exceptions do occasionally occur and become memorable by virtue of their rarity.

8. *Avoid rules.* Avoid telling students spelling "rules." Students discover consistencies and make generalizations for themselves. The teacher's job is to stack the deck and structure categorization tasks to make these consistencies explicit. Instill in students the habit of looking at words, asking questions, and searching for order. Rules are useful mnemonics for concepts already understood. They can be the icing on the cake of knowledge. But memorizing rules is not the way children make sense of how words work. Rules are no substitute for experience.

9. *Work for automaticity.* Accuracy in sorting is not enough; accuracy *and* speed are the ultimate indicators of mastery. Acquiring automaticity in sorting and recognizing orthographic patterns leads to the fluency necessary for proficient reading and writing. Your students will move from hesitancy to fluency in their sorting. Keep sorting until they do.

10. *Return to meaningful texts.* After sorting, students need to return to meaningful texts to hunt for other examples to add to the sorts. These hunts extend their analysis to more words and more difficult vocabulary. For example, after sorting one-syllable words into categories labeled *cat, drain,* and *snake,* a student added *tadpole, complain,* and *relate.* Through a simple word hunt, this child extended the pattern-to-sound consistency in one-syllable words to stressed syllables in two-syllable words.

These 10 principles of word study boil down to one golden rule of word study instruction: Teaching is not telling. In word study, students examine, manipulate, and categorize words. Teachers stack the deck so to speak, and create tasks that focus students' attention on critical contrasts. Stacking the deck for a discovery approach to word study is not the absence of directed instruction. To the contrary, a systematic program of word study, guided by an informed interpretation of spelling errors and other literacy behaviors, is a teacher-directed, child-centered approach to vocabulary growth and spelling development.

GUIDELINES FOR SORTING

When working with picture or word sorts, you will first help your students attend to the targeted feature. Some general guidelines for sorting follow:

1. Use letter cards, letter patterns, or **key words** to head up each category at the top. Select a picture or word to illustrate each category and place it under the corresponding key to start a sorting column. If you are working with sounds, you can emphasize or elongate them by stretching them out. If you are working with patterns, you can think aloud as you point out the spelling pattern. If you are working with syllables, affixes, or derivational relations, you can explicitly point out the unit you are using.

2. Shuffle the rest of the cards and say something like:

   We are going to listen for the sound in the middle of these words and decide if they sound like *map* or like *duck.* I'll do a few first. Here is a *rug. Ruuuuug, uuuug, uuuuuuh. Rug* has the /uh/ sound in the middle so I'll put it under *duck, uuuuck, uuuuh.* Here is a *flag. Flaaaaag, aaaag, aaaah.* I'll put *flag* under *maaaap.*

3. After modeling several sorts, turn the task over to the students or take turns as you sort the rest of the examples. If students make a mistake at the very beginning, correct it immediately. Simply say: "*Sack* would go under *map.* Its middle sound is /ă/."

4. After the students have completed the first sort under your guidance, immediately ask them to shuffle and sort again, but this time cooperatively or independently. Unless your students are in the last two levels of word knowledge (syllables and affixes or derivational relations), ask them to name each word or picture aloud as they sort. If someone doesn't know what to call a picture, tell them immediately. If someone doesn't know a word, discard it. Don't make reading words or naming the pictures into a guessing game.

5. During the second sort, do not correct your students, but when they are through, have them name the words or pictures in each column to check themselves. If there are misplaced cards students fail to find, tell how many and in which column, and ask the students to try to find them.

6. At the end of the sort, be sure to have students verbalize what all the words or pictures in one column have in common, and how that commonality is represented by the letter, pattern, or key word at the top.

Making Sorts Harder or Easier

Picture sorts or word sorts can be made easier or harder several ways. One way is by decreasing or increasing the number of contrasts in the sort. If children are young or inexperienced, starting with two columns is a good idea. As they become adept at sorting into two groups, step up to three categories and then four. Even after working with four categories or more, however, you may want to go back to fewer when you introduce a new concept.

Another way to make sorts easier or harder is by the contrasts you choose. The clearer the distinction, the easier the sort. It is easier to sort short-a and short-i, for example, than short-a and short-e. (The reasons for this will be discussed in Chapter 6.) Meanwhile, remember to start with obvious contrasts first, then gradually move to finer distinctions.

The difficulty of sorts can also be increased or decreased by the actual words you choose as examples within each category. For example, adding words with **blends** and **digraphs** and other consonant units to a short vowel sort can make those words more challenging. Ideally, children should be able to read all of the words in a word sort. In reality, however, this may not always be the case. The more unfamiliar words in a given sort, the more difficult that sort will be. This caveat applies to both being able to read the word and knowing what the word means. A fifth grader studying derivational relations will need easier words to study than a tenth grader, simply because the fifth grader will have a more limited vocabulary. If there are unfamiliar words in a sort, try to place them toward the end of the deck so that known words are the first to be sorted. When new words come up, you can encourage your students to compare the new spelling with the known words already sorted in the columns. In word study you must consider both the word knowledge and the experience of the child.

Finally, the difficulty of a sort can be increased by adding an oddball column and including "exception" words that do not fit the targeted letter-sound or pattern feature.

Oddballs

As students add other words to their sorts, they will undoubtedly encounter **oddballs**— words that are at odds with the consistencies within each category. The word *have*, for example, would be an oddball in a short-a versus long-a vowel sort. The vowel sound of the *a* in *have* is short, yet it is spelled with a long vowel pattern. Oddballs are often high-frequency words such as *have, said, was*, and *again*. Such words become memorable from repeated usage but are also memorable because they are odd. They stand out in the crowd.

The oddball category is also where students may place words if they are simply not sure about the sound they hear in the word. This often happens when students say words differently due to dialectical or regional pronunciations that vary from the "standard" pronunciation. For example, one student in Wise County, Virginia, pronounced the word *vein* as "vine" and was correct in placing *vein* in the oddball column as opposed to the long-a group. To her, the word *vein* was a long-i. Sometimes students detect subtle variations that adults may miss. Students often put words like *mail* and *sail* in a different sound category than *main, wait*, and *paid* because the long-a sound is slightly different. *Mail* may sound more like "may-ul."

Dealing With Mistakes

Mistakes are part and parcel of learning, but not all mistakes are dealt with in the same way. As described in the preceding guidelines for sorting, mistakes made early on in a sort should probably be corrected right away. Sometimes, however, it is useful to find out why a student sorted a picture or word in a particular way. Simply asking, "Why did you put that there?" can provide further insight into a student's word knowledge. If mistakes are made during the second sort, your students will learn more if you guide them to finding and correcting the mistake on their own. If students are making a lot of mistakes it may indicate a need to take a step back or to make the sort easier.

ORGANIZATION OF WORD STUDY INSTRUCTION

What does a word study classroom look like? What kinds of materials do you need? How much time does it take? What exactly do students do? These questions and more about organizing for word study are answered in the sections that follow.

Getting the Classroom Ready for Word Study Instruction

Word study does not require a great investment of money or materials since the basic materials are already available in most classrooms. Access to a copier and plenty of unlined paper will get you well on your way. Copies of word sheets or picture sheets like those in Figure 4-9 can easily be created by hand using the templates and pictures in this

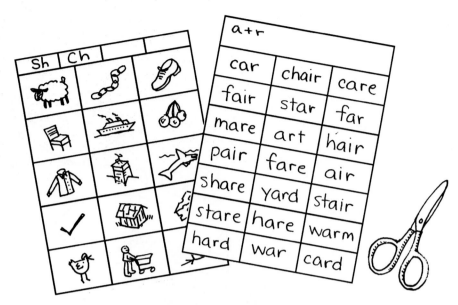

FIGURE 4-9   Sample Word Study Handouts

book or they can be created by computer (use the tables format and set the margins at zero all around). The copies are given to students to cut apart for sorting activities, the heart of the word study program. Students quickly learn the routine of cutting words apart, sorting them into categories, and storing them in a notebook, library pocket, envelope, or plastic bag. Sturdy manila envelopes are recommended for each child because they can be used over and over for storing their sorts.

Sometimes the cut-up words and pictures are kept to be combined with new words or pictures the following week, sometimes they are pasted into a notebook or onto paper, and sometimes they may be simply discarded. Creating these sheets of pictures or words is the first task teachers need to tackle. Sample sorts and tips for the creation of sorts are given in the following chapters and in the appendix.

Planning how to model the categorization procedure you want your students to use is important. In small groups, you may simply use the same cutout words your students will be using as you model on a table or on the floor. For larger groups you may want to model sorts on the overhead transparency using cut-up transparencies of the words or pictures or use large word or picture cards in a pocket chart. Large picture cards are available commercially or can be made by enlarging the pictures in this book and pasting them on cardstock. Some schools have chart-maker copiers that easily enlarge pictures. Magnetic tape can be attached to the back of pictures and word cards for sorting on a metal chalkboard.

You may also want to make your own special set of pictures for sorting by copying the pictures in this book onto cardstock and adding some color to them. Laminating them is optional as cardstock is quite durable. A set of these pictures can be stored by beginning sounds or by vowel sounds in library pockets or in envelopes. They can then be used for small-group work or for individual sorting assignments. For example, you may find that you have one student who needs work on digraphs. You can pull out a set of *ch* and *sh* pictures, mix them together, and then challenge the student to sort them into columns using the pocket as a header. The **sound boards** in the appendix can be copied, cut apart, and used to label the picture sets. It might be useful to have several of these picture sets, especially for resource teachers who work with individual children or small groups. Resource teachers may also want to create word card sets to be used over and over. Index cards can be cut apart or cards can be purchased to make word cards, but

FIGURE 4-10   Students Can Complete Sorts Independently Using Classification Folders

word sheets that are copied and cut apart by students to sort may still be the easiest way to manage word cards. They can be stored in envelopes and reused from year to year to reduce paper consumption.

Many teachers use manila file folders to hold materials and to help students sort their words or pictures into categories as shown in Figure 4-10. Classification folders are divided into three to five columns with key words or pictures for headers glued in place. Words or pictures for sorting are stored in the folder and students sort directly in the columns. Once the folders have been developed, teachers can individualize word study fairly easily by pulling out the folders that target the exact needs of their students. When there is little room in a class for centers, teachers use these folders as a place to store the activities that students can take back to their desks.

Games are appealing for children and encourage them to practice in more depth and apply what they have learned in a new situation. This book contains many ideas for the creation of games, and you will want to begin creating these to supplement the basic word or picture sorts. Look for generic games first since many of them can be used with a variety of word features you will study across the year. For example, the follow-the-path game being played by the boys in Figure 4-11 can be laminated before labeling the spaces and then new letters substituted as they become the focus of study. Label the spaces with a washable overhead projector pen. Over time you can create more specific games.

Word study does not require any dramatic changes to the physical setup of most classrooms. Storage space is needed for the word or picture sheets, large word cards, and games you create but most of these can be stored in folders in a filing cabinet. Word study notebooks might be stored in a common area such as a plastic file box or tub to make it easy for the teacher to access them when checking student work.

Space is needed for group work, individual work, and partner work. Separate areas for word sorting and discussion are needed to convene a group on the floor or at tables in one part of the classroom while other children continue to work at their desks or in

FIGURE 4-11   Board Game for Initial Consonants

other areas of the room. Students' desks provide a surface for individual word sorting. In addition, centers or work stations can be set up where students work individually or with a partner to sort or play a game. A stopwatch is a part of some word study activities and can be placed in the word study center. Many teachers also post chart-size sound boards in this area. Table 4-1 summarizes what you might need, depending on the age and range of developmental word knowledge in your classroom.

Scheduling the Day for Word Study Instruction

The second step to organize word study instruction is to set up a schedule and to develop weekly routines. There are many ways to organize word study. Some teachers conduct word study lessons as part of their reading groups. Other teachers work with two to three separate word study groups and may rotate their students from **circle time** with the teacher to individual **seat work** and **center times.** There may also be settings in which teachers conference individually with children in a workshop routine. In all settings, the focus of word study should be upon active inquiry and discovery where students take much of the responsibility for their own learning. There are a number of things to consider when scheduling word study in your classroom:

1. *Develop a familiar weekly routine with daily activities.*   Routines will save you planning time, ease transitions, and make the most of the time you devote to word study. Several weekly routines described in this chapter will give you ideas about how to create your own. Include homework routines as well. When parents know what to expect every evening they are more likely to see that the work gets done.

2. *Schedule time for group work.*   Students at the same developmental level should work with a teacher for directed word study. During this time, teachers model new sorts, guide practice sorts, and lead students in discussions that stimulate thinking and further their understanding. Chapter 3 offers suggestions for grouping students for instruction.

3. *Keep it short.*   Word study should be a regular part of daily language arts, but it need not take up a great deal of time. Teacher-led introductory lessons may take 15 to 20 minutes, but subsequent activities should last only about 10 minutes a day. Since much

TABLE 4-1 Word Study Materials		
From the Supply Room	**From the Bookstore**	**From Printing Services**
copy paper for sorts cardstock word study notebooks manila folders gameboard materials spinners and dice storage containers library pockets chart paper	student dictionaries rhyming dictionary etymological dictionary homophone books alphabet books phonics readers	photocopied picture cards photocopied word cards student sound boards poster sound boards

of word study can take place without the teacher's immediate attention, it can fit easily into odd bits of time during the day. Children can play spelling games right before lunch or sort their words one more time before they pack up to go home.

4. *Plan time for students to sort independently and with partners.* Students need time to sort through words on their own, and they need time to search for the orthographic features they are studying. Teachers build this independent work into seat work, center activities, and games that students play together. Word study lends itself nicely to many cooperative activities.

Progressive Skill Development

One of the most important decisions a teacher makes is how to schedule activities over the course of a week. Betty Lee, a renowned first grade teacher of 30 years, developed a general progression in word study activities. In this progression, students recognize, recall, judge, and apply their growing word knowledge through the activities.

Recognize

Students are presented a particular feature to consider. With **key pictures** and key words, teachers guide the students as they compare words. For example, when students analyze initial consonants, they compare the picture of a *man* with the key picture of a *mouse*. Students compare the pictures for sound, and the written words for sounds and patterns. They recognize that the words *man* and *mouse* begin with the same sound. To recognize is to be aware of a new orthographic feature. Sometimes it is helpful to post on the wall a record of key words used in sorting. Children can look for similar words throughout the day.

Recall

In this second step in the progression, students recall examples of the features they have studied. A key word or key picture is provided to remind students of the types of words they are trying to recall as they endeavor to generate other examples. After sorting, young children may **draw and label** pictures of things that begin with *m* using the key word *mouse* to stimulate recall. If students' immediate recall stalls, they might be encouraged to look through alphabet books to trigger recall. Students in a later stage of orthographic development may generate rhyming words that follow a specific orthographic pattern. If the key word is *beat*, students might be shown how they can find other words by dropping the beginning consonant and adding another to obtain *seat*, *neat*, or *meat*. These words can then be recorded on a chart or in their word study notebooks.

Judge

In judgment activities, students hunt through word books or picture books for words that match the features they are studying. In a **word hunt,** they make judgments as to which words fit in the categories established in the previous recognize and recall lessons. For example, students studying short-a will have to judge the sound of every *a* word they come to in scanning back through familiar texts. These words are copied into columns under the appropriate category header. Children in the emergent stage may hunt through catalogs or magazines to cut out pictures of things that have a particular sound and paste these into sorts.

Apply

There are many application-type activities. Students apply what they have learned to create something new. Open sorts are application activities because students find and proclaim their own categories. For example, students who have studied the various patterns for long-e can apply this information to sort long-o words. Another form of application involves guided proofreading. Many teachers have children return to their writing folders to look for words they may have written earlier that follow the sound or pattern they have just sorted. Board games and card games that match and categorize word features also provide opportunities for application in an enjoyable context.

One first grade teacher, Susan Smith, has her children "teach a word" at the end of each week. One child, who chose the word *floor,* stood up with an illustrated picture of a house with floors on one side, and the words *floor* and *door* on the other. As he taught the word, he held up his picture and said "first floor, second floor." Then he flipped the card and held up word cards and said "*floor* rhymes with *door.*" Clearly, this student made a creative application of his newfound word knowledge!

As students become wordsmiths, you'll be surprised by the lists of words they create. One class created an illustrated homophone dictionary in a "big book" format (see Figure 4-12). By the end of the year, 250 homophone pairs had been collected, illustrated, and arranged in alphabetical order. The children's spelling and vocabulary were enhanced by this cooperative project.

FIGURE 4-12 Class Homophone Book

Word Study Schedules

Many teachers plan their weekly word study routine around these progressive skills. In the following examples, teachers begin with a directed word study session in which they introduce the categories. Betty Lee's plan works well for children who are in the emergent to early letter name–alphabetic stage where sorting is done with pictures and children cannot be expected to read or spell the printed words.

Betty Lee's Routine for Emergent to Early Letter Name-Alphabetic Spellers

In her first grade class, Betty Lee organized her word study program around a circle-seat-center rotation format. She introduced her spelling concepts with a picture sort at circle time, working with about a third of the class who were at the same developmental level. A second third of the class worked at at their seats drawing and labeling pictures of words they recall from a previous lesson. The remaining students were stationed at different centers where they worked at cutting and pasting, or playing games with a partner. Activities can be organized in a 5-day routine as summarized in Figure 4-13 and described in the following paragraphs, or this routine can be shortened into a 3-day plan for students who are reviewing and need to move more quickly.

Monday–Picture sort.   The teacher models the categorization routine using picture cards and helps students recognize the sounds and letters they are studying. Sound categories are established using a letter card and a key picture which is used repeatedly to help students develop a strong association between the beginning sound of the word and the letter that represents it. Each picture is named and compared to the key picture to listen for sounds that are the same. The sort might be repeated several times in the circle. During their center time the children do the same picture sort on their own or with a partner, or they may have their own set of pictures to sort at their seat.

Tuesday–Draw and label.   Students recall the feature introduced on Monday in drawing and labeling activities. The examples in Figure 4-14 show a student's recall of initial consonants in a draw and label activity. Students are encouraged to write as much of the word as they can using invented spelling, and teachers can use these spellings to judge student progress in hearing and representing sounds. Students may sort again at seats or centers.

Wednesday–Cut and paste.   Children make judgments and extend their understandings to other examples when they look through old catalogs and magazines for pictures that begin with a particular sound. These pictures are cut out, pasted into categories or into an alphabet book (see Chapter 5), and labeled. If children have been working with their own sets of pictures, they might paste these into categories and label them. This takes less time than looking through magazines but it is also less challenging.

Betty Lee's Schedule				
Monday	**Tuesday**	**Wednesday**	**Thursday**	**Friday**
Picture Sorting	Drawing and Labeling	Cutting and Pasting	Word Hunts Word Banks	Games

FIGURE 4-13   Betty Lee's Weekly Schedule of Word Study With Pictures

FIGURE 4-14   Draw and Label Activity

Large retail-store catalogs are particularly useful because the index is arranged alphabetically. Teachers can tear out several pages and place them in a folder for students to look through as they search for pictures to cut and paste and then label.

Thursday—Word hunts.   Children apply what they have learned as they look for more words through word hunts, word bank activities, and other tasks. Children reread nursery rhymes and jingles and they circle words that begin with the same sounds they have been categorizing all week. These words are added to their sorts. (Word bank activities are described in more detail in Chapter 6.)

Friday—Game day.   Children delight in the opportunity to play board games, card games, and other games in which the recognition, recall, and judgment of spelling features are applied.

In Betty Lee's plan, most of the teaching falls into the focus achieved during the recognition and recall activities planned for Monday and Tuesday. The children move on to judgment and application on their own throughout the latter part of the week. Figure 4-15 shows a student's pocket folder which can be used at this level to keep materials organized and guide students to the daily routines. Students can keep their cutout words in the envelope until they are pasted down or discarded. Each folder has a **sound**

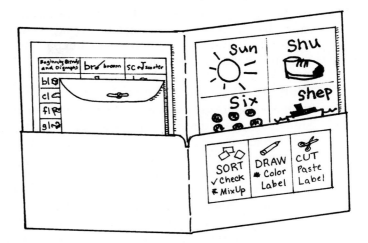

FIGURE 4-15   Pocket Folder for Organizing Materials

FIGURE 4-16   Students Gather With Weekly Word Lists for an Introductory Sort

board (one of three sound charts which can be found in the appendix) to use as a reference and a record of progress. Students can simply color the boxes lightly with crayon to indicate that they have worked with that sound.

A Weekly Schedule for Primary Children in the Letter Name-Alphabetic to Within Word Pattern Stage

The next routine works well for children who are readers and able to spell entire words. In the primary grades, spelling levels often match reading levels closely and teachers may take part of guided reading time to lead a brief word study lesson. While the teacher is working with one group, the other students can be reading independently, writing, or completing other assignments.

Monday—Introduce the sort.   Children receive a word study sheet with words for the week already printed in boxes. Each group has different words, depending on the students' stage of development. During the teacher-guided lesson shown in Figure 4-16, the students read the words aloud to be sure they are known. Word meanings are also discussed as needed. The teacher then models the beginning of the sort using the blackboard, an overhead projector, or large cards so that everyone can see. The children participate in finishing the sort and discussing what the sort reveals about words. They then return to their seats to practice the sort. Before cutting their words apart, they should draw three vertical lines down the backside of their paper using a crayon or colored marker. After the words are cut apart, this color stripe will distinguish their word cards from others as the children work together. The teacher then repeats this procedure with the next guided reading group focusing on a different feature.

Primary Schedule				
Monday	**Tuesday**	**Wednesday**	**Thursday**	**Friday**
Introduce Sort in Group	Re-sort and Write Sort	Buddy Sort Writing Sort	Word Hunt	Testing and Games
Kathy Ganske's Schedule				
Monday	**Tuesday**	**Wednesday**	**Thursday**	**Friday**
Introduce Sort in Group	Speed Sort With Partner	Word Hunts in Trade Books	Speed Sort With Teacher	Testing
Word Study Notebook Assignments Throughout the Week				

FIGURE 4-17   Two Schedules for Use When Students Sort Words

Tuesday—Practice the sort and write it.   On Tuesday, group by group, students bring their words to sort under the teacher's supervision again. Troublesome words may be discussed, and eliminated if necessary. Children are assigned a writing sort for seat work or for homework.

Wednesday—Buddy sorts and writing sorts.   On Wednesday, students work in pairs to do buddy sorts as described earlier in this chapter. After each partner has lead the sort, the pair might do a writing sort in which the partners take turns calling words aloud for the other to write into categories. This can also be a homework assignment in which the parents call the words aloud.

Thursday—Word hunts.   Word hunts are conducted in groups, with partners, or individually. Students search through current reading material to find additional words that fit the categories for the week. When other words are found, they are added to the bottom of the columns created earlier in the week during written word sorts. This can also be homework.

Friday—Assessment and games.   A traditional spelling test format can be used for assessment. If you have two or three groups, simply call one word in turn for each group. This may sound confusing but children will recognize the words they have studied over the week and rarely lose track. It isn't necessary to call out every word studied during the week (10 may be enough) and teachers may even call out some bonus words that were not among the original list to see if students can generalize the principles. It is particularly effective to conduct the spelling test as a writing sort, having students write each word as it is called out into the category where it belongs. One point can be awarded for correct category placement, and one point for correct spelling. Spelling tests conducted as writing sorts reinforce the importance of categorization and force students to generalize from the specific word to the system as a whole. Although games can be played anytime, Fridays might be reserved for them.

This primary schedule is summarized in Figure 4-17 along with a schedule developed by Kathy Ganske for her upper elementary students. Ganske's schedule is described in detail in the next section.

Kathy Ganske's Weekly Schedule for Intermediate Grades

Kathy Ganske's schedule varies in some respects from the primary schedule. This schedule works well for students throughout the upper levels of word study. There is a good deal of small-group work, and **word study notebooks** (see Figure 4-4) become an important part of the word study scene. Word study notebooks are used in five basic activities:

Word Study Notebooks

Weekly activities for this notebook include:
1. Written sorts
2. Draw and label
3. Sentences
4. Words from word hunts

You are expected to:
1. Use correct spelling of assigned words
2. Use complete sentences
3. Use your best handwriting
4. Make good use of word study time

You will be evaluated in this manner:
* Excellent work
√ Good work but could be improved
R You need to redo this assignment

FIGURE 4-18   Expectations for Word Study Notebooks

1. *Writing word sorts.* Students write the words into the same categories developed during hands-on sorting. Key words are used as headers for each column.
2. *Selecting 10 words to draw and label.* Even older students enjoy the opportunity to illustrate words with simple drawings that reveal their meanings.
3. *Changing a letter (or letters) to make new words.* Initial letter(s) might be substituted to create lists of words that rhyme. For example, starting with the word *black* a student might generate *stack, quack, track, shack,* and so on.
4. *Selecting 10 words to use in sentences.* This is especially important as children begin the study of homophones, inflected words (*ride, rides, riding*), and roots and suffixes where meaning is an issue.
5. *Doing word hunts in trade books and response journals.* Students add these words to the written sorts in their notebooks as shown in Figure 4-4.

Work in the word study notebooks is done independently and graded. Kathy Ganske makes her expectations clear by pasting a chart such as the one in Figure 4-18 on the inside cover of the notebook. Composition books with stiff cardboard covers and sewn pages last all year.

One typical year, Kathy Ganske had a fourth grade class of 25 children who exhibited a wide range of instructional levels in reading and spelling. By administering her own spelling-by-stage assessment during the first few days of school, she grouped her pupils into three stages of developmental word knowledge (Ganske, 1994). One group was so large, however, that it was divided in two, making a total of four word study groups that she scheduled for regular small-group meetings. Her weekly schedule follows:

Monday—Introduce the sort.   On Monday morning, every child finds a word study sheet on his or her desk. Different spelling groups get different words for the week. Children sort the words before school even begins in anticipation of the categories they might be sorting later on. These spontaneous, open sorts are interesting for the teacher to observe. They tell her what students already know.

While the rest of the class settles down for independent reading and journal writing, the teacher works with small groups one at a time on the floor or around a table. Everyone brings their cutout word cards with them. The very first thing the teacher does is go through her own stack of words one at a time, pronouncing each one, and talking about meaning. Students also give examples of each word's meaning and share their knowledge of where they have heard or seen the word before.

This teacher presents a weekly word list that will lead to a new sort.

Next the teacher establishes the key words that guide the sorts. She asks students what they think the categories might be and why they think so. In many cases, students have already seen the consistencies in sound or pattern as they cut out the words, and they have anticipated the sort. Nevertheless, the teacher carefully models the sorting, comparing each word to the key word. In each case, the word on the card is pronounced, placed under a key word, and compared to the pronunciation of the key word. In order for the word to be placed in a column, it must match the key word by sound, pattern, or both.

Once the word sort has been demonstrated and discussed, students sort their own word cards in front of the teacher, saying each word aloud. When they are finished, they learn to read through the words in each column to see if there are any changes they would like to make. The teacher checks the sorts and asks students to explain why they grouped the words the way they did. Misconceptions are corrected, and the sorting is remodeled if needed. Afterward, students return to their desks to write the sort in their word study notebooks. Students take their word cards home to practice in anticipation of the speed sorts scheduled for the next day. After all students from the first group have been guided in their first sort of the week, the teacher calls the next groups in turn to work with a different batch of words. At their desks, students work in their word study notebooks, and then return to other reading and writing assignments.

Tuesday–Speed sorts. On Tuesday there is no teacher-directed word study. Instead, students pair for speed sorts, and follow a posted schedule of times and partners. Throughout the day, partners go back to the "sorting table" at 10-minute intervals to sort their word cards for accuracy and speed. One child times the other with a stopwatch kept at the table and then checks for correctness against an answer sheet. Partners work together to solve any discrepancies between their sort and the answer. The partners return to their seats to do additional work in their word study notebooks and then pick up where they left off with other assignments.

Wednesday–Word hunts. On Wednesday, all four word study groups convene at the same time in their respective groups. Students bring the books they are currently reading, and they gather around a large piece of chart or butcher paper spread on the floor. A leader is appointed and the same key words used on Monday and Tuesday are written across the top of the large sheet of paper. Students skim and scan pages in their books that they have already read, looking for words that match the key words according to the feature under study. As examples are found, students share their words. Much discussion may ensue as to whether or not a word contains the spelling feature in question. Often the dictionary is consulted, particularly to resolve questions of stress,

FIGURE 4-19   Cooperative Group Word Hunt

syllabication, or meaning. Once a consensus is reached, the leader writes the word on the paper under the proper key word. The word hunt continues in this cooperative group format for a specified amount of time, and usually several examples are found for each column (see Figure 4-19).

During word hunts, the teacher circulates from group to group and comments on the frequency of one pattern over another. Some patterns are found in virtually every text again and again, whereas others are harder to find. The teacher asks group members to provide reasons for the agreed upon groupings. After this activity, the word hunt is recorded in each member's word study notebook. For homework that night, students find additional examples to add to their notebooks from the books they are reading at home. It is important, however, that students not confuse skimming for word patterns with reading for meaning. The teacher asks her students to use the trade books they have read or are currently reading for word hunts.

Thursday–Speed sorts with teacher.

Thursday is the children's favorite day. If they wish, students can race the teacher in sorting their word cards. Students who are interested in this activity practice the night before. As students meet in their word study groups to practice sorting for speed and accuracy, the teacher circulates from group to group and sorts the word cards while being timed. For the next few minutes, group members try to beat her time. Those who succeed get to put their name on the black-board, and some special prize or privilege is awarded at the end of the day.

Friday–Evaluation and monitoring progress.

Friday completes the cycle for the week. Each group is tested on the spelling features they have examined through their hunting and sorting tasks all week. Not every word is tested, however—only a random sample of words sorted over the week. In this way, the discriminating orthographic feature is emphasized, as opposed to rote memorization of a given list of words.

Knowledge of particular orthographic patterns can also be checked in the form of nonsense words. Students may be asked to spell the word *remblete,* for example, and then the teacher asks what key word they thought of to guide their spelling (*complete*). In this way, she gauges the degree that the studied features generalize to unknown words.

Results of the Friday test as well as observations made during the week influence the teacher's plans for the next week. She may decide that students need to revisit a feature, compare it to another feature, or move on to new features. Group membership may also change depending on a given child's pace and progress.

Integrating Word Study
Into the Language Arts Curriculum

Kathy Ganske's word study program is just one example of how to integrate spelling instruction into a reading-writing, process-oriented classroom. What is remarkable about her routine is its centrality to both reading and writing. Students return again and again to trade books they have already read to analyze the vocabulary. Word study is integrated into other studies as well. Poetry lessons begin with reference to a word study lesson on syllable stress. In a writing lesson, students discuss comparative adjectives from a previous word study lesson that focused on words ending in *er*. During a lesson on parts of speech the students are asked to sort their week's spelling words by nouns, verbs, and adjectives. Whatever routine you choose, your sequence of activities must fit comfortably within your reading/writing/language arts block of instruction. By incorporating a word study notebook as an ongoing activity, you will have a built-in record of activities and progress.

Selecting Written Word Study Activities:
A Caveat Regarding Tradition

There are many long-standing activities associated with spelling that teachers often assign their students such as writing words five times, writing them in alphabetical order, and copying definitions of words from the dictionary. Think critically about whether assignments like these fulfill the purpose of spelling instruction—which is not only to learn the spellings of particular words, but also to learn generalizations about the spelling system itself. Writing a word five times can be a rote meaningless activity, whereas writing words into categories, requires the recognition of common spelling features and the use of judgment and critical thinking. Writing words in alphabetical order may teach alphabetization but it won't teach anything about spelling patterns. Alphabetizing words might be assigned occasionally as a separate dictionary skill, and children will be more successful at it when they can first sort their word cards into alphabetical order before writing them down. Students do need to associate meanings with the words they are studying, particularly in upper level word study when dealing with syllables and affixes and derivational relations. It is reasonable to ask students to look up the meanings of a few words they do not know, but asking students to write the definitions of long lists of words they already know is disheartening and not likely to encourage dictionary use. Writing words in sentences can also be overdone. Kathy Ganske asks her students to choose 10 words (out of 24) each week to use in sentences. This is a more reasonable assignment than writing 24 isolated sentences with the weekly spelling list. Writing just a few sentences per day encourages the application of word use and meaning. She also uses sentence writing to work on handwriting, punctuation, and grammar. Writing sentences is more useful at some levels of development than others. For example, sentences will help students show that they understand homophones or the tense of verb forms when studying inflected endings such as *ed* and *ing*.

Be wary of other traditional assignments that take up time and may even be fun, but have little value in teaching children about spelling. Activities such as hangman, word searches, and acrostics may keep students busy, but they impart little or no information about the English spelling system. Spelling bees reward those children who are already good spellers and eliminate early the children who need practice the most. Word study can be fun, but make good use of the time spent on it and don't overdo it. Remember that written word study activities should be short in duration so that students can devote most of their attention and time to reading and writing for meaningful purposes.

Dear Parents,

Your child will be bringing home a collection of spelling words weekly that have been introduced in class. Each night of the week your child is expected to do a different activity to assure that these words and the spelling principles they represent are mastered. These activities have been modeled and practiced in school, so your child can teach you how to do them.

Monday   Remind your child to *sort the words* into categories like the ones we did in school. Your child should read each word aloud during this activity. Ask your child to explain to you why the words are sorted in a particular way—what does the sort reveal about spelling in general? Ask your child to sort them a second time as fast as possible.

Tuesday   Do a "*buddy sort*" with your child. Lay down a word from each category as a header and then read the rest of the words aloud. Your child must indicate where the word goes without seeing it. Lay it down and let your child move it if he or she is wrong. Repeat if your child makes more than one error.

Wednesday   Assist your child in doing a *word hunt,* looking for words in a familiar book that have the same sound, pattern, or both. Try to find two or three for each category.

Thursday   Do a *writing sort* to prepare for the Friday test. As you call out the words in a random order your child should write them in categories. Call out any words your child misspells a second or even third time.

Thank you for your support. Together we can help your child make valuable progress!

Sincerely,

FIGURE 4-20   Parent Letter

Word Study Homework and Parental Expectations

Classrooms are busy places and many teachers find it difficult to devote a lot of time to word study. Homework can provide additional practice time, and parents are usually pleased to see that spelling is part of the curriculum. A letter sent home, such as the one illustrated in Figure 4-20, is a good way to encourage parents to become involved in their children's spelling homework. Parents are typically firm believers in the importance of spelling because it is such a visible sign of literacy, and many are even taking political action to see it reinstated. Unfortunately, invented spelling is often a scapegoat because parents, politicians, and even some teachers unfairly associate the acceptance of invented spelling with lack of instruction and an "anything goes" expectation regarding spelling accuracy in children's writing at all grade levels. Communicate clearly to parents that their children will be held accountable for what they've been taught. Homework assignments help them see what is being taught in phonics and spelling.

Expectations for Editing and Accuracy in Children's Written Work

Invented spellings free children to write even before they can read during the emergent stage, and children should be free to make spelling approximations when writing rough drafts at all levels. Invented spellings also offer teachers diagnostic information about what children know and what they need to learn. But that does not mean that teachers do not hold children accountable for accurate spelling. Knowing where children are in terms of levels of development and knowing what word features they have studied enable teachers to set reasonable expectations for accuracy and editing. Typical third graders in the within word pattern stage can be expected to spell words like *jet, flip,* and *must,* but it would be unreasonable to expect them to spell multisyllable words like *leprechaun* or *celebration.* Just as students are gradually held more and more accountable for conventions of writing such as commas and semicolons, so too, they are gradually held more accountable for spelling accuracy. Teachers' understanding of how spelling develops over time enables them to make reasonable and individualized expectations. Teachers also need to direct students to a range of spelling resources and help students learn to use them.

When teachers work with students in small groups they often use chart paper to make lists of words which are then posted around the room. Words listed on the walls call attention to the richness and power of a versatile vocabulary. Sometimes these charts chronicle discussions of content studies, and sometimes they focus on the specific study of words: happy words, sad words, holiday or seasonal words, homophones, homographs, synonyms, and antonyms—all provide a ready reference for writing.

Learning to use resources such as word walls (Cunningham, 1995), word banks, personal dictionaries, sound boards, and dictionaries, should be a part of the word study curriculum. Even first graders can use simple dictionaries appropriate for their level to look up some special words, and they can be encouraged to refer to their own individual word banks for words. However, that does not mean you could expect them to look up all the words they need to use. A study by Clarke (1988) found that first graders who were encouraged to use invented spellings wrote more and could spell as well at the end of the year as first graders who had been told how to spell words. This indicates that children are not marred by their own invented spellings or perseverate with errors over time. However, unless teachers communicate that correct spelling is valued, students may develop careless habits.

Many teachers wonder when they should make the shift from allowing children to write in invented spelling to demanding correctness. The answer is: right from the start.

TABLE 4-2 Grading Form for Word Study

Name:	Grading Period:		
	Excellent Effort	Good Effort	Needs Improvement
Weekly Word Study			
Word sorts			
Word study notebook			
Partner work			
Final tests			
Editing Written Work			
Spells most words right			
Finds misspelled words to correct			
Assists others in editing work			
Uses a variety of resources to correct spelling			

A = Excellent work in most areas
B = Good work in most areas
C = Needs improvement in most areas

Recommended Grade _____

Comments:

Teachers must hold children accountable for what they have been taught. What they haven't been taught can be politely ignored. For example, if a child has been taught the sound-to-letter correspondences for *B, M, R,* and *S,* the teacher would expect that child to spell these beginning sounds correctly. However, if the child has not yet been taught the short vowel sounds, these should be allowed to stand as invented spellings. Since the sequence for phonics and spelling instruction is cumulative and progresses linearly from easier features such as individual letter-sounds, to harder features such as Latin-derived *tion, sion,* and *cian* endings, there will always be some features that have not yet been taught. Thus, children (and adults!) will always invent a spelling for what they do not yet know.

Spelling Tests and Grades

Some teachers are expected to assign grades for spelling, or spelling may be part of an overall language arts or writing grade. Ideally such a grade should include more than an average of Friday test scores (which should all be high when children are working on words at their instructional level!). Table 4-2 on page 87 offers a more holistic assessment using a form that can be adapted for any grade level. Some teachers may wish to add a section for students to rate themselves. This one might be used with students in upper elementary who can be expected to spell most words correctly.

MATCHING ACTIVITIES TO DEVELOPMENT

Your final step in setting up a word study program is to develop word sorts and target activities for your students based on the assessments in Chapter 3. The chart in Figure 4-21 outlines the basic word study activities for each stage of spelling. The chart also lists the characteristics of each stage of development in some detail. This chart will help you to focus on the developmental needs of your students. Chapters 5 to 9 offer more detail about planning instruction for each stage.

I. Emergent Stage—Chapter 5

Characteristics
1. Scribbles letters and numbers
2. Lacks concept of word
3. Lacks letter-sound correspondence or represents most salient sound with single letters
4. Pretends to read and write

Reading and Writing Activities
1. Read to students and encourage oral language activities
2. Model writing using dictations and charts
3. Encourage pretend reading and writing

Word Study Focus
1. Develop concept sorts
2. Play with speech sounds to develop phonological awareness
3. Plan alphabet activities
4. Sort pictures by beginning sound
5. Encourage fingerpoint memory reading of rhymes, dictations, and simple pattern books
6. Encourage invented spelling

FIGURE 4-21   Sequence of Development and Instruction

Early Letter Name–Alphabetic

Characteristics

1. Represents beginning and ending sounds
2. Has rudimentary / functional concept of word
3. Reads word by word in beginning reading materials

Reading and Writing Activities

1. Read to students and encourage oral language activities
2. Secure concept of word by plenty of reading in patterned trade books, dictations, and simple rhymes
3. Record and reread individual dictations one paragraph long
4. Label pictures and write in journals regularly

Word Study Focus

1. Collect known words for word bank
2. Sort pictures and words by beginning sounds
3. Study word families that share a common vowel
4. Study beginning consonant blends and digraphs
5. Encourage invented spelling

Middle to Late Letter Name–Alphabetic Stage

Characteristics

1. Correctly spells initial and final consonants and some blends and digraphs
2. Uses letter names to spell vowel sounds
3. Spells phonetically representing all salient sounds in a one-to-one linear fashion.
4. Omits most silent letters.
5. Omits preconsonantal nasals in spelling (BOP or BUP for *bump*)
6. Fingerpoints and reads out loud
7. Reads slowly in a word-by-word manner

Reading and Writing Activities

1. Read to students
2. Encourage invented spellings in independent writing but hold students accountable for features and words they have studied
3. Collect two to three paragraph-long dictations which are reread regularly
4. Encourage more expansive writing and consider some simple editing such as punctuation and high-frequency words

Word Study Focus

1. Sort pictures and words by different short vowel word families
2. Sort pictures and words by short vowel sounds and CVC patterns
3. Continue to examine consonant blends and digraphs
4. Begin simple sound sorts comparing short and long vowel sounds
5. Collect known words for word bank (up to 200)

Characteristics

1. Spells most single-syllable short vowel words correctly
2. Spells most beginning consonant digraphs and two-letter consonant blends
3. Attempts to use silent long vowel markers (NALE for *nail*)
4. Reads silently and with more fluency and expression
5. Writes more fluently and in extended fashion
6. Can revise and edit

Reading and Writing Activities

1. Continue to read aloud to students
2. Plan self-selected silent reading of simple chapter books
3. Write each day, writers' workshops, conferencing, and publication

FIGURE 4-21 Continued

Word Study Focus
1. Complete daily activities in word study notebook
2. Sort words by long and short vowel sounds and by common long vowel patterns
3. Compare words with *r*-controlled vowels
4. After mastering common long vowels, explore less common vowels and diphthongs (*oi, ou, au, ow*)
5. Review blends and digraphs as needed and examine triple blends and complex consonant units such as *thr, str, dge, tch, ck*
6. Examine homographs and homophones

IV. Syllables and Affixes—Chapter 8

Characteristics
1. Spells most single-syllable words correctly
2. Makes errors at syllable juncture and in unaccented syllables
3. Reads with good fluency and expression
4. Reads faster silently than orally
5. Writes responses that are sophisticated and critical

Reading and Writing Activities
1. Plan read-alouds and literature discussions
2. Include self-selected or assigned silent reading of novels of different genres
3. Begin simple note taking and outlining skills, and work with adjusting reading rates for different purposes
4. Explore reading and writing styles and genres

Word Study Focus
1. Examine consonant doubling and inflected endings
2. Focus on unaccented syllables such as *er* and *le*
3. Join spelling and vocabulary studies; link meaning and spelling
4. Explore grammar through word study
5. Sort and study affixes (prefixes and suffixes)
6. Study stress or accent in two-syllable words

V. Derivational Relations—Chapter 9

Characteristics
1. Have mastered high-frequency words
2. Makes errors on low-frequency multisyllabic words derived from Latin and Greek combining forms
3. Reads with good fluency and expression
4. Reads faster silently than orally
5. Writes responses that are sophisticated and critical

Reading and Writing Activities
1. Include silent reading and writing, exploring various genres as interests arise
2. Develop study skills, including textbook reading, note taking, reading rates, test taking, report writing, and reference work
3. Focus on literary analysis

Word Study Focus
1. Focus on words that students bring to word study from their reading and writing
2. Join spelling and vocabulary studies; link meaning and spelling
3. Examine common and then less common roots, prefixes, and suffixes
4. Examine vowel alternations in derivationally related pairs
5. Explore etymology, especially in the content areas
6. Examine content-related foreign borrowings

FIGURE 4-21 Concluded

CHAPTER 5

Word Study for Learners in the Emergent Stage

This chapter presents an overview of the literacy development that occurs during the emergent stage, a period in which young children imitate and experiment with the forms and functions of print. Emergent readers are busy orchestrating the many notes and movements essential to literacy: directionality, the distinctive features of print, the predictability of text, and how all of this correlates with oral language. The emergent stage lies at the beginning of a lifetime of learning about written language.

Emergent children do not read or spell conventionally because they have only very tenuous understandings of how units of speech and units of print are related. Nevertheless, children are developing remarkable insights into written language and with the help of caregivers and teachers they learn a great deal during what has sometimes been called the preliterate stage (Henderson, 1990). Before we go into a thorough description of the emergent stage, we will visit a classroom where 23 kindergartners explore literacy under the guidance of their teacher, Mrs. Collins.

During a unit on animals, Mrs. Collins shared the big book *Oh, A-Hunting We Will Go* by John Langstaff. This book is based on the traditional refrain "Oh, a-hunting we will go, a-hunting we will go. We'll catch a fox and put him in a box and then we'll let him go." The pattern repeats with various animals and places substituting for *box* and *fox*. After reading several pages, Mrs. Collins began pausing to allow her students to guess the name of the place using their sense of rhyme and picture cues. When several students sang out that the *whale* would be put in a *bucket,* Mrs. Collins pointed to the word *pail* on the page and said, "Could that word be *bucket*? What does *bucket* start with? Listen. *Buh-buh-buh-bucket.* What does this word start with?"

In this fashion Mrs. Collins introduced a new book with her children as they enjoyed the silliness of the rhymes and pictures. In the process she drew her students' attention to letters and sounds and modeled directionality and fingerpointing as she read. After enjoying the big book version, she planned a number of follow-up activities to further develop emergent literacy skills.

Mrs. Collins created a chart with the first five lines of patterned text and posted it in the room for children to read from memory. She also wrote each of the first five lines on sentence strips and placed them in order in a pocket chart. After the children had read the lines several times chorally, Mrs. Collins passed out the strips. As a group they put the sentences back in order by comparing them to the chart. Another day, word cards for *fox, box, catch, go,* and *we* were held up one by one as volunteers came up to find the words on the chart or sentence strips. Mrs. Collins observed carefully to see which children were beginning to point accurately as they recited. She made sure the book, chart, and strips were left out where everyone could practice freely with them during the day.

Mrs. Collins had a group of children who were ready to study initial consonants. In previous lessons they had compared words that started with *S* and *M.* Now they looked for words that started with *B* and *F* on the five-line chart and found *fox* and *box.* Mrs. Collins wrote those words on cards as the key words for a picture sort. She brought out a collection of pictures that started with *B* and *F* and modeled how to sort them by beginning sound in the pocket chart. She then invited the children to take turns sorting by choosing from a random assortment of pictures she placed in the pockets below. This sort was repeated by the group and on subsequent days all the children had a number of opportunities to sort on their own, to hunt for more pictures in alphabet books and magazines, and to draw and label pictures with those sounds. After the students compared the sounds for *B* and *F* in several ways, the pictures were combined with *M* and *S,* which had been studied previously, for a four-category sort. The students worked with all four letters and sounds for several days before moving on to a new contrast.

Mrs. Collins used a core book as the basis for teaching a variety of emergent literacy skills in a developmental and appropriate fashion. In Mrs. Collins's class, word study activities address issues critical to emergent literacy in the context of read-alouds and playful language lessons. We will discuss these critical issues and how teachers like Mrs. Collins promote literacy learning.

FROM SPEECH TO PRINT: THE SYNCHROMESH OF UNITS

Learning to read and spell is a process of matching oral and written language structures at three different levels: (1) the global level at which the text is organized into phrases and sentences, (2) the level of words within phrases, and (3) the level of sounds and letters within syllables. For someone learning to read, there is not always an obvious match between spoken and written language at any of these levels. Mismatches occur because of the inflexible nature of print and the flowing stream of speech it represents. Learning to make the match between speech and print is a gradual process, but essential. To learn to read and spell, children must explore the structures of both written and spoken language at these three levels.

The Phrase and Sentence Level

In oral language, the global level is characterized as **prosodic.** This is the "musical" level of language, usually consisting of phrases. Within these phrases, speakers produce and listeners hear intonation contours, expression, and tone of voice, all of which communicate ideas and emotions. For example, a rising note at the end of a statement indicates a question; precise, clipped words in a brusque tone may suggest anger or irritation. Oral language is a direct form of communication where there are partners who fill in the gaps in the incoming message and who indicate when communication breaks down. Written language is an indirect form of communication and must contain complete, freestanding messages in which meaning is clear. Punctuation and word choice are the reader's only cues to the emotions and intent of the writer. Written language tends to be more formal and carefully constructed, using recognizable structures and literacy devices such as "happily ever after" to cue the reader. When children learn to read they must match the prosody of their oral language to the more formal structures of written language.

Words in Phrases

A second level of structures students negotiate are the units of meaning called **words.** In speech, words are not distinct; there is not a clear, separable unit in speech that equates perfectly to individual words. For example, "once upon a time" represents a single idea composed of four words and five syllables. Because of this, when children try to match their speech to print, they often miss the mark. It takes some practice to match words in speech to written words (Morris, 1980; Roberts, 1992).

This mismatch of meaning units between speech and print is most clearly illustrated through an instrument called a **spectrograph.** This acoustic representation of speech reveals a surprising thing: Humans don't speak in words! There are no demarcations for individual words when a person is talking. The only break in a spectrograph coincides with phrases and pauses for breathing. These breaks always occur between syllables. A word is a term specific to print, and according to Malinowski (1952), cultures that have no written language have no word for *word.* This remarkable state of affairs creates an enormous challenge for individuals learning to read.

Sounds in Syllables

Sounds and letters make up the third level of analysis. In learning to read, students must negotiate sounds within syllables. In speech, consonants and vowels are interconnected and cannot be easily separated (Liberman & Shankweiler, 1991). Yet the alphabet and letter-sounds must be learned as discrete units. As children stabilize the match between print and speech at the phrase and sentence level, they come to discover the way the alphabet divides the sounds within syllables. Their first understanding develops through exploring the beginning sounds of words. Later, once they understand how the alphabet represents sounds, children begin to view the writing system—the **orthography**—as a series of patterns that are organized at the level of syllable.

CHARACTERISTICS OF THE EMERGENT STAGE OF READING AND SPELLING

Some emergent children may have well-developed language skills and know a great deal about stories and books; others may not. It is not necessary for children who have difficulty expressing themselves to learn to do that first before learning the alphabet or seeing printed words tracked in correspondence to speech. To withhold these essential components of the learning-to-read process would hold them in double jeopardy. Not only would they be behind in language and story development, but they would also be behind in acquiring the alphabetic principle. Of course all children need to be read to and immersed in the language and literature of their lives. But children can learn about stories *and* learn about words, sounds, and alphabet at the same time as teachers model reading and writing and invite children to imitate and experiment.

Emergent Reading

The reading of the preliterate child is really pretend reading, or reading from memory. Both are essential practices for movement into literacy. **Pretend reading** is basically a paraphrase or spontaneous retelling at the global level which children produce while turning the pages of a familiar book. In pretend reading, children pace their retelling to match the sequence of pictures and orchestrate many other concepts about books and print such as directionality, sequence, dialogue, and the voice and cadence of written language (Sulzby, 1986).

Reading from memory is more exacting than pretend reading and involves an accurate recitation of the text accompanied by pointing to the print on the page in some fashion. Reading from memory helps children coordinate spoken language with print at the level of words, sounds, and letters. This phenomenon, called **concept of word,** is a watershed event that separates the prephonetic, emergent reader from the letter name–alphabetic beginning reader (Morris, 1981).

Emergent children's attempts to touch individual words while reading from memory are initially quite inconsistent and vague. Such children may realize that they should end up on the last word on the page, but the units that come in between are a blur. Their fingerpointing is likewise nebulous. This strategy for reading is mirrored in their writing, in which word boundaries and print distinctions are also obscured, even if some phoneme-grapheme correspondences have been made (see Figure 5-1).

Other children are aware that there are units to be reckoned with while reading, though they are not exactly sure what these units are. Such children may attempt to touch the print in correspondence to stressed beats in speech. Syllables may even be treated as separate words in print. This strategy is revealed in their fingerpoint reading as well as in their writing. In fingerpoint reading, a child might point to the word *man* in the line "Sam, Sam the baker man," while saying the second syllable of *baker* (*ker*), then point to the word *washed* while saying "man." Figure 5-2 illustrates the phenomenon of getting off-track on two-syllable words.

Words gradually begin to evolve as distinct entities with their boundaries defined by beginning and ending sounds. Children's early letter name–alphabetic spelling also provides evidence of this understanding. Early letter name–alphabetic spelling is illustrated in Figure 5-3 and will be described in the next chapter.

Emergent Writing and Spelling

Like emergent reading, early emergent writing is largely pretend. Regardless of most children's culture and where they live, this pretend writing occurs spontaneously wherever writing is encouraged, modeled, and incorporated into play (Ferreiro & Teberosky,

"I like housekeeping"

FIGURE 5–1 Emergent Writing Without Word Boundaries

FIGURE 5-2 Trying to Match Voice to Print

1982). It begins with pictorial representations, then advances to labeling these pictures. Children first approximate the most global contours of the writing system: the top-to-bottom and linear arrangement. Later, smaller segments such as numbers, letters, and words are also imitated. Not until the end of this stage does writing achieve a direct relation to speech, and when it does, conventional literacy will soon follow.

The ability to write emerges in children in much the same way that it first emerged in humankind. Pictures, initially used for decorative purposes, came to be used intentionally as mnemonic devices. Later, a picture of a king and a picture of wood were combined to cue the name Kingwood. A rebus system of this sort led to the invention of the syllabary in which speech sounds were directly represented with hieroglyphs. This direct link to speech heralded the emergence of literacy on the face of the Earth. It was preceded, however, by a period of 40,000 years of prewriting—with pictorial representations (Gelb, 1963).

Like the early humans, the child's first task is to discover that scribbling can represent something and, thereafter, to differentiate drawing from writing and representation from communication. The child must come to realize that a drawing of a flower does not actually say "flower." Writing is necessary to communicate the complete message. Figure 5-4 presents a progression of drawings and their accompanying utterances which show a clear differentiation between picture and writing.

There are many similarities between infant talk and emergent writing. When babies learn to talk, they do not begin by speaking in phonemes first, then syllables, words, and finally phrases. In fact, it is quite the other way around. They begin by cooing in phrasal contours, approximating the music of their mother tongue. Likewise, children begin to

i K hskpen

"I like housekeeping"

FIGURE 5-3 Early Letter Name–Alphabetic Spelling With Word Boundaries

FIGURE 5-4   The Evolution of Emergent Writing

"She jumped up and caught the ball"
FIGURE 5-5   Emergent Writing

write by approximating the broader contours of the writing system; they begin with the linear arrangement of print. This kind of pretend writing has been called "mock linear" (Clay, 1975). Later, as some letters and numbers are learned, these are interchanged along with creative hieroglyphics or "symbol salad" as children experiment with the distinctive features of print.

When babies move into what is conventionally recognized as baby talk, they give up their melodious cooing to concentrate on smaller segments, usually stressed syllables. "Dat!" is hardly as fluid as babbling "Ahee-hee-hee," but these awkward exclamations will be smoothed out in time. Likewise, global knowledge of writing and letter forms is temporarily abandoned as children concentrate their attention on the specifics of letter formation and the representation of the most salient sounds of speech. Such attention sometimes leads children to spit out parts of words on paper, often using single consonants to stand for entire syllables. As Figure 5-5 illustrates, the message is often indecipherable because children do not understand the purpose or need for spaces and tend to run their syllables and words together on paper.

Here is where the similarity between spoken and written language breaks down. Humans don't really talk in words, and there is no such thing as an isolated phoneme. Both words and phonemes are artifacts of print and do not naturally coincide with acoustic realities such as syllables. The concept of word and the concept of a phoneme must be taught; both will emerge as children gradually acquire the alphabetic principle and coordinate the units of speech with printed units on the page.

Emergence of Invented Spelling

By the end of the emergent stage, children are beginning to use letters to represent sounds in a systematic way as shown in the last box in Figure 5-4. These partially phonetic invented spellings represent a number of critical insights and skills. In order to invent a spelling, children need to know some letters—not all, but enough to get started. Second, children need to know how to write some of the letters they know. Third, children need to know that letters represent sounds. Again, they don't have to know all of the letter-sounds; indeed, if they know the names of the letters, they might use those as substitutes. Fourth, children need to attend to the sounds within syllables and match those sound segments to letters. This ability to divide syllables into the smallest units of sound is called **phonemic awareness.** To invent a spelling, a child must have some degree of phonemic awareness and some knowledge of letter-sounds. By the time children gain insight into all four of these aspects of sound and print, they are at the end of the emergent stage.

When literacy development has occurred in a balanced environment, phonemic awareness and the ability to invent a spelling go hand in hand. That is, if children are able to discern only the most salient sound, then they usually will put down only one letter: for example, S for *mouse*, N for *and*, or T for *mitten*. Until terms about language segments like "beginning sound" are sorted out, emergent children rely on the feel of their mouths as they analyze the speech stream. In the phrase "once upon a time," for example, the tongue touches another part of the mouth only for the /s/ sound of *once*, the /n/ sound of *upon*, and the /t/ sound of *time*. The lips touch each other twice: for the /p/ sound in the middle of *upon* and for the /m/ sound at the end of *time*. Emergent children pay attention only to those tangible points of an utterance where one part of the mouth touches another or the most forcefully articulated sounds which receive the most stress. To emergent children, this translates as "the loudest," and they choose this loudest or most prominent sound of stressed syllables to segment in their analysis of speech. If some letters are known, these will be matched accordingly. Figure 5-6 presents a few examples of Lee's phonemic analysis of phrases in her elephant story relative to her knowledge of the alphabet and letter-sounds. As children begin to achieve a concept of word, they become more able to pay attention to sounds that correspond to the beginning and the end of word units. Such children will usually put down one or two letters, as in D for *dog* or KT for *cat*. The goal of phonological awareness instruction for emergent readers is to help them classify the sounds they know into categories that coincide with printed word boundaries—beginnings and ends. If children know how to write their letters, their invented spelling will reflect their degree of phonemic awareness. As the spelling samples in Figure 5-7 depict, the phonemes represented are always the most salient, but the most salient are not always at the beginning of a "word." Notice also that word boundaries are confused with syllables, suffixes, and articles. When letter names are coordinated with word boundaries in a consistent fashion, a child is no longer an emergent speller. Spelling that honors word boundaries is early letter name–alphabetic.

Teaching children the names of the alphabet letters and the sounds they represent is enormously helpful during the emergent stage. But children don't have to get them all straight before they begin to read and write. As with oral language learning, written language learning involves forming and testing hypotheses as new bits of knowledge are

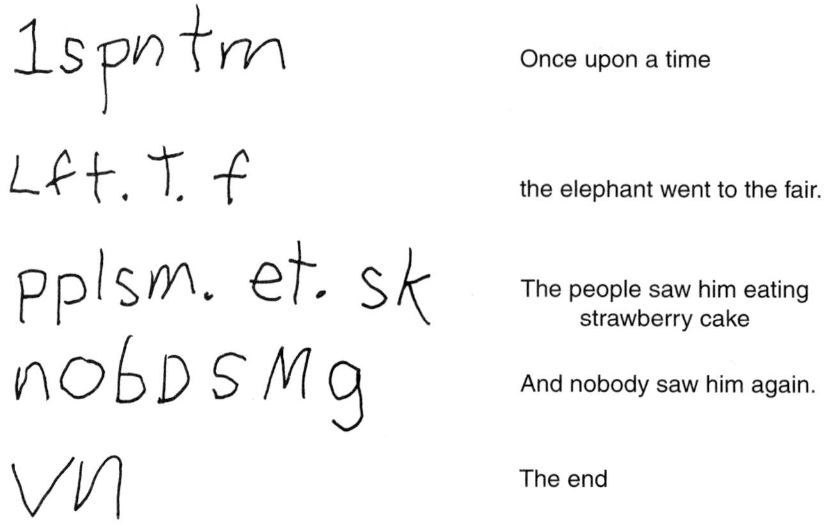

1spntrn   Once upon a time

Lft. T. f   the elephant went to the fair.

pplsm. et. sk   The people saw him eating
                                               strawberry cake

nobDSMg   And nobody saw him again.

Vn   The end

FIGURE 5-6 Lee's Elephant Story

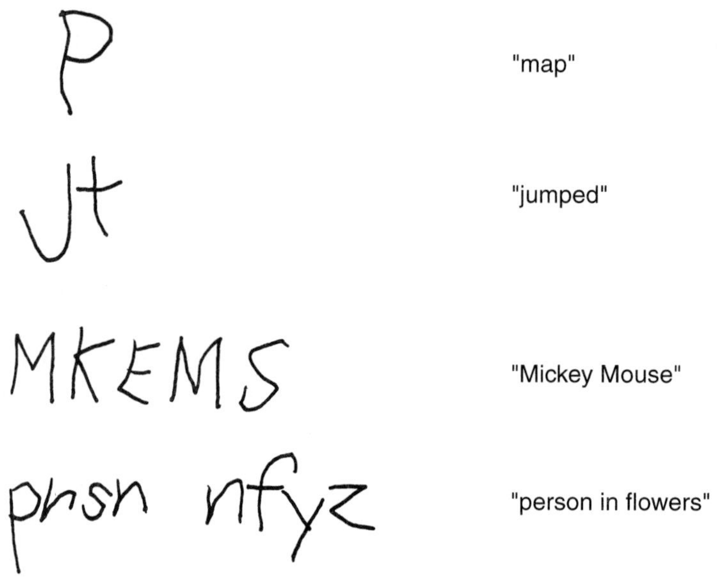

P   "map"

Jt   "jumped"

MKEMS   "Mickey Mouse"

phsn nfyz   "person in flowers"

FIGURE 5-7 Emergent Spelling Sample

perceived and internalized. And like the incessant chatter of the growing child, it is the extensive practice in approximating the writing system that extends the child's reach. Pretend writing and pretend reading must come first, and as they evolve, real reading and real writing naturally follow (Chomsky, 1971).

Early Literacy Learning and Instruction

To move from emergent to beginning reading, students must have many opportunities to see and experiment with written language. They must see their own spoken language transcribed into print, and they must be supported in making the speech-to-print match by choral recitation and fingerpoint **memory reading.** They must be encouraged to write, even if this writing is little more than scribble. The most important condition for emergent literacy to blossom is the opportunity to practice, no matter how closely the child may approximate the standard.

Emergent children will write, or pretend to write, well before they learn to read, provided they are encouraged to do so (Chomsky, 1971). The trick in developmental literacy instruction is how to give that encouragement. The mere act of leaving one's mark on paper (or walls and furniture!) has been called the "fundamental graphic act" (Gibson & Yonas, 1968)—an irresistible act of self-fulfillment. As the teacher, you have to do little more than provide immediate and ready access to implements of writing (markers, crayons, pencils, chalk) and provide a visible role model by drawing and writing yourself. Creating a conducive environment for writing also helps: a grocery store play area where grocery lists are drawn and labeled; a restaurant where menus are offered and orders are written; a writing center with a variety of paper, alphabet stamps, and markers. Outfitted and supported accordingly, writing will happen spontaneously without formal instruction and well before children can spell or properly compose (Strickland & Morrow, 1989).

Emergent reading instruction consists of modeling the reading process as teachers read aloud from big books and charts. Early literacy instruction also consists of talk about where one begins to read and where one goes after that. Teachers demonstrate the left-to-right directionality and the return sweep at the end of each line. Of course, all the talk and demonstration in the world won't get very far without hands-on practice. Early literacy instruction includes lots of guided practice with fingerpointing to familiar texts in a left-to-right progression. In the process, pretend reading or reading from memory gradually becomes real reading.

The reading materials best suited for emergent readers are simple predictable books, familiar nursery rhymes, poems, songs, jump rope jingles, and children's own talk written down. Familiarity with songs and rhymes helps bridge the gap between speech and print and cultivates the sense that what can be sung or recited can be written or read. Recording children's own language in the form of picture captions and dictated experience stories also nurtures the notion that print is talk written down. The ownership that comes with having one's own experiences recorded in print is a powerful incentive to explore the world of written language.

Useful techniques for fostering early literacy development include rebuilding familiar rhymes and jingles with sentence strips in pocket charts and matching word cards to individual words on the sentence strips as an explicit way to direct attention to words in print. Sorting objects, pictures, and words by beginning sounds draws attention to letter-sound correspondences. But, reading and rereading is the technique of choice. As is true with all of the stages of word knowledge described in this book, the best way to create a reader is to make reading happen, even if it's just pretend.

Through these activities, the word study instruction for the emergent reader must aim toward the development of five main components of the learning-to-read process:

1. Vocabulary growth and concept development
2. Phonological awareness
3. Alphabet knowledge
4. Letter-sound knowledge
5. Concept of word in text

These five components constitute a balanced diet for early literacy learning and instruction. If all five components are addressed on a daily basis, no matter how far along the emergent continuum a child may be, reading should inevitably follow.

COMPONENTS OF EARLY LITERACY LEARNING

This section examines the wondrous ways in which emergent spellers analyze speech and apply it to what they know about print. Bear in mind, however, that emergent understandings of how units of speech correspond to units of print operate within a larger context of concept, language, and vocabulary growth (Snow, 1983). For this reason, we will first take a look at emergent vocabulary growth and concept development. Then we will describe the other components of early literacy learning.

Vocabulary Growth and Concept Development

A flourishing child who is 4 or 5 years old has acquired a working oral vocabulary of over 5,000 words. The child has mastered the basic subject-verb-object word order of the English language, and may take great delight in the silliness of word sounds and meanings. Many children have learned to recite the days of the week, and some, the months of the year. But to assume that these children need no further experience with the vocabulary of time is to stunt their conceptual understanding of the larger framework of time—how days, weeks, months, and years relate to one another. Ask some precocious 5-year-olds to name the four seasons of the year, and nine out of ten will recite the names of the months instead. Ask kindergartners to tell you what season of the year December falls in, and many will no doubt tell you "Christmas." These are the answers from children who know the names of the days, the months, and the seasons, but don't really understand the relationships among them.

Young children use many words whose meanings they do not fully comprehend. Their knowledge of words is only partially formed by the information gleaned from their few years of life. In order to extend the partial understandings of words they already have, and to acquire new word meanings as well, children must be given experiences that allow them to add new information to their existing store of word knowledge. Basic concept-development tasks are a surprisingly simple way to provide such experiences.

Concept Sorts

The human mind appears to work by using a compare-and-contrast categorization system to develop concepts and attributes. The sorting activities appropriate for emergent readers build on and reinforce this natural tendency. By stacking the deck with familiar objects, ideas, animals, and things, teachers can devise sorting tasks to help children differentiate and expand existing concepts and labels for those concepts. Fruits can be grouped separately from vegetables, and new vocabulary and interesting concepts are developed along the way.

One bright 5-year-old knew about tables, chairs, sofas, beds, ovens, refrigerators, microwaves, and blenders. But, in her mind these were all undifferentiated "things in a house." Simply by sorting these items into two different categories—tables, chairs, sofas, and beds; and refrigerators, ovens, microwaves, and blenders—she was able to differentiate the characteristics of furniture from those of appliances. In this way the concept of things in a house was refined to include the new concepts of furniture and appliances. The words followed shortly thereafter.

Read-alouds play a critical role in the development of vocabulary and concepts. Books provide background knowledge which some children may not have experienced. For example, books about seasons, weather, transportation, and how seeds grow provide basic vocabulary and information that are essential to comprehending written texts. After listening to Ruth Heller's book, *Chickens Aren't the Only Ones,* children might be provided picture cards to sort into groups: birds, mammals, and reptiles. In this way children may build upon a simple conceptual understanding of where eggs come from to include other attributes of the animal kingdom. Concept sorts based on daily life experiences and information gleaned from books develop and expand children's understandings of their world and their language to talk about it. For example, during a unit on animals, a teacher could introduce children to a concept sort such as the one shown in Figure 5–8.

There are many things in daily life that, for the child, remain unclassified in a sea of unrelated variety. Since language is concept-based, children of diverse cultures may have different conceptual foundations. Teachers must be particularly sensitive to ethnic and cultural diversity in the classroom. They cannot expect children to learn words that label notions unconnected to their experience. Teachers should provide opportunities

FIGURE 5-8 Concept Sort With Farm Animals and Zoo Animals

for children to categorize familiar objects from their surroundings and from experiences in their daily lives at home and in the classroom according to similarity and difference. Read-alouds provide a common frame of reference to further concept development and vocabulary growth for everyone.

The concept sorts described in the activities section (starting on page 112) are all variations on the theme of categorization tasks. In addition to basic sorting, concept-development activities are generally followed by **draw and label** or **cut and paste** procedures. As always, we recommend having children write at every possible opportunity during or following the concept sorts. As a culminating activity for a unit on animals, one teacher helped her children create their own books in which they drew pictures of their favorite animals. Many of her children were able to label these pictures or write stories about the animals with either pretend writing or invented spelling. Her children's efforts ranged from scribbles and random letters to readable approximations such as I LIK THE LINS N TGRS.

Phonological Awareness

Phonological awareness refers to the ability to pay attention to, identify, and manipulate various sound segments of speech. It is the umbrella term for a range of understandings, including a sense of alliteration, rhyme, syllables, and the ability to segment words into sounds and to blend sounds into words. Phonemic awareness is a subcategory of phonological awareness and is quite difficult to achieve. It refers to the ability to identify and reflect on the smallest units of sound within syllables: individual phonemes. Children can hear and use these phonemes easily at a tacit level—they can talk and can understand when others talk to them. Bringing tacit subconscious awareness of individual phonemes to the surface to be examined consciously and explicitly is a critical goal of emergent literacy instruction. Conscious awareness is necessary to learn an alphabetic writing system.

Phonological awareness is critical to reading success, and training in phonological awareness activities has a positive influence on beginning reading (Ball & Blachman, 1988). Phonological awareness activities in the classroom can be fun oral language activities that benefit all students. Classroom teachers should work to include some of the instructional components that have been identified as successful and effective (Blachman, 1994; Lundberg et al., 1988; Smith et al., 1995). Students should work with a unit that most closely matches their developmental level, beginning with listening skills and rhyme. As children's phonological skill develops, they should participate in activities that focus attention at the beginning sound and phoneme level.

FIGURE 5-9 "See You Later Alligator" Odd-One-Out

Listening for Sounds

Very young children need to develop general listening skills because listening becomes crucial as students attempt to differentiate among speech sounds. Students' early attempts at spelling often reflect the sounds they "hear" as they say a word aloud. Activities that promote careful listening by students often involve closing their eyes and identifying various noises made by the teacher. These kinds of activities can be made more difficult by making the same sound in various locations of the room and having students guess where it is coming from, or by making a series of noises and having students recall their sequence (Invernizzi, Meier, Swank, & Juel, 1998).

Rhymes and Jingles

Rhyme awareness activities are an easy, natural way for children to play with words and to begin to focus on speech sounds. Songs, jingles, nursery rhymes, and poems fill children's ears with the sounds of rhyme. Many children develop a sense of rhyme easily whereas others need more structured activities that draw their attention specifically to rhyming words. The easiest activity involving rhyming books and poems is simply to pause and let the children supply the second rhyming word in a couplet. When picture books such as *Oh, A-Hunting We Will Go* are used, children have the support of the illustration to help them out. Other favorites include *I Can't Said the Ant* by Polly Cameron and *Each Peach Pear Plum* by Janet and Alan Ahlsberg. Many others are listed in the activities section.

Rhyming book read-alouds can be followed by picture sorts for rhymes. For example, Barbara Straus and Helen Friedland's *See You Later Alligator* features simple rhymes such as "See you eating honey, bunny." Children can create their own "See you later" rhymes by laying out pictures of assorted animals and rhyming foods or objects (see Figure 5-9). To make it easier for beginners, lay out just two pictures that rhyme and one that does not. This odd-one-out setup enables children to identify more readily the two rhyming pictures. They have only to pick up an animal and the rhyming food. As children grow in their ability to listen for rhymes, the number of possibilities can be increased from three to four sets of pictures at a time.

Songs are naturally full of rhythm and rhyme and hold great appeal for children. Several songs recorded by Raffi, a popular singer and songwriter for children, are particularly well suited for language play. Rhyme is featured prominently in the song "Willaby Wallaby Woo" from the taped collection *Singable Songs for the Very Young* (Raffi, 1976). It goes like this:

Willaby Wallaby Wee, an elephant sat on me.
Willaby Wallaby Woo, an elephant sat on you.
Willaby Wallaby Wustin, an elephant sat on Justin.
Willaby Wallaby Wanya, an elephant sat on Tanya.

The song continues, creating a rhyme starting with *W* for everyone's name. After hearing the song played several times, the children can begin to sing it using the names of their classmates around the circle, perhaps passing along a stuffed elephant to add to the fun. The song can be changed to focus on alliteration by holding up a particular letter to insert in front of every word. *B*, for example, would result in "Billaby Ballaby Boo," and *F* would produce "Fillaby Fallaby Foo."

As children become more adept at listening for rhymes, they can play a variety of categorization and matching games. Traditional games such as Bingo, Lotto, and Concentration are always winners in which picture cards are matched to other picture cards that rhyme. More ideas for games and activities can be found later in this chapter.

Alliteration and Beginning Sounds

Alliteration refers to a series of two or more words that begin with the same sound. Activities that play with alliteration focus children's attention on beginning sounds which mark word boundaries in print and spoken language. This awareness of beginning sounds supports children as they learn to separate the speech stream into individual words. A number of activities help promote children's understanding of beginning sounds, starting with books such as *Dr. Seuss's ABC* in which "Willy Waterloo washes Warren Wiggins who is washing Waldo Woo."

Beginning-sound segmentation games can be played with puppets or stuffed animals who have a funny way of talking. The puppet teaches the children how to isolate the initial phoneme from the remaining portion of the word. The children are then asked to repeat what the puppet said. The children get to manipulate the puppet themselves as they segment words given to them by the teacher. For example, the teacher says "fin" and asks the child to repeat it in "puppet talk." The child responds with "f . . . in" (Treiman, 1985).

Riddles such as I Spy or I'm Thinking of Something can be used here too. The hints given by the teacher should accentuate the initial sound. "This thing I'm thinking of begins with /mmmmm/. This thing is small and gray. It is an animal." As the children respond "mouse" or "mole," the teacher asks them to exaggerate the beginning sound. As children become proficient at playing this game, they create their own riddles. Always encourage students to stretch, or elongate, the beginning sounds of the words they guess as the answer to the riddles. Look for more ideas in the activities section of this chapter.

Children must become aware that speech can be divided into smaller segments of sound before they will advance in literacy and they must learn some of the terminology used to talk about these sounds. Without this insight, instruction in phonics or letter-sound correspondences will have little success. Children have no trouble hearing sounds but they may be mystified by directions such as "Listen for the first sound." In response to the question "What sound does *cow* start with?" one puzzled child tentatively replied, "Moo?" Without a stable concept of word, "first" is a relative notion. Phonological awareness activities at the emergent level should help students attend to sounds and learn to label and categorize these sounds in various ways.

Alliteration or beginning-sound awareness is further developed as children sort pictures by beginning sound, an activity that will be described shortly. At this point, oral language activities cross over into the learning of letter-sound correspondences. Children can learn these associations at the same time they are learning to reflect on their oral language. Phonological awareness does not have to precede or follow alphabet knowledge or other components of emergent literacy instruction. Awareness of sounds is heightened by print, and because of this, it is a reciprocal, ongoing by-product of the learning-to-read process. Although phonological awareness is a key component of early reading acquisition, phonological awareness activities need not be conducted as isolated tasks. As children develop phonological awareness, teachers should seek to make connections between sounds and letters in the context of daily reading and writing.

Alphabet Knowledge

Among the reading readiness skills that are traditionally studied, the one that appears to be the strongest predictor of later reading success on its own is letter naming (Snow, Burns, & Griffin, 1998). There is a great deal to learn about letters and it can take a long time. Letters have names and shapes, and they must be formed in particular ways. Unlike other aspects of life, directional orientation is vital. In the three-dimensional world, a chair is a chair whether you approach it from the front or from the back, whether you approach it from the left or from the right. Not so with letters. A *b* is a *b* and a *d* is a *d*. Print is one of the few things in life where direction makes a difference. Figure 5-4 shows emergent writing in the early stages of alphabet acquisition. Note the mixture of numbers and letters and backward formations in the child's efforts to spell *macaroni*.

Many letter names share similar sounds. The letter name *B*, (bee), for example, shares the vowel sound of the letter name *E*, as do *P, D, T, C, G, V,* and *Z*. There are visual similarities as well. There are verticals with circles in *p, q, d,* and *b*. Verticals and horizontals intersect in *T, L, H, F, E,* and *I*. Intersecting diagonals are shared by *K, A* (which also share parts of letter name sounds), *M, N, V, W, X,* and *Z*. Even movements overlap in the formation of letters: the up-down-up-down motion is basic to *M, N, W,* and *V*; a circular movement is required of *B, C, D, G, O, P, Q, R, U,* and *S*; and the direction of these movements hinges critically on where one begins on the page (see Clay, 1975, for a detailed discussion of the acquisition of these distinctive features of letters).

Students in the emergent stage appear to practice these distinctive features on their own, provided they are given a model. First efforts at a global level mimic the kinds of letters children know best such as the letters in their own name (see Figure 5-10). Meanwhile, letters that share distinctive visual features will continue to be confused for some time; *B*s may be mistaken for *D*s, *N*s for *U*s, and so forth. Provided with the incentive to practice and the means to do so, emergent children will rehearse letter names, practice letter writing, and match uppercase to lowercase with delight.

Learning the names of the letters is an important first step toward learning the sounds associated with the letters. Most of the letters have names that include a sound commonly associated with it and can serve as a mnemonic device for remembering the sound. *B* (bee), *K* (kay), and *Z* (zee) have their sounds at the beginnings of their names, and *F* (eff), *L* (ell), and *S* (es) have their sounds at the end. The names of the vowels are

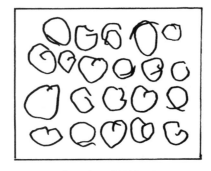

Connie's "Writing"   Ellie's "Writing"

FIGURE 5-10   Connie's and Ellie's Emergent Writing

their long sounds. Only *H* (aich), *W* (doubleyou), and consonant *Y* (wie) have no beginning-sound association and they are often the most difficult to learn. Letter names serve as the first reference point many children use when writing and explain some of the interesting invented spelling they create during the letter name–alphabetic stage discussed more in the next chapter.

Most mainstream, middle-class children take a good 5 years to acquire all this alphabet knowledge at home and in preschool. Magnetic letters on the refrigerator door, alphabetic puzzles, and commercial alphabet games are staples in many middle-class homes (Adams, 1990). Truly advantaged youngsters also have attentive parents at the kitchen table modeling letter formation and speech segmentation as they encourage their child to write a grocery list using invented spelling. Yet many of these children also require the directed instruction provided by formal schooling to fully understand the complexity of the alphabet. The best way to share 5 years of accumulated alphabet knowledge with those who have not been privy to this information is to teach it directly, in as naturalistic, fun, and game-like a manner as possible (Delpit, 1988). The word study activities described in the next section are designed to do just that.

Alphabet Games and Matching Activities

The alphabet is learned the same way that concepts and words for concepts are learned—through active exploration of the relationships between letter names, the sounds of the letter names, their visual characteristics, and the motor movement involved in their formation. By noting the salient, stable characteristics of *B* in many contexts and across many different fonts, sizes, shapes, and textures, a rudimentary concept of *B* is formed (see Figure 5-11). Every new encounter with *B* adds new attributes to the concept of *B*. Like concepts, the distinctive features entailed in a letter's name, look, feel, and formation must be actively manipulated to be identified and grouped.

Many alphabet activities begin with the child's name: building it with letter tiles, cutting it out of play dough, or matching it letter for letter with a second set. Writing or copying their own name, and the names of other family members or friends, is alluring to emergent writers and a great introduction to the alphabet as well as to writing. Letters take on personalities: *K* is Katie's letter and *T* is Tommy's letter. Familiar phrases like "I love you" and "Happy birthday" are frequently requested and demonstrate the compelling need for personalization, ownership, and purpose (Ashton-Warner, 1963).

The alphabet games and activities described at the end of this chapter build on the basic theme of compare-and-contrast categorization routines. Letters will be matched and sorted according to similarities and differences. The activities are designed to develop all

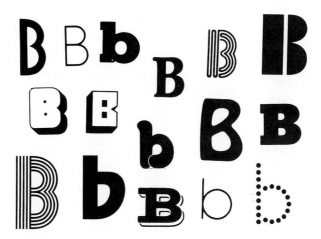

FIGURE 5-11 Different Print Styles

aspects of alphabet knowledge including letter naming, letter recognition (both upper- and lowercase), letter writing, and letter-sounds. To develop letter recognition skill, letters must be matched: uppercase to uppercase, lowercase to lowercase, and finally uppercase to lowercase. At the end of this chapter, you will see variations of many traditional games such as Bingo and Concentration. A writing component has been added to many of these games to incorporate letter formation. Sorting tasks, matching games, picture labeling, and writing are as important to acquiring the alphabetic principle as seeing letters in meaningful print.

Toward the end of the emergent stage of word knowledge, children will have made the connection that letters can represent sound segments in speech. As this connection is developing, have your students sort picture cards into groups under letters that correspond to the beginning sound. It is important to have them do a lot of writing as well.

Letter-Sound Knowledge

During the emergent stage, children learn their letters, attend to speech sounds, and begin to make connections between letters and sounds. Toward the end of the emergent stage many children will begin producing semiphonetic spellings which contain one or two letters for each syllable (see Figure 5-6). **Picture sorting** by beginning sounds secures these tentative efforts and moves children along in acquiring more knowledge of letter-sound correspondences through a game-like, manipulative phonics activity.

Some teachers choose *M* and *S* for their students' first consonant contrast because both letters have **continuant** sounds that can be isolated and elongated without undue distortion (mmmmoon and ssssun). They also feel very different in the mouth in terms of how they are articulated and this makes it easier for children to judge the categories while sorting. On the other hand, the sound for *B* cannot be elongated or isolated without adding a vowel to it (buh); but it is still fairly easy to learn, perhaps because it has a distinctive feel as the lips press together. However, to contrast *B* and *P* in an early sort would be confusing because they are both articulated the same way. The only difference between them is that the sound for *B* causes the vocal chords to vibrate and *P* does not. Try placing two fingers on your larynx and feel the difference in **voiced** *B* and **unvoiced** *P*. Other groups of letter-sounds that share the same place of articulation in the mouth are shown in each row of Table 5-1. The letters in each row are best not contrasted in the very first letter-sound sorts. Remember the sixth principle of word study: begin with obvious contrasts first!

TABLE 5-1 Pronunciation Chart of Beginning Consonant Sounds

Unvoiced	Voiced	Nasals	Other	Place of Articulation
p	b	m		lips together
wh	w		qu	lips rounded
f	v			teeth and lips
th (the)	th (this)			tip of tongue and teeth
t	d	n	l	tip of tongue and roof of mouth
s	z			tongue and roof of mouth
sh			y	sides of tongue and teeth
ch	j			sides of tongue and roof of mouth
k	g	ng	x	back of tongue and throat
h				no articulation—breathy sound

Understanding something about how sounds are produced may seem unnecessarily complicated, but it explains so many of the interesting things children do in their invented spellings during the emergent and letter name–alphabetic stages. Use the chart to see the logic in the invented spelling JP for *chip*, VN for *fan*, and PD for *pet*. Knowledge of sound articulation also helps teachers make decisions about setting up picture sorts.

Guidelines for Beginning Sound Picture Sorts

There are a number of other things to keep in mind when organizing sorts for beginning letter-sounds:

1. *Start with meaningful text.* Choose several sounds to contrast that represent key words from a familiar rhyme, patterned book, or dictation. One of the advantages of teacher-directed word study over published programs is that teachers can integrate phonics and the variety of print used in emergent classrooms.

2. *Make sorts easier or harder as needed.* Start with two obvious contrasts, then add one or two more for up to four categories. Look for fast and accurate sorting before moving on. Be ready to drop back to fewer categories if a child has difficulty.

3. *Use a key word and a letter as headers* so that children will associate the letter and sound. The key words may be words selected from familiar text or they may be the same as the key words used on the sound boards in the appendix. Whatever key word you use, be consistent and use the same one every time.

4. *Begin with directed sorts.* Discuss both the sound and the letter name, and model the placement of two or three words in each category. Be very explicit about why you sort the way you do. Say something like "*Fence, fffffence, ffffox. Fence* and *fox* start with the same sound, *ffff*. I will put *fence* under the letter *F*." Over time, as children catch on to what it is they are to attend to, you can be less directive. Figure 5-12 shows how this sort would look after several pictures are sorted.

5. *Use sets of pictures that are easy to name and sort.* Introduce the pictures to be sure that children know what to call them. Use pictures that are easy to identify and do not start with consonant blends or digraphs. Single-syllable words are better than two-syllable words because they have fewer sounds that need attention.

6. *Correct mistakes* on the first sort but allow errors to wait on subsequent sorts. Show children how to check their sorts by naming the pictures down the columns, emphasizing the beginning sounds. Then ask if there are any pictures that need to be

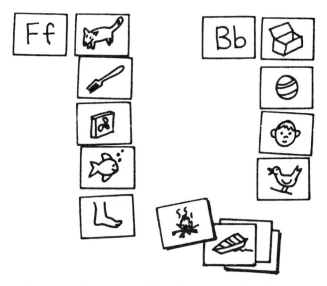

FIGURE 5-12 *Sound Sort for Comparing B and F*

changed. Ask children to check their own work using the same process and praise them when they find their own errors. If they don't, prompt them by saying, "There is a picture in this row that needs to be changed. Can you find it?"

7. *Vary the group sorting.* Put out all the pictures face up and let children choose one that they feel confident of naming and sorting correctly. Ask them to name the picture and the letter by saying "_____ begins with the _____ sound and goes under the letter _____." Another time pass out the pictures and call on children to come up and sort the card they were given. Then turn the pictures face down in a stack or spread them out on the floor and let children turn over the picture they will sort. Children enjoy the anticipation of not knowing which picture they will get. Include an "oddball" or "not sure" category headed by a question mark and add pictures to the sort that don't fit the established categories.

8. *Plan plenty of time for individual practice.* After group modeling and discussion, put sets of pictures in centers or create copies of picture sets for children to cut apart for more sorting. Sheets of pictures for sorting can be created by copying pictures from this book, cutting them apart, and pasting them in a mixed-up fashion on a template.

9. *Plan follow-up activities* like cut and paste, draw and label, and word hunts through familiar chart stories, nursery rhymes, or little books. These activities require children to recognize, recall, judge, and apply (see Chapter 4).

10. *Encourage invented spelling.* In the process of inventing spellings, children exercise their developing letter-sound knowledge in a meaningful activity.

All the phonological awareness, alphabet, and letter-sound knowledge in the world will not help children learn to read if they do not have a chance to apply this knowledge in context. Units of sound and the letters that represent them must be coordinated with printed word boundaries. This match must be synchronized with the flow of language over time and two-dimensional space. Beginning sounds depend upon a child's concept of word.

Concept of Word in Text

Emergent readers do not have a concept of word in print. What they point to as they recite may not coincide with printed word units at all. Like the babbling infant imitating the intonation contours of speech, the preliterate child points in a rhythmic approximation of the memorized text with little attention to word boundaries or even, perhaps, direction on the page. Prior to achieving a concept of word, emergent children, as well as emergent adults, have great difficulty identifying individual phonemes within words (Morais, Cary, Alegria, & Bertelson, 1979). There is an interaction between alphabetic knowledge, the ability to match speech to print, and phonemic awareness (Tunmer, 1991).

Through the teacher's demonstrations, children's fingerpointing behaviors change. Left-to-right movement becomes habitualized, though children may not routinely use letter or word units to guide their tracking. As white spaces are noted and much talk about words is introduced, children begin to track rhythmically across the text, pointing to words for each stressed beat in the recitation. As children become aware that print has something to do with sound, their fingerpointing becomes more precise and changes from a gross rhythm to a closer match with syllables. This works well for one-syllable words, but not so well for words of two or more syllables. For example, in the traditional ditty "Sam, Sam the Baker Man," children may pronounce "ker," the second syllable of *baker*, but point to the next word, *man*. Later, as children learn the alphabet and the sounds associated with the letters, beginning sounds will anchor the children's fingerpointing more directly to the memorized recitation: They realize that when they say the word *man*, they need to have their finger on a word beginning with an *M*. If they don't, they must start again. These self-corrections herald the onset of a concept of word in print. Figure 5-13 shows the progression of fingerpointing accuracy in relation to the orthographic development during this emergent to early letter name–alphabetic stage of word knowledge.

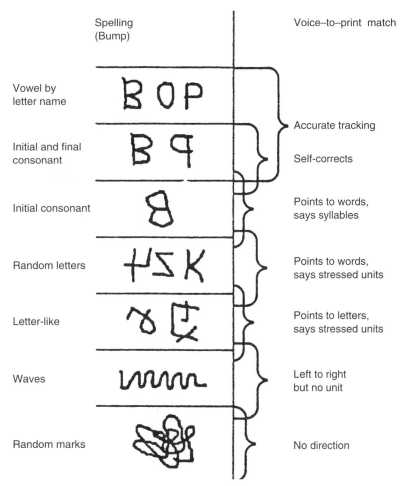

Spelling
(Bump)   Voice–to–print match

Vowel by
letter name   B O P

                                                    Accurate tracking

Initial and final
consonant   B q   Self-corrects

Initial consonant   B   Points to words,
                                                    says syllables

Random letters   H Σ K   Points to words,
                                                    says stressed units

Letter-like   ɣ Ʊ̷   Points to letters,
                                                    says stressed units

Waves   ᴜɴɴɴᴜ   Left to right
                                                    but no unit

Random marks   No direction

Adapted with permission from Gill (1992).

FIGURE 5-13   Voice-to-Print Match in Relation to Spelling Development

Fingerpoint Reading and Tracking Words

The best way for children to achieve a concept of word is to have them point to the words of a familiar text. These texts might be picture captions, dictated experience stories, poems, songs, simple patterned books, or excerpts from a favorite story printed on sentence strips or chart paper. Once these texts become familiar, children can be encouraged to memory-read them, pointing to each word as it is spoken. We call this **fingerpoint reading** or **tracking.**

Rhythmic texts are particularly appealing to young children and, like picture captions and dictated accounts, are easily memorized. Eventually, knowledge of initial consonant sounds will provide the necessary anchor to track accurately, even in the face of two-syllable words. At such times, though, rhythmic texts may throw children off in their tracking, and a move to less rhythmic, less predictable texts may be in order (Cathey, 1991). No matter what the source of text, the important thing from a word study point of view is to focus on individual words within the text. Fingerpointing, repeated reading, cut-up sentences, and word-card matching activities call attention to words and their letter-sound features.

One of the easiest ways to help children make connections between speech and print is to write captions beneath the pictures they draw. First have the children draw a picture of their favorite toy or Halloween costume and encourage them to include as much detail as possible. While they are finishing their drawings, walk around and ask each child to tell something about his or her picture. Choose a simple phrase or sentence that the child speaks, and write it verbatim beneath the picture (see Figure 5-14). Say each

FIGURE 5-14   Drawing With Dictated Caption

word as you write it, drawing attention to the sounds and letters. Read the caption by pointing to each word. Ask the child to read along with you and then to read it alone while pointing. Later, the child may attempt to reread the caption to a buddy.

Like picture captions, spoken or dictated accounts of children's experiences also help them link speech to print. This approach has traditionally been referred to as the language experience approach, or LEA (Hall, 1980; Nessel & Jones, 1981; Stauffer, 1980). Field trips, cooking activities, playground episodes, and class pets all provide opportunities for shared experiences in which the children's own language abounds. Their

> The Fire Station
> Amanda said, "We went to the
>   fire station yesterday."
> Jason said, "We rode on a
>   big orange bus.
> Clint said, "I liked the
>   ladder truck. It was huge!"
> D. J. said, "The firemen told
>   us how to be safe."
> Beth said, "Firemen wear
>   big boots and a mask."

FIGURE 5-15   Dictated Language Experience Chart

Children's books encourage sound and word play.

observations and comments can then be written down next to each child's name. (Daniel says, "The pumpkins were rotten.") In this format, attention to words and to their boundaries will be highlighted in a meaningful context. For example, children may be asked to locate their own name in the dictated account or to find a word that starts with the same letter as their own name (see Figure 5-15). One teacher we know writes dictated accounts using carbon paper, then later has her children cut out individual words from the carbon copy to paste right on top of the original. Other activities for focusing on words and word boundaries are described in the activities section.

Activities for Emergent Readers

In this section, specific activities have been arranged by these categories: concept sorts, phonological awareness, alphabet knowledge, letter-sound knowledge, and concept of word. Within each category the activities are roughly in order of increasing difficulty. However, as noted earlier in this chapter, it is not the case that concept sorts must precede sound awareness, which in turn must precede alphabet. In reality, all of these develop simultaneously during the emergent years and many activites cut across the categories. Many of the games are generic to all stages of developmental word knowledge as indicated by the generic symbol used throughout the book:

Generic

CONCEPT SORTS

The activities for concept sorts are all variations on the theme of categorization tasks. In addition to the basic sorting tasks, activities are generally followed by draw and label, then cut and paste procedures as discussed in Chapter 4. As always, we recommend having children write at every possible opportunity during or following the concept sorts. Categories and examples can be labeled with invented spellings.

Beginning With Children's Books and Concept Sorts 5–1

Books make great beginnings for concept sorts. Here are just a few examples to get you started.

Materials

Gregory the Terrible Eater, by Marjorie Sharmat, tells the story of a young goat who wants to eat real food while his parents constantly urge him to eat "junk food." In this case the goats' favorite foods really are junk from the local dump: tires, tin cans, old rags, and so on. Collect real objects or pictures of items suggested by the story—for example, fruits, vegetables, newspaper, shoe laces, spaghetti, and pieces of clothing.

Procedures

1. After enjoying this story together the children can be introduced to a **concept sort** categorized by real food and junk food. Gather the children on the rug, around a large table or pocket chart, and challenge them to group the items by the things Gregory liked and the things he didn't like.

2. After deciding where everything should go, ask the students to describe how the things in that category are alike. Decide on a key word or descriptive phrase that will label each category. *Real food* and *junk food* are obvious choices, but your children might be more inventive. As you print the selected key words on cards, model writing for the children. Say each word slowly and talk about the sounds you hear in the words and the letters you need to spell them. Each child in the group might also be given a card and asked to label one of the individual items using invented spelling.

3. Plan time for individual sorting. Keep the items and key word cards available so that children will be free to redo the sort on their own or with a partner at another time, perhaps during free time or center time.

4. Draw and label or cut and paste activities should follow the sorting. This may be done as a group activity, in which case a section of a bulletin board or a large sheet of paper is divided into two sections and labeled with the key words. If children do it individually, each child can be given a sheet of paper folded into two sections. The children might be asked to draw items or they might be given a collection of magazines or catalogs to look through for pictures to cut out and paste into the correct category (seed catalogs are great for fruits and vegetables). Again, they can be encouraged to use invented spelling to label the pictures.

Variations

Other books will also serve as the starting point for concept sorts of many kinds. Here are just a few suggestions:

Noisy Nora by Rosemary Wells—sort pictures that suggest noisy activities or objects with pictures that suggest quiet activities.*

The Country Mouse and the City Mouse by Jan Brett and various authors—sort pictures of things you would see in the country and things you would see in the city.

Alexander and the Wind-Up Mouse by Leo Lionni—sort pictures of real animals and toy animals or imaginary animals.

Amos and Boris by William Steig—sort pictures of things that Amos would see on the land and things that Boris would see in the ocean.

Is It Red? Is It Yellow? Is It Blue? by Tana Hoban—one of many books that suggest sorting objects and pictures by color.

My Very First Book of Shapes by Eric Carle—one of many books that lead into a sorting activity based upon shapes.

Paste the Pasta and Other Concrete Concept Sorts 5-2

Categorizing pasta by size, shape, and color is a good hands-on activity that introduces the idea of sorting to young children. It was first shown to us by Ann Fordham in the McGuffey Reading Center. Many early childhood curricula include the study of pattern, but being able to categorize by particular attributes must come first. It is difficult for

*Thanks to Elizabeth Schuett for this idea.

FIGURE 5-16   Paste the Pasta

young children to stay focused upon a single attribute of interest. They may begin sorting by color and then switch to shape in midstream. They will need many activities such as this one, sorting real, concrete objects that have different features.

Materials

You will need three to six types of pasta that vary in size and shape. You may find pasta of various colors or you can dye your own by shaking the pasta in a jar with a tablespoon of alcohol and a few drops of food coloring. Lay it out on newspaper to dry. If you dye your own, make sure that any one color has a variety of shapes and sizes. Two or three colors is enough. Children can sort onto paper divided into columns or simply into piles as shown in Figure 5-16.

Procedures

1. Prepare a mixture of all the dried pasta and give each child a handful and a sorting paper.
2. Begin with an open sort in which you invite the students to come up with their own way of grouping. This will give you an opportunity to evaluate which of the children understand attribute sorting and who will need more guidance. Ask the children to share their ideas and show their groups. Discuss the different features or attributes by which they can sort.
3. Ask them to re-sort using a category different from their first one. You might end up this activity by letting the students glue the pasta onto their paper by categories and labeling their chosen sorts.

Variations

There is no end to the concrete things you can sort with your students as you explore the different features that define your categories. Here are some suggestions:

Children—male/female, hair color, eye color, age, favorite color
Shoes—girls/boys, right/left, tie/Velcro/slip-on
Mittens and gloves—knit/woven, right/left
Coats—short/long, button/zip, hood/no hood
Buttons—two holes/four holes/no holes, shapes, colors, size
Bottle caps—size, color, plastic/metal, plain/printed, ribbed/smooth

Lunch containers—boxes/bags, plastic/metal/nylon
Legos—color, shape, number of dots, length
Blocks—shape, color, size
Toys—size, color, purpose, hardness
Food—sweet/sour/bitter

All My Friends Photograph Sort 5-3

This is another example of an open-ended sort that involves guessing each other's categories. Pat Love passed this one along to us from Hollymead Elementary School in Charlottesville, Virginia.

Materials

You will need copies of the children's school photographs made into a composite sheet. These can usually be copied quite successfully on a photocopy machine so that you can have a complete set for each child or small group. The students will also need a sheet of construction paper to divide into columns for sorting.

Procedures

1. Brainstorm with the children some of the ways that the pictures might be grouped (by hair length, hair color, clothing, boys/girls, facial expressions).
2. Let them work in groups to sort by these or other categories they discover. After pasting their pictures into the columns on their paper, each group can hold up their effort and ask the others in the class to guess their categories. The category labels or key words should then be written on the papers.

Variations

Photographs from home may be sorted according to places (inside/outside, home/vacation, holidays, and so forth), number of people in the photograph (adults, sisters, brothers), number of animals in the photograph, seasons (by clothing, outside trees/plants), age, and so forth.

As children learn to recognize their classmates' names, have them match the names to the pictures. Later, these names may be sorted by beginning letter, then placed under the corresponding letter of an ABC wall strip to form a graph.

THEMATIC UNITS AS A STARTING POINT FOR CONCEPT SORTS

Teachers of young children often organize their curriculum into thematic units of study. Such units frequently lend themselves to concept sorts which will review and extend the understandings central to the goals of the unit. Here are some examples.

Food Group Unit 5-4

Gregory the Terrible Eater serves as an excellent introduction to the study of healthy eating. The same pictures the children have drawn or cut out can serve as the beginning pictures for categories such as meats, grains, fruits and vegetables, and dairy products. After categorizing the foods in a group sorting activity, the students should be asked to draw or cut out pictures of additional foods for a wall chart or individual sheet which is then labeled with invented spellings.

FIGURE 5-17   Vehicle Draw and Label

Animal Unit 5-5

The study of animals particularly lends itself to concept sorts and can be used as a way of introducing a unit. Lay out a collection of pictures of animals and ask the students to think of ways that they can be grouped together. Such an open sort will result in many different categories based on attributes such as what color they are, how many legs they have, whether they have fur or feathers, and so on. A lively discussion will arise as students discover that some animals will go in different categories.

The direction you eventually want this activity to go will depend upon the goal of your unit. If you are studying animal habitats, then you will eventually guide the children to sorting the animals by the places they live. If you are studying classes of animals, then the students must eventually learn to sort them into mammals, fish, amphibians, and birds. If you are focusing on the food chain, your categories may be carnivores, herbivores, and omnivores.

Transportation Unit 5-6

Here is another open sort to start off a unit on transportation. A collection of toy vehicles (planes, boats, cars, and trucks) can be laid on the floor or table and the children invited to think of which ones might go together. Encourage them to think up a variety of possibilities that will divide everything into only two or three categories. After each suggestion, sort the vehicles by the identified attributes, and write the key words down on a chart or chalkboard. Some possibilities include plastic/metal, big/little, old/new, one color/many colors, windows/no windows, wheels/no wheels, and land/air/water.

After exploring this open sort thoroughly, have the children select the suggestion they liked the best. They can then be given construction paper to label their categories and draw or cut out pictures for each. As always, they should be encouraged to label the pictures with invented spelling as shown in Figure 5-17.

Variations

Other concept sorts might be developed along the same lines. The following list of categories represents some that are frequently confused by preschool, kindergarten, and first grade children.

real, imaginary
smooth, rough
kitchen tools, office tools, shop tools
plastic, wood, metal
hard, soft
holidays and seasons

PLAYING WITH SOUNDS TO DEVELOP PHONOLOGICAL AWARENESS

Phonological awareness is made up of an array of understandings about sounds which include a sense of rhyme, a sense of alliteration, a sense of syllables, phonemic segmentation, and blending. Rhyme and alliteration are easier than others to develop and many activities for developing these are included here. There are also some activities in this section for syllable sense, segmenting, and blending, but they are also addressed as part of other activities such as Morning Message (5-38) and Starting with Children's Names (5-20).

Beginning With Rhyme in Children's Books 5–7

Filling children's heads with rhyme is one of the easiest and most natural ways to focus their attention on the sounds of the English language. Books written with rhyme provide one way to do this.

Materials

Many of the books enjoyed by children in the emergent stage feature rhymes. Here are just a few:

Ahlsberg, J., & Ahlsberg, A. (1978). *Each peach pear plum: An "I spy" story.* New York: Scholastic.
Cameron, P. (1961). *I can't said the ant.* New York: Putnam Publishing.
Crews, D. (1986). *Ten black dots.* New York: Greenwillow.
Degan, B. (1983). *Jamberry.* New York: Harper.
Florian, D. (1987). *A winter day.* New York: Scholastic; (1990). *A beach day.* New York: Greenwillow.
Guarina, D. (1989). *Is your mama a llama?* Illustrated by Steven Kellogg. New York: Scholastic.
Hennessy, B.G. (1989). *The missing tarts.* Illustrated by T.C. Pearson. New York: Scholastic.
Macmillan, B. (1990). *One sun.* New York: Holiday House; (1991). *Play day.* New York: Trumpet.
Strickland, P., & Strickland, H. (1994). *Dinosaur roar!* New York: Scholastic.

Procedures

1. As you read books with rhyme aloud, pause to allow the children to guess the rhyming word. The text in *Is Your Mama a Llama?* is set up to facilitate children's input as it poses a rhyming riddle and a page break right before the animal's identity is revealed. *I Can't Said the Ant* is a favorite rhyming tale that invites student participation with each line cued by an illustration. You will find many books in which you can use this **cloze** procedure to let children supply the rhyming words.

2. Some rhyming books are so repetitive and simple that children can easily memorize them and read them on their own. *Play Day* and *One Sun*, by Bruce Macmillan, are some of the simplest rhyming books available. They feature "hinkpink" rhymes such as *white kite* or *bear chair* with a vivid photograph to cue

the child's response. Douglas Florian has a series of books, including *A Beach Day* and *A Winter Day,* that feature only two or three words on a page. These books can also be used to introduce concept sorts in which summer/winter and city/country can be contrasted. After hearing these books read aloud two or three times, young children may be able to recite the words or track the print successfully for themselves and will get great satisfaction from the feeling that they can read.

Matching and Sorting Rhyming Pictures 5–8

After reading rhyming books aloud, you can follow up with an activity that has the children sorting or matching rhyming pictures.

Materials

Rhyming pictures are available commercially or you can create your own. The appendixes of this book contains pictures grouped by initial sounds and by vowel sounds. These can be copied, colored lightly, and glued to cards to make sets for sorting. The following list is of pictures you can find to make sets of at least four rhyming words. Most of them are in the vowel sets but the consonant and blend pictures contain some as well.

boat coat float goat	chop top mop hop shop	bell well shell smell yell
plane train chain cane rain	glue zoo shoe two	sleep jeep sheep sweep
nail whale pail snail sail mail	lip ship drip zip whip	spill grill hill mill
fan can pan man van	cat mat rat bat hat	wing ring swing king sting
drive hive five dive	bee tree pea key three	fly tie fry cry pie
shed bed sled bread	trap clap map cap snap	block clock rock lock
chick brick stick kick	nose rose hose toes	track quack crack sack jack pack

Procedures

1. After enjoying the story together several times, Mrs. Collins introduced her group to a collection of animal pictures from the story (fox, mouse, goat, whale) and pictures of the places they were put (box, house, boat, pail) for the children to match by rhyme. To make it easier for beginners, just put out three pictures at a time: two pictures that rhyme and one that does not.
2. After sorting pictures as a group, put the book and the pictures in a center for children to reread on their own and play the matching game.

Variations

Simply set up two categories and lead the children in sorting pictures by rhyming sound. For example, lay down *cat* and *bee* as headers and sort other pictures in turn under the correct header. Add a third and fourth category when children are comfortable with two.

Inventing Rhymes 5–9

Nonsense rhymes and books with rhyme and word play are a delightful way to cultivate awareness of sounds. Word play directs children's attention to the sounds of the English language and can stimulate children to invent their own words. Jan Slepian and Ann Seidler's *The Hungry Thing* comes to town begging for food but has trouble pronouncing what he wants; *shmancakes* (pancakes), *feetloaf* (meatloaf), and *hookies* (cookies) are among his requests. It is only a small boy who figures out what he wants. After reading the book, children can act it out. As each takes the part of the Hungry Thing, they must come up with a rhyming word for the food they want: *blizza, bandwich, smello?*

Making up one's own rhymes is likely to come after the ability to identify rhymes. Thinking up rhyming words to make sense in a poem is quite an accomplishment, requiring a good sense of rhyme and an extensive vocabulary. Children need supported efforts to create rhymes, and a good place to start is pure nonsense. No one was a greater master of this than Dr. Seuss. *There's a Wocket in My Pocket* takes readers on a tour of a young boy's home in which all manner of odd creatures have taken up residence. There is a *woset* in his closet, a *zlock* behind the clock, and a *nink* in the sink. After reading this to a group, ask children to imagine what animal would live in their cubby, under the rug, or in the lunchroom. Their efforts should rhyme, to be sure, but anything will do: a *rubby*, *snubby*, or *frubby* might all live in a cubby.

Patterned text can be used to create rhymes. The rhyming pattern in *Ten Black Dots* can be extended to eleven, twelve, and so on. "Twelve dots can make ice cream cones or the buttons to dial a _____." In the supportive framework of a familiar patterned sentence, children are likely to be more successful at creating their own rhymes.

Using Songs to Develop a Sense of Rhyme and Alliteration 5–10

Earlier we mentioned how appropriate the singer/songwriter Raffi is for young children. Teaching these songs by Raffi can lead to inventive fun with rhymes and sounds, and some are available as books:

> "Apples and Bananas" (from *One Light, One Sun*)
> "Spider on the Floor" (from *Singable Songs for the Very Young*)
> "Down by the Bay" (also available as a book, from *Singable Songs for the Very Young*)

Another song that features names, rhyme, and alliteration is "The Name Game," originally sung by Shirley Ellis. It has apparently passed into the oral tradition of neighborhood kids and may be known by some children in your class. Sing the song over and over, substituting the name of a different child on every round. It goes like this:

> *Sam Sam Bo Bam, Banana Fanna Bo Fam, Fee Fi Mo Mam, Sam!*
>
> *Kaitlyn Kaitlyn Bo Baitlyn, Banana Fanna Bo Faitlyn, Fee Fi Mo Maitlyn, Kaitlyn!*

Lend an ear to the playground songs and chants your children already know and encourage them to share them with you. Generations of children have made up variations of "Miss Mary Mack Mack Mack . . ." and a new generation with a taste for rap is creating a whole new repertoire. You can take an active role in teaching these jingles to your students—or letting them teach them to you! Write them down to become reading material. Here are some printed sources of traditional chants and jingles:

Cole, J. (1989). *101 jump-rope rhymes.* New York: Scholastic.
Cole, J., & Calmenson, S. (1990). *Miss Mary Mack and other children's street rhymes.* Illustrated by Alan Tiegreen. New York: Morrouno.
Schwartz, A. (1989). *I saw you in the bathtub.* New York: Harper Collins.
Withers, C. (1948). *Rocket in my pocket.* New York: Holt, Rinehart.
Yolan, J. (1992). *Street rhymes from around the world.* New York: Wordsong.

RHYMING GAMES

There are many commercially made games and computer software that feature rhyming words. The two games described here are easy to make and based on familiar formats.

Rhyming Bingo 5-11

Materials

Prepare enough Bingo gameboards for the number of children who will participate (small groups of three to five are probably ideal). An appropriate gameboard size for young children is a 9-by-9-inch board divided into nine 3-by-3-inch squares; for older students, the gameboard can be expanded up to a 4-by-4-inch or 5-by-5-inch array. Copy sets of pictures from the appendix and form rhyming groups such as those listed in Activity 5-8. Randomly paste all but one of each rhyming group in the spaces on the gameboards, then laminate them for durability. Each gameboard must be different.

Prepare a complementary set of cards on which you paste the remaining picture from each rhyming group. These will become the deck from which rhyming words are called aloud during the game. You will need some kind of marker to cover the squares on the gameboard. These may be as simple as 2-inch squares of construction paper, plastic chips, bottle caps, or pennies.

Procedures

1. Each child receives a gameboard and markers to cover spaces.
2. The teacher or a designated child is the caller who turns over cards from the deck and calls out the name of the picture.
3. Each player searches his or her gameboard for a picture that rhymes with the one that has been called out. Players can cover a match with a marker to claim the space.
4. The winner is the first player to cover a row in any direction, or the first player to fill his or her entire board.

Variation

When children are able to read, this game can be played with word cards instead of picture cards.

Rhyming Concentration 5-12

Materials

This game for two or three children is played like the traditional Concentration or the more current Memory game. Assemble a collection of six to ten rhyming pairs from the pictures in the appendix (listed in Activity 5-8). Paste the pictures on cards and laminate for durability. Be sure the pictures do not show through from the backside.

Procedures

1. Shuffle the pictures and then lay them facedown in rows.
2. Players take turns flipping over two pictures at a time. If the two pictures rhyme, the player keeps the cards to hold to the end of the game. The player who makes a match gets another turn.
3. The winner is the child who has the most matches at the end of the game.

Variation

When children are able to read, this game can be played with word cards instead of picture cards.

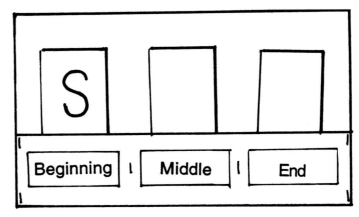

FIGURE 5–18   Sound Boxes

Beginning-Middle-End: Finding Phonemes in Sound Boxes 5–13

Phonemic segmentation is best developed as teachers model writing and as children try to invent spellings, but there may be times when you want to give some added emphasis to phonemic segmentation using sound boxes. Originally developed by Elkonin (1973), sound boxes serve as a concrete way to demonstrate how words are made up of smaller pieces called sounds (or phonemes). Here is a variation developed by Erica Fulmer, a Title I teacher, who has made up a song she and her children sing as the children try to find the location of each sound in the word.

Materials

You will need large letter cards and a three-pocket holder such as the one shown in Figure 5-18.

Procedures

1. Place the letters needed to spell a three-letter word in the pocket backwards so the children cannot see the letters. Announce the word, such as "sun." Choose words from a familiar book, poem, or dictation when possible. Words that start with continuants such as *M, S,* or *Sh* work well because they can be said slowly.
2. Sing the song to the tune of "Are you sleeping brother John?"

   Beginning, middle, end; beginning, middle, end
   Where is the sound? Where is the sound?
   Where's the ssss in sun? Where's the ssss in sun?
   Let's find out. Let's find out.

3. Children take turns coming forward to pick the position and check by turning the letter card.

Variations

Add a fourth box when children are able to do three sounds with ease. Draw sound boxes on the board anytime you want to model the sounding out process when writing a word. For example, as you take a group's dictation the word *fast* might come up. Draw four boxes and invite the children to help you say the word slowly in order to figure out what letters need to go in each one.

It's in the Bag—A Phoneme Blending Game 5-14

Materials

You will need a paper bag (gift bags are attractive) and an assortment of small objects collected from around the classroom, from outside, or from home: chalk, pen, paper clip, tack, key, rock, stick, and so on. You might use a puppet to add interest.

Procedures

Lay out a dozen or so objects and name them with the children. Explain that you will use them to play a game. Introduce the puppet. The puppet will name an object in the bag, saying it very slowly, and the children will guess what it is saying.

Variations

Use objects or pictures related to a topic of study. For example, if you are teaching a unit on animals, you could put pictures of farm animals in the bag. You could also use plastic toy animals. This can be a sensory activity by letting children reach into the bag, figure out an object by touch, and then say it slowly for the other children to guess. Objects that begin with the same beginning sounds can also be put into the bag to sort.

Incorporating Phonological Skills Into Daily Activities 5-15

Teachers of emergent children can incorporate sound play into many daily activities and routines.

1. Lining up, taking attendance, or calling children to a group:

   Call each child's name and then lead the class in clapping the syllables in the name.
   Announce that everyone whose name has two syllables can line up, then one syllable, three, and so on.
   Say each child's name slowly as it is called.
   Make up a rhyme for each child's name that starts with a sound of interest: Billy Willy, Mary Wary, Shanee Wanee, and so on.
   Substitute the first letter in everyone's name with the same letter: Will, Wary, Wanee, Wustin, and so on.

2. During read-alouds:

   Pause to let children fill in a rhyming word, especially on a second or third reading. If they have trouble, say the first sound for them with a clue: "It rhymes with *whale* and starts with /puh/."
   Draw attention to a long word by repeating it and clapping the syllables: "That's a big word. Let's clap the syllables: hip-po-pot-a-mus, five syllables!"
   You might also pause while reading and say a key word very slowly before asking the children to repeat it fast: "The next day his dad picked him up in a red . . . . jeeeep. What's that? A jeep, right." You might point to the letters as you do this.

There are many other published resources on the topic of phonological awareness and what teachers can do to facilitate it. The following are particularly worthwhile:

Adams, M.J., Foorman, B.A., Lundberg, I., & Beweler, T. (1998). *Phonemic awareness in young children.* Baltimore, MD: Paul H. Brooks Pub. Co.
Blevins, W. (1997). *Phonemic awareness activities for early reading success.* New York: Scholastic.

Ericson, L., & Juliebo, M. F. (1998). *The phonological awareness handbook for kindergarten and primary teachers.* Newark, DL: International Reading Association.
Fitzpatrick, J. (1998). *Phonemic awareness: Playing with sounds to strengthen beginning reading skills.* Cypress, CA: Creative Teaching Press.

ALPHABET ACTIVITIES AND GAMES

The activities presented in this section are designed to develop all aspects of alphabet knowledge, including letter recognition (both upper- and lowercase), letter naming, letter writing, and letter-sounds. You may notice that these activities address more than one letter at a time: For children who haven't cut their teeth on alphabet letters and picture books, one letter per week is not enough. We must deal with more than one letter at a time.

Beginning with Alphabet Books 5–16

Share alphabet books with a group as you would other good literature and plan follow-up activities when appropriate. Some books are suitable for toddlers and merely require the naming of the letter and a single accompanying picture, such as Dick Bruna's *B Is for Bear.* Others, such as Graeme Base's *Animalia,* will keep even upper elementary children engaged as they try to name all the things that are hidden away in the illustrations. Look for alphabet books, such as the ones listed here, to draw children's attention to beginning sounds through alliteration.

Base, G. (1986). *Animalia.* New York: Harry Abrams.
Bayor, J. (1984). *A: My name is Alice.* Illustrated by Steven Kellogg. New York: Dial.
Berenstain, S., & Berenstain, J. (1971). *The Berenstain's B book.* New York: Random House.
Cole, J. (1993). *Six sick sheep: 101 tongue twisters.* New York: Morrow.
Obligado, L. (1987). *Faint frogs feeling feverish and other terrifically tantalizing tongue twisters.* New York: Viking Penguin.
Seuss, Dr. (1963). *Dr. Seuss's ABC.* New York: Random House.

Many ABC books can be incorporated into thematic units, such as Jerry Pallotta's many content alphabet books or Mary Azarian's *A Farmer's Alphabet.* Some alphabet books present special puzzles such as Jan Garten's *The Alphabet Tale.* Children are invited to predict the upcoming animal by showing just the tip of its tail on the preceding page. Following is a list of some outstanding ABC books for school-age children:

Anglund, J. W. (1960). *In a pumpkin shell.* (Alphabet Mother Goose). San Diego, CA: Harcourt Brace, Jovanovich.
Anno, M. (1975). *Anno's alphabet.* New York: Crowell.
Aylesworth, J. (1992). *Old black fly.* Illustrated by Stephen Gammell. New York: Scholastic.
Azarian, M. (1981). *A farmer's alphabet.* Boston: David Godine.
Baskin, Leonard. (1972). *Hosie's alphabet.* New York: Viking Press.
Fain, K. (1993). *Handsigns: A sign language alphabet.* New York: Scholastic.
Falls, C.B. (1923). *ABC book.* New York: Doubleday.
Gág, W. (1933). *The ABC bunny.* Hand lettered by Howard Gág. New York: Coward-McCann.
Geisert, A. (1986). *Pigs from A to Z.* Boston: Houghton Mifflin.
Hague, K. (1984). *Alphabears: An ABC book.* Illustrated by Michael Hague. New York: Holt, Rinehart & Winston.
McPhail, D. (1989). *David McPhail's animals A to Z.* New York: Scholastic.
Musgrove, M. (1976). *Ashanti to Zulu: African traditions.* Illustrated by Leo and Diane Dillon. New York: Dial.
Owens, M. B. (1988). *A caribou alphabet.* Brunswick, ME: Dog Ear Press.
Pallotta, J. (1989). *The yucky reptile alphabet book;* (1991). *The dinosaur alphabet book.* Illustrated by Ralph Masiello. New York: Bantam Doubleday, Dell. (There are many more in this series.)
Thornhill, J. (1988). *The wildlife A-B-C: A nature alphabet book.* New York: Simon & Schuster.
Tryon, L. (1991). *Albert's alphabet.* New York: MacMillan.

Alphabet Book Follow-Ups 5–17
Procedures
1. Discuss the pattern of the books, solve the puzzle, and talk about the words that begin with each letter as you go back through the books a second time.
2. Focus on alliteration by repeating tongue twisters and creating a list of words for a particular letter. Brainstorm other words that begin with that letter, and write them under the letter on chart paper.
3. Make individual or class alphabet books. You might decide on a theme or pattern for the book. Refer back to the alphabet books you have read for ideas. One idea might be a noun-verb format, for example, ants attack, bees buzz, cats cry, and dogs doze.
4. Look up a particular letter you are studying in several alphabet books or a picture dictionary to find other things that begin with that sound. This is an excellent introduction to using resource books.*

Chicka Chicka Boom Boom Sort 5–18

The book *Chicka Chicka Boom Boom* (Martin & Archambault, 1989) is a great favorite and provides a wonderful way to move from children's books to alphabet recognition and letter-sound activities. After reading this delightful book with her children, Pat Love demonstrates how to match foam "Laurie Letters," one at a time, to the letters printed in the book. Pat's boom boards (Figure 5-19) can be used for sorting letters and pictures by beginning sounds. Other teachers have created a large coconut tree on the side of their filing cabinet so that children can act out the story and match upper- and lowercase forms using magnetic letters.

Starting With Children's Names 5–19

Children are naturally interested in their own names and their friends' names. Names are an ideal point from which to begin the study of alphabet letters. We like the idea of

---

*Thanks to Jennifer Sudduth for these ideas.

FIGURE 5-19 Chicka Chicka Boom Boom Board

a "name of the day"* so much better than a "letter of the week." Many more letters are covered in a much shorter time!

Materials

Prepare a card for each child on which his or her name is written in neatly executed block letters. Put all the names in a box or can. Have additional blank cards ready to be cut apart as described.

Procedures

1. Each day, with great fanfare, a name is drawn and becomes the name of the day. The teacher begins with a very open-ended question, "What do you notice about this name?" Children will respond in all sorts of ways depending upon what they know about letters: "It's a short name." "It has three letters." "It starts like Taneesh's name." "It has an *O* in the middle."

2. Next children chant or echo the letters in the name as the teacher points to each one. A cheer led by the teacher is lots of fun:
   Teacher: "Give me a *T*."   Children: "*T!*"
   Teacher: "Give me an *O*."   Children: "*O!*"
   Teacher: "Give me an *M*."   Children: "*M!*"
   Teacher: "What have we got?"   Children: "*Tom!*" (repeat three times)

3. On an additional card, the teacher writes the name of the child as the children recite the letters again. Then the teacher cuts the letters apart and hands out the letters to children in the group. The children are then challenged to put the letters back in order to spell the name correctly. This can be done in a pocket chart or on a chalkboard ledge and repeated many times. The cut-up letters are then put into an envelope with the child's name on the outside. The envelope is added to the name puzzle collection. Children love to pull out their friends' names to put together.

4. All the children in the group should attempt to spell the featured name. This might be done on individual chalkboards or on pieces of paper. This is an opportunity to offer some handwriting instruction as the teacher models for the children. Discuss the details of direction and movement of letter formation as the children imitate your motions.

5. Each day the featured name is added to a display of all the names that have come before. By displaying them in a pocket chart they can be compared to previous names and used for sorting activities:
   Sort the names by the number of letters.
   Sort the names by the number of syllables.
   Sort the names that share particular letters.
   Sort the names that belong to boys and girls.
   Sort the names by alphabetical order.

6. Create a permanent display of the names and encourage children to practice writing their own and their friends' names. If you have a writing center, you might put all the names on index cards in a box for reference. Children can be encouraged to reproduce names not only by copying the names with pencils, chalk, and markers, but also with rubber stamps, foam cutout letters, link letters, or letter tiles. The display of children's names becomes an important reference tool during writing time.

---

*For more information on using students' names to develop alphabet knowledge, see *Phonics They Use: Words for Reading and Writing* by Pat Cunningham.

One Child's Name 5-20

Some children may need additional help learning the letters in their names. For them, the following activity is valuable:*

1. Spell out a child's name with letter cards, tiles, foam, or plastic letters using both upper- and lowercase.
2. Spell it with uppercase letters in the first row and ask the child to match lowercase letters in the row below, as shown in Figure 5-20.
3. Mix up the top row and have the child unscramble the letters to form the name once again. Have the child name the letters as this is done. Mix up the bottom row and repeat.
4. Rematch the upper- and lowercase tiles, letter for letter, naming each letter again as they are touched.
5. Next take blank cards and place one blank card beneath each letter. Write each letter on each blank card, discussing the details of direction and movement in letter formation as you do. Give the child a piece of paper to imitate your letter formations. Alternate this activity for upper- and lowercase.
6. Play Concentration with the set of capitals and lowercase letters needed to spell a child's name.*

---

*Darrell Morris presents this activity in the context of a tutoring session for an emergent leader in his excellent book *Case Studies in Teaching Beginning Readers: The Howard Street Tutoring Manual.*

FIGURE 5-20   Brandon's Name Puzzle

FIGURE 5-21   Alphabet Scrapbook

Alphabet Scrapbook 5-21

Materials

Prepare a blank dictionary for each child by stapling together sheets of paper. (Seven sheets of paper folded and stapled in the middle is enough for one letter per page.) Children can use this book in a variety of ways (see Figure 5-21).

1. Practice writing uppercase and lowercase forms of the letter on each page.
2. Cut out letters in different fonts or styles from magazines and newspapers and paste them into their scrapbooks.
3. Draw and label pictures and other things which begin with that letter-sound.
4. Cut and paste magazine pictures onto the corresponding letter page. These pictures, too, can be labeled.
5. Add sight words as they become known to create a personal dictionary.

The Alphabet Song and Tracking Activities 5-22

Every early childhood classroom should have an alphabet strip or chart at eye level. Too often these strips are put up out of the children's reach. The best location for the strips is to be posted on desktops or tabletops for easy reference. Here are activities that make active use of these charts.

Materials

Commercial or teacher-made alphabet strips for both wall display and for individual children and individual letters.

Procedures

1. Learn the ABC song to the tune of "Twinkle Twinkle Little Star." Sing it many times!
2. Model pointing to each letter, as the song is sung or the letters are chanted. Then ask the children to fingerpoint to the letters as they sing or chant.
3. When students know about half of the alphabet, they can work on putting a set of letter cards, tiles, or link letters in ABC order from A to Z. Use capital letters or lowercase, or match the two (see Figure 5-22). Keep an ABC strip or chart nearby as a ready reference.

FIGURE 5-22   Alphabet Link Letters

Alphabet Eggs 5-23

Materials

Create a simple set of puzzles designed to practice the pairing of capital and lowercase letters. On poster board, draw and cut out enough 4-inch egg shapes for each letter in the alphabet. Write an uppercase letter on the left half and the matching lowercase letter on the right portion. Cut the eggs in half using a zigzag line (see Figure 5-23). Make each zigzag slightly different so the activity is self-checking. Students should say the letters to themselves and put the eggs back together by matching the upper- and lowercase form.*

Variations

There are many other shapes that can be cut in half for matching. In October, for example, pumpkin shapes can be cut into two and in February, heart shapes can be cut apart the same way. There is no end to the matching possibilities. Acorn caps can be matched to bottoms, balls to baseball gloves, frogs to lily pads, and so on. These matching sets can also be created to pair letters and a picture that starts with that letter, rhyming words, contractions, homophones, and so on.

Alphabet Concentration 5-24

This game works just like Concentration with rhyming words as described in Activity 5-12. Create cards with capitals and lowercase forms of the letters written on one side. Be sure they cannot be seen from the backside. Use some letters the children may need to work on as well as some they know quite well. Do not try this with all 26 letters at once or it may take a long time to complete; eight to ten pairs is probably enough.

Variations

To introduce this game or to make it easier, play it with the cards faceup. As letter-sounds are learned, this game can be played by matching consonant letters to pictures that begin with that letter-sound.

Letter Spin 5-25

Materials

Make a spinner with six to eight spaces, and label each space with a capital letter. If you laminate the spinner before labeling, you can reuse it with other letters. Just write in the letters with a grease pencil or nonpermanent overhead transparency pen. Write the lowercase letters on small cards, creating five or six cards for each letter (see Figure 5-24).†

---

*Thanks to Elizabeth Schuett for this idea.
†Thanks to Alison Dwier-Selden for this idea.

FIGURE 5-23   Alphabet Eggs

Procedures

1. Lay out all the lowercase cards faceup.
2. Each player in turn spins and lands on an uppercase letter. The player then picks up one card that has the corresponding lowercase form, orally identifying the letter.
3. Play continues until all the letter cards have been picked up.
4. The winner is the player with the most cards when the game ends.

Variation

Students can be asked to not only name, but write the upper- and lowercase forms of the letter after each turn. This game can be adapted to any feature that involves matching—letters to sounds, rhymes, vowel patterns, and so on.

Alphabet Cereal Sort 5–26

Materials

For this sorting activity, you will need a box of alphabet cereal—enough to give each child a handful. Prepare a sorting board for each child by dividing a paper into 26 squares. Label each square with an upper- or lowercase letter.

Procedures

1. Allow the children to work individually or in teams to sort their own cereal onto their papers (see Figure 5–25). Discard (or eat) broken or deformed letters.
2. After the children are finished they can count the number of letters in each category (e.g., A-8, B-4). This could become a graphing activity.
3. Eat the cereal! (Or glue it down.)*

Variation

Have the children spell their names or other words using the cereal.

---

*Thanks to Janet Brown Watts for this idea.

FIGURE 5–24   Letter Spin Game

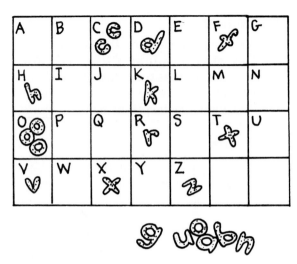

FIGURE 5–25   Cereal Sort

Sorting Letters With Different Print Styles 5–27

Children need to see a variety of print styles before they will be readily able to identify their ABCs in different contexts. Draw children's attention to different letter forms wherever you encounter them. Environmental print is especially rich in creative lettering styles. Encourage the children to bring in samples from home—like the big letters on a bag of dog food or cereal—and create a display on a bulletin board or in a big book.

Materials

Get a collection of different print styles by cutting letters from newspapers, catalogs, magazines, and other print sources. You can also search your computer fonts and print out letters in the largest size you can. Cut the letters apart, mount them on small cards, and laminate for durability. Use both capitals and lowercase, but avoid cursive styles for now. You may want to set up a sorting board with labeled categories as shown in the illustration in Figure 5-26, or simply have the children sort on any surface.

Procedures

1. After modeling the sort with a group of children, place the materials in a center where the children can work independently.
2. Don't put out too many different letters at any one time—four or five is probably enough, with eight to twelve variations for each.

Variation

If you have created alphabet scrapbooks (Activity 5–21), children can paste in samples of different lettering styles.

WORKING WITH BEGINNING SOUNDS

Specific guidelines for creating and using picture sorting for initial sounds were described earlier in this chapter and general guidelines were presented in Chapter 4. Picture and word sorts are at the heart of word study and the procedures will be revisited throughout this book. Games can be used to review beginning sounds after children have already practiced categorizing targeted sounds in basic picture-sorting activities.

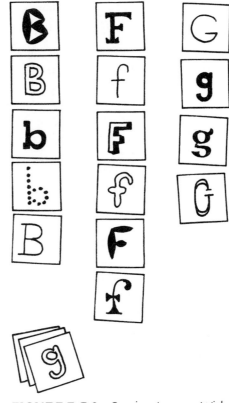

FIGURE 5-26   Sorting Letters With
Different Print Styles

Using Books to Enhance Beginning Sounds 5-28

Since alphabet books often include one or more examples of words that start with a targeted letter, they are a natural choice to use when teaching beginning sounds. Such books can be used to introduce an initial sound, or they can be used as a resource for a **word hunt** as children go searching for more words that start with targeted letters. Watch out for the choices authors and artists sometimes make, however. The C page may have words that start with the digraph *Ch* (*chair*), hard-c (*cat*), and soft-c (*cymbals*). Children will eventually need to sort out these confusions, but this is not the time.

Soundline 5-29

This classic activity can be used to focus on letter matching or letter-sound correspondences.

Materials

Rope, clothespins, markers, tagboard, glue, pictures, scissors, and laminating film.

Procedures

1. Write upper- and lowercase letters on the top of the clothespins.
2. Glue a picture beginning with each letter on a square of tagboard and laminate.
3. Students can match the picture card to the clothespin and hang it on the rope (see Figure 5-27).*

---

*Leslie Robertson contributed this activity.

FIGURE 5-27   Soundline

Letter Spin for Sounds 5-30

This is a good game to review up to eight beginning sounds at a time. It is a variation of the letter spin described in Activity 5–25.

Materials

You will need a spinner divided into four to eight sections and labeled with beginning letters to review. You will also need a collection of picture cards that correspond with the letters, with at least four pictures for each letter.

Procedures

1. Lay out all the pictures on a table or on the floor faceup.
2. Two to four players take turns spinning. The player can select one picture that begins with the sound indicated by the spinner. The next player spins and selects one picture. If there are no more pictures for a sound the player must pass.
3. Play continues until all the pictures are gone. The winner is the one with the most pictures at the end.

Variation

A large cube could be used like a die instead of a spinner.

Object Sorting by Sounds 5-31

Rule off a large sheet of poster board into squares and label each one according to the initial sounds you want to review. Collect miniature toys and animals or small objects (a button, bell , box, rock, ring, ribbon, etc.) that begin with the sounds of interest. Children are asked to sort the objects into the spaces on the board.

Initial Consonant Follow-the-Path Game 5-32

This game is simple enough that even preschoolers can learn the rules and it can be used throughout the primary grades to practice a variety of features. You'll see this game adapted in many ways in Chapters 6 and 7.

Materials

You will need to make a copy of the two halves of a follow-the-path gameboard found in the appendix. To make the game in a folder that can be easily stored, just paste each half on the inside of a manila folder (colored ones are nice) leaving a slight gap between

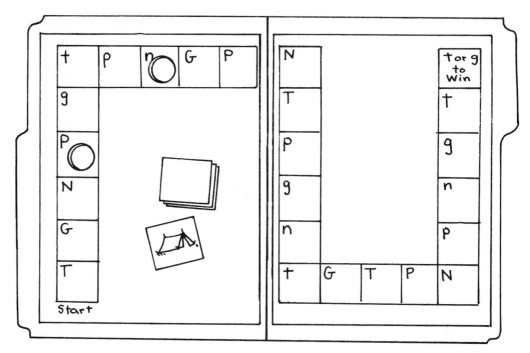

FIGURE 5-28 *Follow-the-Path Game*

the two sides in the middle (so the folder can still fold). Add some color and interest with stickers or cutout pictures to create a theme like "trip to the pizza parlor" or "adventure in space." Label each space on the path with one of the letters you want to review, using both upper- and lowercase forms (see Figure 5-28). Sets of four letter-sounds at a time work best. Reproduce a set of picture cards that correspond to the letters. Copy them on cardstock or glue cutout pictures to cards. You will need two to four game pieces to move around the board. Flat ones like bottle caps or plastic disks store well. You might want to put the pictures and playing pieces in a labeled plastic zip-top bag inside the folder.

Procedures

1. Turn the picture cards facedown in a stack. Players go in alphabetical order.
2. Each player draws a picture in turn and moves the playing piece to the next space on the path that is marked by the corresponding beginning consonant.
3. The winner is the first to arrive at the destination.

Variations

This game can be adapted for alphabet, blends and digraphs, short vowels, and vowel patterns.

HELPING CHILDREN ACQUIRE A CONCEPT OF WORD

When children are learning about letters and sounds at the same time they are finger-point reading from memory, there is a complementary process at work. Learning one gives logic and purpose to learning the other. Fingerpoint reading to familiar rhymes and pattern books is the best way to achieve a concept of word. Emergent readers need a lot of support in learning how to track print in correspondence with their speech. The following activities provide a few ways to go about getting kids connected to the words on the page.

FIGURE 5-29   Rhymes for Reading

Rhymes for Reading 5-33

After playing with the sounds in rhyming songs and jump rope jingles, an important further step is to let the children see and interact with the printed form. From such experiences children will begin to develop the concept of a printed word. Here is an example making use of a classic fingerplay which children will quickly be able to read from memory.

Materials

Record the words to a well-known jingle such as "I had a little turtle" on a sheet of 24-inch-wide chart paper—big enough for all to see (see Figure 5-29). Some teachers have special pointers (variations we have heard of include the rib bone of a cow and the beam of a flashlight), but a finger will do fine when the chart is at eye level.

Procedures

1. Teach the children the words to the song and show them how to do the fingerplay if you know it. Sing it over and over until everyone knows it well.
2. Display the words to the song and model for the children how to point to the words as they are said. Invite children to take their own turn at tracking the words as they or their classmates chant the words. From repeated opportunities, teachers can easily monitor the children's developing concept of word, from vague left-to-right sweeps, to self-corrected, careful matching of speech to print.
3. Make smaller copies of the text and photocopy them so that every child can get their own finger on the print. Modeling with a large chart for a group is only a starting point. Nothing beats individual practice. Copies of familiar songs and poems can be left posted in the room and small copies can be put into **personal readers** (described in Chapter 6).

Cut-Up Sentences 5-34

Write sentences or phrases from a familiar piece of text on a sentence strip. Sentences might come from a book or a poem the group has read together such as the turtle rhyme

FIGURE 5-30 *Cut-Up Sentences*

in the previous activity. The sentences can then be used in the group to rebuild the text in order using a pocket chart. Individual copies of text can be cut apart so that each child gets to practice.

A further step is to ask the students to cut apart the words in the sentence and then challenge them to reconstruct the sentence. Hand out scissors and call out each word as the children cut it off. The spaces between words are not obvious to emergent children so be prepared to model for them. Demonstrate how to find the words in order to rebuild the sentence: "What letter would you expect to see at the beginning of *swam?*" Leave the word cards and model sentence strips with a pocket chart in a center for children to practice in their spare time. Put individual words into an envelope with the sentence written on the outside (see Figure 5-30). These can be sent home with the children to reassemble with their parents.

Be the Sentence 5–35

Children can also rebuild familiar sentences by pretending to be the words themselves. Write a familiar sentence on a chart or on the board. Start with short sentences such as "Today is Monday" or "I love you." Then write each word from the sentence on a large card. Give each word to a child, naming it for them. "Stephanie, you are the word *Monday;* Lorenzo, you are the word *is.*" Ask the children to work together to arrange themselves into the sentence. Have another child read the sentence to check the direction and order. Try this again with another group of children, then leave the words out for children to work with on their own.

Pulling It All Together As You Share the Pen 5–36

The act of writing for children offers teachers the opportunity to model the use of the alphabet, phonemic segmentation, letter-sound matching, and concept of word as well as conventions such as capitalization and punctuation all in the context of a meaningful group activity. As the teacher writes on the chalkboard, chart paper, or an overhead projector, children see their own ideas expressed in oral language transformed into print. What began as a key feature of the language experience approach to reading has undergone a recent transformation in the form of "shared writing" (McKenzie, 1985) or "interactive writing" (Button, Johnson, & Furgerson, 1996).

During interactive writing, children share the pen and are invited to come forward to add a letter, a word, or a period. Such writing can take place any time of the day and for any reason—for example, to list class rules, to make a shopping list, to record observations from a field trip, to create a new version of a familiar text, or to list questions for a classroom visitor. The following activity is a favorite form of group writing in which the teacher and children compose sentences that report on daily home and school events which are of importance to the class.

The Morning Message 5-37

Each morning the teacher talks with the entire group to discover bits of news which can be part of the morning message. In preschools or early kindergarten, this may be only one sentence, but over time, it can grow to be as long as the teacher and children desire.

Materials

Large chart paper or chalkboard with markers or chalk, white tape for covering mistakes.

Procedures

1. Chat with children informally, sharing news from home or the classroom. Select a piece of news to record in the form of a single sentence.
2. Recite the sentence together with the children to decide how many words it contains, holding up a finger for each word. Then, draw a line for each word on the board or chart (see Figure 5-31).
3. Repeat each word, emphasizing the sounds as it is written and invite the group to make suggestions about what letters are needed, "The first word we need to write is *we*. *Wwwwwweeeeee*. What letter do we need for the first sound in *wwweee*?" A child might suggest the letter *Y*. "The name of the letter *Y* does start with that sound. Does anyone have another idea?" Every letter in every word need not be discussed at length. Focus on what is appropriate for the developmental level of your students.
4. You can do the writing in the beginning but as children learn to write their letters you can share the pen. White tape is used to cover any mistakes. Let children take turns writing—usually just one child per word at this level.
5. Model and talk about concepts of print such as left to right, return sweep, capitalization, punctuation, as well as letter formation. Clap the syllables in longer words, spelling one syllable at a time.

FIGURE 5-31 Morning Message

6. After each sentence is completed, read it aloud to the group, touching each word. If your sentence contains a two- or three-syllable word, touch it for every syllable, helping children see how it works. Invite children up to fingerpoint as they read.

7. The morning message should be left up all day. Some children may want to copy it or you might want to use it for the cut-up sentence or be-the-sentence activities described earlier.

8. A collection of all the morning messages for a week can be sent home on Friday as a summary of class news which children will have a good chance of proudly reading to their parents.

The word study activities for the emergent stage promote concept and vocabulary development, awareness of sounds, concept of word, and the alphabetic principle. These activities spring from and return to children's books and are extended through writing. Once children achieve a concept of word in print and can segment speech and represent beginning and ending consonant sounds in their spelling, they are no longer emergent, but beginning readers. This is also when they move into the next stage of spelling, the letter name–alphabetic stage. Word study for the letter name–alphabetic speller/beginning reader is described in Chapter 6.

CHAPTER 6

Word Study for Beginners in the Letter Name–Alphabetic Stage

The letter name–alphabetic stage of literacy development is a period of beginnings. Students begin to read and write in a conventional way. That is, they begin to learn words and actually read text, and their writing becomes more readable by themselves and others. However, this period of literacy development needs careful scaffolding because students know how to read and write only a small number of words. The reading materials and activities you choose should provide rich contextual support. In word study, the earliest sorts are pictures. Later, students work with words in families or words known by sight. In the following discussion of reading and writing development and instruction, we will look closely at the support teachers provide and the way word knowledge develops during this stage. We suggest instructional practices that help teachers plan word study programs for beginners. Word study for letter name–alphabetic spellers helps beginners acquire a sight vocabulary through reading and **word banks,** construct phonics generalizations through picture and word sorts, and create ever more sophisticated, if not completely accurate, spellings as they write. Before we describe this stage of word knowledge in detail and provide guidelines for word study instruction, let's visit the first grade classroom of Mr. Perez.

During the first weeks of school, Mr. Perez observed his first graders as they participated in reading and writing activities and he used an inventory described in Chapter 3 to collect samples of their spelling for analysis. Like most first grade teachers, he had a range of ability in his classroom but he learned to manage three instructional groups for reading and word study and to use children's spellings as a guide to appropriate phonics instruction. Mr. Perez had each group meet daily for guided reading. Some days, he used part of that group time for teacher-directed word study.

Cynthia was typical of the children in one group who wrote slowly, often needing help sounding out a word and confusing consonants such as *v* and *f* and *s* and *c*. The results of their writing efforts were limited primarily to consonants with very few vowels as shown by Cynthia's spellings in Table 6-1. Cynthia had memorized the words to jingles such as "Five Little Monkeys Jumping on the Bed" but often got off-track when she tried to point to the words as she read. Mr. Perez decided to take a step back with this group and planned a review of beginning sounds. Each Monday he introduced a set of four initial consonants such as *b,m,r,* and *s*. After modeling the sort and practicing it in the group, he gave each child a handout of pictures to be cut apart for individual sorting practice such as the one in Figure 6-1A. The next day they sorted the pictures again and Mr. Perez observed how quickly and accurately they worked. On subsequent days of the week the children drew and labeled pictures beginning with those sounds, cut and pasted pictures, and did word hunts (follow-up routines described in Chapter 4).

Each day when Mr. Perez met with this group of children they read chart stories, jingles, and big books with predictable texts. To help the children in this group develop a sight vocabulary, Mr. Perez started a word bank for each child. Words the children could quickly identify he wrote on small cards for their collection. The children added a few new words several times a week and reviewed their words on their own or with classroom volunteers.

Tony was part of a large group who had beginning and ending consonants under control, but he was not spelling blends and digraphs or short vowels with much accuracy. Tony pointed to the words as he read "Five Little Monkeys" and self-corrected if he got off-track on words with more than one syllable like *jumping* and *mama.* Mr. Perez decided to introduce the digraphs *sh, ch, th,* and *wh* using picture sorts, and then began the study of word families such as *at* and *an* using word cards. He knew that Tony and the other children in that group could already read words like *cat, can,* and *man,* and they served as the basis for the study of other words in the same family. Mr. Perez spent 10

TABLE 6-1   Invented Spellings of Three First Graders

Word	Cynthia	Tony	Maria
fan	VN	FAN	FAN
pet	PD	PAT	PET
dig	DK	DKG	DEG
wait	YT	WAT	WAT
chunk	JK	HOK	CHOK
stick	CK	SEK	STEK

A. Beginning Consonant Sort			
Bb	Mm	Rr	Ss

B. Word Family Sort		
cat	man	can
rat	fan	hat
pan	sat	pat
that	tan	bat
van	mat	than
fat	ran	

C. Short Vowel Sort		
cap	pig	hot
sit	hat	shop
ship	stop	fast
camp	fish	lock
mad	job	will
him	trap	not
got	that	pin

FIGURE 6-1   Word Study Handouts for Letter Name–Alphabetic Spellers in Three Different Instructional Groups

minutes in group word study several times a week introducing new word families, modeling how to sort them into categories, and leading discussions which helped the children focus on the features common to the words in each column. The children then got their own set of words (Figure 6-1B) to cut apart for sorting, and worked alone and with partners to practice the sort, write the words, illustrate the words, and play follow-up games.

Maria represented a third group who used single consonants accurately, as well as many blends and digraphs as shown in Table 6-1. This group used vowels in most words but the short vowels were often incorrect. Maria could read some books independently and was quickly accumulating a good size sight vocabulary simply from doing lots of reading. Mr. Perez worked with word families for several weeks, making an effort to include words with blends and digraphs, but he soon saw that word families were just too easy and decided to move on to the study of short vowels in nonrhyming words. Each Monday he introduced a collection of words that could be sorted by short vowels into three or four groups. This group also got a sheet of words as shown in Figure 6–1c to cut apart and use for sorting. They learned to work in pairs to do buddy sorts, writing sorts, word hunts, and games on other days of the week.

LITERACY DEVELOPMENT OF LETTER NAME–ALPHABETIC STUDENTS

Letters have both names and sounds. Children typically learn the names of the letters first and use them to spell. This phenomenon accounts for the name of this stage. Letter name–alphabetic spellers are operating in the first layer of English, the alphabetic layer. They understand that words can be segmented into sounds and that letters of the alphabet must be matched to these sounds in a systematic fashion. At first these matches may be limited to the most salient or prominent sounds in words, usually the beginning and ending consonants. By the middle of this stage, students include a vowel in each stressed syllable, and they spell short vowels by matching the way they articulate the letter names of the vowels. By the end of the letter name–alphabetic stage, students have learned how to spell words with short vowels, and they can read most single-syllable words in their reading.

Letter name–alphabetic spelling develops in synchrony with the beginning stages of reading and writing. As you can see in Figure 2-1, spelling development is matched with reading and writing behaviors. The next section describes how students read and write during this stage.

Reading and Writing in the Letter Name–Alphabetic Stage

Students who are in the letter name–alphabetic stage of spelling have recently acquired a **concept of word**—the ability to "track" or fingerpoint read a memorized text. Students who have a concept of word can read familiar rhymes, familiar pattern books, and their own dictations. Beginning readers read slowly, except when they read well-memorized texts, and are often described as word-by-word readers (Bear, 1991b). Students' fluency is constrained by their lack of word knowledge. They do not remember enough words, nor do they know enough about the orthography to read words quickly enough to permit fluent reading or writing. Often beginning readers' reading rates are painfully slow. For example, a beginning reader may reread a familiar text, either a dictation or a pattern book, at fewer than 50 words per minute compared to mature readers who average 250 words per minute.

Most beginning readers fingerpoint to the words when they read, and they read aloud when they read to themselves. This helps them keep their places and also buys processing time. While they hold the words they have just read in memory, they read the next word, giving them time to try to fit the words together into a phrase. Silent reading is rarely evidenced. If you visit a first grade classroom during sustained silent reading (SSR) or during drop everything and read (DEAR), you are likely to hear a steady hum of voices. Disfluency, fingerpointing, and reading aloud to oneself are natural reading behaviors to look for in beginning readers.

There is a similar pattern of disfluency in beginning writing because students usually write slowly, and they often work through spelling words sound by sound (Bear, 1991a). As in reading, orthographic knowledge makes writing easier and more fluent. The more students know about how words are spelled, the more easily and fluently they can write. Consequently, they can give more time to working with and expressing ideas.

In the previous stage of development, the emergent stage, writers are often unable to read what they have written because the letter-to-sound correspondences are lacking or very limited. Students in the letter name–alphabetic stage can usually read what they write depending upon how completely they spell, and their writing is generally readable to anyone who has worked with children in this stage and understands the logic of their letter-to-sound matches.

Supporting Beginning Literacy Learning

Letter name–alphabetic spellers are beginning readers who need support to make reading happen. Support can come from two sources: (1) from the text, and (2) from the teacher. Support from the text comes from its degree of predictability and from its degree of familiarity. Predictability means a child can predict what is coming up next because of certain recurring elements. A rhyming pattern may repeat: "Five little monkeys jumping on the bed, one fell off and bumped his head." A refrain may reoccur: "Have you seen my cat?" (Carle, 1987). A cumulative sequence may reoccur: "This is the cat that caught the rat that ate the malt that lay in the house that Jack built." Or specific words and spelling patterns may reoccur: "The cat sat on the mat. The dog sat on the mat. The goat sat on the mat" (Wildsmith, 1982). **Familiarity** makes the text predictable as well. Familiarity with the subject, the language, and the words, supports students as they read. Text becomes familiar when children have heard it many times before, or because they have read it many times. Texts also become familiar when the words are about an event experienced firsthand by the students, as in dictated stories.

Support from the teacher comes from the many ways a teacher may scaffold the reading experience. For example, the teacher may provide an oral book introduction (Clay, 1991) before the reading. Book introductions use the language of the text and anticipate difficult words and concepts. A teacher may also scaffold the reading experience by modeling the reading process and by encouraging students to reread the same text many times. Asking the children to read in unison (**choral reading**) or immediately after the teacher reads (**echo reading**) are additional methods of scaffolding. The teacher can also provide support by recording a child's experiences in print (language-experience stories).

There is a tension between these two forms of support. The more predictable a text is, the less support is needed from the teacher. Conversely, the less support provided from recurring elements of text, the more scaffolding is needed from the teacher. Because early letter name–alphabetic spellers require support to make reading happen, we often call these beginners "support readers." As students develop as readers, they will need less support from either teacher or text and will benefit from reading text that is not so predictable.

Support readers do not recognize many words by sight, nor is their letter-sound knowledge enough to sound out words. Word recognition needs to be supported by offering students text that is predictable and memorable. As children read and reread these beginning texts, words are gradually remembered out of context as **sight words.** Rhyming books, nursery rhymes, simple decodable texts, group experience stories, and individual dictations, support beginning readers as they rely upon their memory and their limited knowledge of letter-sounds to track their way through text. The redundancy provided by recurring letter-sounds, rhymes, or refrains, helps beginners feel successful. Textual support of this nature is necessary until students acquire a corpus of words they recognize automatically at first sight. For example, in the familiar rhyming book *Five Little Monkeys Jumping on the Bed* by Eileen Christelow (Christelow, E., 1989), beginning readers can point to the words using their memory for the rhyming pattern and their knowledge of beginning sounds /f/, /l/, /m/, /j/, and /b/. The words *fell* and *bed* might even be recognized out of context by virtue of their beginning and ending sounds alone. But in another context, partial phonetic cues alone will not suffice. *Fell* might be confused with *fall* or *fill*, and *bed* might be confused with *bead* or *bad*. Partial information about the alphabetic code is not enough to support unerring word recognition.

Support reading must be accompanied by **word study,** the systematic categorization of known words by letter-sound correspondences. Students in the letter name–alphabetic stage learn about letter-sound correspondences needed for reading and spelling by working first with picture cards and then with words they know. We emphasize the use of *known words* because it is difficult for students to study the orthography when they have to work hard at simply reading the word to begin with. Learning to read and spell is the process of matching the mother tongue to the spelling patterns that represent it. To facilitate that process, it helps to be able to pronounce the words under study. This chapter provides detailed instructions on how to use support reading materials to create **word banks,** a collection of known words that form the corpus of words to be studied. The chapter also discusses the process of collecting known words from familiar reading materials, and procedures for managing word banks. Children who do lots of reading and writing and who also examine words carefully in word study will gradually acquire the orthographic knowledge they need to remember words out of context, to recognize words fully, and to read and spell them quickly and automatically.

CHARACTERISTICS OF ORTHOGRAPHIC DEVELOPMENT

Students in the letter name–alphabetic stage provide a wonderful example of how learners construct knowledge in an attempt to make sense of the world of print. Without a mature knowledge of orthography they carefully analyze the sound system more vigorously than adults do, and they make surprisingly fine distinctions about the way sounds and words are formed in the mouth. They match segmented sounds to the letter names of the alphabet in ways that may seem curious and random to the uninformed adult. Teachers and parents need help in understanding the special logic of letter name–alphabetic spellers as described in this section.

The letter name–alphabetic stage describes students who use their knowledge of the actual names of the letters of the alphabet to spell phonetically or alphabetically. For example, to spell the word *jeep*, students are likely to select *g* as the first letter because of its name (gee) and *p* for the final letter because its letter name (pee) offers a clear clue to the sound it represents. GP for *jeep* is a typical spelling of the early letter name–alphabetic stage. According to letter name logic, there is no need to add the vowel because it is already part of the letter name for *g*. Sometimes early letter name–alphabetic spellers do include vowels, especially when they spell long vowels that "say their name." For example, students might spell *jeep* as GEP. Using a strategy of letter names, students can luck out and include the correct long vowel, but early letter name–alphabetic spelling is largely consonantal. During the middle part of this stage, children's spellings gradually include more vowels.

Some letter names do not cue students in to the sounds they represent. For example, the letter name for *w* is "double you," which does not offer any clue to its /wuh/ sound. Consequently, early letter name–alphabetic spellers may spell *when* as YN. Why do students use a *y*? When you say the letter name for *y*, you can feel your lips moving to make the shape of the /wuh/ sound. *Y* is the letter whose pronounced name is closest to the sound at the beginning of *when*. In Table 6-2 you can get a sense of what the letter names offer students in terms of sound matches.

How Consonant Sounds Are Articulated in the Mouth

Letter name–alphabetic students rely not only on what they hear in the letter names, but also on how the letters are articulated, or formed in the mouth, when they spell. An example to demonstrate this point is the way students spell the blend *dr* in *drive*. Students are misled in their spelling by the similarity between *dr* and *jr*, and they may spell *drive* as JRV. Test this yourself. Say *drive*, and then say *jrive*. Don't they sound and feel alike? Linguists call these sounds **affricates,** made by forcing air through a small closure at the roof of your mouth. This creates a feeling of friction (*friction*, af*fric*atives—see the meaning connection?). In English there are several other letters and letter combinations that create the affricate sound and these are often substituted for each other: *j*, *g* (as in *gym*), *ch* (as in *chip*), *dr* (as in *drive*), *tr* (as in *trap*), and the letter name for *h* (aich). In their writing, students use the consonant blends and digraphs they know best. For example, children who are familiar with words that begin with *ch* may spell *train* as CHRAN.

There are several other ways in which students relate sounds to the ways the sounds are made. Basing a decision on the way a sound feels, students may spell *brave* as BRAF, or *oven* as OFN. What is the difference between the consonant sound spelled by *v* and that spelled by *f*? Both sounds feel exactly the same but one is **voiced** and the other is

TABLE 6-2   Names of the Letters of the Alphabet

A	A	H	Aich	O	Oh	V	Vee
B	Bee	I	I	P	Pee	W	Double You
C	See	J	Jay	Q	Kue	X	Ecks
D	Dee	K	Kay	R	Are	Y	Wie
E	Ee	L	Ell	S	Es	Z	Zee
F	Ef	M	Em	T	Tee		
G	Gee	N	En	U	You		

unvoiced. When voiced phonemes are created your vocal chords vibrate. You can feel this if you place your fingers on your larynx as you say them. Compare the way *v* and *f* feel in the words *van* and *fan*. There are similar voiced and unvoiced pairs listed in the pronunciation chart in Table 5-1. One implication for instruction is that students in the letter name–alphabetic stage benefit from saying the words they are sorting so that they can feel the shape of their mouth as they say the words.

The Issue of Vowels

Vowels pose special problems for letter name–alphabetic spellers who rely on the name of letters and how a sound feels in their mouth. Try saying the word *lip.* You can feel the initial consonant as your tongue curls up toward your palate and you can feel the final consonant as it explodes past your lips, but did you feel the vowel? Unlike the consonants—articulated by tongue, teeth, lips, and palate—the vowels are determined by more subtle variations: the shape of the mouth and jaw, the opening of the vocal tract, the force of air from the lungs, and the vibration of the vocal cords.

Vowels are elusive but central to every syllable humans speak. When consonants are electronically separated from vowels, they sound like noise, a click, or a snap of the fingers, and nothing like speech. Try to say a consonant such as *b.* What vowels did you attach to the *b?* If you said the letter name (bee), then you would have said the long-e vowel. Now say the sound associated with *b: /*buh/ or /bə/. The vowel this time is the **schwa,** a vowel made in the middle of the mouth. Now try to say a /b/ sound without a vowel. Try to whisper *b* and cut your breath short in a whisper. The whisper is as close as you come to separating a vowel from a consonant.

Studies in acoustical phonetics have demonstrated that vowels are like musical tones when separated from the consonants. Without the music of the vowel, the consonants become just noise. Because vowels are so closely wedded to the consonants around them, spellers in the early letter name–alphabetic stage have difficulty separating vowels from consonants in order to analyze them and make letter matches. It is as if the consonant were the proverbial squeaky wheel; at first, the consonants seem to demand more attention than the vowel and are more easily examined.

Talking About Vowels

Linguists refer to the distinctive sounds within a given vowel according to its tenseness or laxness. The vocal chords are tense when producing the long-a sound in the middle of the word *shake.* Conversely, the vocal chords relax a bit in producing the short-a sound in the middle of *shack.* The difference in the medial vowel sounds in the words *shake* and *shack* can be described linguistically as **tense** and **lax.**

In phonics instruction, teachers have traditionally taught students the differences between long vowels (which say their name) and short vowels. This distinction between five long and five short vowels may be derived from the 10 central long and short vowels of classical Latin (*a, e, i, o,* and *u*). Supposedly, long vowel sounds are longer in duration than short vowel sounds (Fromkin & Rodman, 1993) but this is not always the case. Even short vowel sounds vary in duration. For example, the vowel in *bad* is different than the vowel sound in *bat.* In the first case, did you notice that the short-a in *bad* was longer than the short-a in *bat?* As a matter of fact, in many dictionaries you can find *bad* written as *ba:d,* meaning that the *a* has a longer duration than expected.

Although **long vowels** and **short vowels** may not be the most accurate terms linguistically, they are more common than *tense* and *lax* and teachers understand each other when these terms are used. The simplest way to talk about vowels is probably the best. For example, teachers can talk about the beginning and middle sounds in words: "Find a picture of a word that sounds like *ball* at the beginning" or "*Bet* and *best*—Do they sound alike in the middle?" Descriptions like "in the middle" may suffice to draw students' attention to the vowels at first, but students have no trouble learning terms like

vowel and **consonant.** Teachers do need to establish a common language to use in word study discussions and such terms make it easier.

Students may be taught to use terms to describe sounds, but the important thing to look for is their ability to read and write words quickly and easily enough to create meaning in their reading and writing. What students can do with words is certainly more important than mastering terms about words. Orthographic knowledge should come forward easily and tacitly. Experience has shown that the long-short distinction provides an adequate description for initial discussions with students about vowels.

How Vowels Are Articulated in the Mouth

Over the course of the letter name–alphabetic stage, students become adept at segmenting words into phonemes, even the vowel, and they use the alphabetic principle to represent each sound with a letter. Long vowel sounds are easiest because they say their name and the choices are obvious. Students spell *line* as LIN, *rain* as RAN, and *boat* as BOT. Perhaps what is most interesting about the invented spelling in the letter name–alphabetic stage is the way students spell the short vowels. They turn to the names of the letters but find no clear letter-sound matches for the short vowel sounds. For example, there is no letter name that says the short-i sound in *bit* or the /uh/ sound in *cup*. They might use *f* (ef) or *s* (es) for short-e but they seldom do. How do students choose a letter name for a short vowel? They use their knowledge of the alphabet to find the letter name closest to the place of **articulation** of the short vowel sound they are trying to write.

Since it has probably been some time since you analyzed sounds at this level, take a moment to consider the vowels and where they are made in the vocal tract. The position of the words in Figure 6-2 illustrates some of the basic contrasts among vowels in English. The vowels are drawn in this space to mimic the general area where speakers can feel the articulation of the vowel. To talk about articulation is to describe the shape of the mouth, the openness of the jaw, and the position of the tongue while the word is being said. Compare the vowels in this figure by feeling the air pass through the oral cavity and the position of the mouth as the following words are said in a sequence from *beet* to *boot:*

beet   bit   bait   bet   bat   bite   but   bah   ball   boat   book   boot

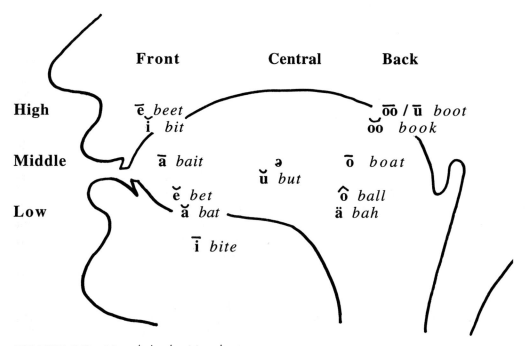

FIGURE 6-2   Vowels in the Mouth

Try saying this string several times, saying only the vowel sounds in each word. Feel how the production of the vowels moves from high in the front of the oral cavity (*beet*) to low in the oral cavity (*bite*) to the back of the oral cavity (*boat*), down the front, back, and up (*boot*). As you read the words *boot, foot,* and *boat,* do you feel how the vowels are rounded? Feel how the tongue is raised in the back and how the lips are pursed as the words are pronounced. Contrast the rounded vowel in *boot* with the way your lips feel when you say the high front vowel sounds in *beet* or *bit.*

The way a word is pronounced may vary by dialect. For example, many people say *caught* and *cot* the same way. Some native speakers of English pronounce *bought, bore, roof,* and *stalk* with different vowels. Teachers need to be aware of dialectical differences when students sort and talk about words. These differences do not interfere with word study and learning to spell, but an awareness of these differences enhances word study. Everyone speaks a dialect.

Letter Name Spelling of Short Vowels

How do students choose a letter name to represent a short vowel? Without being consciously aware that they are doing this, letter name–alphabetic spellers spell short vowels with the letter name closest in articulation to that short vowel. There are five letter names to choose from: *a, e, i, o,* and *u.* How would an alphabetic speller spell the word *bed?* What letter name is closest to the short-e sound in *bet?* Try saying *bed-beet* and *bed-bait* to compare how the short vowel sounds and the long vowel or letter names feel in your mouth. Repeat the pairs several times and pay attention to how the mouth is shaped. The long-a or letter name for *a* is closer in place of articulation to the short-e sound than to the letter names for *e, i, o,* or *u.*

Students in the letter name–alphabetic stage use their knowledge of letter names and the feel of the vowels as they are produced in the vocal tract to spell *bet* as BAT. What letter name is closest to the short-i sound in *ship?* Compare the vowel sound in the middle of *ship* with the letter names for *i* and *e.* Children often spell *ship* as SHEP because the letter name for *e* is closer in place of articulation to the short-i sound than the letter name for *i.* The wondrous aspect of these letter name substitutions for short vowels is that they are so predictable. Charles Read (1975) found that nearly all children go through a period of time when they substitute the short vowels in this way. Note that short-a does not pose much of a problem for spellers because the short-a sound and the letter name for *a* are already close in place of articulation. Say *bat* and *bait* to test this. The following chart will help you remember how the letter names of vowels are substituted for the short vowel sounds beginning readers try to spell.

Invented Spelling			Logical Vowel Substitution		
BAT	for	*bat*	None, short-a is closest to *a*		
BAT	for	*bet*	*a*	for	short-e
BET	for	*bit*	*e*	for	short-i
PIT	for	*pot*	*i*	for	short-o
POT	for	*put*	*o*	for	short-u

Through word study in the letter name–alphabetic stage, students do learn to spell short vowel words correctly and they see that short vowels follow a specific pattern, a **consonant-vowel-consonant** (CVC) pattern. This **CVC** pattern stretches across all short vowels from the short-a in *pat* to the short-u in *stuck.* In their study of short vowels, students notice that, regardless of how many consonant letters are on either side of the single vowel, one vowel letter in the pattern signals the short vowel sound. Children's sight words, their known words, provide a base for studying the CVC pattern. In reading and directed word study, these known words provide the tension between what is and what they think about the orthography. The CVC pattern provides a basis for learning about vowel patterns.

As they mature and learn more sight words, students face the ambiguities of the **homographs**—words that are spelled the same but pronounced differently. For example, students in the letter name–alphabetic stage may spell *bent, bet, bat,* and *bait* the same way: BAT. The burden of so many homographs is a catalyst for change, a good problem. Letter name–alphabetic spellers are also readers, and when they reread their own spelling of *bait* as BAT, a word they know spells something else, they experience disequilibrium. This forces them to find other ways to spell a word like *bait.* When students are able to spell these basic short vowel patterns, and they begin to experiment with long vowel patterns, they have entered the next spelling stage, within word pattern.

Other Orthographic Features

Students work through three other features during this stage:

1. Influences on the vowel from certain consonants
2. Consonant blends and digraphs
3. Preconsonantal nasals

Although these features are usually studied toward the end of this stage, they can be studied whenever students have enough examples in their word banks or whenever they show an interest in these features. For example, the influence of the letter *r* on the short vowel sounds is profound and may become a topic of study when students realize that a word like *car* does not fit with other short-a sounds even though it follows the CVC pattern.

Influences on the Vowel

The letters *r, w,* and *l* influence the vowel sounds they follow. For example, the vowel sounds in words like *bar, ball,* and *saw* are not the same as the short vowel sounds in *bat* and *fast.* They cannot be called short-a, yet all of these words have the CVC pattern. The consonant sounds /r/ and /l/ are known in linguistics as **liquids.** Both can change the pronunciation of the vowel they follow. These spellings are often known as *r*-controlled and *l*-controlled.

R-influenced vowels can be difficult to spell by sound alone. For example, *fur* and *sir* are said the same way. *R*-influenced vowels that follow a CVC pattern are examined during the letter name–alphabetic stage and can be compared to short vowels in word sorts. Students might contrast consonant **blends** with an *r* (*fr, tr, gr*) and *r*-influenced vowels (e.g., *from–farm, grill-girl, tarp–trap*).

Consonant Blends and Digraphs

Letter name–alphabetic spellers often struggle with consonant blends and digraphs. A **blend** is a spelling unit (sometimes called a consonant cluster) composed of two or three consonants that retain their identity when pronounced. The word *blend* contains two blends: *bl* and *nd.* When the blend is said, the individual sounds can still be heard. Although each of the sounds in a blend remains distinct they are tightly bound and not easily segmented into individual phonemes, making them difficult for children to spell accurately. The *st* blend in *stick* may be spelled simply as SEK or SEC. Blends can occur at the beginning or end of words and are represented by the bold letters in the following words.

(*Note:* In the *qu* blend the *u* represents the consonant sound of *w.*)

black, **cl**ap, **fl**ash, **gl**ad, **pl**ug, **sl**ip, **pl**us (l-blends)
brag, **cr**ash, **dr**eam, **fr**og, **gr**eat, **pr**ize, **tr**ee (r-blends)
scout, ta**sk**, **sm**all, **sn**eeze, li**sp**, li**st**, **sw**eet, **spl**ash, **str**eet, **squ**are (s-blends)
twice, **qu**ick

A consonant **digraph** is slightly different. A consonant digraph is two letters that make a new sound or a single sound. The word *digraph* ends with a digraph, the *ph* that stands for the single sound of /f/. Other digraphs include the bold letters in:

thick, **fish**, ea**ch**, **wh**en, **ph**one

Throughout the letter name–alphabetic stage, students refine their understanding of consonant blends and digraphs. Students become more consistent in the frequency with which they use them in their spelling. In their reading, they recognize words with consonant blends and digraphs with greater accuracy and fluency (Bear, 1992). Students' tacit understanding of consonant blends and digraphs grows along with their sight vocabularies and their understanding of the basic CVC patterns that contain consonant blends and digraphs.

Preconsonantal Nasals

Some letter-sound combinations are more subtle than others. **Nasal** sounds, associated with *m, n,* and *ng,* are made by air passing through the nasal cavity in the mouth. The **preconsonantal nasals** are nasal sounds that come right before a final consonant such as the *m* in *jump* or the *n* in *pink.* In the pronunciation of preconsonantal nasals, it is as if the second consonant dominates and absorbs the nasal. Try saying *ban* and then *band.* Can you feel both the *n* and the *d* in *band?* Preconsonantal nasals are often omitted during the letter name–alphabetic stage (*bump* may be spelled BOP and *pink* may be spelled PEK). When students begin to spell words with preconsonantal nasals correctly they are usually at the end of the letter name–alphabetic stage.

WORD STUDY INSTRUCTION
FOR THE LETTER NAME–ALPHABETIC STAGE

The focus for word study in the letter name–alphabetic stage begins with initial consonants and continues through consonant digraphs, blends, and the study of short vowels. Word study during this stage makes use of pictures and words from students' word banks. This section discusses the sequence of word study throughout the letter name–alphabetic stage, presents ways to use word banks, and offers some tips for how to lead group sorting activities.

Sequence of Word Study

The sequence of word study is based on the alphabet, pattern, and meaning principles that have been observed in students' spelling. During this stage of development, students focus primarily on the alphabetic principle of matching sounds to letters. Consider the invented spellings in Table 6-1 and what they reveal about how students experiment with the orthography. There is an order to their experimentation. Teachers can take the lead from their students' invented spellings in designing word study instruction. The sequence of word study instruction is designed to complement the natural course of learning.

Initially, students use beginning consonants in their writing, so this is a good place to begin word study. After students have learned to use most of the consonants, they add vowels in each stressed syllable. When they start placing a vowel in each syllable, it is time to study short vowels. When students begin to use long vowel patterns in their spelling, they are ready to examine long vowel word patterns and move

TABLE 6-3 Using Spelling Errors to Plan Word Study in the Letter Name–Alphabetic Stage

Spelling Samples	Characteristics of Spellings	Appropriate Word Study
fan = F *pet* = PSLD *dig* = DK *wait* = YT *junk* = GK	Some consonant sounds are represented but incomplete or confused.	Picture sorts of beginning sounds.
fan = FN *pet* = PT *dig* = DG *rope* = ROP *shine* = CIN *sled* = SD	Single beginning and final consonants correct for the most part. Blends and digraphs not correct. Few, if any, vowels in middle.	1. Picture sorts of digraphs and blends. 2. Compare word families with the same vowel using words and pictures.
dig = DEG *pet* = PAT *junk* = JOK *sled* = SLAD *dream* = JREM *shine* = CHIN	Single beginning and final consonants correct. Blends and digraphs may still be confused. Short vowels are used but confused. Long vowel markers are absent or rare. Missing preconsonantal nasals.	1. Compare word families with mixed vowels using word sorts. 2. Compare short vowels. 3. Include words with blends, digraphs, and preconsonantal nasals in word sorts.

Adapted from Johnston, Invernizzi, & Juel, 1998.

on to the next stage. Table 6-3 summarizes how spellings should be used to make instructional decisions.

Although there is a predictable pattern of development, the exact sequence and pace will not be precisely the same for every student. There are three factors that impact the sequence and the pace of the word study:

1. Utmost is the students' development. Although the general sequence will be the same, the pace varies and teachers need to vary the length of time they spend on word study activities with different students. For this reason, membership in word study groups must be fluid.
2. Because word study always works with known words, word study during this stage is constrained by students' sight vocabularies. This is why picture sorts are so effective. Children seldom have enough sight words for the study of initial consonants, blends, or digraphs.
3. The third factor is the curriculum. Some school districts and schools specify through their curriculum guides what orthographic features should be studied. The developmental outline presented in this book provides clear guidelines for what features to study in what order. Teachers can use the following sequence and still cover the features specified in most districts' curricula.
   a. Review beginning sounds with picture sorts.
   b. Introduce consonant blends and digraphs with pictures.
   c. Introduce short vowels in word families.
   d. Continue to study consonant blends and digraphs in word families.
   e. Study short vowels as CVC patterns outside of rhyming families.
   f. Integrate the study of blends, digraphs, and preconsonantal nasals with short vowels.

The following in-depth discussion focuses on each of these areas of word study instruction.

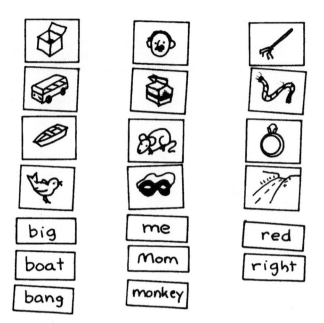

FIGURE 6-3   Initial Consonant Picture and Word Sort

The Study of Beginning Sounds

Word study starts with the study of initial sounds for students in the early letter name–alphabetic stage. Simple picture sorts give students an opportunity to compare pictures based on how they "sound at the beginning." Pictures are sorted and contrasted, starting with frequently occurring initial consonants where the contrasts or differences are clear both visually and by sound. Figure 6-3 is an example of a sort that started with pictures and then included sight words from the student's word bank.

Mr. Perez, whom we met at the beginning of this chapter, was wise in deciding to "take a step" back to firm up Cynthia's understandings of consonants. Many children benefit from a fast-paced review of consonants at the beginning of first grade to clear up some lingering confusions or to secure some tentative letter-sound matches. There is no particular order to the sequence of sounds, but starting with frequently occurring initial consonants where the contrasts or differences are clear both visually and by sound is recommended. Many teachers have found the following sequence to be effective. Chapter 5 offers suggestions for how to plan and carry out these sorts.

B	M	R	S
T	G	N	P
C	H	F	D
L	K	J	W
Y	Z	V	Q

Modify this sequence if there are connections you can make to reading materials or classroom themes of study. In October you might want to focus on *h, j, p,* and *g* to tie in with words like *Halloween, jack-o-lanterns, pumpkins,* and *ghosts.* Picture sorts with initially occurring short vowels can also be included here as a way to introduce those letter-sound correspondences. Pictures for these beginning short vowels can be found in the appendix right after the beginning consonant pictures.

A few final consonants might be introduced and studied, but once students have learned the frequently occurring initial consonants and phonemic segmentation, most of them can easily use their knowledge of letter-sound matches to spell final consonants. When students consistently omit final consonants in their writing, you can draw their attention to them through word study activities that are similar to the initial consonant sorts. For example, your students could hunt for words and pictures of words that end like *bat*. However, the study of final consonants is covered when the students examine word families and this is probably enough for most children.

Some children may have a few lingering confusions even when they are in control of most consonant matches. Don't hesitate to move on to other features since consonants will be reviewed again in word family comparisons. However, you may want to address lingering consonant confusions in sorts that contrast what students are using with what they are confusing. If a child spells *fan* as VN, you may want to pull out pictures of words that start with *v* and *f* to help work out the correct associations. Such close comparisons should not, however, be the child's first introduction to those letter-sounds.

Word Banks

Word banks play a special role for beginning readers, helping them learn specific words as well as how words work in general. What children know about particular words during this period of time may only be partial. For example, as they read, they may substitute *leopard* for *lion* in a story of big cats at the zoo. From such errors, it appears that they are attending to the beginning letters for cues. This is also evident in the way they spell during this time. *Lion* is often spelled as LN. Ehri (1997) has described these readers as "partial alphabetic" because they use partial letter-sound cues—usually consonant cues—to identify and spell words. Children will acquire sight words, or words they know out of context, slowly during the early letter name–alphabetic period and they will need frequent exposure to those words. Examining words out of context makes a difference in how well they learn those words (Ehri & Wilce, 1980) and how many words they learn over time (Johnston, 1998).

Acquiring a sight vocabulary is critical for progress in reading. Automatic word recognition makes it possible to read fluently and to devote attention to comprehension rather than to figuring out words. A sight vocabulary also provides a corpus of known words from which students begin to discover generalizations about how words work.

A word bank is a collection of words chosen by the students (not the teacher) that they remember well enough to identify in isolation (Stauffer, 1980). The words are written on small cards and are added to a collection over time. They are reviewed regularly and words that have been forgotten are discarded. Sometimes we are asked why children need to review words they already know. The answer is, they don't know them the same way adults do; they know them only partially and tentatively. Children reviewing their word bank may confuse *ran* and *run, stop* and *sip, lost* and *little*. They may get *gingerbread* every time because it is the only long word they have that starts with *g*, but when you ask them to spell it (GNRBRD) you get a better idea of what they really know about that word. Regular review of word bank words encourages students to look more thoroughly at words and to note individual letter-sound correspondences.

For children in the early letter name–alphabetic stage, word banks support their growing sight word knowledge and their growing knowledge of letter-sound correspondences. As they study initial sounds they can be asked to find words in their word bank that have those same sounds. This will help them make connections between the pictures they sort and the words they read. Later in the letter name–alphabetic stage the word bank becomes a source of known words to be used in word sorts. It is crucial that students work with known words because it's easier to look across words for similarities and differences in sounds and letters. There is an added burden in word study if students must labor to pronounce words before analyzing their features and relationships to other words.

FIGURE 6-4   Personal Reader With Word Bank

Developing and using word banks and personal readers.   The words in a word bank come from any source where a child can find known words. Usually, these words come from dictations, small-group experience charts, rhymes, poems, and the simple books and preprimers that they read. Words can come from students' names and from labels (like Wendy's, or BUM Equipment), but it is best if the words in the word banks can be traced back to meaningful and familiar text. By using words that come from familiar readings and by numbering the stories and rhymes and the word cards, students can be encouraged to return to the primary source to find a forgotten word and to match the word bank card to its counterpart in print.

Personal readers, such as the one in Figure 6-4, are individual student copies of group experience charts, rhymes and jingles, individual dictations, and selected passages from simple books that students can read independently or with some support from a teacher or partner. Except for the individual dictations, many of the selections in personal readers are the same among many students. The stories in the personal readers are numbered, and the date they are introduced is recorded. Students are enormously proud of their personal readers and they reread them many times before taking them home to read some more. Personal readers are an ideal place for students to collect words from their word banks. They can simply underline the words they know best and these words can then be transferred to small cards.

In Figure 6-4, the child's word bank is a plastic bag that can be stored in the personal reader. You can also see that simple pattern books can fit inside the front pocket. The personal reader also contains a page that lists the words in the child's word bank. A reduced sound board of short vowels is included for the student to refer to in word study and writing.

Word banks increase slowly and steadily. At first, students do not have enough words in their banks to use them much for sorting. Gradually, word banks increase to 50 words, and then there are plenty of words for many sorts. Once the word banks grow to between 150 to 250 words, they become clumsy to manage. It takes students too long to hunt through their banks for examples of a particular short vowel. There are three signs to look for to tell when to discontinue word banks:

1. The student is at the end of the letter name–alphabetic stage of spelling.
2. There are at least 200 words in the word bank.
3. It is possible to create word sorts in which students recognize nearly all of the words easily.

Word banks take extra work but are well worth the time, particularly for students in the beginning of this stage. Word banks support students' sight word development and growing word knowledge. They are also motivating for students because they offer tangible evidence of their word learning and literacy growth (Johnston, 1998). Guidelines for making and using word banks, individual dictations, and group experience charts can be found in the first part of the activities section of this chapter.

The Study of Digraphs and Blends

After students study initial consonants, they are ready to learn about initial consonant digraphs and blends. The goal of word study of consonant blends and digraphs is to, not only master those combinations, but to have students ready to look at the "vowel and what follows" (Henderson, 1990). Most of the consonant blend and digraph study is done with pictures, primarily because students do not have many sight words to bring to the sorts. Of course, words are added as soon as possible.

The first digraphs to be studied are *ch, sh, th,* and *wh.* Sorts for digraphs need to compare words "that do" with words "that don't." What contrasts are best? The answer lies in children's invented spellings. Some children will substitute *j* for *ch* as they spell words like *chin* as JN or they may confuse the letter name of *h* (aich) with *ch* and spell *chin* as HN. These confusions suggest that a good sort to study *ch* would include words that start with *ch, h,* or even *c* and *j. Th* might be compared to single *t; sh* to single *s,* and *ch* to single *c.* Note, however, that it would be very difficult to sort pictures by *w* and *wh* since many words beginning with *wh* do not have a distinctive sound (which *witch* is *which*?). You might compare *wh* to *th, sh,* and *ch* in a culminating digraph sort. Possible contrasts for digraphs include:

1. *c / ch / h*
2. *s / sh / h*
3. *t / th / h*
4. *ch / sh / th*
5. *j / ch*
6. *wh / sh / th / ch*

Consonant blends come in three major groups. There are the s-blends (*sn, sm, st, sk,* etc.), the r-blends (*br, cr, dr, fr, gr, pr, tr*), and the l-blends (*bl, cl, fl, gl, pl, sl*). The easiest group of blends is the s-blends because *s* is a continuant (the /s/ sound continues), and because with the exception of *sl,* the s-blends do not contain the slippery *l* or *r.*

The study of initial consonant blends begins with the easiest contrasts of single initial consonants with its blend. For example, pictures that begin with *st* may be contrasted with pictures that begin with *s* for spellers like Tony who spell *stick* as SEK. After studying several blends in this fashion, it is best to pick up the pace and introduce other blends in groups. Some suggested contrasts are listed as follows, but as always, modify these in accordance with the kinds of words students are encountering in their reading. Once children catch on to how blends work and learn to segment the sounds in blends, they may move quickly through a sequence of study or skip some contrasts altogether. Possible contrasts for blends include:

1. *s / st / t*
2. *sp / s / p*
3. *st / sp / sk / sm*
4. *sl / sn / sc / sw*
5. *bl / b / l*
6. *gl / pl / bl / cl*

| **7.** t / tr / r | **9.** gr / tr / dr / pr | **11.** cl / cr / fl / fr |
| **8.** d / dr / r | **10.** bl / br / gl / gr | **12.** k / qu / tw |

The procedures and routines for the study of digraphs and blends are the same as for other beginning-sound sorts. Composite sheets of pictures can be created for individual practice at desks or students can work in centers with pictures for additional practice. Pictures needed for the study of digraphs and blends can be found in the appendix. Chapter 4 describes follow-up activities, such as **cut and paste** and **draw and label,** that are appropriate for digraphs and blends. Many of the games described for beginning consonants in Chapter 5 and in this chapter can be easily adapted to review digraphs and blends.

Unlike initial consonants, students in the early part of the letter name–alphabetic stage are not expected to acquire great fluency or accuracy in spelling and sorting consonant blends and digraphs because they will be revisited throughout the stage. The study of blends can be alternated with the study of word families. Words chosen to sort for word families or short vowels should include words that begin and end with blends and digraphs. Knowledge of blends and digraphs will help students understand the CVC as the basic short vowel pattern. Even a word like *flash* is a CVC word in which *fl* is the first unit, *a* is the medial vowel, and *sh* is the final unit. Students also work through sorts in which they consider features like the double *l* in *ball,* and the *nd* in *blend* or *stand.*

The Study of Word Families to Introduce Short Vowels

Once letter name–alphabetic spellers have a firm, if not complete, mastery of beginning and ending consonant sounds, and a stable concept of word they are ready to examine the medial vowel. The study of vowels begins with word families or **phonograms** when vowels are still missing or used only occasionally in children's invented spellings. Once children are using short vowels consistently, they can be asked to compare short vowels in word sorts that examine the **CVC** pattern across a variety of vowels. This will happen toward the end of the stage. Refer again to Table 6-3 to see how to use children's spellings for planning instruction during this stage.

Word families offer an easy and appealing way to introduce the issue of vowels. Students are supported in their first efforts to analyze the vowel because the vowel and the ending letter(s) are presented as a chunk or pattern. In linguistic terms, the **rime** consists of the vowel and what follows. What comes before the vowel is known as the **onset.** Examples of onset-rime breaks are *m-an, bl-and, m-at,* and *th-at.* Dividing words into onsets and rimes is easier and more natural for children than dividing them into individual phonemes (Treiman, 1985).

The study of word families makes sense for several other reasons. First of all, 37 rimes can be used to generate 500 different words children encounter in primary reading materials (Wylie & Durrell, 1970). In addition, these same rimes will be familiar chunks in thousands of multisyllabic words; the *an* chunk can be found in *canyon, incandescent,* and *fantastic.* Second, vowel sounds are more stable within families than across families (Adams, 1990; Wylie & Durrell, 1970). For example, the word *dog* is often presented as a short-o word in phonics programs. But in some regions of the United States it is pronounced more like *dawg.* If you say it that way, then you probably pronounce *fog* as *fawg, frog* as *frawg,* and *log* as *lawg.* In the study of word families the actual pronunciation of the short vowel does not matter. It is the *og* chunk that is examined and compared.

There is no particular order to the study of word families, but starting with short-a families (*at, an, ad, ap, ack*) seems to be a good choice because these words abound in early reading materials, and children are likely to already know several words from these families by sight. In addition, short-a is the least likely short vowel to be confused when children try to make matches based on letter names and place of articulation. Knowing that children initially have trouble isolating and attending to the medial vowel, it is a good idea to compare word families that share the same vowel before contrasting different vowels. This supports children's first efforts to read and spell those words. What they really must attend to are the beginning and ending consonants in order to sort and spell the words. The study of same-vowel word families serves to review those features. In sorting words like *mat* and *man*, for example, students must attend to the final consonant more than any place else. Move quickly, however, to comparing words that have different vowels. The difference between *mit*, *met*, and *mat* lies in the medial vowel and it is through such contrasts that students are forced to attend to the vowel sound itself.

Table 6-4 offers a suggested sequence for the study of word families but it is offered only as a model from which to plan your own course of study. Each of the words listed is intended to be an example of a particular word family and you would need to collect additional words to create the sorts. You will find lists of words for each family in the appendix. As always, you should consider the words that your students have in their word banks and the kinds of words they encounter in their reading.

Word sorting to compare two or more word families.
In the following procedure for sorting two or more word families, the phonograms for *ig*, *ag*, and *og* are used as examples.

1. Make a collection of word cards to model the sort on a tabletop, pocket chart, or overhead projector. Students should be able to read two or more words in each family.
2. Begin by laying down a known word as a header for each family. Choose words you are sure the students can read such as *big*, *dog*, and *bag*. Explain that the rest of the words need to be sorted under one of the headers.

TABLE 6-4   Possible Pace and Sequence of Word Family Study

Slow Pace / Introductions	Moderate Pace	Fast Pace / Review
Use single initial consonants and some digraphs in words chosen.*	Use some blends and digraphs in words chosen for sorts.	Use plenty of blends and digraphs in words chosen for sorts.
Same-Vowel Word Families		
at family with pictures and words	*at & an*	*at, an, ad, ap*
an and *ad* with pictures and words	*ag, ad, ap*	*in, ip, ick, ing*
ap and *ag* with pictures and words	*ip, ig, in, ill*	*ub, ug, ush, unk*
ot and *og* with pictures and words	*ot, og, ock*	
ip, ig, ill with pictures and words	*ug, ub, uck, unk*	
ug, ub, ut		
ed, et, eg, ell		
Mixed-Vowel Word Families		
at, ot, it	*at, ot, ag, og*	*an, in, et, ot*
ag, og, ap, op	*an, en, un*	*ag, ig, eg, ug, og*
ill, ell, all	*ip, ap, op, up*	*ink, ank, unk*
ap, ip, op, up	*ack, ock, ick, uck*	*all, ell, ill*
an, un, en	*ing, ish, ang, ash*	*ack, ock, ick, uck, eck*
all, ell, ill	*ang, ing, ung, ong*	
ag, eg, ig, og, ug	*ink, ank, unk*	
ack, ock, ick, uck		
ish, ash, ush		

*Add blends and digraphs to sorts as they are studied, especially to later sorts.

3. Pick up another word such as *frog* and say something like this: "I am going to put this word under *dog*. Listen, *dog, frog*." Continue to model one or two words in each category, always sorting first and then reading down, starting with the header.

4. Invite students to try sorting the next word. They should sort first and then read from the top of each column. They are not expected to sound it out first and then sort. Instead their sense of rhyme will support them as they read the new word by simply changing the first sound of a word they already know. The final sort might look like this:

big	dog	bag
dig	frog	wag
pig	hog	flag
wig	bog	rag
	fog	tag
	log	

5. After all the words have been sorted, lead a discussion to focus your students' attention on the common features in each word, "How are the words in each column alike?"

6. Reread the words in each column and then lead the students in sorting a second time. Any mistakes should be left until the end and checked by reading down the columns.

7. Students should be given their own set of words to sort such as the one in Figure 6-1B. Appropriate follow-up routines include buddy sorting, writing sorts, word hunts, and so on. These are described in Chapter 4 in the primary schedule.

Word family sorts can be made easier or harder in a number of ways. The study of word families can begin with the matching of words to pictures. Some of the short vowel pictures in the appendix can be used for these. However, pictures are not really necessary and you can create sheets of word cards or sorting folders. Word sorts are presented in the appendix. During the study of word families, it is appropriate to modify one of the 10 principles of word study described in Chapter 4—*use words students can read.* Since the words are in rhyming families, students are supported in their reading of the words, as long as the guide word and the first few words are familiar. Students will read unknown words by blending different onsets with the familiar rime. Be sure to include words with blends and digraphs as a review of those features and a chance to see them in another context. The *ack* family can grow to be quite large when you include *black, track, shack, quack, stack, snack, crack*, and so on.

With the publication of research on onsets and rimes and renewed interest in word families, there has been a recent flood of reading materials designed around phonograms. Little phonics readers have been created that feature a particular family or short vowel. Some of these little books are engaging and well written, offering students support in the form of patterned or rhyming text. Such books can be used as a starting point or as a follow-up for word study, and students can use them to go on **word hunts** for additional words that follow the same phonics feature. However, choose these books carefully. Stories featuring sentences like "The tan man ran the van" change reading from the making of meaning into exercises in word calling. Some phonics readers are better done than others.

There are lots of activities and games to use in connection with the study of word families. Board games designed to study beginning sounds can be adapted to word families. Sound wheels, flip charts, and the Show Me game are favorites and are included in the activities to follow. From this point on students are expected to be able to spell the words they sort in their entirety. Word study notebooks can be used to record writing sorts and the results of word hunts or brainstorming sessions.

FIGURE 6-5   Picture Sort by Short-a and Short-i

The study of word families can take a long time if you feel compelled to study every one in a thorough fashion, but this should not be the case. Some children will quickly pick up the notion that words that sound alike probably share similar rimes and are spelled alike. They will also be able to use this knowledge to figure out new words by analogy; noting the *and* in *stand,* they quickly decode it. However, these students may still make errors in spelling short vowels.

The Study of Short Vowels

Once students are using but confusing short vowels on a regular basis in their invented spelling and work with word families easily and accurately, they are ready for the study of short vowels in nonrhyming words outside of word families. This study will ask them to look at words in a new way, not as two units with various rimes (*m-ad, fl-ag, tr-ack*) but as three units with the same CVC pattern (*m-a-d, fl-a-g, tr-a-ck*) and the same short vowel sound. This ability to see words as patterns is the key feature of the next stage, within word pattern. Over the course of studying the short vowels, students come to see that CVC is the basic pattern for all short vowels.

When beginning the study of short vowels, plan contrasts that are fairly distinct from each other. We recommend that students compare short-a to short-i or short-o. Do not try to move directly from a short-a to a short-e or from a short-e to a short-i since those are the very sounds students are most likely to confuse. Save these contrasts for later. Picture sorts such as the one shown in Figure 6-5 can be revisited at this point to focus students' attention on the vowel sounds. Pictures for this purpose can be found in the appendix.

Be prepared to spend some time on short vowels as they pose special problems for young spellers and persist as problems beyond first grade. However, short vowels will be reviewed when they are compared to long vowels in the next stage so do not expect 100% accuracy.

Word sorting to compare two or more short vowels.   Most sorting for short vowels will be done with words. Consider what words your students already know from familiar texts and word bank words. Lists of CVC and CVCC words spelled with short vowels can be found in the word lists in the appendix and can be used to create

handouts like the one in Figure 6-1C. Additional short vowel words can be selected from the word family lists. Here is the basic procedure for sorting words by short vowels:

1. Make a collection of word cards to model the sort on a tabletop, pocket chart, or overhead projector.
2. Model the sort with a group of students. Begin by laying down a well-known word as a header for each vowel. Read each word and isolate the vowel by saying something like this: "Here is the word *cap*. Listen, *cap, ap, a*. We will listen for other words that have the same vowel sound in the middle." Repeat for each category.
3. Pick up a new word such as *fast* and say something like this: "I am going to put this word under *cap*. Listen, *cap, fast*." Continue to model one or two words in each category, reading each new word and comparing it to the header.
4. Invite students to try sorting next. Correct any errors made during the first sort. The final sort might look something like this:

cap	pig	hot
fast	ship	stop
camp	fish	lock
hat	sit	shop
mad	hill	job
trap	him	not

5. After all the words have been sorted, lead a discussion to focus your students' attention on the common features in each word: "How are the words in each column alike?"
6. Reread the words in each column and then lead the students in sorting a second time. Any mistakes should be left until the end and checked by reading down the columns.
7. Students should be given their own set of words to sort at their seats, with partners, or for homework.
8. Appropriate follow-up routines include buddy sorting, writing sorts, word hunts, games, and so on. Since it is easy to simply sort the words visually by attending to the vowel letters, the **buddy sort** described in Chapter 4 is particularly important as a follow-up activity. Model this **sound sort** first in the group and then let partners work together. One partner reads each word aloud while the other partner indicates where it goes without seeing the word.

If students are still making errors in the spelling of blends and digraphs, which is very likely, include words that have those features in the short vowel sorts. At this time, they have many more sight words that contain beginning and ending consonant blends and digraphs. Preconsonantal nasals can also be included in this study. You might even plan a sort that can be sorted two ways, first by vowel sounds and second by blends or digraphs:

First Sort by Vowel			Second Sort by Blends		
trap	trick	drug	trap	drag	crack
crack	trip	crumb	track	drip	crash
drag	trim	truck	trick	drum	crumb
crash	drip	drum	trim	drill	crab
track	crib	crush	truck		crib
crab	drill				crush

Sorts such as the preceding one help students see that the CVC pattern encompasses two-letter consonant units that work the same way as single consonants. Lead discussions that help students see that these words all have a similar pattern—a single vowel surrounded by one or more consonants. This pattern will be more fully understood as students begin to contrast it with long vowel patterns in the next stage. Here is a sort that focuses on the expanded idea of the CVC pattern across these consonant units:

Single Consonants	Double Initial	Double Final	Double Initial and Final
hot	shop	lost	block
job	stop	pond	clock
rob	chop	sock	stomp
top		soft	

During the study of short vowels is a good time to establish the **oddball** or miscellaneous category. This category will accommodate variations in dialect and spelling. Some children may hear a short-o in *frost,* but others will hear a sound closer to /aw/. Some children hear a different vowel in *pin* and *pen,* but others consider them homophones. Rather than forcing students to doubt their own ear, the oddball category offers an alternative and acknowledges that people do not all speak quite the same way nor does spelling always match pronunciation. Some words, which initially go in the oddball category, will become regular categories of their own after enough words are accumulated.

Further Study of Vowels at the End of the Letter Name–Alphabetic Stage

Words like *car* and *ball* look as though they follow the CVC pattern but they do not have the short-a sound. Because words spelled with *ar* and *all* are common in beginning reading materials, it is worthwhile to spend some time with them. *R*-controlled vowels form a major subcategory of vowels that will need to be examined closely during the next stage. For now these words can be treated as word families and added to short vowel sorts as oddballs that challenge students to listen carefully for the sounds and not just attend to the letters they see. Here is a special sort that might examine words with a single *a* in the middle:

Short-a	ar	all	Oddballs
clap	car	ball	saw
jam	star	hall	was
black	park	fall	
sand	yard	stall	
camp	jar	call	

This chapter has presented many examples of teacher-directed sorts or **closed sorts.** The teacher selects the words and leads a group sorting activity accompanied by a discussion of the features of interest. Student-centered sorts or **open sorts** as described in Chapter 4 allow students to establish their own categories, and offer the teacher diagnostic information that will help to determine how much students understand about the orthography.

Figure 6-6 is an open sort by a student in the late letter name–alphabetic stage. Jeff was asked to go through his word bank, find the word cards that had an *a* in them, and sort them into categories. His first sort resulted in three categories: short-a, long-a, and a large pile of miscellaneous words. He was then challenged to take the miscellaneous words and sort them into a number of piles. His new categories include short-a, *l*-controlled, broad-a, *r*-controlled, schwa, and long-a. Figure 6-6 shows that Jeff has developed quite a good ear for vowel sounds and understands that *a* is used to represent a variety of sounds.

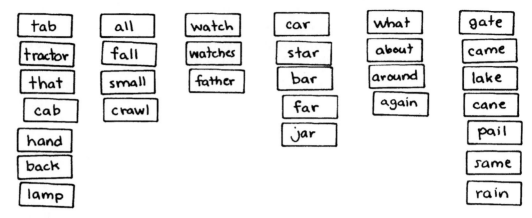

FIGURE 6-6   Jeff's Open Sort

Routines and Pacing for the Letter Name–Alphabetic Stage

Word study during the letter name–alphabetic stage begins with picture sorts for initial sounds and ends with word sorts for short vowels. During this transition there are a variety of routines and generic activities to help students explore features of study in depth (see Chapter 4). Betty Lee's schedule is particularly appropriate for students who are doing picture sorts, and the schedule for primary children has ideas for routines that work well with the study of word families and short vowels. Word study notebooks can be started at any stage, but work best when word study involves the reading and writing of words as in the study of word families and short vowels.

In the letter name–alphabetic stage there is much to cover, so you might want to create 2- or 3-day cycles. For example, you might introduce two word families on Monday, another two on Wednesday, and then combine them both for several days. Pacing is an important issue. There are many blends and many word families and if every one were studied in depth it could take many months. Be ready to pick up the pace by combining a number of blends or families into one sort (up to four or five) or by omitting some features altogether. Only your own observations can dictate the particular pace appropriate for your students.

The letter name–alphabetic stage easily spans kindergarten through second grade as children master the reading and spelling of beginning sounds, blends and digraphs, and short vowels. While most achieving students will be through the stage by at least the middle of second grade, a handful of students in third grade and even a few students in grades four through six will still need to work on the features that characterize this stage. It may be tempting to rush through this stage, but word study in the letter name–alphabetic stage helps to build a solid foundation for the study of long vowels and other vowel patterns in the next stage.

Activities for Beginning Readers in the Letter Name– Alphabetic Stage

In this section specific activities for students in the letter name–alphabetic stage have been organized into several categories:

1. The development and use of personal readers and word banks
2. The review of initial sounds including digraphs and blends
3. The study of word families
4. The study of short vowels

These categories begin with ideas for supporting beginning readers and continue with word study games and activities that correspond to the hierarchy of features students study through picture and word sorts. Some of the games and activities are generic and can be adapted to a variety of features at different stages. These are indicated by the generic symbol 📖

THE DEVELOPMENT AND USE OF PERSONAL READERS AND WORD BANKS

Harvesting Words for Word Banks 6–1

Students need to have a stock of sight words that they can read with ease. The following activities help students develop and maintain a word bank. Through the use of familiar rhymes and small-group and individual dictations, students begin to harvest sight words.

Materials

1. Copies of personal readers, dictations, familiar books, and so on.
2. Blank word cards. Tagboard and index cards can be cut to a size that is large enough to hold easily, yet small enough so that students can work with them on a desktop when sorting—1¼ by 3 inches is about right. Teachers can also

select words from a story or poem read by a group of students and create a sheet of words that can be reproduced and cut apart. These words can then be quickly handed out as students identify them.

3. Something in which to store words for each child. The word bank is kept in a manila envelope, a box, a small margarine container, a can, or a fast-food container. Plastic and metal index card file boxes are nice to have if they are available. When file boxes are at a premium, you can start with margarine containers for the first 50 words and then move to a box. At any given time in either a first or second grade classroom, there are no more than a third of the students who need these smaller containers, and a third who need the larger boxes. In first grade, there may be as many as two thirds of the class who use margarine containers for their long-term word banks.

Procedures

There are several ways to harvest words for the word bank:

1. *From personal readers.* If students have an individual copy of dictations, jingles, parts of stories, and so on, they can simply be asked to underline the words they know. Many children will be tempted to underline every word, but over time they will begin to understand the procedure and realize they need to be selective and underline only words they really know. Suggesting that they scan through the text backwards can help some children find known words more accurately.

A teacher, assistant, or classroom volunteer points to the underlined words in a random fashion to check if the child can indeed name the word quickly. Known words are then written on word cards. Who does the writing is something of a personal choice. Having an adult write the word will ensure that it is neat and accurate. The student can be asked to spell it aloud as the adult writes. On the back of each card write the number of the page in the personal reader. This will make it possible for the children to go back and use context clues to name the word if they forget it. The children can be asked to write their initials on the back of each card in case words get mixed up during word bank activities.

2. *From familiar books.* Students can also collect sight words independently from books they have read. Some of the words from the book are put on word cards that are stored in a library pocket in the back of the book. After reading the text, students are taught to read through the words in the pocket to see which ones they know at sight. Students write the words they know onto their own cards which are placed in their word banks. Unknown words are matched back to their counterpart in the text.

3. *From any text.* The easiest procedure for harvesting words is to simply ask the children to point to words in a book or from a chart that they would like to put in their word bank. After several words have been written on cards, the teacher or helper can hold them up to check for recognition.

Variations

To ensure that unknown words do not enter students' word banks, a short-term word bank can be developed as a holding spot for words students want to harvest into their permanent or long-term word banks. A short-term word bank can be made from a 6-by-8-inch envelope or small plastic bag stored inside students' personal readers (see Figure 6-4). These envelopes are for words students recognize from the latest stories and dictations. Periodically, sometimes once a week or when new materials are added to students' personal readers, teachers work with students in small groups to have them read through the words in their **short-term word banks.** Words they know from memory go into the permanent word bank.

Collecting Individual Dictations and Group Experience Stories 6-2

Recording students' individual or group dictations as they talk about personal or group experiences is a key feature of the language experience approach or LEA (Stauffer, 1980). The text created makes especially good reading material for beginning readers because it is inherently familiar and easy to remember. When dictations are collected in groups, up to 10 children contribute one or two sentences, but dictations need to be kept to a reasonable length to be sure beginning readers will be able to read them back. This activity is divided into a 4-day sequence, but it can be accomplished in fewer days with smaller groups.

Materials

Chart paper, overhead projector, computer, or other way to record dictation so that students can observe as the teacher writes.

Procedures

Day 1: Share an experience and collect dictations.

Find a stimulus (a box turtle, fall leaves, parts of a flashlight) or experience (a trip to the bakery, a classroom visitor, the first snowfall) to share with students. It should be an interesting and memorable experience that encourages students to talk. For some individual dictations, students can be prompted to tell a personal experience without a prop or special event.

After a discussion that stimulates ideas and vocabulary, ask each student to tell you something to write down. Say each word as you write it and invite the group to help decide some of the letters or spellings you need. Talk about conventions such as capitals and punctuation. Reread each sentence and make any changes the speaker requests. Decide on a title at the end as a kind of summary of the ideas. Then reread the entire dictation. Reread it again as the students read along with you in a **choral reading** fashion. Then have them repeat after you, sentence by sentence in the manner of **echo reading,** as you point to each word.

Before day 2, make a copy of the dictation for each child in the group. Computers make it easy to create these copies. Select a font that has the type of letters easily recognized by young readers and enlarge it as much as possible. Without a computer it is still easy to make copies by writing neatly in your best manuscript handwriting. These copies will go into each child's personal reader and should be numbered.

Day 2: Reread dictations and underline known words.

Choral read the dictation again on day 2 and encourage the students to follow along on their own copies, pointing to words as they read. Individual children can be called on to read a sentence. Once children can read the dictation successfully, they are invited to underline known words for their word bank. You can point to the underlined words randomly to make sure they know the words they underline. Students might also make an illustration to go with the dictation.

Day 3: Choral read and make word cards of known words.

Students can work together or individually to read the dictation again. Make word cards for underlined words that are recognized accurately and quickly.

Day 4 and on: Choral read and review new word cards.

Students continue to reread their dictations, review the words in their word banks, and complete their pictures. A new dictation or story cycle is begun when students can read their new readings with good accuracy and modest fluency.

In our Reading Buddies tutoring programs, students have personal readers that they take with them back and forth from the tutoring sessions to their classrooms. Students also take the personal readers home, where they show their parents how to offer support when they read, and how the parent should check them on their word bank words, go on word hunts, and sort words and pictures (Caserta-Henry, Bear, & Del Porto, 1997). In Book Buddies, tutors store the personal readers in their tutoring boxes (Johnston, Invernizzi, & Juel, 1998).

Support Reading With Rhymes and Pattern Stories 6-3

Rhymes and jingles and predictable patterned texts make good reading materials because they provide support for beginning readers and can then be used to harvest known words for word banks.

Materials

Find a rhyme, jingle, or predictable story that students will find memorable and readable. You can focus on one major pattern or verse. Find a big book or make a chart or overhead of the text for group work, and make copies of the rhymes and patterns for students' personal readers.

Procedures

Day 1: Introduce and read the text.

Talk about the title and cover and look at the pictures (if applicable) with the students for information about the rhyme or pattern story. Read the rhyme or story to students, running a finger underneath the text. Read fluently and with expression but not too fast. Stop periodically to discuss and enjoy the story. Lead students to reflect on the story by asking general questions like: "What did you think of the story? What was your favorite part?" Ask students to help you return to a few favorite pages. Reread these parts of the text and point to a few words to see if some students are able to recognize words at sight. Invite students to **choral** or **echo** read the entire text if it is short or parts of the text. Decide which parts of the text will be compiled for personal readers. Type the text onto a single page or two that can be duplicated for each child. Number and date this entry.

Days 2, 3, and 4: Reread the rhyme or story and harvest words for word bank.

The same procedures described in Activity 6-2 for dictations can be done as follow-ups for rhymes and predictable text. Sentences from the text can also be written on sentence strips, and the students can work to rebuild the text in a pocket chart.

The Grand Sort With Word Bank Words 6-4

This is an important sort in which students review their individual word banks. In this sort, students simply go through their word cards, saying the words they know, putting them in one pile, and placing the unknown words to the side. The student tries to move quickly through the pile. The words that students put in the "I know" pile can be used in subsequent sorts.

The unknown words can be discarded, but this can be a touchy point for some students who are hesitant to throw away words. There is no harm in letting a few temporarily unknown words remain, but the big mistake is when a student proceeds to another word study activity with a number of unknown words. Working with so many unknown words makes students' work hesitant, prone to errors, and frustrating.

Students in the early letter name–alphabetic stage do not have the word knowledge they need to sound out unknown words, so the teacher should show them how to figure out an unknown word by using context. Referring to the number on the back of the card, the students return to their personal reader and find the word. Their familiarity with the story and the context usually ensures that they can figure out the unknown word. Since this procedure can be time consuming it is important that only a small percent of words in a word bank are unknown.

Variations

Students can do this sort under the teacher's supervision, with a partner or classroom volunteer, or independently. This is a good opportunity for heterogeneous groups.

Reviewing Word Bank Words 6–5

There are other ways to review and work with the words in the word bank.

1. *The Pick-up game.* Lay out a collection of 5 to 10 words faceup. Those words that the student does not know or frequently confuses are good candidates. A teacher, assistant, classroom volunteer, or another student calls out the words randomly for the student to find and pick up.
2. *I'm Thinking Of.* This is similar to Pick-up but the student is given clues instead of words: "I am thinking of a word that rhymes with *pet*" or "I am thinking of a word that starts like *play.*"
3. *Concentration.* Make a second set of words and play this classic game as described in Activity 5-12.
4. *Word hunts.* Students look through their word banks for words that have a particular feature: words that start with *t,* words that end in *m,* words that have an *o* in them, and so on.
5. *Concept sorts.* Students look through their word banks for words that fit given semantic categories: words that are animals, words that are people, color words, things in a house, and so on. An example of a concept sort is shown in Figure 6-7.

Note: You might want to keep a supply of low-tension rubber bands or library card envelopes to wrap or store selected words. In this way, word sorts can be started on one day and continued on the following day.

Alphabetizing Word Banks 6–6

Materials

Make a large alphabet strip up to 6 feet long (see Figure 6-8) and laminate it.

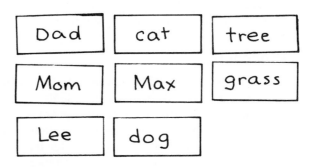

FIGURE 6-7   Concept Sort

FIGURE 6–8   Alphabetizing With an Alphabet Strip

Procedures

A student lays out the alphabet strip and using his or her word bank words, places the words under the beginning letter.

Variations

1. Pictures can be included.
2. Later students can alphabetize by second and third letters.

ACTIVITIES FOR BEGINNING SOUNDS, INCLUDING DIGRAPHS AND BLENDS

A number of activities or games in Chapter 5 are appropriate for students in the letter name–alphabetic stage working to master single consonants, digraphs, and blends: Soundline (5-29), Letter Spin for Sounds (5-30), Object Sorting by Sounds (5-31), and Follow-the-Path Games (5-32). Concentration is another game that can be adapted. Any two pictures that begin with the same sound(s) make a match that can be claimed.

Sound Boards 6–7

Sound boards are references for letter-sound features and can be found in the appendix. They provide a key word and picture for each letter-sound match, helping students internalize the associations. There are sound boards for beginning consonants, blends and digraphs, and vowels in the appendix.

Procedures

1. A copy of the sound boards can be placed at the front of students' writing folders. These boards make it easy for students to find letters to stand for the sounds they want to use. Reduced copies of relevant sound boards can be taped to students' desks.
2. Teachers often post charts of various letter-sound features. Recently, the new technology of chart printers has made it possible to take the individual sound boards and enlarge them to poster size. The sound board posters can be displayed in a prominent place in primary classrooms. This gives beginning writers the opportunity to refer to the enlarged sound boards for the letters of a word they want to write.

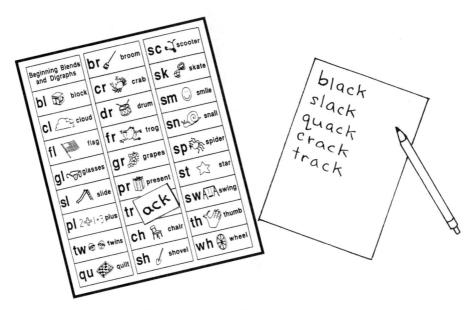

FIGURE 6-9   Expanding a Word Family Using a Sound Board

3. A sound board can serve as a word study record. In Figure 4-1 a sound board is part of a student's word study folder. Students can indicate which features they have studied by coloring the boxes lightly.

4. Sound boards can be used to generate more words to add to a word family. The **rime** of the family is written on a small card and slid down beside the beginning sounds. In Figure 6-9 the word family *ack* has been expanded by the addition of many different blends and digraphs.

Word Hunts 6-8

Word hunts can be done several different ways and at different times in the letter name–alphabetic stage.

Procedures

1. In the early letter name–alphabetic stage, students hunt for words that begin with the particular initial consonants, blends, or digraphs they are studying. They should look for words they know in familiar reading materials such as their personal reader or by going through their own word banks. Word hunts can be done independently, with a partner, or in small groups.

2. Students can also hunt for pictures that correspond to beginning sounds. Pictures can be cut out of magazines or catalogs and pasted onto individual papers, group charts, or into alphabet books. When hunting for pictures, it helps if the teacher, aide, or student helper rips out pages on which there are pictures that contain the feature being hunted. Students can be asked to label the pictures they find by spelling as best they can.

3. Students can also hunt for words or pictures that sound like the short vowel they are studying. For example, a student could be asked to find words that sound like "red" in the middle.

4. Word hunts can be made into a game when teams of two or three students hunt for words in a given time period. Students read the words to the teacher or group.

5. One to three students can walk around the room hunting for words they know. Students write down the words they find that are in their word banks.

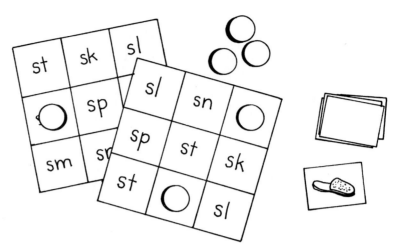

FIGURE 6-10   Blend Bingo Boards

Initial Sound Bingo 6–9

In this version of Bingo, students discriminate among the initial sounds. This is another generic activity that can be expanded to consonant blends, digraphs, and vowels.

Materials

Make Bingo cards with 9 or 16 squares. In each square write a letter(s) that features the sounds students have been studying in sorts (see Figure 6-10). You also need Bingo markers and picture cards to match sounds.

Procedures

Work in a center or with small groups of two to four children. Each student gets a Bingo card and markers. Students take turns drawing a card from the stack and calling out the picture name. Students place a marker on the corresponding square. Play continues until someone gets Bingo.

Gruff Drops Troll at Bridge 6–10

This is a special version of the basic follow-the-path game that reinforces r-blends.* It was developed after reading Paul Galdone's *The Three Billy Goats Gruff.* This book was part of a class study of books about monsters. Many of the books yielded a great crop of consonant-plus-*r* words such as *growl, groan,* and *fright.* These were sorted into categories by beginning blends.

Materials

Manila folder with a game path filled in with consonant-plus-*r* blend letters (as shown in Figure 6-11), four button markers, and picture cards of the features being studied. Follow-the-path templates and directions for preparing the boards can be found in the appendix.

*Esther Heatley developed this board game as a literature extension.

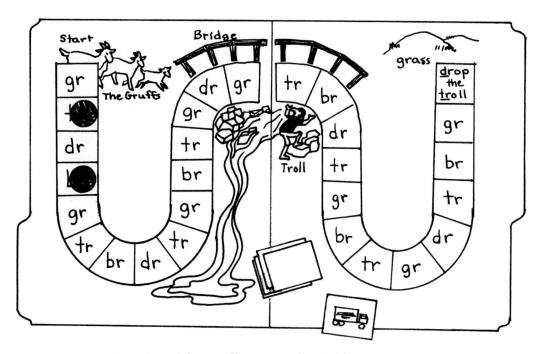

FIGURE 6-11   Gameboard for Gruff Drops Troll at Bridge

Procedures

1. Each player selects a button marker. Students turn over picture cards containing the consonant-plus-*r* blend pictures. Players move the marker to the correct space as turns are taken.
2. Winner drops the troll from the bridge by drawing a picture that begins with *dr* (for *drop*) for the last space.

Sea World Diorama 6-11

Students create a sea world diorama while they study the *sh* digraph.

Materials

Pictures and things that begin with *s* and *sh*. To make a diorama, students will need a shoe box, construction paper, colorful tissue paper, glue, scissors, markers, sand, and tiny shells or cut-up natural sponges.

Procedures

1. After sorting pictures that begin with *s* and *sh*, have students think of animals and things in the sea that begin with those sounds and make a list of them. Here is an abbreviated list: starfish, seals, sea horses, sunfish, swordfish, scuba divers, sunken ships, sea snakes, sharks, sea anemone, seaweed, sponges, shrimp, and shells.*
2. Introduce students to how a diorama is constructed (see Figure 6-12).
3. Students find or draw and cut out pictures of things that belong in the sea and begin with *s* and *sh*. Students might work in groups to glue, tape, or hang these items in their shoe boxes. Small shells or some natural sponges add decoration. Cover the bottom of the "sea" with sand.

---

*Cindy Booth developed this activity.

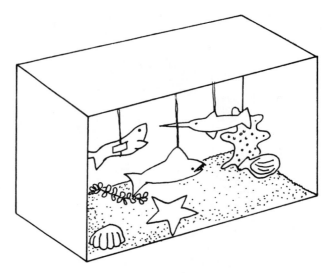

FIGURE 6-12   A Diorama for Sea World

Variations

Expand the sea diorama with sea blends (e.g., *st, sc, sw*) or create other types of dioramas. Similar books can be used. Elizabeth Schuett recommends *Sheep on a Ship* by Nancy Shaw.

Match! 6–12

In this game, similar to the card game War, students look for matches of the beginning sounds they have recently studied.

Materials

Create a set of cards that feature pictures with four to eight different beginning sounds. Include at least four pictures for each sound. Pictures can be copied from the appendix, glued on cardstock, and laminated.

Procedures

Each student has half the deck of pictures. Students turn a picture card faceup from their deck at the same time. If the pictures begin with the same sound, the first person to recognize and say "match!" gets the pair. If the pictures do not match, another set is turned over until a match occurs. There can be penalties for calling out "match" carelessly.

Variations

This game can be played with word families, short vowels, and long vowel patterns.

Beginning and End Dominoes 6–13

This is a picture sort to match initial and final consonants (e.g., *lamp* matches *pig*).

Materials

Pictures for these matches can be found in the appendix. Wendy Brown put together a fine list of words. Divide a 2-by-4-inch card in half and paste a picture from each of the following pairs on each side.

ghost-tub	book-leg	gate-pin	nurse-goat	ten-log
dishes-map	pencil-bed	desk-mop	pig-nut	tent-bed
rain-dog	goat-zip	pin-sit	tie-mad	door-pear
two-hat	toes-road	doll-sick	key-lips	seal-boat
pen-bug	gas-sun	net-belt	tail-sink	kite-jeep

Procedures

Students are given a set of five pairs mixed up and challenged to match the pairs as in the traditional game of dominoes.

Variations

Students compete to make the longest string they can with a collection of pictures. For example, tub/book-kite/toad-doll/lip-pig/game-mad/door-rope/pen.

ACTIVITIES FOR THE STUDY OF WORD FAMILIES

Once students begin the study of word families, they are expected to read and spell the words they sort. Many word games can be adapted as follow-up activities for word sorting and there are some activities that are especially designed to enhance students' understandings of how families work.

Word Family Wheels and Flip Charts 6–14

Wheels and flip charts, as shown in Figure 6-13, are fun for students to play with independently or with partners. The wheels and flip charts are used to reinforce the patterns. Prior to using the wheels and charts, students have worked in small groups to sort words from the various families.

Materials

To make word family wheels, follow these three steps:

1. Cut two 6-inch circles from tagboard. Cut a wedge from one circle and write the vowel and ending consonants or rime to the right of it. Make a round hole in the center.
2. On the second tagboard circle, write beginning sounds that form words with that family. For example, the *op* family can be formed with *b, c, h, l, m, p, s, t, ch, sh, cl,* and *st.*

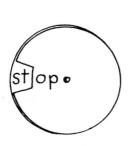

FIGURE 6-13   Word Family Wheel and Flip Book

This student uses word maker cards to study blends.

Space the letters evenly around the outside edge so that only one at a time will show through the "window" wedge. Cut a slit in the middle of the circle.

3. Put the circle with the wedge on top of the other circle. Push a brass fastener through the round hole and the slit. Flatten the fastener, making sure the top circle can turn.

To make flip books:

1. Use a piece of tagboard or lightweight cardboard for the base of the flip book. Write the family or rime on the right half of the base.
2. Cut pages that are half the length of the base piece and staple to the left side of the base. Write beginning sounds or onsets on each one.

Variation

Students can draw a picture to go with each word.

Show Me 6–15

This activity is a favorite with teachers who are teaching word families and short vowels.*

Materials

Make each student an individual pocket to hold letter cards. To make a pocket, cut paper into rectangles about 7 by 5 inches. Fold up 1 inch along the 7-inch side, then fold the whole thing into overlapping thirds. Staple at the edges to make three pockets (see Figure 6-14). Cut additional paper into cards 1½ by 4 inches to make 14 for each student.

---

*This excellent activity is attributed to Margery Beatty who taught in the Waynesboro, Virginia, Public Schools many years ago.

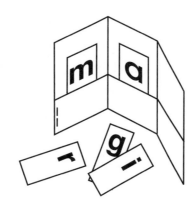

FIGURE 6-14 *"Show Me" Game*

Print letters on the top half of each card making sure the entire letter is visible when inserted in the pocket. A useful assortment of letters for this activity includes the five short vowels and *b, d, f, g, m, n, p, r,* and *t.* Too many consonants can be hard to manage.

Procedures

Each student gets a pocket and an assortment of letter cards. When the teacher or designated caller names a word, the students put the necessary letters in the spaces and fold up their pockets. When "show me" is announced, everyone opens their pocket at once for the teacher to see. The emphasis is on practice, not competition, but points for accuracy could be kept if desired.

Start with words having the same families such as *bad, sad,* or *mad,* where the students focus primarily on changing the initial consonants. Move on to a different family and different vowels. For example, you could follow this sequence: *mad, mat, hat, hot, pot, pet.*

Variations

1. The Show Me pockets are used just for beginning sounds and/or ending sounds.
2. Long vowel patterns are spelled using a four-pocket folder.

Word Maker With Initial Consonants, Blends, and Digraphs 6–16

Students match blends and digraphs with word families to make words.*

Materials

Create a collection of cards that have onsets on half (single consonants, blends, and digraphs) and common short vowel rimes on the other. For students in the later letter name–alphabetic stage, include rimes with ending blends, digraphs, and preconsonantal nasals such as *ish, ash, ush, ing, ang, ast, ust, ank, ink, ump, amp, ack, ell,* and *all.*

Procedures

1. Each student begins by drawing five cards from the deck. With the five cards faceup, each student tries to create words as shown in Figure 6-15.

---

*Katherine Preston contributed to this activity.

FIGURE 6-15 Word Maker Cards

2. Once the students have made one or two words from their first five cards they begin taking turns drawing cards from the deck. Every time they make a word they can draw two more cards. If they cannot make a word they draw one card.
3. Play continues until all the letter cards are used up. The player with the most words is the winner.

Variations

Students can work independently with the word maker cards to generate and record as many words as possible.

Sorting R-Influenced Vowels 6–17

The *r* has a distinct influence on the pronunciation of words. The sounds of the vowels often differ from similar words, for example, *bar* and *bat.* In the appendix there are sample sorts for *r*-influenced words.*

Procedures

1. The best way to study the influence of *r* is to brainstorm or hunt for any and all words containing a single vowel followed by an *r*. The only rule is that there can be no *e* at the end. Any word that your students can recognize is fair game. A student-generated word list might look like this: *farm, nerd, firm, form, fur, far, perm, fir, for, hard, herd, first, cord, word, war, hurt, turn, dart, term, bird, dirt, world, born, curd.*
2. Start with a sound sort. Choose three words that are distinguishable by sound. In the brainstorming used in this example, *car, her,* and *for* represent three distinct sounds and could be used as the guide words at the top of three columns.
3. Call out the other words, one at a time, and have students judge which category to place them in using sound as the sole criterion. After the students have made the decision as to which category, give one of them the word card to place in the proper column (see Figure 6-16). They will notice that most words that sound like *car* are consistently spelled only with the *ar* pattern.

Roll the Dice 6–18

This game is for two to four players. It reinforces word families and builds automaticity.

---

*Neva Viise contributed this sort from her work with adults.

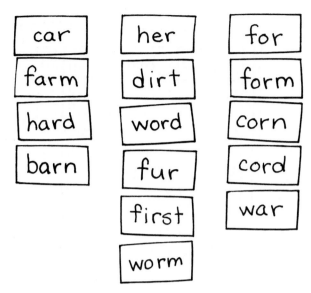

FIGURE 6-16   An *R*-influenced Word Sort

Materials

You need a cube on which to write four contrasting word families, for example, *an, ap, ag,* and *at.* A blank side is labeled *lose a turn,* and another is labeled *roll again* (see Figure 6-17). You will also need a blackboard or paper for recording words.

FIGURE 6-17   Cube for Roll the Dice Game

Procedures

Students roll the die. If it lands on a word family space, the student must come up with a word for that family and record it on chalkboard or paper. Students keep their own lists and can use a word only once—although someone else may have used it. If a player is stumped or lands on *lose a turn,* the die is passed to the next person. If the student lands on *roll,* he or she rolls again. The person who records the most words at the end of the allotted time wins.

Variations

1. Play with two dice and have two teams for a relay. Each team has a recorder. The first person of each team rolls the dice and quickly calls out an appropriate word. The recorder records the words on the board. The player hands the dice over to the next player and goes quickly to the end of the line. With this variation you would not need to lose a turn or roll again.
2. This game can also be used with vowel patterns, beginning consonants, or blends.

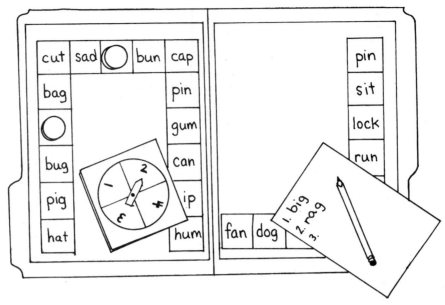

FIGURE 6-18   Gameboard for Word Families

Rhyming Families 6-19

Materials

Prepare a follow-the-path gameboard like the one shown in Figure 6-18. You will also need a single die or a spinner, pieces to move around the board, pencils, and paper for each player. Directions for making gameboards and spinners as well as gameboard templates are in the appendix. Write a word from each word family you have been studying in each space on the board. You can also write in special directions like *roll again, free space, go back 2 spaces, write two words,* and so on.

Procedures

The object is to make new words to rhyme with words on the gameboard that do not match the other players'.

1. Spin to determine who goes first. Play proceeds clockwise.
2. The first player spins and moves the number of places indicated on the spinner.
3. The player reads the word in the space where he or she lands. All players write a rhyming word by changing initial letter(s). Players number their words as they go. Play continues until someone reaches the end of the path.
4. Beginning with the player who reaches the end first, each player reads the first word on his or her list. Players who have a word that does not match the other players' words get to circle their word. For example, if players have *cat, bat, cat,* and *splat,* only the players having *bat* and *splat* would circle their words. Continue until all words have been compared.
5. Each circle is worth one point, plus the player who reaches the end first receives two extra points. The winner is the one with the most points.

Variations

Label each space on the gameboard with the rime of a family you have studied (*at, an, ad, ack*). Use no more than five different rimes and repeat them around the path. Prepare a set of cards that have short vowel pictures that correspond to the families. Students

FIGURE 6-19 *Playing Cards for Go Fish*

move around the board by selecting a picture and moving to the space it matches. For example, a student who has a picture of a hat would move to the next space with *at* written on it.

Go Fish 6–20

This classic game has been adapted to word study and can be played by two to four players. This version can be used as a review of word families.

Materials

Create decks of blank cards with four words from different word family words written on them. For example: *that, bat, fat,* and *hat* are written on four cards. Write each word at the top of the card so that the words are visible when held in the hand as shown in Figure 6-19.

Procedures

1. Five cards are dealt to each player and the remainder placed in the middle as a pool from which to draw. The first player asks any other player for a match to a card in her hand: "Give me all your words that rhyme with *hat.*" If she receives a matching card, she may put the pair down and ask for another card. If the other player does not have the card requested, he tells the first player to "go fish," which means that she must draw a card from the "fish pond." The first player's turn is over when she can no longer make a match.
2. Play continues around the circle until one player runs out of cards. Points can be won by the first person to go out and by the person who has the most matching cards.

Variations

Go Fish can be adapted for beginning sounds and blends using pictures, or it can be used with vowel patterns.*

---

*Janet Bloodgood adapted this word study game from the familiar game of Go Fish.

ACTIVITIES FOR SHORT VOWELS

Once students are automatic with word families it is time to study short vowels in non-rhyming CVC words. After this feature has been explored through word sorts and weekly routines, games can provide additional practice.

Hopping Frog Game 6–21

This game for two to four players reviews all five short vowels.*

Materials

1. Use a gameboard or make your own course with a manila folder. Cut green circle lily pads for each space and write CVC words students have used in word sorts on each one (e.g., *pin, get, hot, bad, leg, run, bug, wish*).
2. You'll need four frog markers. The spinner is marked into five sections, with a vowel and illustrating picture in each (*a*, apple; *e*, ten; *i*, fish; *o*, frog; *u*, sun). See the appendix for directions on how to make a spinner. Figure 6-20 shows you a sample board for the game.

---

*This game was developed by Janet Bloodgood and has become a favorite.

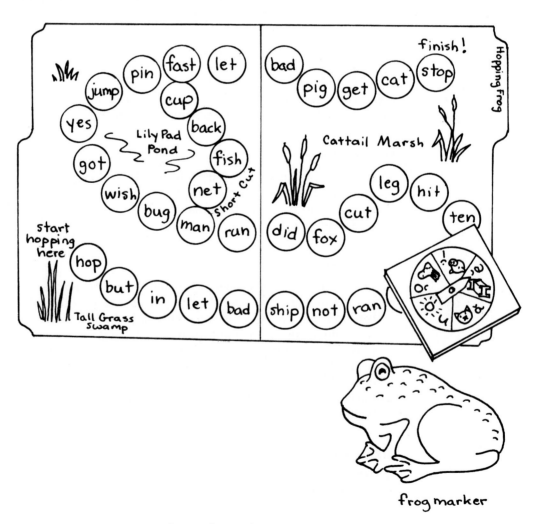

FIGURE 6-20   Frog Marker and Hopping Frog Game

Procedures

Each child selects a frog marker. Players take turns spinning, and place their marker on the first word that matches the vowel sound they land on (e.g., *e, get*). They then pronounce this word and must say another word with the same vowel sound to stay on that space. The next player then spins and plays. The first player who can finish the course and hop a frog off the board wins.

Variations

1. Students can write down the words they land on and organize them in columns by short vowel.
2. The same game plan could be used for long vowel patterns and inflected endings.

Making-Words-With-Cubes Game 6–22

Short vowel words are built with letter cubes in this game and it can be used for many other vowels as well.

Materials

Letter cubes that can be found in many games (Boggle and Perquackery) are needed. Playing pieces can also be made from blank wooden cubes. Write all the vowels on one cube to be sure that a vowel always lands faceup. Put a variety of consonants on five or six other cubes. (Pairs like *qu* and *ck* might be written together.) The students need a sand clock or timer, paper and pencil, and a record sheet such as the one shown in Figure 6-21.

Procedures

1. In pairs, students take turns being the player and the recorder. The recorder writes the words made by the player.
2. Letters are shaken and spilled out onto the table and the timer is started.
3. The word maker moves the cubes about to create words and spells them to the scribe. The letters can be moved around to make more words. Errors should be ignored at this point. Write the words in columns by the number of letters in the words.

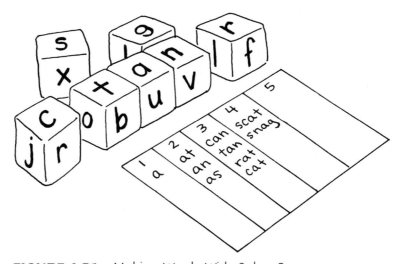

FIGURE 6-21 *Making-Words-With-Cubes Game*

4. At the end of the timer the students review the words and check for accuracy. Words are then scored. Count up the total number of letters used. Multiplication can be used (e.g., four 3-letter words = 12). Students soon realize that the bigger the words they make, the greater their score.

Variation

Students in the within word pattern stage should work with two vowel cubes. On a second cube, write vowel markers such as *e* (put two or three), *a, i,* and *o.*

The Bug Race 6–23

This is a variation of the basic follow-the-path game and reviews any combination of short vowels. This example uses a bug theme but it can be adapted to many other themes such as the zoo, space travel, comic characters, or vehicles. Use stickers and cutouts to add interest to the basic path templates found in the appendix.

Materials

Use one of the follow-the-path gameboards and label the spaces with *a, e, i, o,* or *u.* Add pictures of leaves, grass, and so on to make it resemble a bug's world. Make copies of short vowel pictures on tagboard and cut them apart or paste paper copies of the pictures onto cards. It is important that the pictures do not show through the card. On several additional cards write commands such as *skip a turn, go back 2 spaces,* and *move ahead 3 spaces.* Make bug-like playing pieces from bottle caps by drawing in eyes, antennae, and spots with a permanent fine-tip marker.

Procedures

1. Shuffle the picture and command cards and turn them facedown in a pile. The players move around the board by turning over a picture and moving their playing piece to the next free space on the board that has the corresponding short vowel.
2. The student who reaches the end first is the winner.

Variation

Long vowel pictures can be used for students in the within word pattern stage.

The Spelling Game 6–24

This is another variation of the basic follow-the-path game that works as a follow-up to word sorts for short vowel words.

Materials

Use one of the follow-the-path templates in the appendix. Make reduced copies of short vowel pictures (about half size or 50% should work). Cut the pictures out and paste them in the spaces on the game path. Use two, three, four, or all five short vowels. You will also need playing pieces to move along the path and a spinner or single die. In some spaces you can write *roll again, go back 2 spaces,* and so on. Include a card on which all the words are written in the same order they are pasted to settle any arguments about spelling.

FIGURE 6-22 Slider for Slide-a-Word

Procedures

1. Students take turns spinning for a number. Before they can move to the space indicated by the spinner, they must correctly spell the word pictured. If they cannot spell the word, they must stay where they are for their turn.
2. The student who reaches the end first is the winner.

Variations

Any pictures can be pasted on the gameboard. Long vowel pictures can be used for students in the within word pattern stage.

Slide-a-Word 6–25

Students can be asked to list and then read all the CVC words they are able to generate using the slider created by Jeradi Cohen and shown in Figure 6-22. As different short vowels are studied, the central vowel letter can be changed.

Materials

Tagboard or posterboard, ruler, marker, single-edge razor blade, and scissors.

Procedures

1. Cut a piece of tagboard or posterboard into strips 8½ by 2½ inches. Using the razor, cut a pair of horizontal slits on each end 1½ inches apart. Write a vowel in the center.
2. Cut two 12-by-1½-inch strips for each slider. Thread them through the slits at each end and print a variety of consonants, blends, or digraphs in the spaces as they appear through the slits. Turn the strips over and print additional beginning and ending sounds on the back.

Word Study for Transitional Learners in the Within Word Pattern Stage

Orthographic development and word study instruction during the within word pattern spelling stage is the subject of this chapter. We open with a discussion of the reading, writing, and spelling behaviors that are characteristic of transitional learners. This is followed by a discussion of why and how to plan word study instruction. Then activities are presented, arranged in order along the developmental continuum for the within word pattern stage of spelling. Before we discuss development, let's visit the classroom of Mrs. Holmes, a second grade teacher who has eight students in the early part of this stage of development.

It is Monday, and the goals for word study instruction today are to show students a new sort, observe how well they can read the words, have them try the sort, and then store the words away to sort tomorrow. The children have studied long-a thoroughly, and they are familiar with the word study routine as well as some of the spelling patterns, like the common CVV and CVVC patterns (i.e., *say* and *nail*). Mrs. Holmes has prepared word study sheets like the one in Figure 7-1a as well as a collection of the words written on index cards which she will use to model the sort in a pocket chart.

"I'd like to study long- and short-e words with you this week." This is how Mrs. Holmes moves to the word study part of her lesson with a small group of students. They just shared their entries in their dual entry diaries (Barone, 1989) in response to what they had read in *Fantastic Mr. Fox* by Roald Dahl (Dahl, 1988). "Let's begin by reading these words together." As each of the words is read, she places it randomly at the bottom of her pocket chart. There is some discussion of *read* when Jason points out that it can be read two ways. They agree for now to pronounce it as "reed."

Mrs. Holmes introduces the sort by saying, "What do you notice about all of these words?"

"They all have *e*s in them," explains Troy.

"But do they all have the same sound in the middle?" asks Mrs. Holmes. She puts up pictures of a web and a queen as key words. "We'll sort these words by how they sound in the middle. Put all the words that sound like *web* in the middle here, under this picture of a web. Put words that sound like *queen* here, under this picture of a queen. Place words that don't fit either under the oddball column." She places a blank word card down as a third column. "Let's try a few. Jean, show us how you would figure out where to put this word."

Jean places the word *bed* underneath the picture of the web while she says, "Web. Bed."

"Fine, Jean. Why did you put *bed* under the web?"

"Because they sound alike in the middle. They both say 'eh' in the middle."

"Yes. David, where would this word go?" Mrs. Holmes hands David the word *team*. "Say the word and name the pictures and decide which two sound alike in the middle."

David takes the word card and checks out the fit as he talks himself through this sort: "Team, web. Team, queen. . . . Team, queen." He places the word *team* underneath the picture of the queen.

The students decide that *been* does not fit under either picture and should go in the oddball column. After all the words have been sorted, Mrs. Holmes and the children check each category by reading the words from top to bottom. Then Mrs. Holmes poses the next important question, " How are the words in each column alike?"

David notes that the words under the web all have one *e*. Jean points out that the words in the second column all have two vowels. This leads to the next question, "Do you see some words in the second column that look alike or are spelled alike?" Mrs. Holmes invites Jason to come up, and he quickly pulls out all the words spelled with *ee* and puts them in a new column leaving the words spelled with *ea*. Once more Mrs. Holmes asks the children how the words in each column are alike. Then she removes all the cards from the pocket chart leaving only one word in each of the three categories as a key word. She mixes up the words and passes them out to the students. They then take turns coming up to sort their own three words. The final sort looks like the one in Figure 7-1b.

Mrs. Holmes ends this lesson by giving each student a copy of the word study sheet in Figure 7-1a. The students go back to their seats, cut apart the words, and sort them independently while Mrs. Holmes checks in with another reading group. When she returns she moves among the children and asks them, "Why did you put all these words together?"

To close this word study activity, students store their word cards in plastic bags. The next day they will sort again when they convene in their group, and Mrs. Holmes will watch to see how quickly and accurately they sort. Later they will write the sort in their word study notebooks before returning to reading and writing activities.

FIGURE 7-1a Long-e and Short-e Word Study Sheet

🕸	🧒	Long E Short E Sort 1
web	queen	team
seat	bed	seen
yes	jeep	read
meal	tree	leg
treat	bell	sheep
jet	cream	seed
eat	been	feel

FIGURE 7-1b Pattern Sort for Long-e and Short-e

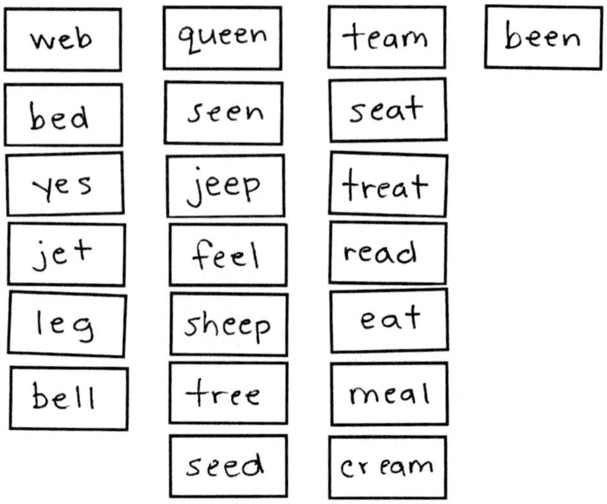

web	queen	team	been
bed	seen	seat	
yes	jeep	treat	
jet	feel	read	
leg	sheep	eat	
bell	tree	meal	
	seed	cream	

LITERACY DEVELOPMENT AND INSTRUCTION FOR STUDENTS IN THE WITHIN WORD PATTERN STAGE

This is a fragile period of development between the beginning stage when students' reading and writing are quite labored, and the intermediate stage when students can read nearly all texts that come before them, including newspapers and magazines. Orthographic development during this period is fresh and interesting, and students make rapid progress in their understanding of single-syllable orthographic patterns. During this stage of development, students learn to spell long vowel patterns, and they read most single-syllable words accurately and with increasing fluency. Transitional readers also can read many two-syllable words when there is enough contextual support in the text.

Reading and Writing

As noted in Figure 2-1, students in this transitional stage read and write with increasing fluency and expression compared to the disfluent reading of the beginning readers (Bear, 1992; Bear & Cathey, 1989). This stage begins when students stop reading in the word-by-word and inexpressive fashion apparent in the beginning stage of literacy. Transitional readers begin to read in phrases (Bear, 1991b), pausing at the end of sentences, and they read with greater expression by emphasizing particular words and by reading some short phrases with a rise or fall in intonation.

Transitional readers also begin to read silently when they read to themselves. They no longer need the support that oral reading contributes; the phrases are read fast enough for students to bypass reading aloud. Students read silently to themselves during sustained silent reading (SSR) or drop everything and read (DEAR). In silent reading, transitional readers approach rates of 100 words per minute in easy material. Teachers observe that most of the fingerpointing characteristics of the beginning stage drop away.

Writing also becomes more fluent during this period of development and there is greater sophistication in the way transitional writers express their ideas. The physical act of writing is performed with greater speed and less conscious focus on the explicit act of writing (Bear, 1991a). This added fluency gives transitional writers more time to concentrate on ideas, and this may account for the greater depth and complexity in their expression. Cognitively they compose with a better sense of the reader's background knowledge. In style, transitional writers learn to do more than present sequences of events; their stories often have morals or themes that build from the central activities of the major characters. Transitional writers also use a greater variety of story devices to begin and end their stories. When transitional learners write responses and reactions to what they read and do, they continue to retell and summarize their experiences and the events in a story, and they begin to include generalizations and analyses which show the reader the deeper processing of the writer (Barone, 1989).

Literacy Learning and Instruction

To promote fluency and expression at the beginning of this stage, transitional readers read and reread support materials like lengthy pattern books and individual dictations with good fluency and expression. These materials are at an independent reading level. However, in easy, but unfamiliar and less predictable texts, transitional readers are more hesitant and slower in their reading and writing. Well-written readers, folktales, and pattern books are good reading materials for transitional readers because they promote fluency.

By the middle of this stage, there are many books that students can read at an independent level such as the *Frog and Toad* books by Arnold Lobel. The support provided by individual dictations and pattern books is no longer required. At an instructional level, there are many books that students can read with good understanding as well as moderate accuracy and fluency such as *Amelia Bedelia* by Peggy Parrish.

By the end of this stage, students can read easy chapter books like *Nate the Great* by Marjorie Sharmat or the *Boxcar Series* by Gertrude Warner. Transitional readers also explore different genres, and informational text becomes more accessible. For example, they read informational books from the *Let's Find Out* series as well as the easy informational magazines like *Ranger Rick.*

Students in the transitional stage work in small groups for reading and writing workshops where they discuss their reading and writing in greater depth than they did as beginners. Students discuss the stories they have read, and they look into their reading materials to share specific ideas and language they think is interesting. Independently and with partners, they can read books without a teacher's support. This independence makes it possible to use reading conference time to share and discuss ideas in more detail.

In writing conferences and directed lessons, teachers help transitional writers through the steps of the writing process. Because they have often written more and written with greater clarity and detail than beginning writers, writing conferences and workshops include more of the revision and editing parts of the writing process. Students use capitals and sentence punctuation and may be ready for conventions such as quotation marks for dialogue.

Teachers may find transitional stage students in the middle part of first grade, but the greatest number of transitional students are in the second, third, and beginning of fourth grades. You will also certainly find corrective and remedial readers in the secondary grades who are in this stage of orthographic development. Perhaps 25% of the adult population in the United States is stunted at this point of literacy proficiency. Many students who progress no further than the transitional stage revert back to beginning behaviors as their knowledge atrophies.

Some college and university students who are poor spellers need to return to this transitional stage of orthographic development. These are the adults who can read at sight many of the words they see regularly, but they may have difficulty reading fairly common polysyllabic words like *repetition.* They also spell many two-syllable words incorrectly, for example, double consonants (*betting* as BETING) or the schwa in the second syllable (*label* as LABLE). It is important to take a step back and conduct word study activities that help them cement their knowledge of vowel patterns in single-syllable words to get a running start as they study two-syllable words.

Lots of experience reading and writing is crucial during this stage. Students must read for at least 25 to 30 minutes each day in instructional- and independent-level materials. They need this practice to propel them into the next stage; otherwise, they will stagnate as readers and writers. This puts word study into perspective. If students are not doing plenty of reading, all of the word study in the world will not help.

CHARACTERISTICS OF ORTHOGRAPHIC DEVELOPMENT

Students in the within word pattern or transitional stage are experimenting with the spellings of the many vowel patterns of English. They "use but confuse" these patterns (Invernizzi, Abouzeid, & Gill, 1994). For example, they no longer spell *boat* sound by sound to produce BOT but rather as BOTE, BOWT, BOOT, or even BOAT as they experiment with possible patterns for the long-o sound. When spellers begin including silent letters, they are ripe for instruction in long vowel patterns.

In the letter name–alphabetic stage, students learned about straightforward letter-sound matches like consonants, blends, and short vowels, and employed a linear strategy in which each letter represented one sound. In contrast, students in the within word pattern stage move beyond a letter name strategy to a higher level of abstraction. They have mastered the alphabetic principle and are learning that sound alone does not govern spelling. Pattern must be considered as well and English has many vowel patterns. These patterns as well as other aspects of orthographic development are discussed in this section.

The Complexities of English Vowels

Vowels are certainly one of the most challenging aspects of learning to read and spell English. Short vowels are a problem because they do not match to a letter name, but once students have learned to associate the five common short vowel sounds with *a, e, i, o,* and *u,* the relationship is usually one letter to one sound. However, students must come to understand that although sound will enable them to spell short vowels in a reliable fashion, this is not true for the many other vowel sounds.

The study of vowel patterns characterizes much of the word study during the within word pattern stage and accounts for the name selected to label it. Word study at this level requires a higher degree of abstract thinking because children face two tasks at once. They must (1) segment words into phonemes, and (2) choose from a variety of patterns that involve silent letters (*cute, suit*) or special consonant patterns (co*ld, i*tch). Mastery of vowels is complicated by a number of factors:

1. There are many more vowel sounds than there are letters to represent them. Each designated vowel as well as *y* are pressed into service to represent more than one sound. Listen to the sound of *a* in these words: *hat, car, war, saw, father, play.* To spell the additional sounds, vowels are often paired up such as *oa* for long-o in *boat,* or *ou* for the diphthong in *shout;* or a second vowel or consonant is used to mark or signal a particular sound. The silent-e in *ride,* the *y* in *play,* and the *w* in *snow* are examples of silent **vowel markers.**

2. Not only are there more vowel sounds than vowels, many of those sounds are spelled a number of different ways. Some of these long vowel patterns are more frequent or common than others as indicated in Table 7-1.

3. In addition to short vowels and long vowels, there are many more vowel sounds, all of which are spelled with a variety of patterns. These include *r-***influenced vowels** (*car, sir, earn*), **diphthongs** (*brown, cloud, boil, toy*), and other **vowel digraphs** that are neither long nor short (*caught, chalk, straw, thought*). The vowel patterns involve either a second vowel or the vowel is influenced by a letter that has some vowel-like qualities. The /l/ and /w/ sounds are examples of consonants that influence the sound of the vowel (*bulk, crowd*). These additional vowel patterns are also shown in Table 7-1.

TABLE 7-1   Vowel Patterns

Long Vowel Patterns

Common long-a patterns: *a-e* (*cave*), *ai* (*rain*), *ay* (*play*)
         Less common: *ei* (*eight*), *ey* (*prey*)
Common long-e patterns: *ee* (*green*), *ea* (*team*), *e* (*me*)
         Less common: *ie* (*chief*)
Common long-i patterns: *i-e* (*tribe*), *igh* (*sight*), *y* (*fly*)
         Less common: *i* followed by *nd* or *ld* (*mind, child*)
Common long-o patterns: *o-e* (*home*), *oa* (*float*), *ow* (*grow*)
         Less common: *o* followed by two consonants (*cold, most, jolt*)
Common long-u patterns: *u-e* (*flute*), *oo* (*moon*), *ew* (*blew*)
         Less common: *ue* (*blue*), *ui* (*suit*)

Consonant-Influenced Vowels

R-controlled vowels
    a with *r*:   *ar* (*car*), *are* (*care*), *air* (*fair*)
    o with *r*:   *or* (*for*), *ore* (*store*), *our* (*pour*), *oar* (*board*)
    e with *r*:   *er* (*her*), *eer* (*deer*), *ear* (*dear*), *ear* (*learn*)
    i with *r*:   *ir* (*shirt*), *ire* (*fire*)
    u with *r*:   *ur* (*burn*), *ure* (*cure*)

    Note: er (*her*), *ir* (*shirt*), and *ur* (*curl*) often spell the same sound.

W exerts an influence on the vowels that follow it: *wa* (*wash*), *war* (*warn*), *wor* (*word*).

L exerts an influence on *a* as heard in *all*. The sound is spelled with *al* (*talk*), *aw* (*saw*), and *au* (*haul*).

Diphthongs and Other Vowel Digraphs

oy (*boy*) and *oi* (*boil*), and *ou* (*cloud*) and *ow* (*brown*)
         Double *o* represents two sounds: long-oo (*moon*) and short-oo (*book*)

---

4. The history of the English language explains why there are so many patterns. English has been enriched with the addition of vocabulary from many different languages, but it has imported diverse spelling patterns as well. In addition, certain patterns represent sounds that have changed over the centuries. For example, *igh* was once a guttural sound different from long-i, but over time pronunciation tends toward simplification while spelling tends to stay the same. Therefore, one long vowel sound is spelled many different ways.

5. English is a language of infinite dialects, and the difference between dialects is most noticeable in the pronunciation of vowels. In some regions of the United States the long-i sound in a word like *pie* is really more of a vowel glide or **diphthong** as in "pi-e." *House* may be pronounced more like "hoo-se" in some areas and *roof* may sound more like "ruff" than "rue-f." Sometimes the final *r*s in *r*-controlled vowels are dropped, as in Boston where you "pahk the cah" (park the car). In other regions a final *r* is added to words as in the "hollers" (hollows) of southwest Virginia. Such regional dialects add color and interest to the language but teachers may be worried about how speakers of such dialects will learn to spell if they can't pronounce words "right." These children will learn to associate certain letter patterns with their own pronunciations. The value of word sorting over packaged phonics programs is that children can sort according to their own pronunciations, and a miscellaneous or oddball column can be used for variant pronunciations.

6. Many words in English do not match even one of the many patterns listed in Table 7-1. These words have sometimes been called exceptions or rule breakers. We prefer to put them in the miscellaneous or oddball category. During word study in the within word pattern stage the oddball category will get a lot of use. Sometimes these words are not exceptions at all but just part of a little known category. An example of these are words like *dance*, *prince*, and *fence* which may look like they should have long vowel patterns, but in these words the *e* is there to mark the /c/ sound "soft" (consider the alternative: *danc, princ,* and *fenc*). Such exceptions should not be ignored and in fact a few such words should be deliberately included in the sorts you plan. They become memorable because they deviate from the common patterns.

Despite the complexity of vowels, by the end of the within word pattern stage, students have a good understanding of vowel spelling patterns. This knowledge is prerequisite to the examination of the way syllables are joined during the next stage of development, the syllables and affixes stage. For example, when students have immediate recognition of words like *bet* and *beat* they soon begin to see that *betting* has two *t*s and *beating* has one *t*.

The meaning connection is emphasized in the study of **homophones** (*meat* and *meet*) and **homographs** (*tear*). Homophones will inevitably turn up in the study of long vowel patterns and can be included in the word sorts you plan even at the beginning of this stage, but an intensive look at homophones at the end of this stage is also recommended. At this point students know most of the vowel patterns and are ready to focus on the meaning of the words. Also during the within word pattern stage, students create semantic sorts that are collections of words on a particular topic (e.g., baseball words, space words, or government words). This focus on meaning and spelling prepares students for the next stage of spelling when the meaning of syllables is examined.

The Influence of Consonants on Vowels

In English, vowel patterns often consist of two vowels, one of which marks or signals a particular sound for the other vowel. Common examples are the silent-e in words such as *bake* and *green*. But consonants are also vowel markers, such as the *gh* in *night* and *sigh* which signals the long-i sound. Children who have come to associate the CVC pattern with short vowels may be puzzled when presented with *car, joy, hall,* or *saw*. *R* retains its identity as a consonant in *car* but the preceding vowel has a sound quite different from short-a. *Y, l,* and *w* are no longer acting as consonants at all but are taking on vowel-like qualities. These words may look like they are exceptions to the CVC rule, but are in fact simply additional patterns that are very regular. This is why it is so important to learn patterns at this stage rather than rules. The influence of *r* is particularly common and deserves further discussion.

R-Influenced Vowels

As our friend Neva Viise says, "*R* is a robber!" The presence of an *r* following a vowel robs the sound from the vowel before it. This causes some words with different short vowels to become homophones (*fir/fur*) and makes vowel sounds spelled with *er, ir,* and *ur* indistinguishable in many cases (*herd, bird, curd*). Even long vowel sounds before the robber *r* are not as clear as the same vowels preceding other consonants (*pair* vs. *pain*). These behaviors of *r*-influenced vowels cause spelling confusions.

The *r*-influenced vowel sorts draw students' attention to the location of the *r* and to the subtle difference in sound which location creates. Word study of *r*-influenced words during the within word pattern stage can begin with activities that contrast initial consonant r-blends (*grill*) and digraphs, with *r*-influenced vowels (*girl*). For example, in a word hunt, students found these contrasts: *crush/curl, fry/first, price/purse, bruise/burn, cream/care, dry/dark,* and *wrap/war*. From here, pairs of students focused on one *r*-influenced word and hunted for related words. One group found *curl, burl, purr, fur,* and *sure*. They included *twirl, pearl,* and *funeral* as "sounding alike but spelled differently."

Note that the presence of a *w* before certain combinations like *or* and *ar* results in a different sound: *w-ar* sounds like "wor" (*war, warm*) and *w-or* sounds like "wer" (*worm, word, world*). The study of *r*-controlled vowels can get quite complex.

Consonant Patterns and Another Look at Blends and Digraphs

During this stage of development, students make single consonant sound-symbol correspondences easily and know many beginning and ending consonant blends and digraphs (*frost, smash*). Some lingering confusions can exist however, and three-letter blend and digraph clusters may pose problems for some spellers: *spr* (*spring*), *thr* (*throw*), *squ* (*square*), *scr* (*scream*), *shr* (*shred*), *spl* (*splash*), and *str* (*string*). Words can be sorted by these combinations or included in other sorts over time. The hard and soft sounds of *g* and *c* can also be explored. Continued study of blends and digraphs at this stage is quite successful because students have many sight words to draw on when they sort words. As you may recall, this is one of the problems that letter name–alphabetic spellers have when they examine consonant digraphs and blends.

What is of special interest in this stage are some of the other characteristics of consonants. Based on Venesky's work (1970), Henderson called these **"complex consonant patterns"** (1990). For example, students in the within word pattern stage can examine words that end in *ck* (*kick*), *tch* (*catch*), and *edge* (*ledge*). By collecting plenty of examples of these final consonant patterns, they see that these patterns are associated with short vowels whereas *k* (*lake*), *ch* (*coach*), and *ge* (*page*) are associated with long vowel patterns. Contrasting these pairs will enable students to make interesting discoveries:

tack versus *take*	*coach* versus *scotch*	*rage* versus *badge*
smock versus *smoke*	*peach* versus *fetch*	*huge* versus *fudge*

Homophones and Homographs

Once students understand the basic differences between long and short vowels, they also become aware of the numerous mismatches between pronunciation and spelling. These inconsistencies are in the spelling for various reasons. It is not helpful for teachers to tell students that this is just the way English spelling is. In some words, as noted earlier, the spelling pattern is a remnant of the way the word used to be pronounced. Often, when students hunt for words that are alike, they find there are not so many inconsistencies as they once thought.

Students enjoy creating lists of homophones (*bear/bare, Mary/marry/merry*) and homographs (*wind* up string/listen to the *wind, read* [present tense]/*read* [past tense]). There is perhaps a good reason why words that sound alike are spelled differently. The different spelling may make the reading easier and the meaning clearer. Perhaps you can see the need to spell words differently in a sentence in which homophones are substituted for one another:

> The weigh Peat cot the bare was knot fare. (The way Pete caught the bear was not fair.)

You will find in discussions of homophones and homographs that you also talk about the meaning and grammatical function of words. Pairs of homographs and homophones differ grammatically as well as semantically. For example, when discussing the homophones *read* and *red*, it makes sense to talk about the past tense of the verb *to read* and the color word *red*. Look at the curriculum and plan to integrate grammar and word study instruction.

WORD STUDY INSTRUCTION FOR THE WITHIN WORD PATTERN–TRANSITIONAL STAGE

Word sorts and word study notebooks are the most common (and crucial) activities to use during this stage. Three brief reminders are useful at this point: (1) Students must be able to read the words before sorting. (2) Do not just plug students into these word sorts; choose sorts that match their development and represent what they use but confuse. (3) Avoid rules. Instead, have students find reliable patterns. Although it is common to teach students rules about silent-e and "when two vowels go walking," often these rules are less reliable than the categories of patterns themselves (the rule about two vowels works for *oa* but not for *ie* in *field* or *chief*).

Sequence of Word Study

The sequence of word study in the within word pattern–transitional stage begins by taking a step back with a review of short vowels as they are compared to long vowels. Then the focus shifts to common long vowel patterns and *r*-influenced vowel patterns. Less common patterns and vowel diphthongs are addressed after the common patterns are well established. Complex consonant patterns and homophones and homographs can be addressed as they appear in vowel sorts. For example, a sort for long-a might include both *pale* and *pail*. A suggested sequence is summarized in Table 7-2 where one word is used as an exemplar for the categories you would set up.

TABLE 7-2   Possible Sequence for the Study of Single-Syllable Vowel Patterns

Slow Pace / Introductions	Moderate Pace	Advanced Pace / Review
Focus on most common patterns and use easy words. Less common patterns may be oddballs.	Use oddballs and some words with blends and digraphs.	Use more words spelled with blends and digraphs, oddballs, and less common patterns.

Long Vowels (and some vowels that are neither long nor short)

hat face	*hat face pay*	*chat place stray train*
hat face paid	*hat face paid pay*	*train sleigh great*
face paid pay		
pet feet	*nest sleet cream*	*nest bread sleet cream*
pet feet seat	*nest bread cream*	*chief sleigh pie*
pet feet seat me		
sit like	*ship prize slight*	*chick prize slight fly*
sit like light	*ship prize lie fly*	*chick child find*
sit like fly	*sick sight wild find*	
like light fly lie		
pot nose	*sock stove toast*	*stock stove groan grow*
pot nose road	*sock stove toast grow*	*stock sold ghost*
pot nose road grow	*sock sold post*	*grow plow cloud*
pot road grow go	*grow plow*	*cloud boil*
	loud boy boil	
rug cute	*drum flute glue suit*	*drum flute glue flew*
rug cute new	*flute shoot group*	*shoot group brook could*
cute boot book	*drum rough group*	
rug book boot flew		

TABLE 7-2	Possible Sequence for the Study of Single-Syllable Vowel Patterns (*continued*)	
Slow Pace / Introductions	**Moderate Pace**	**Advanced Pace / Review**
Focus on most common patterns and use easy words. Less common patterns may be oddballs.	Use oddballs and some words with blends and digraphs.	Use more words spelled with blends and digraphs, oddballs, and less common patterns.
R-Controlled Vowels		
hat car	*hat car face fare*	*shark stare chair warm*
hat car face fare	*car fare fair war*	
pet her	*pet her screen cheer*	*clerk learn clear cheer*
feet deer seat fear	*feet cheer cream fear*	
her deer fear learn	*her fear cheer learn*	
pot for	*for more*	*short store pour word*
nose more	*for more pour poor*	
for more your		
sit girl	*girl her fur learn*	*swirl burn fern learn*
like fire		
girl fur her		
Complex Consonant Clusters		
shr thr sh th	*shr thr spr str*	*include words with these clusters in*
scr squ str spl	*scr spl squ*	*all sorts*
spr thr shr str	*kn wr gn*	
kn wr gn		
Diphthongs and Other Vowels		
cot boy boil	*float boy boil*	*boil brown cloud*
hat ball saw	*boil brown loud*	*salt hawk fault cough*
	hat ball saw fault	
	grow grew saw	

Syllable Patterns Across Vowels   Use a variety of vowels and sort by the pattern rather than by the vowel sound. For example, *game, like, cute,* and *cone* all go under CVCe.

CVC CVCe	CVC CVCe CVVC	CVC CVCC CVCe CVVC
CVC CVCC CVVC	CVCe CVVC CVC CVCC	
Complex Consonants and Vowel Patterns		
hard/soft c (*cent, cut*)	hard/soft g (*gym, goat*)	hard/soft g (*gym, goat*)
hard/soft g (*gym, goat*)	hard/soft c (*cent, cut*)	hard/soft c (*cent, cut*)
ck (*luck*), k (*leak*), ke (*like*)	ck (*luck*), k (*leak*), ke (*like*)	g (*log*), ge (*age*), dge (*edge*)
	g (*log*), ge (*age*), dge (*edge*)	ce (*once*), ve (*glove*), ge (*age*)
	ce (*once*), ve (*glove*), ge (*age*), dge (*edge*)	ch (*each*), tch (*itch*), k (*leak*), ck (*luck*)
	ch (*each*), tch (*itch*)	

Remember to use children's spellings to determine where in this sequence to start. Observations of students' writings and the inventories described in Chapter 3 can help you pinpoint the features students have under control and those that pose problems. The vowels you choose to study first should be ones you see students using but confusing.

You may spend as much as a month on the first long vowel. It takes time to introduce the long vowel patterns, to contrast the long vowel patterns with the CVC short vowel pattern, and to set up word study notebooks to incorporate these new patterns. The extensive repertoire of vowel patterns for each long vowel sound requires equally extensive instruction. Low-frequency patterns are explored toward the end of study for each vowel (e.g., *height* as a long-a word). Subsequent long vowels can be covered more quickly. Pacing can be adjusted by adding more categories to a single sort (up to four or five) or dropping back to fewer categories when students exhibit confusion. A sense of the pacing of word study during this time can be seen in the three pacing sequences in Table 7-2. Late first graders would probably need a slow introduction to long vowel patterns, whereas achieving fourth graders might benefit from a very fast-paced review with more challenging words. There is a lot to cover in this stage—2 years is not too long to address the range of features.

The suggested sequence of word study during this stage is as follows:

1. Sort pictures of words by long and short vowel sound (pictures in appendix). These sorts help students focus on the sounds of the vowels and where in the word to focus their attention.
2. Study one vowel by comparing the long and short sounds and then by exploring the common patterns for that long vowel sound (long-a = CVCe in *cake*, CVVC in *rain*, and CVV in *say*).
3. Study each long vowel in the same fashion. As you study additional vowels, help students examine similarities between them (e.g., *bay* and *key* are CVV words, and *nail* and *feet* are CVVC patterns).
4. Study other vowel sounds and less common patterns. Vowel sounds that are neither long nor short include ambiguous vowel digraphs such as *mouth* and *taught*, diphthongs such as *boil* and *loud*, and r-influenced vowels and l-influenced vowels like *car* and *chalk*. Contrast these less common patterns to the familiar long and short vowel patterns. For example, *dart* and *share* can be contrasted to *trap* and *face*.

Conducting Word Sorts

In small-group teacher-guided activities, students are shown some of the fundamental ways to examine the vowel patterns. Chapter 4 has guidelines for sorting you may want to review. The steps will also be described briefly here.

1. *Introduce the sort in groups.* After reading all the words and talking about the meaning of any unfamiliar words, a teacher may direct the sort or invite students to look for their own categories in an open sort. A teacher-directed sort is helpful when students are new to word sorts or when starting a new feature. The teacher introduces the **key words** and then says something like this: "Find all the words you can that sound like *fish* in the middle and words that sound like *kite* in the middle." After sorting, lead a discussion to focus students' attention on the distinguishing features: "How are the words in this column all alike?"

2. *Students sort independently.* Students can use sets of words or word sheets prepared by the teacher or classification folders like those discussed in Chapter 4. These manila folders have the key words or pictures at the top, and the words to sort are in a plastic bag attached to the folder. In Figure 7-2, the student is shown isolating the long-e sound in *leaf* before placing it in the column with the picture of the feet at the top. Saying the words aloud and comparing them in this way is a necessary strategy when students begin a sort. The steps for independent sorting are:

    a. Read through the words and discard unknowns.
    b. Place the key words at the top of each column.
    c. Sort the rest of the words using the words at the head of each column as guides. Observe how fluently and accurately students sort their words.
    d. Shuffle, re-sort, and store the words for more sorting on another day.

FIGURE 7–2   Long Vowel Sorts: Student Sorts by Sound

3. *Students work independently across the week.* As part of the language arts block, word study sessions usually last 20 minutes. There are numerous follow-up activities that extend students' studies. As was discussed in Chapter 4, weekly routines incorporate spelling activities and word study games as a regular part of the word study program. Buddy sorts, which involve students sorting words by sound as a partner reads them aloud, are particularly recommended. Games give enjoyable practice in reading the words and thinking about their patterns. Many games are described in the activities section at the end of this chapter.

The word study notebook is used across the week for a number of activities. Students write their sorts into word study notebooks as well as the results of word hunts. Word study notebooks are used to document activities, and they serve as handy references that preserve continuity from one small-group word study session to another. More ideas for the use of word study notebooks are described later.

Dialects and sorting.
The pronunciation of vowel sounds in words varies because of individual as well as regional dialectical differences. Teachers need to accept differences in pronunciation. This means that some students will sort words slightly differently than the teacher or other classmates. There is no harm in this. Let students sort in ways that make sense to them, and observe what students do differently but consistently. The goal is for students to associate patterns with their own pronunciations.

Disputes may sometimes arise among the children about whether words are oddballs. Some students say *again* with a long-a whereas others say it with a short-i. *Poem* has a long-o to some folks and an /oi/ sound to others. Some people pronounce *bear* and *bar* as homophones. Students find these dialectical contrasts interesting and teachers should treat them as variations, not as issues of right or wrong. You will find that the fourth grade social studies curriculum in many parts of the United States is a great place to discuss dialects as students study the diverse groups that have settled the state in which they live.

Creating Word Sorts in the Within Word Pattern-Transitional Stage

In this section, you will learn more about creating materials for students in the within word pattern stage of development. Word sorts that contrast sounds and patterns are the key to effective word study. To create these sorts you need to decide what kind of words or feature you will contrast and then find words that exemplify these features.

Ideas for contrasting features are listed in Table 7-2. You will find many sample sorts in the appendix. The contrasts in these sorts are used in the games, as well. As students explore the patterns of each long vowel, choose words that contain the different patterns you want to contrast. For example, if a student is studying long-a, then you may choose the words *trade, rain,* and *day* to head the columns of the sort. If students are studying the common orthographic patterns across vowels, then the words *day, free, seat,* and *mail* might be chosen as the heads of columns. This would then lead to an examination of the CVV and CVVC patterns of both of these long vowels; in this example, *day* and *free* are both CVV words and *mail* and *seat* are both CVVC words.

Once you have decided upon the features or patterns you are going to contrast, you will need words for each category. The appendix lists words by vowel sounds and patterns. Many teachers use their school district's adopted spelling program to find words in weekly lists. Often these published programs pace instruction very fast and cover a lot of patterns at one time. You can adjust these lists by postponing the study of some patterns and adding other words for students who need a slower pace.

You can also look for words in your students' writing and reading materials. The words students spell correctly in their writing will suggest to you words that can be omitted, words that are useful to study, and words that are too difficult and should be studied a little later. Ask your students to brainstorm a list of words that have a particular vowel, and see what words they call out easily and can spell to you as you record them on chart paper.

Preparing Word Study Sheets

You can write the words for sorts on the blank word study sheets found in the appendix or enter them on a word processor by creating your own word study template. Set your margins at zero and create three columns and six to seven rows. Choose a clear font and size to fit your cells. Some teachers like to indicate the key words students will be using for the sort by posting them at the top of the page or highlighting by underlining or bolding. Other teachers like the key words to be established as part of the group discussion and students can then underline them.

Guidelines for Creating Word Sorts

Some of the principles of word study listed in Chapter 4 have particular importance in this stage:

1. *Sort by sight and sound.* Plan sorts that ask students to contrast vowels by how they *sound*. Long vowels should be introduced by comparing them to their corresponding short vowels as Mrs. Holmes did in the vignette at the beginning of this chapter. *R*-influenced vowels (such as the *ar* in *car*) can be compared to the short CVC patterns (such as short-a in *cash* or *trap*). Sound sorts are very important because sound is the first clue spellers use. Long and short vowel pictures can be used for sound sorts, but most of these sound sorts are done with words at this stage.

After sorting by sound, sort by sight—look for the different orthographic spelling patterns used to spell long vowel sounds as well as other vowels in English. An example of a complex consonant sort which begins with sound and moves to pattern can be found in Chapter 4 (sorting first by hard-g and soft-g and then by patterns at the ends of words: *dge, ge,* and *g*).

2. ***Don't hide exceptions.*** Include two or three oddballs whenever they are appropriate (too many oddballs can mask the regularity that students should find). For example, a long-o sort could include *love* and *some* which look as though they fit the CVCe but whose vowel sounds are not long.

Word Study Notebooks in the Within Word Pattern Stage

As you learned in Chapter 4, word study notebooks can serve as a record of some of the routine word study activities used throughout the week and as such they provide documentation of student work for assessment and grading. Chapter 4 has a scoring system for word study activities. The word study notebook can also serve as an organized collection of words students examine for different purposes. Word study notebooks have a long instructional life in learning. Students become accustomed to bringing them to small-group sessions, along with their reading materials and response journals or logs.

The notebooks can be divided into separate sections, and for word study during this stage, each vowel comprises a small section. Post-it notes make it easy to refer to specific sections of the notebook. As students become familiar with the spelling patterns, they assign separate pages to these patterns. For example, in the study of long-o, there may be two pages of words that all have the short-o sound, followed by separate pages for the various long-o patterns—a page of CVVC *coat* words and CVCe *joke* words. Students are challenged to be on the lookout for new words all the time. In this way the sounds and patterns are constantly revisited.

You may also designate a section of the notebook for new vocabulary that students encounter in books and other readings. Whenever they find a new word, they write it in their notebook along with the page number where they found it. Students can share new words and hypotheses about their meanings as part of the general discussion after reading. After checking the dictionary to confirm word meanings, students can record a definition in their own words in their notebooks.

Other entries you might see as you thumb through word study notebooks of students in the within word pattern stage include pages dedicated to content areas and **concept sorts.** This relational type of thinking about vocabulary can be used to usher in the vigorous study of spelling and meaning in subsequent spelling stages. As examples, you might see a science web on pandas, a list of concepts related to immigration to summarize a discussion in social studies, and a page comparing soccer terms to football terms. Many activities for word study notebooks evolve out of the word sorts and small-group brainstorming sessions. You may also see a section of word study pages devoted to grammar studies, for example, a page of nouns and adjectives. More advanced students in the syllables and affixes stage are likely to have pages of lists dedicated to words with double consonants or words that begin with a particular prefix. A complete word study program addresses the spelling, phonics, *and* vocabulary curricula.

Written Reflections

At times, it is useful to have students write about why they sorted the way they did. As fairly fluent writers, within word pattern stage spellers can spend just a few minutes at the end of a sort to summarize discoveries. Such is the case in Figure 7-3, which shows what Graciela has learned about long vowels. It is clear that she is aware of the various patterns for long-i. This reflection shows that she has made a generalization about the *imb* and *ind* words, "*Climb* is the same as *bind, wind,* and *hind.*" These written reflections help teachers assess students' progress. They also give students a starting place at the beginning of small-group word study lessons.

Graciela
10/22/99

I that say his name

shine	climb	sky	right	wind
bite		try	slight	find
slide		my	sigh	blind
slime	2	3	night	hind
spine				
1			4	
				5

1. This word Say i by the e at the end.

2. Climb is the same as bind, wind and hind.

3. a i tarn's into an y.

4. The i is with gh we can not hear it.

5. This word all got an i-n-d.

FIGURE 7-3   A Page From Graciela's Word Study Notebook

What About High-Frequency Words?

Currently there are a number of commercial spelling programs that feature high-frequency or high-utility words. The authors of these programs argue that spelling instruction should focus on a small core of words students need the most, words such as *said, because, there, they're, friend,* and *again.* Unfortunately, this narrow view of word study reduces spelling to a matter of brute memorization and offers students no opportunity to form generalizations, which can extend to the spelling of thousands of unstudied words.

Many of these high-frequency words do not follow common spelling patterns but can be included in word sorts as oddballs. For example, the word *said* is usually examined along with other words that have the *ai* pattern such as *paid, faint,* and *wait.* It becomes memorable because it stands alone in contrast to the many words that work as the pattern would suggest. It is also likely to be spelled correctly by most children because they have seen it so often when they read. Some words in English, however, do persist as problems for young writers. There are also some words children need to write frequently in the lower grades that are not included in the weekly lessons designed to meet their developmental needs. An example of this is the word *because,* which occurs often in the writings of first graders. Many teachers will accept children's inventions for such words (BECUZ, BECALZ, BECAWS) but some teachers grow tired and concerned about such errors, especially beyond the primary grades. Although we feel confident that such errors will be worked out over time, some teachers may wish to consider these guidelines when they study high-frequency words.

We offer this way of studying words with some caution. Studying low-frequency words should not replace the developmental study of words by features but can supplement such study, occasionally. The words chosen should be highly functional words seen in your own students' writing and should be kept small in number. The words should also not be too far in advance of your students' developmental level. Interesting content or theme words which children need for short periods of time such as *Thanksgiving, leprechaun,* and *tyrannosaurus* can simply be posted for easy reference.

Guidelines for the Optional Study of High-Frequency Words

1. Select six to ten words for 1 week out of each 9-week period for a total of 24 to 40 words a year. (Short weeks of 2 to 3 days might be good for these.) A list developed in a second grade class might include *know, friend, again, our, went, would,* and *once.* Students can take part in this selection by choosing words they have difficulty spelling and by choosing words from the teacher's master list. A cumulative list of these words in alphabetical order is posted in the room for reference with the understanding that students are expected to spell those words correctly in all their written work once they have been studied (Cunningham, 1995). Individual student copies of these words in alphabetical order can also be distributed. Students may place the individual lists in their writing workshop folders, in the back of their journals, or as an entry in their word study notebooks.

2. Develop routines to help children examine and study the words carefully. Here are some suggestions:
   - *Introduction and discussion.* As the teacher writes the words on the board the children copy them on their own paper in a column. (Be sure that everyone copies correctly!) The teacher should then lead a discussion about each word. "What part of this word might be hard to remember and why?" (For the word *friend* the discussion would focus on the fact that it has a silent-i.) "What might help you remember how to spell this word?" (Students might note that it ends with *end.*)
   - *Self-corrected test method.* After each word has been written and discussed, students should fold their paper over so that the list is covered. The teacher calls the words aloud while the children write them again. The children then check their own work by unfolding the paper to compare what they copied to what they spelled. Any words spelled incorrectly should be rewritten again. This method has been well researched (Horn, 1954).
   - *Self-study method.* The self-study method is another long-standing activity that appears in most published spelling books. This process above can be used independently, but children need to be taught to follow these steps: (1) look at the word and say it, (2) cover the word, (3) write the word, (4) check the word, and (5) write the word again if it was spelled wrong.
   - *Practice test.* The words are called aloud. Children spell the word and then immediately check it by looking at the chart posted in the room. This gets them familiar with using the chart as a reference. Students can call the words to each other in pairs or small groups, or the teacher may lead the practice test.
   - *Final test.* The chart is covered and children spell the words as they are called aloud. Since the number of words is kept small the chance of 100% success is high. Once students have been tested they are responsible for those words from then on. The teacher will undoubtedly need to remind students often to reread a piece of written work to check for the posted words in the editing stage. Any word that continues to be a problem can reappear on the next list, but students will have about 8 weeks to work at getting it under control.

Activities for Students in the Within Word Pattern Stage

This section begins with three model word sorts and several routines to summarize the basic approach to word study and to highlight the importance of categorizing and discovery in the study of words. Games are offered as follow-ups designed to extend and reinforce students' understandings, not to substitute for instruction. In addition, many games from the previous chapter—particularly the ones marked with the "generic" logo—can be adapted simply by using different words. The activities for students are grouped according to difficulty, with common long vowel games coming before less common vowel sounds and patterns.

Generic

Picture Sorts to Contrast Long and Short Vowels 7–1

This is an excellent bridge activity for students in the early part of this stage. Students work individually and in small groups to examine the basic sound differences among short and long vowel patterns.

Materials

Focus on one vowel and choose 14 short vowel pictures and 14 long vowel pictures. You can find pictures in the appendix as well as in graphics programs.

Procedures

1. Students say the names of the pictures and discard pictures they do not recognize.
2. The teacher places a picture at the top of the first two columns to fit the categories the students are to use in their sorting. An oddball column is established for words that for various reasons do not fit.

3. Students sort the pictures underneath the column heads.
4. Students read their completed sorts by column, at which time they make any changes they wish. At the end of reading each column, students declare the reason why they sorted as they did.

Variations
This same activity can be conducted as an open sort with pictures.

Teacher-Directed Word Sorts for Long Vowels 7–2
Start word sorts early in this stage. Here is the basic procedure for setting up and carrying out a sort that begins with sound and moves to pattern.

Materials
Using the word lists in the appendix or other resources, select about 20 short-a and long-a words that are spelled with the CVVC pattern (*rain, pail*) and the CVCe pattern (*cake, tape*). Select words that you believe your students will already know how to read. You may also include one or two words that do not fit the expected sound or pattern (*was* or *have* for example). Prepare word cards or write the words randomly on a word study handout template for students to cut apart for independent sorting.

Procedures
1. Introduce the sort by reading the words together and talking about any whose meaning may be unclear. Invite students to make observations about the words: "What do you notice?"
2. Sort the words first by the sound of the vowel in the middle.
3. After discussing the rationale for the sort, ask students to look for patterns in the long-a column and separate them into two categories.
4. Again talk about how the words in each column are alike.
5. Scramble the words and re-sort a second time under designated headers or key words. The categories will look something like the following sort.
6. Ask students to sort independently.
7. Store words for more sorting and activities on subsequent days.

Short-a	Long-a		Oddballs
cap	cape	chain	have
gas	came	rain	was
back	name	pail	
fan	lake	pain	
has	gate	paint	
fast	safe		
rake			

Variations
Study sounds and patterns for *e, i, o,* and *u* in the same manner.

Open Sort Using R-Influenced Vowels 7–3
Many vowels which are neither long nor short should be examined as well. After students are familiar with listening and looking for the vowel patterns, they can be very successful at open-ended sorts such as the one described here.

Materials

Using the word lists in the appendix or other resources select about 20 words that are spelled with *ar* (*bark*), *are* (*bare*), or *air* (*chair*). Select words that you believe your students will already know how to read. You may also include one or two words that have the same sound but not the same spelling pattern (*pear* and *fair* for example). Write the words randomly on a word study handout template for students to cut apart for independent sorting.

Procedures

1. Introduce the sort by reading the words together and talking about any whose meaning may be unclear. Invite students to make observations about the words: "What do you notice?"
2. Ask the students to sort the words into categories of their own choosing. Call on different children to describe the rationale for their sorts. Accept all reasonable categories.
3. Designate key words or headers and ask all the students to sort the same way. The categories will look something like the following sort. Discuss the categories and oddballs.
4. Ask the students to scramble their words and re-sort a second time.
5. Ask students to identify the homophones (*fare/fair, bare/bear, hare/hair*) and define them or use them in sentences.
6. Store words for more sorting and activities on subsequent days.

bark	bare	air	war	pear
chart	share	chair	warm	bear
yarn	stare	pair	warn	
large	scare	hair		
sharp	square	fair		
	hare			
	fare			

Variations

Any number of sounds and patterns can be explored in a similar fashion.

Word Study Notebooks 7-4

The notebook is a diary and collection of words students have studied. The notebooks document students' word study and vocabulary program, and help teachers to assess student activity and growth. Words are grouped by sound, orthographic patterns, and meaning. Word study notebooks are begun early in this stage of development if not before. Refer to the previous discussion of word study notebooks for more ideas.

Materials

You can use spiral notebooks or sewn notebooks with stiff covers, but the notebook can also be several pieces of paper folded and stapled.

Procedures

Word study notebooks are used almost daily. Students bring them to small-group meetings to share their discoveries and to add to their lists as they read. They write the sorts they complete into their word study notebooks under the appropriate long vowel, and they share the results of their hunts.

Word Hunts 7-5

Word hunts are excellent seat work activities. Students can work independently or with a partner. They enjoy going back into familiar texts to look for words that fit a particular pattern. Word hunts will usually turn up many miscellaneous words or oddballs, and interesting discussions arise as students work together to decide where certain words should be categorized.

Procedures

1. Ask students to go through what they have recently read to find words that fit a particular sound or pattern: "Find all the words you can that sound like *cake* in the middle."
2. Words that fit the desired patterns are written down in notebooks.
3. Students meet together in small groups and read their words aloud. The children or the teacher may record the words on chart paper for display.
4. Students are asked what words could be grouped together.
5. Students check to see what words they can add to their word study notebooks.

Variations

1. Students can hunt for sight words, similar vowel patterns, words to which inflected endings or plural forms may be added, or compound words.
2. Use a newspaper for the hunt. Teams are sent in search of various long vowel patterns (an *ai* team, an *ay* team, a CVCe team, etc.). Words fitting the desired patterns are circled in crayon or highlighted, written down, and shared in small-group instruction.

Train Station Game 7-6

This easy board game for up to four people is used to emphasize automaticity with common long vowels.*

Materials

Use a basic pathway board found in the appendix and decorated like the one shown in Figure 7-4. Write in words that have been studied in word sorts. Many more words are listed in the appendix. There are four special squares incorporated into the gameboard:

1. Cow on the track. Lose 1 turn.
2. You pass a freight train. Move ahead 2 spaces.
3. Tunnel blocked. Go back 1 space.
4. You lost your ticket. Go back 2 spaces.

Procedures

Each child selects a gamepiece. The first child then spins or rolls the die and places the gamepiece on the appropriate space. The child pronounces the word and identifies the vowel. In addition, the child must say another word containing the same vowel sound to stay on that space. Play continues in this fashion until someone finishes the course.

If students have studied the long vowel patterns within each long vowel, they can be asked to say what the pattern is, for example, "*Nail* is a long-a with a CVVC pattern."

---

*Thanks to Janet Bloodgood for this activity.

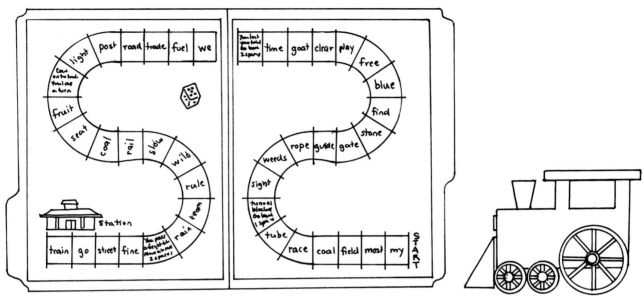

FIGURE 7-4   Train Station Game: Long Vowel Patterns

Variations

Divide a spinner into five sections and label each with a vowel. Students move to the next word with the vowel sound they spin.

Turkey Feathers 7-7

This is a game in which two players compare visual patterns across a single long vowel.*

Materials

Two paper/cardboard turkeys without tail feathers, such as the one in Figure 7-5; 10 construction paper feathers; and word cards representing the long vowel studied, for example, for long-a, CVCe, *ai*, and *ay*. Word cards should have pairs (*cake/bake, mail/pail*).

Procedures

1. One player shuffles and deals five cards and five feathers to each player.
2. Remaining cards are placed facedown for the draw pile.
3. Each player puts down pairs that match by pattern. For example, *cake/bake* would be a pair, but *pain/lane* would not. Each time a pair is laid down, the player puts one feather on his or her turkey.
4. The dealer goes first, says a word from his or her hand, and asks if the second player has a card that has the same pattern.
5. If player 2 has a card that matches the pattern, player 1 gets a feather; if not, player 1 must draw a card. If the player draws a card which matches any word in hand, the pair can be discarded, and a feather is earned. Player 2 proceeds in the same manner.
6. The player using all five feathers first wins. If a player uses all the cards before earning five feathers, the player must draw a card before the other player's turn.

---

*Marilyn Edwards developed this easy game.

FIGURE 7-5 Turkey Feathers: Comparing Vowel Patterns

Variation

Upon using all five feathers, a player must correctly pronounce words. If a word is mispronounced, the player loses a feather and the game continues.

The Racetrack Game 7–8

Players move around a track and match words in their hand with words on the track. This is a great way to examine long vowel patterns. A racetrack template can be found in the appendix. A sample gameboard appears in Figure 7-6.*

Procedures

This game for two to four players is played on an oval track divided into 20 to 30 spaces. Different words following particular patterns are written into each space, and a star is drawn in two spaces. For example, *night, light, tie, kite, like, my, fly, wish,* and *dig* could be used on a game designed to practice patterns for long- and short-i. A collection of 40 to 50 cards is prepared with words that share the same patterns. A number spinner or a single die are used to move around the track.

1. Shuffle the word cards and deal six to each player. Turn the rest facedown to become the deck.
2. Playing pieces are placed anywhere on the board and moved according to the number spinner or die.
3. When players land on a space, they read the word and then look for words in their hand that have the same pattern. For example, a player who lands on *night* may pull *sign* and *right* to put in the winning pile. If they move to a space with a star, they dispose of any oddballs they might have (such as *give*).
4. The cards placed in the winning pile are replaced by drawing the same number from the deck before play passes to the next player.
5. A player who has no match for the pattern must draw a card anyway.
6. The game is over when there are no more cards to play. The winner is the player with the most word cards in the winning pile.

*Darrell Morris developed this game and has written extensively on word sorting (Morris, 1982, 1992).

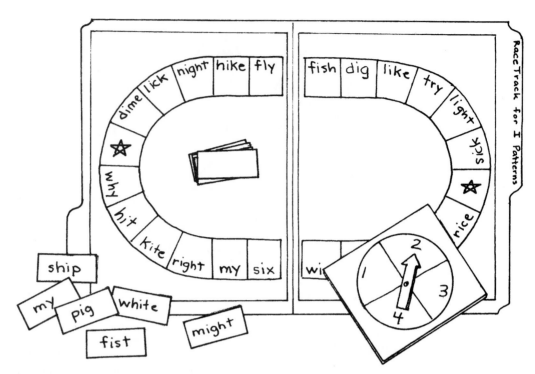

FIGURE 7-6   Racetrack Games Are Popular, Easy to Make, and Simple to Play

Variations

This game can be used for any vowel patterns and serves as a good review of the many patterns for the different vowels. Generally limit your categories to five or six.

The Classic Card Game 7-9

This card game is a favorite for two to five players; three is optimal. The many variations show how versatile this game is.*

Materials

Use known words representing the vowel patterns you wish to review. For card games, write the words at the top of the word card. This makes it easier for students to see the words when they are held in their hands. If children have trouble holding the cards in one hand as a fan, the players usually agree to lay them out and not to look at each other's words. You may actually prefer that students play in this way so that they get more practice with the words.

Procedures

1. Seven cards are dealt to each player.
2. Roll the dice to see who goes first.
3. The first player places a card down, reads the word, and designates the vowel pattern to be followed, for example, *rain, ai.*
4. The next player places a card down with the *ai* pattern and reads it out loud.

---

*This game is a McGuffey Reading Center classic that has been recorded by Cindy Aldrete-Frazer.

5. The play continues going around the circle until all of the players are out of *ai* pattern word cards.
6. Players pass if they do not have a word card to match the category.
7. Players forfeit a turn if they do not read their contribution correctly.
8. The player who last played the pattern card gets to begin the new round. This player chooses a different card from his or her hand, places it in the middle, and declares what vowel pattern is to be followed.
9. The object of the game is to be the first player to play all your cards.

Variations

1. Students who do not have a match can be forced to draw from the remaining cards until a match is found.
2. Wild cards can be added so players can change categories in midstream.
3. Write words arranged by pattern in the word study notebooks.
4. The rules of the game can be expanded to include parts of speech (e.g., nouns, adjectives, verbs).

Word Sorting and Computer Software 7–10

There are two types of word study software: (1) sorts on computer, and (2) instructional materials that teachers print and reproduce.

Word Sort

Students in the within word pattern stage sort words on the computer with a software program called Word Sort. This software was developed several years ago by Ed Henderson, his son, and several students. It is suitable for students in the within word pattern stage because the 215 sorts all focus on long vowel patterns. A student report form is included as well as ways for teachers to compile ongoing class profiles. Teachers also can check students' accuracy and fluency in sorting. The teacher's guide and disk contain a management system. Analyses of students' sorts and printouts of class profiles are possible. Students enjoy this independent activity, especially the timed version. Mac and PC versions are available. For information on obtaining the software (a limited number of sorts are free), check out the Web site at www.hendersonedsoft.com.

Finding Words in Dictionaries

The dictionary on word processors may be a wonderful place to find words to use in sorting. Look to see how you and your students can search the dictionary for specific letter strings and word patterns. For example, the *American Heritage Dictionary* can be searched for letter strings placed between two asterisks, or preceded by a number of question marks. To locate words with *oa* in them, *oa* would instruct the computer to search for words with letters on both sides of the *oa*. Or, for a narrower search, use question marks. Searching with ?at will find three-letter words ending in *at*, ??at will find four-letter words ending in *at*, and so on.

Rhyming dictionaries also come in handy during the within word pattern stage. The single-syllable lists are where the various orthographic patterns for each of the long vowels can be found. Toward the end of this stage, two-syllable rhyming words can be included in sorts and word lists as long as students can read the words.

Computer Word Games

There are many computer word games that can be useful. Word Muncher (MECC) is especially good and asks students to listen for sounds as well as look for patterns. In choosing software, be sure that the games use words students can read, patterns they need to study, and allow a fast enough pace. Look for software in which students match words by sound and spelling patterns. In the classroom be sure that the word study games do not take away time students need for writing and reading.

The ways students use software can be adapted so that they examine spelling and sounds. Many games ask students to recognize whether or not two words rhyme. In such games, students can write down the words and arrange them by columns in their word study notebooks according to orthographic patterns, for example, CVVC, CVV, and CV.

Letter Spin 7–11

Players spin for a feature and remove pictures or words from their gameboards that match the feature. For pictures, the features are sounds (long-o, short-o, long-i). For words, the features are patterns (*o, oa, o-e, ow*).

Materials

1. A spinner divided into three to six sections and labeled with the pattern to be practiced. (See directions for making the spinner in the appendix.)
2. A collection of picture or word cards.
3. Playing boards are divided like a Tic-Tac-Toe board. Use a 9-by-9-inch board for 3-by-3-inch pictures (see Figure 7–7).

Procedures

1. Players draw cards and turn them faceup on their boards or in a three-by-three array if they do not have playing boards.
2. The first player spins and removes all those picture or word cards that fit the sound indicated by the spinner. The cards go into the player's "point pile." That same player draws enough cards from the pile to replace the gaps in the playing board before play moves to the next player.
3. Play continues until a player has removed all cards and there are no more to be drawn as replacements. The player who has the most cards in the point pile wins.

Variations

1. This is a Tic-Tac-Toe version: Players prepare boards as described, but when they spin they can turn facedown one picture that has that feature. The winner is the one who turns down three in a row. Blackout is a longer version of Tic-Tac-Toe. Players turn over their cards. The player who turns over all of the words on the board wins.
2. This game can be used to study initial sounds and blends. The spinner and the pictures change accordingly.
3. A large cube (1-inch square would do) is used like a die instead of a spinner. Use sticky dots to label the sides with the different features.

Board Game With *Sheep in a Jeep* 7–12

This activity features *Sheep in a Jeep* by Nancy Shaw and illustrated by Margot Apple. This is a game for two people to examine two CVVC patterns (e.g., *ee* and *ea*).* The gameboard appears in Figure 7-8 on page 208.

---

*Alison Dwier-Selden developed this game.

FIGURE 7-7   Letter Spin Game: Finding Words to Match the Spinner

Procedures

1. After reading *Sheep in a Jeep* and sorting words with the *ee* and *ea* patterns, players move to the board game and place game markers at the start position (see Figure 7–8).
2. One player spins and moves that number of spaces on the board.
3. The player reads the word on the space. A player moves back a space if the word landed on is read incorrectly. Students add a sheep to the jeep by saying or writing a word that rhymes with the word they have landed on.
4. Players alternate turns. The first player to the finish wins.

Variations

1. Players can move two or three times around the board.
2. Students hunt for these words or words that follow the same patterns in other texts.

Green Light! Red Light! A Sorting Game 7-13

This is a speed game for two or more players to review long vowel patterns.*

Materials

Word cards vary with the students' word studies. There must be at least 10 words for each player and 10 word cards for the draw pile.

---

*Mary Ellen McGraw developed this game. She notes that this is more competitive than most games, and that it is enjoyed by many upper elementary and secondary students at this stage of development. Be sure that students are close in terms of development. She also notes that students like to carry the game over from one day to another and wait a few days to declare a winner.

FIGURE 7-8 Board Game for *Sheep in a Jeep*

Procedures

The object of the game is to be the first player to say "red light," write words on the chalkboard, and score more points than other players. Players need to be attentive to challenge incorrect word-sorting choices by others.

1. The leader writes the column pattern headings on the chalkboard. This is an example for long-a word study:

   Long-a CVCe   Short-a CVC   Long-a CVVC   Short-a CVCC

2. Players face the chalkboard, and each player is dealt seven cards. The remainder are placed in the draw pile.

3. The leader writes numbers 1 through 5 at random under the word sort headings and says "green light" as a signal for players to pick up their cards and search for words to match the numbered categories. For example, a leader may have numbered the patterns this way:

Long-a CVCe	Short-a CVC	Long-a CVVC	Short-a CVCC
2	5	1	3
		4	

4. The first player to find all five examples says, "red light." Searching halts. Other players turn their cards facedown as this player goes to the board and writes the words beside the numbers. After writing all five words, the player reads aloud each heading as well as the words.

   The player then goes to the score section on the chalkboard and writes his or her name and score (5). The player discards the five cards and draws five from the draw pile. (After several rounds of play, the words in the draw and discard piles can be shuffled.)

5. Other players may challenge the word sort choices by going to the board, pointing out any incorrect choices, and substituting their own words. The validity of the challenge is decided by the leader. The score is adjusted to account for corrections.

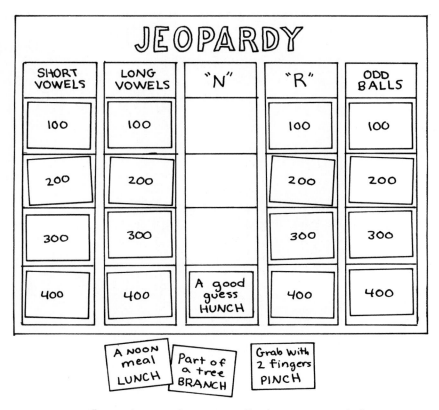

FIGURE 7-9 Word Jeopardy Game: "I'll Take Long Vowels for 100"

For example, Jon has five points. Lisa correctly challenges two words. Lisa would have two points and Jon would be left with three. The challenger must discard the used cards and draw an equal number of cards from the draw pile.

6. The leader starts another round by writing 1 through 5 at random under the headings. Play continues until all word cards are used or until time is called. The player with the most points is the winner.

Jeopardy Game 7-14

In this game for four or five students, students recall and spell words that follow a particular pattern. In this example the final *ch* pattern is reviewed. A posterboard is divided into 5-by-5-inch sections such as the one shown in Figure 7-9, and clue cards are placed in each space.* On one side of each card a clue is written about a word in that category. On the other side an amount is written (100–500).

Procedures

1. One player is the moderator or game host. The others roll the dice to determine who goes first.
2. The game begins when the first player picks a category and an amount for the moderator to read, for example, "I'll take short vowels for 100." The moderator reads the clue and the player must respond by phrasing a question and spelling the word. For example:

Moderator: "When struck it produces fire."

Player: "What is a match? m-a-t-c-h."

---

*This game was contributed by Charlotte Tucker.

Word study notebooks are useful tools for vocabulary and spelling learning.

3. The player receives the card if the answer is correct. This player chooses another clue. (A player can only have two consecutive turns.) If the player misses, the player to the left may answer.
4. The game continues until all the clue cards are read and won or left unanswered. Players add their points, and the one with the highest amount wins.

Word Lists

Here are a few words that would be used to study words ending in *ch* and *tch*. More complete list of words can be found in the appendix.

R	N	Short Vowels	Long Vowels	Oddballs
march	bench	stitch	beach	much
perch	lunch	watch	teach	such
porch	branch	sketch	roach	rich
torch	pinch	witch	coach	

Word Study Scattergories 7–15

This is an independent activity for three to five students for review of patterns. Students make a list of words that follow a pattern (*at*/*flat*). Students read their answers and earn a point when their word is different than the other players' words.*

Materials

Prepare gamecards such as the one in Figure 7-10 that could be used for five games. An answer sheet is provided that could be used for three games.

Procedures

The game is played in three rounds.

---

*Brenda Reibel adapted Scattergories by Milton Bradley Company for this fast moving word study game.

GAMECARD

ONE	TWO	THREE	FOUR	FIVE
1. at	1. et	1. ig	1. og	1. ug
2. ad	2. en	2. in	2. ot	2. ut
3. an	3. est	3. it	3 op	3. us
4. al	4. el	4. ing	4. ope	4. ute
5. ame	5. ea	5. ice	5. or	5. ew
6. ai	6. ear	6. ite	6. oo	6. ur
7. ay	7. ee	7. ile	7. oi	7. ue
8. ar	8. ie	8. igh	8. ow	8. ui
9. aw	9. ew	9. ir	9. ou	9. un
10. atch	10. er	10. y	10. oy	10. ush

ANSWER SHEET

ONE	TWO	THREE
1. (flat)	1. hat	1. chat
2. (glad)	2. had	2. mad
3. man	3. (plan)	3. tan
4. walk	4. chalk	4. (final)
5. game	5. blame	5. same
6. (pain)	6. wait	6. straight
7. pay	7. play	7. today
8. car	8. star	8. farther
9. (claw)	9. saw	9. straw
10. match	10. catch	10. hatch
TOTAL 4	3	4

FIGURE 7-10   Word Study Scattergories Gamecard and the Answer Sheet

1. Each player has a Scattergories word study gamecard and an answer sheet.
2. The timer is set for 2 minutes.
3. All players quickly fill in the first column of their answer sheet using the patterns in the first column of the gamecard. Answers must fit the category and must use the vowel pattern given.
4. Scoring a round: Players take turns reading their answers aloud for each number. Players score their own answer sheets by circling an acceptable answer that does *not* match any other player's answer. Continue reading answers until all 10 categories have been scored. Score one point for each circled answer. Record the score at the top of the column of the answer sheet.
5. Starting a new round: Set the timer again; continue playing using the *same* category list as in the previous round. Fill in the next column with new answers.
6. Winning the game: After three rounds have been played, players total the three scores on their answer sheets. The player with the highest score is the winner.
7. Rules for acceptable answers: The exact same answer *cannot* be given twice in one round. A player cannot answer *push* for *us* and *ush.*
8. Challenging answers: While answers are being read, other players may challenge their acceptability. When an answer is challenged, all players vote on whether it is acceptable. Players who accept the answer give a thumbs-up sign. Players who do not accept the answer give a thumbs-down sign. Majority rules. In the case of a tie, the challenged player's vote does not count.

Variations

Create other cards to use to play Word Study Scattergories.

Building Word Categories 7–16

Word cards are the playing cards in this matching game. Up to four students practice grouping short and long vowel words by pattern (sight, sound, and meaning). Older students like this game because they add their poker terms.*

Materials

A deck of 45 cards is needed. The patterns can vary. A good starting combination is a blend of five cards of each short vowel (CVC) and five cards of each long vowel except for CVCe (e.g., *Pete*).

Procedures

1. Five cards are dealt to each player. Players look in their hands for patterns.
2. Unwanted cards are discarded, and new cards are drawn to keep a hand of five cards. For example, *bone, rope, rat, pet, rake* could be one player's hand. This player may want to discard *rat, pet,* and *rake,* and draw three other cards to create a better hand, possibly.
3. Each player has a chance to draw up to four cards from the deck one time to create a better hand.
4. The possible combinations are a pair (*hat, rat*); two pairs (*hat, rat, bone, tone*); three of a kind (*bone, phone, tone*); four of a kind (*phone, bone, tone, cone*); three of a kind plus a pair (*bone, phone, tone, rope, mope*); or five of a kind (*phone, bone, tone, cone, drone*). In poker the three of a kind plus a pair combination is a full house, and five of a kind is like a flush.
5. Determining winners: Five of a kind beats a three of a kind with a pair, four of a kind, three of a kind, two pairs, and a pair. Four of a kind beats everything except five of a kind. Two pairs beats three of a kind and a pair. Three of a kind beats two pairs and a pair wins if it is the highest matching family.
   In case of ties, players can draw from the deck until one player comes up with a card that will break the tie.

Variations

1. Using guide words, students sort the words in their hands.
2. Pictures can be sorted with the words.
3. Wild cards can be included.

Declare Your Category! 7–17

One player finds a way to match a guide word and the other players have to guess how the words are categorized. This game is for two to five players (three is optimal) to study long vowel patterns.

Materials

Combine long vowel words from the word lists in the appendix. You will need 45 word cards from the vowels students have studied.

Procedures

This is similar to the Classic Card Game in Activity 7-9, but it's a little more complex and works best with students who have had some experience playing games. In this game, players guess the first player's category.

---

*Fran deMaio recorded the directions to this traditional game.

1. Seven cards are dealt to each player and the remainder are placed facedown as a draw pile. Players lay out their seven cards. Players should always have seven cards.

2. The first player turns up a card (*home*) from the draw pile in the middle and looks for a word in his or her hand to match (*bone*). If the player can match the guide word in some way, he or she puts the card underneath the guide word. This player becomes the judge for the other players as they try to match the guide word and the way this first player matched the words. The player who started the category keeps the sorting strategy a secret, and waits until the last player puts a card down and declares the category. To keep the starter from changing categories, he or she can write down the reason for the match: "*Home* and *bone* are both long-o words and have the same pattern, the CVCe."

3. The next player places a card down underneath the guide word and reads the new word aloud. (*Tone* would be acceptable because they are both long-o and CVCe words. *Gone* would be unacceptable because it only looks like *home,* but does not have the long-o sound.)
   What happens if the person who set up the category does not think the next player put down an acceptable card? The person who established the category is the judge and can send a card back and give that player another chance. Mistakes by the judge are discussed at the end of the game.

4. The play continues going around the circle until players stop putting words down to fit the pattern. Players can pass when they wish.

5. The player who plays the last card reads the list and then has to declare the category. If the last player has correctly guessed the category established by the first player, then the last player to lay down a card keeps the words. If the last player's guess is wrong, the previous player gets a chance to declare the category.

6. At the end of each round, students are dealt enough cards to get them back to seven. The player to the left of the winner of the round turns up a card from the pile, and is the person who makes up the category.

7. The player with the most cards wins.

Variations

1. Add wild cards to the pile. Wild cards can be used to change categories in midstream. The person who establishes a new category must guess the original category correctly. This player becomes the new judge: "Your sort was by words that sound like *bone* and look like *bone.* I am putting down my wild card, and laying down *loan.* Guess my category."

2. The rules of the game can be expanded to include semantic (e.g., types of birds) and grammatical (e.g., nouns) categories.

Word Study Trivial Pursuit 7–18

This game is designed for up to four players and one referee. After initial introduction by the teacher, students can play the game independently. This game works particularly well when two or more long vowels are part of the list.*

Materials

Posterboard, $1\frac{1}{2}$-inch squares of construction paper in four different colors, word cards with exemplars for the spelling concept being studied, envelopes made from the four colors of construction paper (or plastic bags), die or spinner, and gamepiece markers.

---

*This version of Trivial Pursuit was developed by Rita Loyacono.

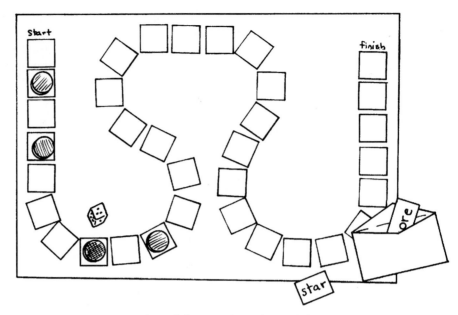

FIGURE 7-11   Gameboard for Word Study Trivial Pursuit

How to Make It

1. To construct the gameboard, glue squares of colored construction paper onto the posterboard, alternating colors and making a trail from start to finish covering the entire board.

2. Make four envelopes to hold four different packets of word cards out of construction paper corresponding to the four colors on the gameboard (red squares and red envelope, orange squares and orange envelope, brown squares and brown envelope, green squares and green envelope as shown in Figure 7-11). You can also use color swatches on plastic bags.

To Play

1. Players pick order by spinning or tossing the die. The winner chooses what color to be. Each player in turn selects a color.

2. Players take the packet of word cards corresponding to their color and call these words out when another player lands on their respective color. If players land on their own color, they may take another turn.

   For example, suppose Adam spins a five and lands on a green square. If he is not holding the green packet, the person with the green packet calls out a word. Adam spells the word correctly, and the card is placed faceup next to the caller. Bonnie takes a turn and also lands on a green square. After successfully spelling her word, she must decide if it is to be placed on top of the first word (follows the same pattern) or beside it (is a different pattern).

   The players continue, starting a new pile whenever necessary. In this way, they spell the words as well as sort them by pattern. Whichever color the player lands on is the packet from which the word is chosen for the player to spell and sort, unless it is the player's own color.

3. Players who misspell the word must go back one square and try a word from that color providing it is not their own color (in which case they move back two squares). If players are unable to spell that word, they remain where they are and lose one turn. If players are unable to sort the word properly, they must move back

one space (again providing it is not their color and if so, two spaces), but do not lose a turn. The first player to get to the finish square is the winner and will be referee the next time. Since the students have been previously exposed to the pattern in the pockets and are approaching automaticity, there should be few spelling or sorting mistakes.

Variations

1. This game is used simply for word sorting (without the spelling practice). In this variation, players present the word instead of calling it out for another player, and the player reads the word and sorts it.
2. The game is played with four different categories of words, one for each envelope, or with three categories and the fourth color being the free space, or with two patterns divided up between the four envelopes.
3. Since neither the gameboard nor the envelopes would be marked, the board can be used for any word patterns that are being studied.

Having several sets of the game allows different groups of five students to play the same game while practicing different patterns. Refer to the word-sorting lists to develop sets.

Word Study UNO 7-19

This game uses word cards, and students group patterns together. This game is for two to four players.*

Materials

Make six wild cards, six *skip* cards, six *draw 2* cards, and 27 word cards. Use the word lists in the appendix. For example, if students are studying word families across vowels, the following *skip* and *draw 2* cards could be made:

Skip	*ane*	Draw 2	*ane*
Skip	*ale*	Draw 2	*ale*
Skip	*ean*	Draw 2	*ean*
Skip	*eel*	Draw 2	*eel*
Skip	*ent*	Draw 2	*ent*

Procedures

1. Model this game in a small group. Cards are shuffled and the dealer deals five cards to each player. The remaining cards are placed facedown and the top card is turned faceup.
2. Players alternate and discard a card that changes only one letter at a time, or by playing one of the special cards (*skip, draw 2, wild*).
   Here is a good example: If the beginning card was *sale,* the player could discard *sale, tale,* or *bale.* A player who did not have one of those cards, or chose not to use one of those, could discard *skip ale* or *draw 2 ale.* The *skip ale* card allows the player to play a second card. The *draw 2 ale* card forces the other player to pick two cards from the pile until that player has two *ale* words, and no cards may be discarded. The player who discarded the *draw 2* card may then take another turn (if only two are playing).
3. *Skip, draw 2,* and wild cards may be used successively to move from one pattern to another. A player who cannot discard must draw from the pile. Unless it is a *draw 2* situation, the player may discard if the card drawn follows the pattern.

---

*Rita Loyacono developed this word study version of the UNO game.

4. As players alternate turns, they are attempting to discard all their cards. A player who has only one card remaining must say, "UNO." If the player forgets, another player can tell the player with one card to draw another card.
5. The first player to "go out" wins the game.

Homophone Win, Lose, or Draw 7–20

Four or more students work in teams to draw and guess each others' words in a game that resembles charades.* A list of homophones can be found in the appendix.

Procedures

1. Write homophone pairs on cards and shuffle.
2. Students divide the group into two equal teams, and one player from each team is selected as the artist for that round. The artist must draw a picture representing the given homophone which will elicit the homophone itself, the spelling, and the meaning.
3. A card is pulled from the deck and shown simultaneously to the artists for both teams. As the artists draw, their teammates call out possible answers. When the correct word is offered, the artist calls on someone to spell both words in a pair.
4. A point is awarded to the team that provides the correct information first. Play proceeds in the same fashion.

Homophone Rummy 7–21

This activity is suitable for two to six students. The object of the game is to discard all of the cards in one hand as well as to get the most number of homophone pairs or points (Figure 7-12).

Materials

Prepare several decks of homophone pairs (52 cards, 26 pairs). A list of homophones can be found in the appendix. Select words your students know.

---

*Barry Mahanes based this on the television show.

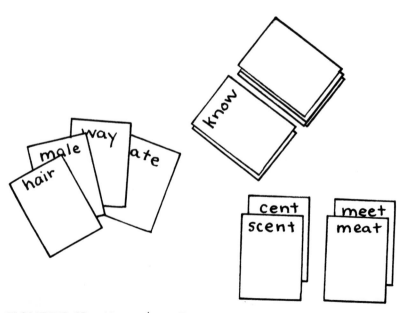

FIGURE 7–12   Homophone Rummy

Procedures

1. Each player is dealt ten cards (two players); seven cards (three to four players); six cards (five to six players).
2. Players check their hands for already-existing pairs. Once a pair is discovered, the meaning for each word is given in order to receive points. In giving definitions, the players may use the actual word in a sentence to show the meaning until they become well versed in homophone definitions; then, they must give a definition of the word separate from its use in a sentence or a synonym for the word. Each pair receives one point; any other additional homophone for the pair receives one additional point.
3. The remainder of the deck is placed in a central location as the drawing pile in which the first card is turned up.
4. The person on the left of the dealer goes first. Each player draws from the deck or the discard pile. The player lays down any pairs as described in number 2, above. The player must then discard one card to end the turn. *Note:* If a card is taken from the discard line, all cards appearing below the card wanted also have to be taken. Also, the top card must be used.
5. The game is over when one player has no cards left. That person yells "rummy!" Then the pairs are counted up.

Variations

1. Rather than having a random mix of homophone pairs, the decks can be divided into homophones by sound or homophones by syllable accent. This creates an opportunity to examine homophones by both sound and spelling patterns as well as syllable and accent patterns. Each deck of cards can consist of two to four contrasting sound patterns or syllable/accent patterns which the children have to sort.
2. A player can be challenged by someone else disagreeing with the definitions. The person who challenges looks up the words in the dictionary. Whoever is right gets to keep the pair.
3. Each player can play off of other players' cards, receiving additional points for each homophone found.
4. If a player has a card that can be added to a set or sequence but does not realize it and discards it, another player detecting what happened can pick up the card discarded, and add it to a sequence. That player then gets to discard one card.
5. Homophone synonyms can be used in this game. For each homophone, a child has to come up with at least one synonym. For example, if the pair was *through* and *threw,* synonyms corresponding to this pair might be *finished* and *pitched.*

Terse Verse Rhyme 7–22

In small groups, students think of rhyming pairs that describe an object, for example, *pink/sink, bear/lair, sled/bed.**

Procedures

Read *One Sun* by Bruce McMillan (1990) to the group. Discuss the structure of the language and the book. Students will see how the author uses photographs to illustrate the "terse verse."

---

*Carolyn Melchiorre developed this literature extension.

FIGURE 7-13   Terse Verse: Create a Clever Rhyme

Work with students to create a terse verse. First, think of an object (e.g., sink, bear, bed). Then ask the group to think of rhyming words that correspond with the object (see Figure 7-13). Accept all responses and write them on a chart. Continue this process with the group until they are confident they understand the task.

Students can create their own terse verse to challenge the group. They might opt to omit one word in the sequence:

There's a _____ in the pail. (whale)
The _____ is sad. (Dad)

Rhyming pairs collected from terse verse may be sorted by sound and pattern and may serve as the basis for other games.

Variations

1. Challenge students to draw a picture card and exchange with a friend who must figure out the terse verse.
2. For a real challenge, students use multisyllabic words.

Homophone Decks 7–23

There are a variety of games that can be played with decks of homophone cards. "The Homophone Deck" is a series of decks arranged by difficulty. Developed by Marilyn Pryle and Jeff Cantrell, these decks are used by students to play a variety of games in which they match the words by patterns including Homophone Rummy, Homophone Go-Fish, and Homophone Memory. Decks are available from Dr. Jeffrey Cantrell, PAN 142, Scranton, PA 18510-4603, phone 570-941-7421 (e-mail cantrellr1@uofs.edu).

Semantic Brainstorms 7–24

This is a small-group activity that focuses on the meaning of the words. This is a great game for content studies.

Procedures

1. Choose a topic for students to study. Topics can be chosen by students and can be related to content studies. Start with easy, familiar topics like sports and locations (countries, animal life, clothes, furniture, sports, modes of transportation).

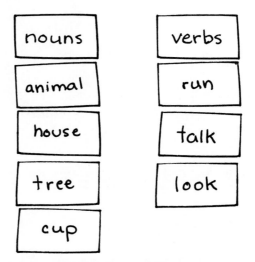

FIGURE 7-14 Grammatical Relations Can Be Examined in Semantic Sorts

2. Students brainstorm related words and write them down. Look for fluency of the brainstorming to assess success.
3. Students share their findings and see if they can come up with subcategories from their brainstorming. Categories can be circled by color or written over into columns.

Variations

Look in magazines, newspapers, and catalogs. Circle words that express feelings, color words, people's names, or parts of speech.

Semantic Sorts 7–25

Students work with content-related words to compare and contrast.

Procedures

1. Look through a chapter or unit in a textbook and make a list of the key terms. Often, they are listed at the end of a unit. Make word cards for the words.
2. Students sort the words in an open sort, establishing their own categories. Start with easy, familiar topics like sports, locations, animal life, clothes, furniture, and modes of transportation.
3. The sorts are copied into word study notebooks in a separate section for that content area.

Variations

Grammatical Sorts is a variation in which students sort by parts of speech (see Figure 7-14). For example, students can collect nouns and then divide them into different types of nouns (e.g., things that move/animate vs. stationary/ inanimate nouns).

cow	rock
boat	uranium
cats	plants

When students look for differences in the concepts, they begin to debate. In just this easy example, one could argue that there is something quite active about both uranium and plants.

CHAPTER 8

Word Study for Intermediate Readers and Writers: The Syllables and Affixes Stage

The intermediate stage is a time of expanding reading interests and fine-tuning of reading strategies. In previous developmental stages, the challenges posed by what the children are reading stem more from children's level of word knowledge than from their background knowledge about the topic or genre. At the intermediate and advanced levels, the challenges they encounter in reading will come more from the conceptual load in whatever they are trying to read. The nature of students' word knowledge allows them to read more fluently, exercising and expanding their increasing level of cognitive and language sophistication.

Students will be reading, writing, and thinking about polysyllabic words for quite some time before they have developed into intermediate readers and writers whose word knowledge is characterized by what we have termed **syllables and affixes.** Because their knowledge of vowel and consonant patterns within single-syllable words has become so automatic, reading and writing are much more fluent. This knowledge of pattern can now support students' learning about two types of features within simple polysyllabic words: (1) how these consonant and vowel patterns are represented in polysyllabic words, and (2) what occurs where syllables join together. When students examine polysyllabic words, attending to these two types of features, they are building their spelling efficiency. They are also developing a more efficient word identification routine for reading, because the ability to perceive syllables rapidly within polysyllabic words contributes to reading efficiency.

LITERACY LEARNING AND INSTRUCTION

Word study at the intermediate level should demonstrate to students how their word knowledge can be applied to advance their spelling knowledge, their vocabulary, and their strategies for figuring out unknown words. At the intermediate and middle grades, the following principles should guide instruction:

- If students are actively involved in the exploration of words, they are more likely to develop a positive attitude toward word learning and a curiosity about words.
- Students' prior knowledge should be engaged; this is especially important if they are learning the specialized vocabulary in different disciplines or content areas.
- Students should have many exposures to words in meaningful contexts, both in and out of connected text.
- A sequence of teaching about structural elements should be followed: syllables, affixes, and the effects of affixes on the base words to which they're attached.

Teachers can model for students how to focus on what they need to attend to in examining many polysyllabic words. Listen in as one teacher models this skill for her students.

> While standing at an overhead projector, Ms. Lee begins:
> "Kids, a number of you have been trying out words in your writing that end with an /er/ sound. This sound can be spelled different ways, so I'd like to focus on thinking about the spelling for a moment. Now, here's how one of you spelled the word *tractor* in your writing [writes TRACTER on the transparency]. Let's see, now. You correctly spelled *t, r, a, c, t,* and *r.* You knew almost all of the word! Here's the only letter that caused some problems [pointing to *e*]. Actually, the letter right here should be *o.* You can't hear this sound clearly, so you need to remember this spelling. Concentrate on this letter as you examine this word and some other words this week that end with the /er/ sound. Remember, this one letter is all you have to remember because you already know how to spell the rest of the word."

This simple, straightforward explanation does two important things:

1. It demonstrates to children how much they already know about spelling a particular word—spelling is not an all-or-none affair where they "get a word wrong." Usually they will get most of the word correct, and teachers need to remind and reassure students about this.
2. It demonstrates to children what they need to focus on when they look at a word; because they already know most of the word, they need attend to the part that is still challenging.

Teachers can begin to engage students in examining how important word elements—prefixes, suffixes, and base words—combine. This understanding is a powerful tool for vocabulary development, spelling, and figuring out unfamiliar words during reading. Once again, listen to Ms. Lee as she models for her students how to take a word apart to analyze its meaning:

> "I've underlined one of the words in this sentence: They had to <u>redo</u> the programs after they were printed with a spelling error. What does *redo* mean? Yes, Adrienne?"
>
> "When you have to do something over again?"
>
> "Okay! So you already had done something once, right? Now, let's cover up this first part of the word [covers *re*]. What word do we have? Right—*do.* Now, let's look at these words."
>
> Ms. Lee writes the words *join, tell,* and *organize* on the board.
>
> "When we join the prefix *re* to each of them, what happens? Right! We are going to be doing these things again—we can rejoin a group, retell a story, reorganize our classroom." Ms. Lee writes the prefix *re* in front of each base word as she pronounces the new word. She then asks the students what they think the prefix *re* means. After a brief discussion, she asks a student to look up the prefix in the dictionary to check their definitions.

Beginning in second and third grade for some students, and in fourth grade for most, cognitive and language potential allows children to make new and richer connections among the words they know and the words they will learn. As you teach students at these levels, you will find the whole enterprise of learning about words to be fascinating—as well as never-ending. This awareness can sustain your interest and delight in words and in what your students will be learning about words. As at earlier stages, you will facilitate students' word explorations to help them discover the patterns of sound, spelling, and meaning that link thousands of words within word families. This knowledge will help them read, write, and spell much more effectively.

At the intermediate and middle grade levels, word study should be fun, but it should also be systematic, and it should be related effectively to the reading and writing that students are doing. It should also come to emphasize how the structure or spelling of words is a direct clue to learning and remembering the meaning of words. The intermediate and middle grades are a critical time for consolidating knowledge about the spelling of words with knowledge about how this spelling represents meaning. As you learned in Chapter 2, the stages of word knowledge through which most students will move during these years are termed *syllables and affixes* and *derivational relations.* In this chapter addressing syllables and affixes, and the next chapter addressing derivational relations, you will learn how teachers can establish a firm foundation in spelling and in vocabulary development as they facilitate students' move into understanding the role of structure and meaning in the spelling system.

CHARACTERISTICS OF ORTHOGRAPHIC DEVELOPMENT DURING THE SYLLABLES AND AFFIXES STAGE

Children in the syllables and affixes stage are already familiar with single-syllable patterns. During this stage, they will learn how these single-syllable patterns also apply in polysyllabic words. In addition, they will learn how these patterns influence spelling at the **juncture** of syllables—where syllables join within printed words.

Table 8-1 presents some representative errors by students in the early and middle/late syllables and affixes stage. These students will continue to examine less common vowel patterns (such as *crawl*) and revisit common vowel patterns in two-syllable words (such as *early*). They will examine the junctures of syllables (*rabbit, hoping, hopping*), the spelling of vowels in **unaccented** syllables (*organ, barber, helmet*), and the spelling of some more complex consonants (the spelling of the /j/ sound in *damage*).

While students are spending time examining and consolidating their word knowledge at the level of the syllable, part of their focus will naturally include attention to **base words** and simple **prefixes** and **suffixes**—the meaning or morphemic aspects of the syllables. This examination provides the basic understanding of how these important word

TABLE 8-1	Examples of Spelling at the Syllables and Affixes Stage		
Early		**Middle/Late**	
hopping	HOPING	barber	BARBAR
crawl	CROLL, CRAUL	helmet	HELMIT, HELMENT
dollar	DOLER	skipping	SKIPING
useful	USFUL, USFULL	ugly	UGLEY
circle	CIRCEL, CIRCILE	hurry	HEARY, HURREY
early	ERLY, EIRLY	traced	TRAISSED
keeper	KEPER, KEPPER	parading	PERADDING, PARRADING
		damage	DAMIGE, DAMADGE

parts combine to form words and their meaning. It is important that students encounter and learn to read many, many words that are constructed from these meaning or morphemic elements; for example: *unlock = un +* lock; likable = *like + able; uneventful = un + event + ful.*

Concepts to Be Learned at the Syllables and Affixes Stage

There are several important concepts that student learn during this stage. We explore these concepts here in a way that will allow you to introduce the concepts to your students.

Open and Closed Syllables

To double or not to double? Answering this question depends on whether you're dealing with an open or a closed syllable. **Open syllables** end with a long vowel sound (*labor, reason*), and **closed syllables** contain a short vowel sound that is usually closed by two consonants (*rabbit, racket*). Let's see how this works at a basic level first: When students in second and third grade examine what happens when the inflected endings *ed* and *ing* are added to short and long vowel pattern words, they are learning the basics of open and closed syllables. Consider these examples:

hop + ing = hopping   hope + ing = hoping
strip + ing = stripping stripe + ing = striping

When you are uncertain about whether to double the consonants at the juncture of syllables, say the word and listen to the vowel sounds. If you hear a long sound, the syllable is open and will be followed by a single consonant. If you hear a short vowel sound, the odds are likely that the syllable will need to be closed by two consonants. For example, if you are writing about how a rabbit moves along the ground (*hopping*) and do not double the *p,* you'll wind up with an entirely different meaning (*hoping*).

Whereas within word patterns include the vowel and what follows within a single syllable, **syllable patterns** extend across the juncture—the point where syllables join—thus including parts of two syllables. Table 8-2 lists the common syllable patterns.

The first two syllable patterns, the open VCV pattern and the closed VCCV pattern, are the most frequent. The third pattern, the closed VCV pattern, occurs less frequently than the others. The fourth pattern, the closed VCCCV pattern, is quite frequent. Words that follow this pattern include a consonant digraph or blend at the syllable juncture. If a blend occurs at the juncture, the word is divided before the blend (*pil-grim*); if a digraph is at the juncture, the word is divided after the digraph (*laughter*). The VV pattern has each vowel contributing a sound; the word is usually divided after the long vowel sound (*ri-ot, du-el*).

TABLE 8-2 Syllable Patterns		
Label	**Type**	**Examples**
VCV	Open	lazy, coma, beacon, bacon
VCCV	Closed	skipping, button, rubber, window
VCV	Closed	river, robin, cover, planet
VCCCV	Closed	laughter, pilgrim, instant, complain
VV	Open	create, riot, liar, fuel

Accent

Some syllables are accented or emphasized more than others. Dictionaries use bold apostrophes to show which syllables are stressed. Intermediate dictionaries often bold-face the stressed syllable: for example, *rabbit* = /**răb′** ĭt/; *deposit* = /dĭ **pŏz′** ĭt/. Just as with open and closed syllables, however, accent is first thought of in terms of sound rather than print. Start with your first name (if it contains two or more syllables) or the name of a friend. When you pronounce it, where are you putting most emphasis? Which syllable seems to sound louder than the others? If your name is Molly, you pronounce it as MOLLee—not moLEE. If your name is Jennifer, you say JENifer, not jeNIfer or jenniFER.

Now try this with certain **homographs**—words that are spelled alike but whose meaning changes with a shift in accent:

You give someone a PRESent, not a presENT.
You reCORD a message, you don't RECord it.
You are conTENT when you are with someone you care deeply about, not CONtent.

Thinking about accent as it works with names and then with certain homographs should help solidify this concept for you. This is also the sequence you should follow with your students, beginning in the upper elementary grades.

When examining words of more than one syllable, knowing about accent helps students identify what they know about the spelling of a polysyllabic word and what they don't know: what they will need to pay particular attention to. For example, when students pronounce *market*, they realize they know the spelling of the accented syllable (*mar*) yet may be uncertain about the vowel spelling in the second unaccented syllable. When students grasp the concept of an accented syllable, therefore, they also learn about the other side of this concept: the unaccented syllable. The unaccented syllable is the one in which the spelling of the vowel (the schwa) is unclear, so students will need to pay close attention to it. As we'll see a little later, the spelling of the schwa in the unaccented syllable can often be explained in terms of meaning.

Vowel Patterns

There are a number of vowel patterns within single-syllable and polysyllabic words that are not sorted out until the upper elementary years:

/ô/ as in *haul, straw, thought*
/oi/ as in *enjoy, embroider*
/ou/ as in *mountain, chowder*

Students must also explore vowel spellings in unaccented syllables. As you learned in Chapter 7, by paying attention to the position of many ambiguous vowels, students can often determine which spelling pattern occurs most often. For example, *aw* and *oy* usually occur at the end of words or syllables (*straw, boycott*), whereas *au* and *oi* are found within syllables (*fault, voice*).

By the middle of the syllables and affixes stage, vowel patterns for the /əl/ and /ər/ sounds at the end of words are examined. In word study, students learn the relations between spelling and grammatical functions and meaning:

/ər/ as in *winter, motor, dollar*
/əl/ as in *nickel, middle, metal*

They also examine the /chə r/ and /j/ sounds in various spelling patterns in unstressed syllables:

/chər/ as in *lecture, puncture*
/j/ as in *village, bridge, damage*

Base Words and Affixes

Research in vocabulary instruction has underscored the critical importance of students' understanding how prefixes and suffixes combine with base words and **word roots** to create new words. This understanding can help students analyze unknown words they encounter in their reading and lead to a rich expansion and elaboration of their vocabularies. Attention to the spelling and the meaning of these word parts reinforces this understanding. Teachers begin to facilitate students' examination of these features when students are farther along in the syllables and affixes stage. The groundwork for this examination is laid when students begin to investigate the addition of plural and inflectional endings to base words. They will then examine the meaning and spelling effects of combining simple prefixes, suffixes, and base words. For example:

Prefixes *un, re, dis*
Suffix *er* as in *better* and *longer* denotes a comparison of some type.
Suffixes *er* as in *baker* and *farmer* and *or* as in *professor, generator* both denote
    "someone or something who does something"; words that have come from
    Latin use the *or* spelling.
Suffixes *ful, ly, ness*

This type of study will extend to more complex prefixes, suffixes, and Greek and Latin word roots in the derivational relations stage discussed in Chapter 9.

WORD STUDY INSTRUCTION: SYLLABLES AND AFFIXES

Sequence of Word Study

A sequence of word study during this stage is presented in Table 8-3. This sequence touches on the important patterns and features to consider, and is based on what students do developmentally (Ganske, 1994; Templeton, 1992).

Word Study Routines in the Syllables and Affixes Stage

Students in this stage of development are usually ready for a fair amount of individual and small-group work. The classroom organization discussed in Chapter 4 should be considered as you aim for self-direction in student work. You want students to know word study routines well enough for them to become responsible to work toward their personal best. In this way, students become involved in gauging their progress and effort. This personal responsibility and understanding of word study activities leaves time for you to work with small groups of students in your classroom.

TABLE 8-3   Sequence of Word Study: Syllables and Affixes

- Plural endings
  - s/es   *walks, beaches*
- Compound words   *pancake, sidewalk*
- Inflectional endings
  - doubling   *stopping*
  - e-drop   *hoping*
  - no change   *walking, nailing*
- Changing final *y* to *i*   *bunny/bunnies, happy/happily*
- Open and closed syllables
  - VCCV double   *button, cattle*
  - VCCV different   *window, sister*
  - VCV open   *bacon, lazy*
  - VCV closed   *river, cover*
- Vowel patterns in accented and unaccented syllables
  - Vowel patterns in accented syllables   *parading, preparing*
  - Vowel patterns in unaccented syllables   *deposit*
  - Two-syllable homophones   *pedal/petal/peddle*
  - Two-syllable homographs   *PRESent/presENT*
  - Spelling patterns at the ends of words:
    - *el/le; or/er/ar*   *label/middle, doctor, lawyer, lunar*
    - schwa + *r*   *beggar/barber/actor*
    - schwa + *n*   *captain/human/frighten/basin/apron*
    - schwa + *l*   *angel/able/central/civil/fertile*
- The /j/ sound at the middle and end of words   *badger/major, village*
- The /chər/   *culture*
- Base words + simple prefixes
  - *un* not   unlock
  - *re* again   remake
  - *dis* opposite   distasteful
  - *in* not*   inappropriate
  - *non* not   nonfiction
  - *mis* wrong   misfire
  - *pre* before   preview
  - *uni* one   unicycle
  - *bi* two   bicycle
  - *tri* three   tricycle
  - *en/em* make   empower
- Base words + simple suffixes
  - *ful* full of, like   graceful, peaceful
  - *ly* like   gladly
  - *less* without   penniless
  - *ness* condition   happiness
  - *ion/tion* state of, characterized by   perfection

*There are other meanings for *in,* but this is the most frequent and occurs more often in words students at this level are reading.

Grouping students developmentally often results in four or five word study groups in intermediate classrooms. This means that in terms of classroom organization, it will be difficult for you to see each group every day. Therefore, you may decide to meet with students twice a week in small groups, and collect and review their word study notebooks once a week. Some teachers schedule 15 to 20 minutes of a class period when students can work individually or with partners on developmentally appropriate activities.

Students continue to use word study notebooks throughout this stage. These notebooks are divided into various sections. To keep things relatively simple, Tamara Baren has her students divide their word study notebooks into two sections. The first section is titled "Word Study" and contains the developmental sorts. This section includes weekly records of sorts, word hunts, lists generated in small groups, written reflections of sorts, and sorts assigned for homework. The second section is called "Looking into Language" and contains records of related words like lists of words categorized by parts of speech in language arts, student-generated semantic webs of content area studies, and lists of words related to themes and units of study.

Take care to provide a clear model for students as you introduce them to basic word study activities and routines. Some word study routines can be introduced in a whole-class setting with word cards written on transparency chips for an overhead. Students are often sent from these whole-class sessions to explore words in groups and independently. In small-group meetings, you can demonstrate sorts that are geared to students at different developmental levels.

You will want to introduce your students to the fundamentals of sorting and comparing words. The 10 word study activities in the following list give you a sense of the word study routines that are teacher-directed or student-selected. Through these simple activities you can show students that it is easy to take apart and add to words. With a list of words containing patterns that are useful for your students to study, you can show them how to play with words:

1. Choose five words from your list. Circle the base word in each.
2. Make appropriate words on your lists plural.
3. Choose five words on your list. For each word make as many new words as possible using the same letters.
4. Circle any prefixes you find in the words on your list.
5. Underline any suffixes you find in the words on your list.
6. Choose three words on your list. Change at least one letter to create a new word.
7. Add a prefix and/or suffix, when possible, to words on your list.
8. Classify your words according to subject area: art, math, science, language, social studies.
9. Go for speed. See how fast you can sort your words.
10. Generate lists. Write five words with one pattern, then have students find 10 more that follow the pattern.

In the activities section of this chapter, you will find many games and sorts to help your students examine syllable patterns and affixes in both small groups and with a partner.

Word Knowledge in Context: How to Analyze an Unfamiliar Word

As your students explore words at both the syllables and affixes and derivational relations stages, you can directly show them how to apply this knowledge when they encounter unknown words in their reading. Because spelling and vocabulary knowledge underlie the efficient application of word analysis in reading, the following strategy is useful for approaching new words in reading:

1. Examine the word for meaningful parts—base word, prefixes, or suffixes.
   a. If there is a prefix, take it off first.
   b. If there is a suffix, take it off second.
   c. Look at the base or root to see if you know it or if you can think of a related word (a word that has the same base or root).
   d. Reassemble the word, thinking about the meaning contributed by the base or root, the suffix, and then the prefix. This should give you a more specific idea of what the word is.

2. Try pronunciation, looking for familiar patterns and trying out pronunciations of syllables.
3. Try out the meaning in the sentence; check if it makes sense in the context of the sentence and the larger context of the text that is being read.
4. If the word still does not make sense, or if you were unable to break the word down into affixes and base or root—and if it is still critical to the meaning of the overall passage—then look it up in the dictionary.
5. Record the new word in your word study notebook.

Let's take a look at how Ms. Lee might model this process for students, with the following text displayed on a transparency:

To say that Kim was disillusioned when at last she saw their vacation island would be putting it mildly. It did not look like the travel poster at all—there wasn't much of a beach, and what there was seemed to have stringy seaweed all over it. A cold wind blew without letup.

Here is how Ms. Lee guides her students through the process:

"I don't know this word [pointing to *disillusioned*], so I'll try to take it apart. It looks like there's a prefix, *dis.* That leaves *illusioned*, and *ed* is a suffix, so I'll take that off. That leaves *illusion.* I've heard of that—I think it's like when something isn't real. *Dis* usually means 'not' or the opposite of something. I'll think about the context. It sounds like Kim isn't happy. She was expecting something else, whatever it was like in the poster—but here she's found a disappointing beach with stringy seaweed all over it. And, to top it off, it's cold! So, this word [pointing again to *disillusioned*] may have something to do with being unhappy. So, Kim was 'not illusioned'? Hmm . . . let's see if that fits with the context . . . she expected something else, but it was not the way the island really was—kind of like her expectation was an illusion, not real."

It may seem like a lot of work to talk through this process for students and then help guide them through it. Like the development of any other skill, it does take some time at first. However, it's critical to introduce, model, and reinforce this process for students, because as they move through the grades and read more widely, they will encounter many new terms that are not highlighted and supported by a rich context. In addition to helping students read through texts with more ease, this strategy will become one of the most effective means of developing and extending their vocabulary knowledge.

You will notice that authors of many textbooks try to provide a rich context to support new vocabulary as well as highlighting important new terms for the reader. Although students need to learn about these features, they also need to learn the strategy discussed here so that they can grow confidently and competently into independent word learners. This strategy depends critically on the students' knowledge of word structure. Adams (1990) best emphasized this importance:

Learning from context is a very, very important component of vocabulary acquisition. But this means of learning is available only to the extent that children . . . bother to process the spelling—the orthographic structure—of the unknown words they encounter. Where they skip over an unknown word without attending to it, and often readers do, no learning can occur. Acquisition of the meaning of a word from context depends on the linkage of the contextually evoked meaning with the structural image of the word. (p. 150)

Activities for Students in the Syllables and Affixes Stage

This section outlines word sorts, word hunts, and board games for students in the syllables and affixes stage. Several activities are carefully designed sorts to guide students in a discussion of important features that have been outlined in the sequence of instruction. You will enjoy taking your students through these sorts.

Plural Word Sorts 8–1

In this activity, students use a classification to look for words ending in *s* and *es*.*

Procedures

1. Create a word sheet using words such as those in sort 64 in the appendix (e.g., *peaches*, *picks*, and *slices*).
2. Ask students how the words are all alike (e.g., they end in *s* or *es*, are all plurals). Ask them, "What categories can we set up? How do we know when to spell the plural ending *s* and when to spell it *es*?"
3. Students begin a sort for words needing *es* endings in their word study notebooks. They can add new words to each category.

Compound Word Sorts 8–2

By exploring **compound words,** students can develop several types of understandings. First, they learn how different words can combine in different ways to form new words. This is the beginning understanding of the combinatorial features of English words. Second, they lay the foundation for explicit attention to syllables, because so often compound words comprise two smaller words, each of which is a single syllable. Third, students reinforce their knowledge of the spelling of many high-frequency, high-utility words in English, because these words include so many compound words.

*Amy M. Dixon developed this activity.

Procedures

1. Share some common compound words with the students, for example, *cookbook* and *bedroom*. Discuss their meaning, pointing out how each word in the compound contributes to the meaning of the whole word.
2. With the words presented in the appendix, conduct open sorts with a small group—for example, words that have to do with people (*anyone, someone, somebody, nobody, anybody*) or things we find outdoors (*sunshine, airplane, campfire, airport*). Then have the students do open sorts working in pairs.
3. Have students cut words apart. Then have them arrange the single-syllable words in two columns, and challenge them to create as many compound words as they can. Some words will be legitimate, real words; others will be words that do not yet exist, but they could. Share and discuss their words. Students may then write sentences using these pseudo words, and draw a picture that illustrates the meaning of each.
4. An interesting variation is for students to explore how many compound words can be made from one word. For example: *any* plus *time, one, how, body,* and so forth.

VCCV and Doublets Word Sort 8–3

This activity is suitable for small groups, and its purpose is to look at patterns in words when students are deciding how to divide words into syllables. This sort compares VCCV words (*ten-der*) and doublets that also follow this pattern (*kit-ten*).

Materials

Use the syllable patterns sorts in the appendix, e.g., sort 72.

Procedures

1. Explain to your students that you are going to place each word card under the pattern that it matches. Ask the students to attend to patterns as you say each word, and tell them that the patterns they are looking at will help them better remember the spelling of these words.
2. Next, shuffle the word cards and say each word as you place it in the appropriate column, for example, *lum-ber, mar-ket, dol-lar, din-ner*. Sort three to four words into each column. After you have sorted the words, ask the students how the words in column 1 are alike. Encourage the students to look at patterns in column 1, and then ask them if anyone noticed where the words were "divided" when you pronounced them. Then go to column 2 and guide the students' examination in the same fashion.
3. On their own, students can sort these words until they are comfortable with the pattern.
4. On another occasion, you could call out the words and the students would write them in the appropriate column in their word study notebook.

Variations

1. Use the VCCV pattern words and, together with the following V/CV pattern words, sort according to V/CV or VC/CV pattern (exemplars may be *canvas* and *basic*).
   baby, hoping, writer, before, begin, beside
   basic, even, waving, bacon, chosen, moment
   raking, human, pilot, silent, season, navy
   music, female, stolen, robot, prefer
   Guide the students through these questions: In which pattern is the first vowel usually short? Why? In which pattern is the first vowel usually long? Why?

2. Sort the preceding V/CV words with the following VC/V words:
cabin, planet, finish, robin, magic, limit, cousin, prison
habit, punish, cover, manage, medal, promise, closet, camel

Spelling *ed* and *t* Endings 8–4

In these three sorts, students look at past tense spelling patterns.* (See sorts 62 and 68 in the appendix.)

Procedures

1. Establish the three sound categories for words that end in *ed:* /t/ *stopped*, /ed/ *traded*, and /d/ *mailed.* Students try to find common features with each list. Notice that most *ed* words which sound like /t/ have a base word that ends in *k, p, s,* or *x.* In contrast, the base words in the next category combine with the ending to form two syllables. These words can be easily recognized by the /d/ or /t/ ending on the base word. The last category includes base words with a variety of endings. The base word combines with the *ed* ending to form a single-syllable word with a distinctive /d/ sound at the end.
2. In this sort, students sort for word endings.

t	*ed*
knelt	*chased*

3. Ask the students to name the present tense verb for each past tense verb. Place word cards by each column so that the students can make comparisons. If the student is having difficulty producing the present tense verb, use sentences as models (e.g., Mary swept the house yesterday, but today Mary needs to sweep the house again). The cards should look like this:

knelt (kneel)	*chased (chase)*

4. Compare the lists. Most students will easily see that the first column with *t* endings contains verbs where the past tense verb is a completely different word from the present tense verb. In the second column, the students might notice that the *ed* ending is added to the present tense to form the past tense verb, and that you can always find the complete present tense verb in a past tense verb.
5. Ask students to circle the present tense within each of the past tense words in the second column.
6. Ask students to search for the one exception to this pattern in the sort. Most students will discover the present tense verb *deal* in *dealt*, but usually students can remember this exception by the change in vowel sound.

Double Scoop 8–5

This board game will help children develop automaticity in writing words with inflectional endings. It is appropriate for small groups of two to four students.†

Materials

Gameboard (see Figure 8-1), playing pieces, spinner or die, board for writing answers, and sentence cards as shown here:

The bunny was <u>hopping</u> down the road.
The cat is <u>sunning</u> herself on the chair.

---

*Karen Broaddus developed this activity.
†Marilyn Edwards developed this game.

Brittany <u>shopped</u> at her favorite store yesterday.
We go <u>swimming</u> in the summer.
Danny <u>flopped</u> down on his bed.
The child was <u>running</u> through the store.
I don't like people who go around <u>bragging</u>.
I <u>slipped</u> on the ice.
Jerry was so tired he felt like <u>quitting</u>.
The kite string became <u>knotted</u>.

He <u>pushed</u> the cart.
Why are they <u>jumping</u> around?
Stop <u>kicking</u> me!
She <u>pumped</u> her arms up and down.
My dog is good at <u>finding</u> his way home.
The frogs <u>croaked</u> loudly.
I felt like I was <u>floating</u> on the wind.
My brother is <u>sleeping</u> in today.
I <u>peeled</u> the banana.
The bucket <u>leaked</u>.

I enjoy <u>trading</u> baseball cards.
He is <u>diving</u> into the pool.
She <u>glided</u> across the ice.
I like <u>riding</u> bikes.
I <u>hoped</u> you would come.

FIGURE 8–1 Double Scoop Gameboard

I like <u>sliding</u> down water slides.
We went <u>skating</u> across the ice.

He <u>wasted</u> his time at the movie.

Will you please stop your <u>whining</u>?

The paint was <u>flaking</u> off.

Procedures

1. Players put their pieces on the sun to start.
2. Player 1 reads a sentence card and repeats the underlined word.
3. Player 2 then writes the word under the appropriate heading on the writing board.
4. The caller then checks the opponent's answer by comparing it to the sentence card. If it is correct, the writer spins and moves that number of spaces on the playing board.
5. The players then switch roles—one becomes the reader and the other becomes the writer.
6. The first player to reach the double scoop of ice cream wins.

Variations

Sort just the sentence cards by whether or not the final consonant is doubled before the ending is added: for example, *hoped, pinned.*

Freddy, the Hopping, Jumping, Diving Frog 8–6

In this board game for two to four players, students sort words that end in *ing* according to these three categories (see the word list in the appendix):*

No Change	**Double**	**E-Drop**
punching	*bragging*	*trading*

Procedures

1. Use a follow-the-path board marked with these labels: *double, no change,* and *e-drop.* (For an example, see the gameboard in the appendix.)
2. Roll die to determine who goes first. Play proceeds clockwise.
3. Place drawing cards facedown in the center of the board.
4. Player 1 draws one card, reads the card aloud, and moves to the closest space that matches the features of the word. For example, if the card says *hopping,* the player moves to the nearest space that says *double.*
5. A player who draws a penalty or advancement card must follow the directions on the card.
6. Cards are discarded on the sorting board under the correct headings: *double, no change,* and *e-drop.*
7. Upon reaching the home lily pad, a player must correctly read the words on the discard folder in order to win. A player who misreads a word must move back five spaces, and play continues.

Penalty or Advancement Cards

1. You have the strongest legs. Jump ahead to the next lily pad.
2. Skip two spaces if you correctly pronounce the e-drop words on the discard folder.
3. Your croaking made me lose sleep. Move back two spaces.
4. You ate too many flies. Move back two spaces.

---

*This activity is provided courtesy of Barbara Santos.

Variations

1. Discard by sorting *no change* words by sound.
2. Determine the pattern for these *no change* words.
3. Write uninflected forms on cards (*hop, jump, dive*), have players decide how the form should be spelled, and move to the appropriate place. Include an answer sheet with words in alphabetical order to check if there is a disagreement.

Slap Jack 8-7

This card game may be used to contrast open- and closed-syllable words as represented by any of the syllable spelling patterns (V/CV with VCCV; V/CV with VC/V). It is played by two students. The object of the game is for one player to win all 52 cards. If time runs out, the winner is the player with the most cards.

Materials

On 52 small index cards, write the words that you want to be contrasted. There should be 26 words that have a closed-syllable pattern and 26 words that have an open-syllable pattern. For example, 26 words would follow the open-syllable V/CV pattern (*pilot, human*) and 26 would follow the closed-syllable VCCV pattern (*funny, basket*). See lists in the appendix for a V/CV versus VCCV deck. Additional decks may be made from the other lists in the appendix.

Directions

1. The cards are dealt one at a time until the pack is completely dealt. The players keep their cards facedown in a pile in front of them.
2. Each player places a card faceup in a common pile. Whenever two words with either open syllables or closed syllables are turned up together, the first player to slap the pile takes all the cards in the common pile and puts them at the bottom of his or her pile.
3. Turning cards and slapping must be done with the same hand.
4. A player who slaps the common pile when there are not two open- or closed-syllable words must give both cards to the other player.
5. The students must be able to pronounce the words. (*Note*: To ensure that the students can pronounce all of the words in the deck, have them quickly read through the cards first. Have a second deck on hand with the same patterns. Then, if one or both students do not know a particular word, they can draw a card from the second deck. If they know the word they can add it to the first deck. They then insert the unknown word into the second deck.)

Variations

Once students are comfortable contrasting two syllable patterns, an additional pattern may be added to the deck—for example, VC/V (*cabin, water*).

Base Word/Suffix Sorts: Changing y to i 8-8

The purpose of this sort is to look at patterns in words to decide when *y* changes to *i* and when it remains the same. It works well with small groups.

Materials

File folder and word cards; the inside of the file folder is labeled with *carry* and *carried* as column heads. See sort 64 in the appendix.

Directions

1. Explain to your students that you are going to place each word card under either the base word or the related word. After you have sorted the words, ask the students why they think the spelling of the base word changed when *ed* or *es* was added.
2. On their own, students can sort these words until they are comfortable with the pattern. You could then lead a closed sort and have the students write the words down on a paper they have labeled with two columns, *penny* and *pennies*.
3. On another occasion, you could call out the words, and the students would write them in the appropriate column in their word study notebook (e.g., *carry, carried*). See the appendix for a *y* to *i* sort.

Variations

1. Now explore single-syllable base words that end in *y: dry, dried, cry, cries, try, tried, fly, flies.*
2. Add the following base and related words to words from the previous sorts; why doesn't the *y* change to *i? turkey, turkeys, donkey, donkeys, chimney, chimneys.*
3. Sort base words and related words to which the suffixes *er* and *est* have been added: *tiny, tinier, tiniest; pretty, prettier, prettiest; crazy, crazier, craziest; early, earlier, earliest; happy, happier, happiest*
4. In some words, such as *baby*, and *copy*, the spelling of *y* does not change when suffixes beginning with *i* are added. Present the following words, ask the students why they think the spelling doesn't change, then go on a word hunt to find other examples: *baby, babyish; copy, copyist.*

Double Crazy Eights 8–9

This activity is designed to review teacher-directed instruction on consonant doubling and *e*-drop, and at the same time reexamine the various spellings of /k/ in two-syllable words. On the basis of the traditional card game "Crazy Eights," students can play in pairs or in groups of three. The object of the game is to get rid of all the cards in your hand. This is a good follow-up to sort number 70 in the appendix.

Materials

52 word cards comprising four suits: (1) V*ck* pattern (*tacking*), (2) V-*k-e* pattern (*baking*), (3) VV-*k* pattern (*looking; speaking*), (4) VC-*k* pattern (*asking*). 13 words per suit. Four Crazy Eight cards designated by the words *eight, ate,* or the numeral 8. See sort 70 in the appendix for words to use on the cards.

Directions

1. Dealer gives each player eight cards. The remaining cards become the draw pile. The dealer turns the top card of the draw pile over and places it beside the deck. This card becomes the starter card and is the first card in the discard pile.
2. The player to the left of the dealer begins by placing a card that matches the starter card onto the discard pile. Matches may be made in four ways:
   a. By sound—long, short, or neither
   b. By pattern—V*ck*, V-*k-e*, VV-*k*, or VC-*k*
   c. By whether the consonant is doubled, the *e* dropped, or no change made
   d. With a Crazy Eight card, which can change its suit to anything the player chooses
3. If the player does not have a match, he or she must draw from the draw pile until a match is found.

4. If all the cards in the draw pile are used up, reserve the top card from the discard pile, shuffle the rest of the cards, and place them face down on the table as the new draw pile.
5. Play continues until one player has discarded all cards.

Variations

This game can be adapted simply by making up a new deck using words that focus on another spelling feature. Just remember, the deck must have four suits and allow for matching by at least two different elements.

You're Up / Password 8–10

The purpose of the game, which should be played with five students, is to contrast the spellings for the /ure/ sound: *ure* as in *picture* and *cher* as in *preacher,* as well as other incidents of the suffix *ure.* The format is similar to the Password game.

Materials

Scoring pad and pencil; stopwatch; Password covers such as the one in Figure 8-2.

Procedures

1. One student is designated as the recorder, while the other four pair up into two teams of two players. Each team decides who is player A and player B. The recorder flips a coin to see which team will go first.
2. Both players are given the Password covers with the first word to be played showing through the window. (Both teams are given the same word.)
3. Player A from the team that won the coin toss begins by giving player B (on the same team) a one-word clue as to the password on the card. This clue may not be any part of the word to be guessed, or contain the password in any form. If player B does not guess the correct word on the first attempt, the other team has a chance.
4. Play moves back and forth between teams until one team guesses the password. If both teams have given five clues and the password is still not guessed, the referee throws the word out. Players B are given the second word, with the second team's player B leading off with a one-word clue to his or her partner.

FIGURE 8-2 Password Cover for You're Up

5. Each time a team successfully guesses a word, they receive one point. If the same player that guessed the word can also spell the word, the team receives another point (total of two). If the player cannot spell the word, the opposing team has a chance to do so with whichever player was guessing the clues. The team with the most points wins.

6. For the teacher to assess students' knowledge of the targeted feature, and in the interest of fairness, the recorder is to write down the given clues on a sheet provided with the words played. The recorder also acts as referee and timekeeper, making sure only one-word clues are given and that those clues are in keeping with the rule. Keeping time involves allowing each team 15 seconds total for giving clues and guessing the password during each round, as well as a 15-second limit to spell the word.

Variations

1. Have students create their own Password cards with this feature, or another, for their fellow students to use.
2. This game could also be played with *ant/ent* words, providing an engaging way to practice spelling these words as well as sharpen vocabulary (see Chapter 9).

The Apple and the Bushel 8–11

The purpose of this board game is to help students differentiate between *le* and *el* endings. A prerequisite skill is the ability to sort rapidly words with *le* and *el* endings. See the list of *el* and *le* words in the appendix for words to use in this game.*

Materials

1. The Apple and Bushel gameboard (see Figure 8-3).
2. Game marker for each player.
3. Word cards with *le* and *el* endings left off. (Optional additional cards: words with *le* and *el* left on.)

Procedures

1. Students sort words with *le* and *el* endings to review (optional step).
2. Students roll die to determine order of turns.
3. Student draws card from pile and reads word out loud.
4. Student moves the marker to nearest *le* or *el* ending that would complete the word. (If there is disagreement among players about the correct ending, they should consult the dictionary.)
5. The game continues until one player reaches the bushel. (*Note:* To get in the bushel, an *le* word must be drawn. A player who draws an *el* word must move backwards and continue playing from that space.)

Variations

Students may sort word cards as they draw them from the pile. This will reinforce the spelling patterns. You can use *apple* and *angel* as the guide words for sorting.

Add words that end with *il* (*pencil*) and *al* (*pedal*).

---

*This game is courtesy of Charlotte Tucker.

FIGURE 8-3 Apple and Bushel Gameboard

Schwa + R Sounds in Stressed and Unstressed Syllables 8-12

This three-step sort should be conducted over the course of 3 to 6 days. Each sort builds on the previous one, so it is important to conduct them in the order shown. The focus of these sorts is on the *ir, er,* and *ur* spellings of the schwa + r sound in stressed syllables (*circus, certain, further*) and unstressed syllables (*thirteenth, concert, surprise*).

Materials

Word sort category headings (one set per student)
Word sort sheets (see sorts 94 through 96 in the appendix)

Directions

Sort 1: A sound sort.
1. See sort 44 in the appendix.
2. Model the sort with a few words before having students sort on their own:

   Group 1: Words have the sound you hear in *girl, hurt,* and *verb.*

   Group 2: Words will *not* have the sound you hear in group 1 words.

3. Once students understand the sort, have them place their own word cards under the appropriate group heading.
4. Check students' accuracy as they sort or when they finish. Students should check themselves if you provide an answer sheet, or they could write the words under the correct heading on notebook paper to turn in or save.
5. Repeat this sort if students were not 90% to 100% accurate.

Sort 2: A spelling pattern sort.
1. Use words from sort 1, group 1.
2. Tell students they will be sorting the *fur* sound into three different spelling patterns: *ir, er,* and *ur.* Model the sort with a few words before students sort on their own.
3. Ask students to predict which category will have the most and the least words. Revisit their predictions after they have completed the sort.
4. Save the words from this sort.

Sort 3: A spelling-by-syllable sort.   This sort is designed to familiarize students with the frequency of spelling patterns in terms of first- or second-syllable location. The sort has three different sortings using the three groupings from sort 2. Sort the *ir* words first, the *er* words second, and the *ur* words last.

1. Prepare word sort category headings for two groups as follows. If you photocopy the category headers, you can use the same headings three times by inserting the targeted spelling pattern in the blank provided:
   Group 1 words will have the *fur* sound   Group 2 words will have the *fur* sound
   spelled _____ in the first syllable.   spelled _____ in the second syllable.

Variations

1. Have students sort the word groups from the third sort according to stressed or unstressed syllables.
2. Using the word groups from the third sort, have students sort the words into syllable "families" (for example, *ser: servant, service, serpent, sermon*).
3. Have students look up the derivations of the words sorted as suggested in 2, above.
4. Repeat these sorts for speed. Play "beat the clock."

Homograph Concentration 8–13

This game follows the Concentration game format and may be played by two to four students. The object of the game is to collect the most pairs of sentence cards with matching homograph pronunciations.*

Materials

Prepare a sentence card for each of the following sentences. There are four sentences for each homograph—two each for the different meanings and pronunciations.

There was a *tear* in her jeans.	A *tear* ran down his cheek.
Be careful not to *tear* the paper.	The end of the movie brought a *tear* to my eye.
I always enjoyed it when my teacher *read* to us after lunch.	Will you *read* the newspaper tomorrow morning?
I *read* a lot of books last year.	Before I buy some types of food, I like to *read* the ingredients first.
I saw a *live* performance by that band.	I used to *live* in a small town.
We are going to need *live* bait for fishing.	I *live* close to my best friend.
We plan to *sow* many new seeds in our garden this spring.	That is the largest *sow* I've ever seen at a livestock show.

---

*Credit goes to Elizabeth Harrison, Teliz Blackard, and Lisbeth Kling.

An old saying goes, "You reap what you *sow*."

The *sow* and her piglets played in the mud.

Wind the scarf around your neck.

The *wind* is really cold at this time of year.

I think this road will *wind* around the mountain.

The *wind* blew over the trash cans.

My dad *does* a good job of cooking.

The *does* brought their fawns down to the stream.

She *does* not have my favorite sweater.

Does are not as large as bucks.

The *dove* is often a symbol for peace.

Jerry quickly *dove* into the river.

My favorite birdcall is that of the *dove*.

I was so hungry I *dove* into the spaghetti.

The wind will definitely *buffet* that small boat.

We ate at a terrific seafood *buffet*.

I'm afraid that hard winds will really *buffet* that small tent.

My grandma stores her good dishes in a large *buffet*.

The distant *object* appeared to be approaching quickly.

I *object* to the way you're talking about my best friend.

I don't understand the *object* of this game.

I *object* to your tone of voice.

She set the *record* for the fastest time in the race.

I don't like to *record* my own voice.

There is no *record* of her living in this town.

I can't wait until they *record* their new CD.

Math is my favorite *subject*.

I hope they won't *subject* us to a lot of noise.

That's a *subject* we don't talk about very often.

I don't want to *subject* you to any more discomfort.

I can't wait to find out what my birthday *present* will be.

We would like to *present* you with this award.

She was *present* for every meeting.

The drama club is going to *present* their first play.

Our group *project* was a success.

I try to *project* a confident image.

The new building *project* cost millions of dollars.

You will have to *project* your voice better so we can hear you.

Wait just one more *minute*.

There was a *minute* speck of dust on the lens.

I don't have a *minute* to spare.

Our problems seem *minute* compared to theirs.

The band just signed a recording *contract*.

I hope I don't *contract* a serious illness.

The actor was offered her first movie *contract*.

My muscles *contract* when I get cold.

Directions

1. Select five to eight homographs for each game (32–40 sentences). *Important*: Students should know at least one of the two pronunciations for each homograph.
2. Shuffle the sentence cards. Place the cards facedown on the tabletop.
3. Players take turns at turning over two sentence cards in hopes of locating homographs with matching pronunciations. Players must read aloud the sentence cards they turn over or they do not get to keep the pair if they do match.
4. A player may keep the two sentence cards if (a) the two sentence cards have matching homographs that also have the same pronunciation, *and* (b) the player pronounces the homographs correctly when reading the sentences. The player then gets another turn. The player may *not* keep the sentence cards if (a) they do not have matching homographs underlined *or* (b) they have matching homographs but their pronunciations are different. In both of these cases the cards are turned facedown again and the next player takes a turn.
5. Each pair of sentence cards is worth 10 points. The first player to reach 100 points or the player with the most pairs when play is stopped is the winner.

Homophone Solitaire 8–14

Building on the traditional game of solitaire, this simple card game requires flexible thinking and versatile attention to words. Word cards are matched by homophone, syllable pattern, or whether the homophonic spelling change is in the stressed or unstressed syllable. The object of the game is to end up with all the words in one pile. Refer to sort 97 and the list of homophones in the appendix.

Materials

52 word cards using two-syllable homophones. The cards comprise two suits (1) homophones in the stressed syllable, (2) homophones in the unstressed syllable. There are 13 pairs of matching homophones from each suit. (See the homophone list in the appendix.)

Directions

1. Shuffle the deck; then turn one card over at a time. Say the word, observe the pattern, and place the card down, face up.
2. Turn over the next card. Place it on top of the previously placed card if it matches by any of these features:
    a. Exact homophone (for example, *alter, altar*)
    b. Syllable pattern (VCCV doublet, VCCV different; VCV open, VCV closed)
    c. Homophonic spelling change in the same syllable *(kernal, accept)*
    If there is no match, place the card to the right of the last card played.
3. Continue play in this way, placing cards with no matches to the right of the last card played. Stacks may be picked up and consolidated at any time. The top card played on a stack determines the movement.
4. You may move back no more than four stacks for play.
5. Play continues until the entire deck is played. Then shuffle and play again!

Oygo 8–15

Oygo is a simplified version of Bingo intended for three to four students. It reinforces the spelling patterns *oi* and *oy* for the /oy/ sound. There are different groups of words that may be used in each game.* See sort 92 in the appendix for a sample sort.

Materials

- Word cards (see the *oi* and *oy* sort in the appendix as well as the related word lists.
- Number cards (1–12, five cards for each number).
- Feature cards (*oi* or *oy* spelling).
- Egg carton (1-dozen size); number the egg pouches 1 to 12 and place the number cards into the correct pouch.

Directions

1. Number carton, word cards, and feature cards are placed in center of table.
2. The caller shuffles the deck of cards and then deals out four cards to each player.
3. The players place the cards faceup in front of them.
4. The caller turns up the rest of the cards one at a time, calling out the word and the number of the card. The caller should make sure the cards are in order by placing a number card on top of each called word card.

---

*Credit to Geraldine Robinson; adapted from the game "Bango" by Robert Harbin in the book *Family Card Games*.

The Apple-Bushel Game helps learners differerentiate between *el* and *le* endings.

5. A player who has a card of the same feature turns it facedown. The player then takes a number card of the called word from the number carton and places it on top of the facedown card. Numbers are used to check the winner's cards.
6. The first player to have turned down all cards shouts "Oygo!"
7. The winner's facedown cards can be checked by comparing them to the called words.
8. The players place the number cards back into the carton.
9. The winner becomes the next caller.
10. The game starts over using the same feature or another feature, or a combination of features.
11. The caller can use the word list to choose a different group of word cards illustrating a different feature or a combination of features.

Variations

The game can be changed to OWGO, using words in the first /ou/ sort in the appendix. The game will reinforce the two common spellings for the /ow/ sound—*ou* and *ow*.

Oy! 8–16

This sort involves four basic steps in examining the /oy/ sound in words with oi and *oy*. Students sort by pattern and then by accent.

Directions

Use the lists in the appendix to create sorts.

Procedures

1. Sort the word cards into the *oi* spelling or the *oy* spelling.
   Is there a generalization? When is /oy/ spelled *oi* and when is it spelled *oy*?
2. Sort the two- and three-syllable *oi* word cards into words accented on the first syllable and words accented on the second syllable.
3. Sort the two- and three-syllable *oy* word cards into words accented on the first syllable and words accented on the second syllable.
4. Combine the *oi* and *oy* word cards and sort into words accented on the first syllable and words accented on the second syllable.

Ow! 8-17

The /ow/ sound can be spelled *ow* or *ou*. This sort shows where the accent is with this vowel pattern. Students sort by pattern and then by accent in these four steps:

1. Sort the word cards into the *ow* spelling or the *ou* spelling:
2. Sort the two-syllable *ou* word cards into words accented on the first syllable and words accented on the second syllable.
3. Sort the two-syllable *ow* word cards into words accented on the first syllable and words accented on the second syllable.
4. Combine the *ou* and *ow* word cards and sort into words accented on the first syllable and words accented on the second syllable.

See sort 93 in the appendix.

You Be the Judge 8-18

The spelling of the /j/ sound depends on whether or not the sound occurs in an accented syllable and whether it follows a long or a short vowel sound. The following sorts are designed to help students understand the different conditions that determine the spelling. Use sorts such as 54, 56, and 80 in the appendix.

1. Sort by long versus short:
   stage   badge
2. Sort by long versus short:
   stage   badge   hinge
3. Sort long and short vowels by pattern (VCe/VCCe):
   stage   badge
4. Sort long, short, and *r*-influenced vowels by pattern (VCe/VCCe):
   stage   badge   plunge   large
5. Have students sort words that have /j/ in an unaccented syllable (*baggage*) and contrast them with words that have /j/ in the middle (*budget*). See sort 80, the /j/ sort, in the appendix.

Stressbusters 8-19

The purpose of this board game is to determine the correct placement of accent or stress in a given word. Students can play the game in pairs after they have conducted their initial sorting of the words by accent pattern under the teacher's guidance.* Refer to sorts 86 to 88 for sample sorts.

---

*This activity comes to us courtesy of Brenda Reibel.

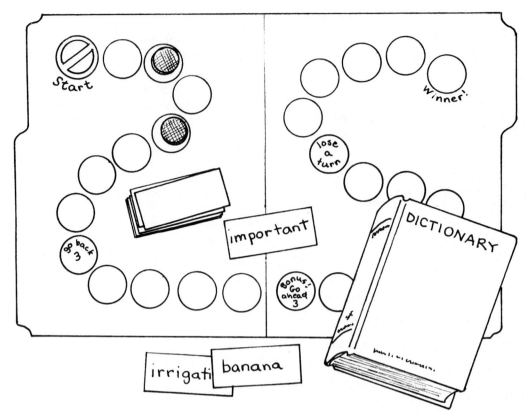

FIGURE 8-4   Stressbusters Gameboard

Materials

Prepared gamecards made from the word lists in the appendix; Stressbusters gameboard (see Figure 8-4); gamepieces; dictionary; word list showing accent in given words.

Procedures

As students identify the placement of accent, they will do the following:

1. If the accent falls in the beginning syllable and is correctly identified, the player moves the penny one space; if the accent falls in the second syllable and is correctly identified, the penny is moved two spaces; if the accent is on the third syllable, the penny is moved three spaces.
2. Player 1 takes a card from the gamecard stack and identifies if the accent falls on the first, second, or third syllable. If unchallenged, player 1 moves the correct number of spaces depending on where the accent falls. If there is more than one accented syllable and the player realizes this (as in CONstiTUtion), the player may choose which syllable to "count"; the player may decide that *constitution* should count for three spaces.
3. Player 2 then takes a card from the gamecard stack, identifies the accent, and moves the correct number of spaces depending on where the accent falls.
4. The game continues until one player reaches the finish circle.
5. *Challenging answers*: Game players may challenge acceptability of accent answers. When an answer is challenged, the challenger looks the words up in the dictionary to determine the accented syllable. If correct, the challenger gets to move the gamepiece forward one, two, or three places, depending on where the accent falls.

If the player is correct, and the challenger is wrong, the challenger must move back one space.

Words that are accented on the third syllable are also accented on the first syllable. These words may be challenged. If a player moves one space for the word *constitution*, for example—not realizing it is also accented on the third syllable—the other player could then challenge. An incorrect challenge, however, costs the challenger the corresponding number of spaces (if the challenger thinks the word is accented on the second syllable and is incorrect, he or she must move back two spaces; if the challenger thinks the accent is on the third syllable and is incorrect, he or she moves back three spaces).

Building Bridges 8–19

Students reinforce spelling of polysyllabic words and recognition of syllable patterns. Two-syllable words are place don each side of the bridge. The object of the game is to span the bridge with a multisyllabic word that includes the syllable patterns in each two-syllable word to the left and to the right.

Materials

Picture board (Figure 8-5)
Syllable juncture word cards:

- Two-syllable cards representing four syllable patterns: VCCV (*basket*), VCCV (doublets, as in *rabbit*), VCV open (*pilot*), VCV closed (*planet*). Select words from the syllable patterns list in the appendix on page 360.
- Multijuncture cards that represent different syllable patterns (for example, *reflection*: VCCV and VCCV; *republish*: VCV open and VCCV)

Other multijuncture words like the following can be added from the lists in the appendix that contain three- and four-syllable words.

recommence	republish	dinosaur	occupation
reflection	commitment	casually	decoration
climactic	renavigate	delightful	identify
collarless	mechanic	government	October
entertain	populate	educate	ecology

FIGURE 8-5 *Building Bridges Gameboard*

Directions

1. Students may play individually or in groups.
2. A two-syllable word card is laid down on each side of the bridge. The words can have the same or different syllable patterns.
3. The student must span the bridge with a multijuncture word that includes the syllable patterns found in each side word. For example:

recommence

VCV/VCCV

civil	*grammar*
VCV closed	VCCV doublet

4. Students keep track of each "bridge" by writing down the side words and bridge word.
5. Students may challenge themselves by setting a time limit to see how many bridges they can span.

Pulling Two-Syllable Words Together 8–20

A word sort that pulls together much of the exploration you have been doing with two-syllable words is a three-step sort. In this type of sort, a group of words is sorted according to three different criteria: accent, sound, and pattern.

1. Locate accent. Sort the words according to which syllable is accented:

First Syllable	Second Syllable
ze' / bra	a / way'
fe' / ver	to / day'

2. Sort by sound. Sort according to the sound you hear in the accented syllable. For example, long vowel versus short vowel:

Long Vowel	Short Vowel
lazy	ladder
climate	better

3. Identify pattern. Sort the sounds according to the pattern in the accented syllable. For example, final long vowel pattern versus medial long vowel:

Final Long Vowel	Medial Long Vowel
today	remain
reply	impeach

Semantic Chart Sorts 8–21

You can use a bulletin board to create an interactive word wall related to content studies. Like the semantic sorts in Chapter 7, students arrange words conceptually. As an ongoing activity, students look for words that are tied to their content studies.

1. Students collect words from unit of study on a word wall. Words selected for the wall are defined and reviewed as an ongoing class activity.

2. These words are given to groups to sort into meaning- or association-based groups. Students write the groups on chart paper with an explanation for each grouping.

Vocabulary Jeopardy 8–22

Students create Jeopardy games after brainstorming terms related to a unit of study.

1. Students generate vocabulary cards from a unit of study. Tamara Baren developed this activity, and she starts with the vocabulary students generate on their own, followed by a scan through texts and materials.
2. With these cards, students make a Jeopardy game. A sample of a gameboard can be found in Activity 7-14. Students write questions on cards that relate to facts and concepts studied. Answers are written on the back upside down. The cards are sorted into categories.
3. Teams of students play the game as a whole-class vocabulary review of unit.

Prefix Sort 8–23

This series of sorts introduces (1) the concept of prefixes and (2) how prefixes can be used to generate a large number of words.

Materials

Copies of sorts 98 and 99 in the appendix.

Directions

Day 1: *Introduce the sort*.

1. Each student does an open sort with the words.
2. Do a closed sort: With *un, re,* and *dis* as the categories, lead the students in sorting several words. Introduce the term *prefix* to describe these categories. Then have the students finish the sort on their own.
3. Ask students for the meanings of the words in each category by first thinking about the base word and then thinking about the word meaning when the prefix is added. Encourage them to think about what each prefix means. For example, "What does the prefix *un* do to the word *usual*? To the word *able*? What does the prefix *re* do to the word *retell*? To the word *play*?"
4. Have the students shuffle their words and sort them again.

Day 2: *Repeat the sort*.

1. Sort the words again by prefixes. Ask the students to use the words orally in sentences. For example, model a sentence in which the base word is used alone and then a sentence in which the derived form is used: "I obey my parents. If I disobey I get in trouble." "After I plug in the iron, I always have to remember to unplug it." "I already counted those but you can recount them if you like."
2. In class or for homework, students write the words in columns in their word study notebook and select some to write in sentences as modeled in class.

Day 3: *Cut-up sort*.

1. Hand out a second copy of the word sheet and ask the students to cut apart the words. Then ask them to cut off the prefixes and recombine prefixes and base words to form new words. Some possibilities include *recover, replug, display, reappear, unarm, recharge,* and *disable.*
2. Have students add the new words to their word study notebook and define them *first* without checking the dictionary. Expect disagreement over "real" words; students can then go ahead and check the dictionary.

Day 4: *Word hunt*.   Have students do a word hunt to find more words with these prefixes. They can also brainstorm more words. The meanings of the words should be discussed as they are added to the class chart and/or word study notebooks.

Day 5: Assessment.

Two options: (1) Call out each word, and then have students write a brief definition. (2) Provide a definition, and then have students write the word that matches.

Variations

1. Use sort 98 in the appendix.
2. During the next few weeks, introduce more common prefixes such as those listed in Table 8-3 on page 226, Sequence of Word Study. Discuss how they affect the base words to which they are attached and discuss their meanings.
3. Common *suffixes* can be introduced and discussed in the same way.

Affix Partner Sort 8–24

This is another open sort that mixes prefixes and suffixes. Students work in pairs and refer to the word study books that are available to them. It is helpful to have an area in the classroom set aside for reference materials. Suggested reference books are listed on pages 397–398 of the resources in the appendix.

Student Directions

1. Work in pairs. Read the words and sort them into columns.
2. Make the meaning connection with four of the roots and affixes.
3. Use the blank word chips to write your own words to fit the categories. Write the sort into your word study notebooks.
4. Choose one word and explore it in the word study reference books.
5. Meet with another pair to see what they learned.

CHAPTER 9

Word Study for Advanced Readers and Writers: The Derivational Relations Stage

As at the intermediate level, word study for specialized readers emphasizes active exploration of words and the application of word knowledge to spelling, vocabulary development, and the analysis of unknown words encountered in reading. The principles for instruction we listed for intermediate readers and writers (p. 227) also guide instruction at the advanced level.

The type of word knowledge that underlies mature reading and writing includes an ever-expanding conceptual foundation and the addition of words that represent this foundation. Mature readers are able to explore the Greek and Latin word roots out of which thousands of words are constructed. In most instances, these words are derived from a single base or root through the addition of **affixes—prefixes** and **suffixes.** In reading, this additional layer of word knowledge makes it possible to perceive polysyllabic words at a fairly sophisticated level. Whereas the intermediate reader (syllables and affixes) picks up syllabic segments in such words, the mature reader (derivational relations) picks up **morphemic** segments (Taft, 1991; Templeton, 1992). For example, an intermediate reader attempting to read the word *morphology* would most likely analyze it syllable by syllable, picking up the letter sequences *mor-pho-lo-gy.* The mature reader would probably pick up the letter sequences *morph-ology,* which cross syllable boundaries.

To see how one teacher guides his students through the increasingly advanced layers of information in the structure of words let's visit the classroom of Mr. Ramirez. He is about to help his students make the spelling-meaning connection.

> Writing the misspelled word *COMPISITION* on the board, Mr. Ramirez comments, "Everything is correct in this word except for the letter *i* in the second syllable. However, there's a word that is related in spelling and meaning that actually provides a clue to the correct spelling. Any ideas what this word might be? [If no one responds, he continues.] Well, let's look at this word [writes *compose* directly above *COMPISITION*]. Are *compose* and *composition* related in meaning? Yes, they are! Can you hear the long-o sound in *compose*? You know how to spell this sound, and because *compose* and *composition* are related in meaning, the *o* in *compose* is the clue to the spelling of what we call the schwa sound in *composition.*
>
> "Keeping this fact in mind can help you spell a word you may not be sure of, like *composition.* Why? Because schwas don't give you any clue to the spelling—they can be spelled with any of the vowel letters. You've got a powerful strategy you can use, though: By thinking of a related word, like *compose,* you can get a clue.
>
> "Remember, words that are related in meaning are often related in spelling as well. So, by thinking of a word that is related to one you're trying to spell, you will often discover a helpful clue to the spelling."
>
> In a follow-up lesson, Mr. Ramirez expands upon the spelling-meaning connection to show his students how Latin roots "work" within words. Using the Latin word roots *fract* and *struct* as examples, Mr. Ramirez writes the following words on the board: *fracture/fraction; construct, structure, instruct:*
>
> "We know what these words are and what they mean. What happens when you *fracture* your arm? What do you do when you divide something into *fractions*? Both of these words have the Latin root *fract* in them. . . What do you think this root might mean? [Students are engaged in a brief discussion in which the meaning 'to break' emerges— bones break, whole numbers are broken down into fractions.]
>
> "Now let's look at these other words: Think about what happens when workers *construct* a building or *structure.* [Students engage in a brief discussion in which the meaning 'to build' emerges.] Right! *Construct* means 'to build something,' and *structure* is another term we often use to refer to a building or something that has been built. How about *instruct*? Can you think of how the meaning 'build' applies here?"
>
> The lesson concludes with the class discussing how knowledge is "built."
>
> On another day, Mr. Ramirez introduces the concept of "absorbed" prefixes:
>
> "Jared, you checked the prefix *in* in the dictionary yesterday and were a little perplexed! You discovered that it said that this prefix is also spelled *il, im,* and *ir.* It seems a little peculiar, doesn't it? Well, let's look at why this is so.
>
> "Let's take the word *immobile.* What does it mean? . . . Right! Something is 'not moving.' The word is constructed from the prefix *in,* meaning 'not,' and the base word *mobile,* which means 'capable of moving.' When we put *in* and *mobile* together, two things happen. First, the word parts combine to mean 'not mobile'—not capable of moving. Second, notice that the spelling of the prefix *in* has changed to *im.* Let's think about why this happened.

"A long time ago, someone realized that instead of always saying something was 'not mobile' they could simply combine the prefix *in* with the word *mobile* to create a new word that meant 'not mobile.' Now, try pronouncing the word like it was pronounced when it first came into existence: ***in**mobile*. Does that feel kind of weird? Does your tongue kind of get stuck on the beginning of *mobile?* Mine sure does! Well, the same thing happened to speakers a long time ago—it became easier for people to leave out the /n/ sound when pronouncing the word. The sound of the *n* became absorbed into the /m/ sound at the beginning of the base word *mobile.* Before long, the spelling of the *n* changed to indicate this change in pronunciation—but it's important to remember that this letter didn't disappear. They knew it was necessary to keep the two letters in the prefix to indicate that it was still a prefix. If the last letter of the prefix had been dropped, then the meaning of the prefix would have been lost.

"Here are some other words that have absorbed the *in* prefix into the base word [writes the words *immeasureable, immodest,* and *immortal* on the board]. These started out as ***in**measureable,* ***in**modest,* and ***in**mortal.*"

CHARACTERISTICS OF ORTHOGRAPHIC DEVELOPMENT AT THE DERIVATIONAL RELATIONS STAGE

Beginning in the intermediate school years, most students are capable of understanding that the way words are spelled can provide clues to their meanings. We begin to explore *spelling-meaning relationships,* helping students become consciously aware of the spelling-meaning principle as it applies in English: *Words that are related in meaning are often related in spelling as well, despite changes in sound* (Chomsky, 1970; Templeton, 1983). Because of this similarity in meaning in similarly spelled words, students at the specialized phase of reading can learn the following strategy: If you're unsure how to spell a word, try to think of a word that is similar in spelling and meaning. For example, a student who is uncertain about the spelling of the schwa in the second syllable of *competition,* can think of the related base word *compete,* which offers a clue: The student clearly hears the long-e vowel sound and knows how to spell that sound.

This spelling-meaning principle applies to thousands of words in English and does so with surprising consistency, and students will encounter more and more of these words in their reading. Teachers can initiate students' examination of these spelling-meaning patterns by observing, "You know, when you first learned to read you had to learn how spelling stands for sounds—now, you're going to be learning how spelling stands for *meaning.*"

Table 9-1 presents examples of misspellings from derivational relations spellers.

TABLE 9-1	**Examples of Spelling at the Derivational Relations Phase**
Early	
enclosed	INCLOSED
confession	CONFESION
resident	RESADENT
confidence	CONFADENCE
opposition	OPPISITION
Middle/Late	
prosperity	PROSPARITY
emphasize	EMFASIZE
criticize	CRITISIZE
prohibition	PROHABITION
indictment	INDITEMENT

At first glance, misspellings at the derivational relations stage appear similar in type to those at the syllables and affixes stage. Errors occur at the juncture of syllables and with the vowel in unaccented syllables. Earlier, at the syllables and affixes stage, students' word study established a secure foundation for what they will explore at the derivational relations stage: Greek and Latin **roots** and affixes, and the application of this knowledge across reading and writing tasks.

Now let's examine more closely some important aspects of the sequence presented in Table 9-2, the spelling-meaning connection and Greek and Latin word elements.

Concepts to Be Learned at the Derivational Relations Phase

Spelling-Meaning Connection

The spelling-meaning connection provides the opportunity to help students learn a strategy for examining words that are related in spelling and meaning as well as to help them become aware of the several different spelling-meaning patterns that characterize so many words in English.

Very often there is a direct visual link between the spelling of related words and their related meanings. For example, consider the "silent/sounded consonants" pattern: consonants that are silent in one word are sounded in a related word, as in *sign* and *signature*. Rather than trying to remember the spelling of one silent consonant in one word, students are given the following strategy: To remember the spelling of a word with a silent consonant, try to think of a related word in which the consonant is sounded.

Another pattern is that of the spelling of the **schwa,** or unaccented vowel sound in words such as *confidence, opposition,* and *prohibition*. This spelling becomes obvious when these words are paired with related words in which the corresponding vowel sound is clearly heard:

conf**i**dence	opp**o**sition	prohi**bi**tion
confide	oppose	prohibit

Again, here is the strategy that is reinforced: To remember the spelling of the schwa in an unaccented syllable, think of a related word in which that syllable is accented.

Students benefit most from their study of the spelling-meaning connection when these patterns are presented in a logical sequence. For example, related words that illustrate vowel alternation begin with simple long-to-short vowel changes such as *revise/revision,* in which the long-i in the base word *revise* changes to a short-i in the derived word *revision.* It's easier for students to understand the long-to-short **vowel alternation** pattern before they explore in depth the long-to-schwa vowel changes as in *oppose/opposition.* Later still, students will examine patterns in which there is a significant spelling change between related words, but this change is predictable. For example, although the spelling of the long-a in *explain* changes from *ai* to simply *a* in the derived word *explanation,* these are not the only words in which this change occurs; it is a predictable pattern that also occurs in many other related words such as *exclaim/exclamation* and proclaim/proclamation. Students are ready to examine these words because they understand the spelling-meaning patterns presented earlier.

The same sequence holds for **consonant alternation.** The earlier patterns in which the sound changes while the spelling remains constant (*sign/signal, critic/criticize*) lay the groundwork for later predictable spelling alternations (*divide/division, confident/confidence*).

The spelling-meaning connection plays a very important role in expanding students' vocabularies. Once students understand how the principle operates in known words, they are ready to learn how it applies in unknown words. Suppose a student has used the word *condemn* in his writing—he knows the meaning of the word and understands it when he runs across it in his reading—but he misspells it as CONDEM. By showing the student the related word *condemnation*, his teacher has the opportunity to address two important objectives. First, the reason for the so-called silent-n in *condemn* becomes clear—the word is related to *condemnation* in which the *n* is pronounced. Second, because the student already knows the meaning of *solemn*, he is able to understand the meaning of the new but related word *solemnity*. The teacher has just used the spelling system to expand this student's vocabulary!

Greek and Latin Elements

After exploring a number of spelling-meaning relationships and playing with the meaning changes accompanying the addition and deletion of affixes to known **base words**, students may be ready to explore the incredibly rich terrain of **word roots**—elements from Greek and Latin. Greek and Latin word roots form a large part of the new vocabulary that students encounter in the intermediate years and beyond. In contrast to base words, word roots cannot stand alone. Still, they are the meaningful anchor to which prefixes and suffixes may attach. It is important to remind students, moreover, that spelling still visually represents the meaning of these elements and preserves the meaning relationships among words that at first may appear quite different. Notice, for example, the consistent spelling *jud* in the words *judge, prejudice,* and *adjudicate.* Students will learn (1) the most frequently occurring Greek and Latin word roots; and (2) how these elements combine within words. This knowledge provides a powerful foundation and productive strategy for continuing vocabulary and spelling growth.

Additional Word Exploration for Derivational Students

Word Origins

Exploring the origins of words and the processes of word creation provides a powerful knowledge base for learning spelling and vocabulary, as well as for facilitating more effective reading and writing. Etymology, the study of word origins, may develop into a lifelong fascination for many students. Many times the spelling of a word may appear odd, but an understanding of its origin provides the most powerful key to remembering the spelling. Knowing that so many words have come from mythology, literature, and historical events and figures provides important background knowledge for students' reading in the various content areas. An interest in word origins provides invaluable insight into the concepts and content of much of their continuing education.

This initial understanding will help tremendously later on when students realize how many of these elements occur in the vocabulary terms that represent core concepts in science, social studies, and math.

These Greek and Latin elements should be sequenced according to the abstractness of their meaning, from concrete to more abstract. For example, the Greek roots *phon* (sound), *auto* (self), and *graph* (writing) and the Latin roots *spect* (to look), *rupt* (to break, burst), and *dict* (to speak, say) are introduced and explored early in the sequence. More abstract roots such as the Latin *fer* (to carry) and *spir* (to breathe) are explored later. In this chapter we present the roots that occur most frequently in the reading material that intermediate and middle grade students encounter. Because of this frequency of occurrence, these roots warrant students' direct attention and exploration.

Assimilated prefixes are primarily Latin in origin. They are addressed later in the instructional sequence because they depend upon considerable prior knowledge about other basic spelling-meaning patterns, processes of adding prefixes to base words, and simple Greek and Latin roots. In the word *attract* the *at* is an absorbed prefix. A long time ago the word began as *adtract*. It was created by combining the prefix *ad*, meaning "to" or "toward," with the word root *tract*, meaning "to draw, pull." Because of the difficulty in pronouncing *adtract* and keeping the /d/ and the /t/ sounds separate, over a period of time the /d/ sound became absorbed into the /t/ sound, in effect disappearing altogether. The spelling of the *d* in **adtract** also changed. Absorbed prefixes should first be presented in the context of base words: *con + respond = correspond; in + mobilize = immobilize.* Once understood in these types of words, they may be taught in the context of word roots: *ad + tain = attain; con + rode = corrode.*

WORD STUDY INSTRUCTION: DERIVATIONAL RELATIONS

Sequence of Word Study

The sequence for derivational relations begins with a straightforward exploration of the spelling-meaning connection. The study moves from Greek and Latin word elements, to predictable spelling changes in related words, and then on to absorbed prefixes. This sequence is presented in Table 9-2.

TABLE 9-2   Sequence of Word Study in the Derivational Relations Stage

The Spelling-Meaning Connection

Words that are related in meaning are often related in spelling as well, despite changes in sound.

1. *Consonant Alternations:* **The spelling of the base word remains the same, despite the change in sound.**

a. silent/sounded	*sign/signal, condemn/condemnation, soften/soft*
b. /t/ to /sh/	*connect/connection, select/selection, attract/attraction*
c. /k/ to /sh/	*music/musician, magic/magician*

2. *Vowel Alternations:* **Words that are similar in meaning are often similar in spelling.**

a. Long to short	*please/pleasant, crime/criminal, ignite-ignition, humane-humanity, gene, genetic*
b. Long to schwa	*compete/competition, define/definition, reside/resident*
c. "Other" to schwa	*locality/local, legality/legal, relativity/relative, metallic/metal, adapt/adaptation*

Greek and Latin Word Elements

1. Start with Greek number prefixes *mono* (one), *bi* (two), *tri* (three), and move to the Greek roots *tele* (far, distant), *therm* (heat), *photo* (light), and *astr* (star). (See lists in Tables 9-3 and 9-4.)
2. Move to frequent Latin roots with the aim of gaining a working understanding of a few frequent roots with relatively constant meanings: *tract* (drag, pull), *spect* (look), *port* (carry), *dict* (to say), *rupt* (to break), and *scrib* (to write).(See lists in the appendix.)
3. Explore additional Latin and Greek prefixes, building on those already taught at the syllables and affixes phase:

Prefix	*Meaning*
inter	between
intra	within
super	over; greater
counter	opposing
ex	out
fore	before
post	after
pro	in front of, forward
co/com	together
sub	under
pre	before
con	with
anti	against
demi	half
semi	half
quadr	four
pent	five

TABLE 9-2   (continued)

4. Explore common Greek suffixes that students will frequently encounter:

crat/cracy:	rule (*democracy*—rule by the *demos*, "people")
emia:	condition of the blood (*leukemia*—the blood has too many white [*leuk*] blood cells)
ician:	specialist in (*dietician*)
ine:	chemical substance (*chlorine, Benzedrine*)
ism/ist:	belief in, one who believes (*communism/communist, capitalism/capitalist*)
logy/logist:	science of, scientist (*geology*—science of the earth, studying the earth; *geologist*—one who studies the earth)
pathy/path:	disease, one who suffers from a disease (*osteopathy*—disease of the bones; *osteopath*, one who suffers from such a disease)
phobia:	abnormal fear (*claustrophobia*—fear of being closed in or shut in [*claus*])

The Spelling-Meaning Connection: Predictable Spelling Changes in Consonants and Vowels

1. *t/c*   *silent/silence*
2. *d/s*   *explode/explosion, erode/erosion, decide/decision*
3. Long to short   *vain/vanity, consume/consumption*
4. Long to schwa   *explain/explanation, exclaim/exclamation, receive/reception, perceive/perception*

Assimilated Prefixes

1. Prefix + base word (*in + mobile = immobile; ad + count = account*)
   base words: *con + respond = correspond; in + mobilize = immobilize.*
   prefix *in*   *il, im,* and *ir. immobile.*
   prefix *in*, meaning "not," and the base word *mobile*, which means "capable of moving."
       immeasurable, immodest, immortal
       irresponsible
       illiterate
2. Prefix + word root
   ad + cept = accept; in + mune = immune

There are some basic points to keep in mind regarding students' word study at this level (Templeton, 1989, 1992):

1. Words and word elements selected for study should be **generative,** which means that whenever possible you should teach about words in meaning "families." This highlights the awareness that particular patterns of relationships can be extended or generalized to other words. For example, an awareness of the long-to-short vowel alternation pattern in the words *please* and *pleasant* can generalize to words such as *wise/wisdom* and *cave/cavity.*

2. The words that you initially choose for exploration by your students should be selected based on how obvious their relationship is. For example, you should teach clearly related words such as *represent/misrepresent* before teaching about words that are less clearly related, such as *expose/exposition.*

3. There should be a balance of teacher-directed instruction with students' explorations and discussions.

Activities for Students in the Derivational Relations Stage

Here we present illustrative activities, word sorts, and games for students in the derivational relations stage. The following materials should always be readily available to students:

- Intermediate and collegiate dictionaries. There should be enough copies for six to eight students to work in a small group.
- Thesaurus collection, enough for six to eight students in small-group work.
- Several word history (etymological) dictionaries and root books like those listed in the appendix.

Generic

Vocabulary Notebooks 9-1

Vocabulary notebooks* are an integral part of students' word learning at the derivational relations phase (Gill & Bear, 1989). They can also be used with many of the activities presented in this section—for example, to record word sorts and add words to the sorts after going on word hunts. Divide the notebooks into two sections:

> *Word study:* A weekly record of sorts, explanations of sorts, and homework.
> *Looking into language:* Records of whole-group word study of related words, semantic sorts, interesting word collections, investigations, and theme study words.

Older students can be taught to follow these steps to collect interesting words:

1. While you are reading, place a question mark above words you find difficult, and place a question mark in the margin for easy reference. When you are through reading or

---

*Thanks to Tamara Baren for suggestions and examples.

studying, go back to your question marks. Read around the word, and think about its possible meaning.

2. Write the word, followed by the sentence it came from, the page number, and an abbreviation for the title of the book. (There will be times when the sentence is too long. Write enough of the sentence to give a clue to meaning.) Think about the word's meaning.

3. Look at the different parts of the word—prefixes, suffixes, and base word or word root. Think about the meaning of the affixes and base or root.

4. Think of other words that are like this one, and write them underneath the part of the word that is similar.

5. Look the word up in the dictionary, read the various definitions, and in a few words record the meaning (the one that applies to the word in the book you are reading) in your notebook or on a card. Look for similar words in the dictionary (both in form and meaning) above and below the target word, and add them to your list.

6. Look at the origin of the word, and add it to your entry if it is interesting.

A realistic goal is to collect 10 words a week. These words may be brought up in class and shared. In addition, record words that consistently present spelling challenges in the notebook or on the cards. For each word, think of related words.

Here's an example:

1. *Word: Orthography*
2. *Sentence:* "English orthography is not crazy, and it carries the history of the word with it." (*Sounds of Language*, p. 22)
3. *Look at word parts: ortho graph* ("may have something to do with writing")
4. *Think of possible related words:*

ortho	*graphy*
orthodontist	graphic
orthodox	graph
orthographer	autograph/photograph
orthographist	
orthomolecular	

Note: These were added from the dictionary (step 5). { orthographer / orthographist / orthomolecular

5. *Definition:* "A method of representing the sounds of a language by letters; spelling."
   Note: This, the third definition, fits most nearly the meaning of *orthography* as it was used in the sentence. The first two meanings are: (1) the art or study of standard spelling (2) the aspect of language study concerned with letters and spelling" (*The American Heritage College Dictionary*, 1993, p. 965).
6. *Origins: ortho:* correct *graph:* something written

Is It *sion* or *tion*? 9–2

This word sort will involve students in small groups or two teams of two each, examining words to determine clues for spelling the *tion* or *sion* suffixes.

Procedures

1. Each team gets a stack of cards to sort (see lists in the appendix). The same words are in each stack. To keep word cards for each team separate, one stack is printed in black letters and the other in red.
2. Each team then sorts the words into two categories: *base words* and *derived words.*
3. After looking closely at the words sorted, each team discusses generalities that they notice about when words took the *tion* or the *sion* ending.
4. After the teams have determined and supported their generalizations, they have a meeting of the minds to compare findings.

Variations

1. Students look for other words with *tion* or *sion* endings, determine the base or root, and then determine whether it fits the spelling generalization the team came up with. This gives students the opportunity to keep a running record in their vocabulary notebook and to monitor their generalization to see if it continues to work for new words that are encountered.
2. This activity will work with other base words, word roots, and derivatives.

Spelling-Meaning Word Sort 9–3

1. Have students sort the following words into categories: base words and derived words.

sign	please	soft	bomb	muscle
signal	pleasant	soften	bombard	muscular
signature	pleasure	softly		

2. Match each base word with its derivative(s).
3. Discuss how the words are related in meaning. Discuss how the sound changes when a suffix is added.
4. Ask students if they can think of additional words that are part of each spelling-meaning family. These may be added to the sort, the vocabulary notebook, or both.

The Long, the Short, and the Schwa 9–4

This word sort helps students focus attention on the major types of vowel **alternation patterns.***

Materials

Word lists with paired examples of each of the three predominant alternation patterns: (1) long to short (*divine/divinity*), (2) long to schwa (*compose/composition*), and (3) "other" to schwa (*similar/similarity*). See the appendix for sorts 109 to 113.

Procedures

1. Before introducing the category labels of *long to short, long to schwa,* or *other to schwa,* lead students through an examination of each of the three word pairs. Ask the students how the sound of the highlighted vowel changes in each word pair: For example, "What happens to this vowel sound [pointing to the *i* in *divine*] when we put the suffix *ity* onto it?" Ask students if they can think of any other words that follow this same type of pattern in which the long vowel changes to the short vowel.
2. Walk through this discussion for each of the alternation patterns.
3. Have students sort or write words from the list into categories:

Long to Short	Long to Schwa	Other to Schwa
divine/divinity	*compose/composition*	*similarity/similar*
sane/sanity	*invite/invitation*	*prohibit/prohibition*
	compete/competition	*mentality/mental*

Select a number of word pairs from the lists in the appendix, and randomly arrange them on a handout for the students.

---

*Thanks to Lisbeth Kling.

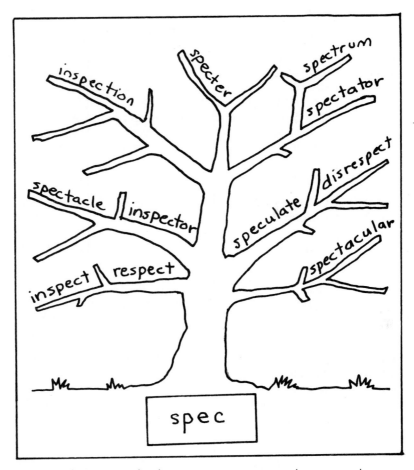

FIGURE 9-1 Word Tree: Words That Grow From Base and Root Words

4. Students may work independently or in pairs. They will later compare their categorizations and record them in their vocabulary notebooks.

Additional spelling-meaning sorts may be constructed from the word lists in the appendix.

Words That Grow From Base Words and Word Roots 9–5

In this whole-class or small-group activity, students see directly how words grow from base words and word roots. It builds on and extends the understanding, begun during the syllables and affixes stage, of how word elements combine.

Materials

Laminated posterboard of tree (see Figure 9-1) and a water-based overhead pen.

Procedures

1. Decide on a base word or a word root to highlight (word roots may be selected from the lists in Tables 9-3 and 9-4). When roots are used, begin with more frequently occurring ones; over time, move to less frequently occurring roots.
2. Write the base word or word root at the bottom of the tree, and think of as many forms as possible. Consult a dictionary for more words.
3. Write the different forms on individual branches.

LATIN ROOT JEOPARDY				
SPECT (to look)	FORM (shape)	PORT (to carry)	TRACT (draw or pull)	DICT (to say, speak)
100 One who watches; an onlooker	100 One "form" or style of clothing such as is worn by nurses	100 Goods brought into a country from another country to be sold	100 Adjective: having power to attract; alluring; inviting	100 A book containing the words of a language explained
200 The prospect of good to come; anticipation	200 One who does not conform	200 One who carries burdens for hire	200 A powerful motor vehicle for pulling farm machinery, heavy loads, etc.	200 A speaking against, a denial
300 To regard with suspicion and mistrust	300 To form or make anew; to reclaim	300 To remove from one place to another	300 The power to grip or hold to a surface while moving, without slipping	300 A blessing often at the end of a worship service
400 Verb: to esteem Noun: regard, deference Literally: to look again	400 To change into another substance, change of form	400 To give an account of	400 An agreement: literally, to draw together	400 An order proclaimed by an authority
500 Looking around, watchful, prudent	500 Disfigurement, spoiling the shape	500 A case for carrying loose papers	500 To take apart from the rest, to deduct	500 To charge with a crime

FIGURE 9-2 Latin Root Jeopardy Board

4. Display the word tree in the classroom for several days, then wipe off, and begin again with the introduction of a new base or word root.

Variation

After making the words, students may use them individually in sentences and/or discuss their meanings. Confirm with the dictionary.

Greek and Latin Jeopardy 9-6

A total of six students are involved in this game. Three students are the contestants, one student is in charge of the answers and questions, one student is the scorekeeper, and one person can be the judge in case of the need to question a decision.

Materials

Enlarge the Latin Root Jeopardy and Double Latin Root Jeopardy boards in Figures 9-2 and 9-3, or make an overhead transparency and project it on a screen. Cover the clues with squares of paper. Use tape to fix them in the correct order on the

DOUBLE LATIN ROOT JEOPARDY				
CRED (to believe)	**DUCT** (to lead)	**FER** (to bear, carry)	**PRESS** (to press)	**SPIR** (to breathe)
200 A system of doing business by trusting that a person will pay at a later date for goods or services	200 A person who directs the performance of a choir or an orchestra	200 (Plants) able to bear fruit; (Animals) able or likely to conceive young	200 A printing machine	200 An immaterial intelligent being
400 A set of beliefs or principles	400 To train the mind and abilities of	400 To carry again; to submit to another for opinion	400 Verb: to utter; Noun: any fast conveyance	400 To breathe out: to die
600 Unbelievable	600 To enroll as a member of a military service	600 To convey to another place, passed from one place to another	600 To press against, to burden, to overpower	600 To breathe through; to emit through the pores of the skin
800 Verb, prefix meaning "not"; word means to damage the good reputation of	800 The formal presentation of one person to another	800 Endurance of pain; distress	800 State of being "pressed down" or saddened	800 To breathe into; to instruct by divine influence
1000 An adjective, prefix *ac*, word means officially recognized	1000 An artificial channel carrying water across country	1000 Cone bearing, as the fir tree	1000 To put down, to prevent circulation	1000 To plot; to band together for an evil purpose

FIGURE 9–3   Double Latin Root Jeopardy Board

chalkboard, with the side on which only the number is written facing out. Turn over the square that is requested during the playing of the game so the answer can be read.

Procedures

The teacher should go over the rules of the game first. The game consists of three rounds: Jeopardy, Double Jeopardy, and Final Jeopardy.

1. The game is modeled after the Jeopardy television game. The answer will appear when uncovered in this version. The players must phrase their answers in the form of a question:
   Answer: Coming from the Latin root meaning "to draw or pull," its definition means "a machine for pulling heavy loads"
   Question: What is *tractor*?
2. Determine who will go first. That player will select the first category and point value. The leader uncovers the clue and reads it aloud.
3. The first player responding correctly adds the point amount of the question to his or her total and chooses the next category and point amount. An incorrect response means that the points are subtracted.

TABLE 9-3   LATIN ROOTS

aud: to hear.	**rupt:** to break.
audible, inaudible, audience, auditory, audio, audition, auditorium	*abrupt, corrupt, disrupt, eruption, interrupt, bankrupt, rupture*
bene: well, good.	**scrib/script:** to write.
benefit, beneficial, benevolent, benefactor, benediction	*inscribe, transcribe, transcript, manuscript, prescription, describe*
cred: to believe, to trust.	**sect/sec:** cut.
credit, credible, credence, discredit	*dissect, intersect, insect, midsection*
dict: to say.	**spect:** to look.
dictate, diction, dictator, dictionary, contradict, contradiction, indict, benediction	*spectator, inspect, prospect, suspect*
duc(t): to lead.	**spir:** to breathe.
conducive, deduce, deduct, educate, induce, introduce, produce, reduce, aquaduct	*respiration, inspire, conspirators*
fac: to do, to make.	**st/sta/stat:** to stand.
fact, factual, factory, facilitate, manufacture, benefactor	*stable, station, constant, establish, statue, arrest, constitute, institute, obstacle*
flec/flex: to bend.	**struct:** to build.
reflection, deflect, flexible	*construct, instruct, destruct*
form: shape.	**tang/tact:** to touch.
formation, formative, deform, formula	*tangible/intangible, tangent, contact, tactile*
fract: to break.	**trac/tract:** to drag, pull.
fracture, refract, fraction	*trace, track, tractable, tractor, detract, extract, distract*
ject: throw.	**vid/vis:** to see.
reject, projectile, eject, inject	*video, invisible, television*
jud: judge.	**vert/vers:** to turn.
judgment, prejudice, adjudicate	*revert, inversion, vertical, convert*
junct: to join.	**voc:** voice, to call.
juncture, junction, conjunction	*vocal, advocate, vociferous*
port: to carry.	**vor:** eat.
import, export, transport, portable	*voracious, omnivore, carnivore, herbivore*

4. When it is time for the Final Jeopardy question, here is the procedure: Players see the category, but not the answer. They then decide how many of their points they will risk. When they see the answer, they have 30 seconds to write the question. If they are correct, they add the number of points they risked to their total; if incorrect, that number of points is subtracted from their total.

Questions for Latin Root Jeopardy

Spect

1. spectator 2. expectation 3. suspect 4. respect
5. circumspect

Form

1. uniform 2. nonconformist 3. reform 4. transform 5. deformity

Port

1. import 2. porter 3. transport 4. report 5. portfolio

Questions for Double Latin Root Jeopardy

Cred

1. credit 2. creed 3. incredible 4. discredit 5. accredited

Duct

1. conductor 2. educate 3. induct 4. introduction 5. aqueduct

Fer

1. fertile 2. refer 3. transfer 4. suffering 5. coniferous

Press

1. press 2. express 3. oppress 4. depression 5. suppress

Spir

1. spirit 2. expire 3. perspire 4. inspire 5. conspire

Tract

1. attractive 2. tractor 3. traction 4. contract 5. subtract

Dict

1. dictionary 2. contradiction 3. benediction 4. edict 5. indict

Variations

1. The gameboard may be copied and given to players who work alone. A sketch of the gameboard may be drawn on the chalkboard with the point amount in the square. Mark off the square chosen before the answer is read by the leader. Daily Doubles may be included, if desired (the number of points for an answer is doubled, and if correct, added to the player's score; if incorrect the doubled number of points is subtracted from the player's score).
2. Develop a Vocabulary Jeopardy to accompany a unit of study:*
   * Students generate vocabulary cards from a unit of study.
   * Students write questions on the cards that relate to facts and concepts studied. Answers are written on the back upside down. The cards are sorted into categories.
   * Teams of students play the game as a whole-class vocabulary review of unit.
3. See Figure 9-4 for alternative items.

"Hidden" Greek Roots 9–7

This word sort is a more advanced activity with Greek roots for one to three students.†

Materials

Using Table 9-4, prepare Greek word root cards (such as *diagram, monogram,* and *telegram*) and definition cards (such as *thing written*). Have a dictionary for reference.

Procedures

1. The teacher initiates discussion and background material for this Greek word root activity.
2. Student(s) sort word cards by Greek word families and match word cards to root definition cards. Through discussion and use of dictionaries, students may "discover" related word families.

It's All Greek to Us 9–8

In this card game, the deck is composed of Greek word cards. Two to four players may participate, one of whom will serve as game master and hold and read definition cards.†

---

*Thanks to Helen McMullen for this activity.
†Thanks to Virgie Anderson for these activities.

1. *val:* to be strong, to be worth.
   a. the worth of a thing in money or goods (noun)
   b. courage or bravery (noun)
   c. to value at less than the real worth (verb)
   d. brave, full of courage (adj.)
   e. priceless, precious (adj.)
2. *sign:* to sign, to seal.
   a. to write one's name on (verb)
   b. a person's name written by himself (noun)
   c. a thing or happening that shows, warns, or points out (noun)
   d. to be a sign of, to mean (verb)
   e. a seal or other mark stamped on a paper to make it official (noun)
3. *nom:* name.
   a. to name as a candidate for election (verb)
   b. a person who is nominated (noun)
   c. in name only (adj.)
   d. a system of names, as those used in studying a certain science (noun)
   e. showing the subject of a verb, or the words that agree with the subject (noun)
4. *rupt:* to break.
   a. to burst forth, as lava from a volcano (verb)
   b. to break in between, as in conversation (verb)
   c. to part violently (verb); a hernia (noun)
   d. a rending asunder, something you don't want in the classroom (noun)
   e. to defile, to taint (verb)
5. *struc(t):* to build.
   a. a building (noun)
   b. "good" criticism (adj.)
   c. ruin (noun)
   d. to teach or train (verb)
   e. that part of the building above the foundation (noun)

a. What is *value?*
b. What is *valor?*
c. What is *undervalue?*
d. What is *valiant?*
e. What is *invaluable?*

a. What is *sign?*
b. What is *signature?*
c. What is *signal?*

d. What is *signify?*
e. What is *signet?*

a. What is *nominate?*
b. What is *nominee?*
c. What is *nominal?*
d. What is *nomenclature?*

e. What is *nominative?*

a. What is *erupt?*
b. What is *interrupt?*
c. What is *rupture?*
d. What is *disruption?*

e. What is *corrupt?*

a. What is *structure?*
b. What is *constructive?*
c. What is *destruction?*
d. What is *instruct?*
e. What is *superstructure?*

FIGURE 9–4   Alternative Items for Latin Root Jeopardy

1. Use the following list to prepare word cards (example: *chronic*) and definition cards (example: *of long duration* or *prolonged*).
2. The game master shuffles word cards, deals 10 cards per player, and places remaining word cards facedown in front of players.
3. The game master reads a definition card. A player who is holding a card to match the definition places it below the corresponding Greek root. Upon discarding, players must draw one word card from the remaining deck. If no player can respond to the definition, the game master places the definition card on the bottom of his or her cards for rereading later in the game. If a player successfully responds and matches a word card and definition, the game master places that definition card to the side.
4. When the word card deck is depleted, the player who discards all word cards first is the winner.

TABLE 9-4 Greek Word Roots

aer: air.
aerial, aerate
agog: leader.
demagogue, pedagogue, synagogue
angel: messenger.
evangelist, angelic
aster/astr: star.
asteroid, astronomer, astronomy, astrology, asterisk
auto: self.
autograph, autobiography
bio: life.
biology, biome, biosphere, biotic
chron: time.
chronic, chonicle, chronology, synchrony
chlor: greenish-yellow.
chlorophyll, chloroplast, chlorine
derm: skin.
epidermis, dermatology
eco: house.
ecology, economy, ecosystem, ecotype
gram: thing written.
diagram, monogram, telegram
graph: writing.
*autograph, biography, photography, telegraph, graphic,
calligraphy*
hydr: water.
hydrant, hydrology, hydroplane
hyper: over, above, beyond.
*hyperacid, hypercritical, hyperkinesia, hypermedia,
hyperopia, hyperthermic*

hypo: below, beneath.
hypodermis, hypodermic, hypothermia, hypotension
logo: word, reason.
logic, analogy, catalogue, prologue, epilogue, monologue
meter/metr: measure.
metric, barometer, diameter, geometry, perimeter, symmetry
micro: small.
microscope, micrometer, microfilm
mono: one, single.
monotone, monotonous, monastery, monk
od/hod: road, way.
episode, method, methodical, exodus
phe/phem: to speak.
blaspheme, emphasis, emphatic, euphemism
phil: love.
philanthropy, Philadelphia, philosophy, philharmonic
phon: sound.
telephone, phonics, symphonic, euphony
photo/phos: light.
photograph, telephoto, phosphorescent
pol/polis: city, state.
police, metropolis, politics, cosmopolitan
scope: instrument for viewing.
microscope, telescope, kaleidoscope
techn: art, skill, craft.
technical, technology, polytechnic
therm: heat.
thermometer, thermostat, thermal, exothermic
zoo: animal.
zoo, zoology

Variation

Students may create additional deck(s) by composing definitions for the additional example words in the Greek roots list in Table 9-4.

Definitions and Word Lists

1. Adj.	1. Of long duration, continuing, constant 2. Prolonged	*chronic*
2. Adj.	Arranged in order of time of occurrence	*chronological*
3. N.	The medical study of the physiology and pathology of the skin	*dermatology*
4. N.	The outer, protective, nonvascular layer of the skin	*epidermis*
5. N.	A design composed of one or more letters, usually the initials of a name	*monogram*
6. Adj.	Without variation or variety; repetitiously dull	*monotonous*

7.	Adj.	1. Bold and definite in expression or action 2. Accentuated; definite	*emphatic*
8.	V.	To speak of God (or something sacred) in an irreverent or impious manner	*blaspheme*
9.	N.	The substitution of an inoffensive term for one considered offensively explicit	*euphemism*
10.	Adj.	Devoted to or appreciative of music	*philharmonic*
11.	N.	A listing of the order of events and other pertinent information for some public presentation	*chronicle*
12.	Adj.	1. Of or pertaining to written or pictorial representation 2. Described in vivid detail	*graphic*
13.	N.	The process of rendering optical images on photosensitive surfaces	*photography*
14.	N.	A movement away; a departure, usually of a large number	*exodus*
15.	N.	A means or manner of procedure; especially, a regular and systematic way of accomplishing anything	*method*
16.	N.	An outlet from a water main consisting of an upright pipe with one or more nozzles or spouts	*hydrant*
17.	Adj.	1. Showing consistency of reasoning 2. Able to reason clearly	*logical*
18.	N.	A short addition or concluding section at the end of any literary work or play	*epilogue*
19.	N.	An instrument for measuring atmospheric pressure, used in weather forecasting and in determining elevation	*barometer*
20.	N.	1. Mathematics—The distance around an enclosed area 2. Military—A fortified strip or boundary protecting a position	*perimeter*
21.	N.	A long speech or talk made by one person	*monologue*
22.	N.	A succession of sounds or words uttered in a single tone of voice	*monotone*
23.	N.	Public park or institution in which living animals are kept and exhibited to the public	*zoo*
24.	N.	The biological science of animals	*zoology*
25.	N.	Science that deals with microorganisms, especially their effects on other forms of life	*microbiology*
26.	N.	A tiny, representative world	*microcosm*
27.	N.	A film upon which documents or photographs are greatly reduced in size	*microfilm*

28.	N.	The scientific study of celestial bodies and phenomena	*astronomy*
29.	Adj.	1. Of or pertaining to astronomy 2. Inconceivably large; immense	*astronomical*
30.	N.	The story of a person's life written by himself; memoirs	*autobiography*
31.	N.	A person's own signature or handwriting	*autograph*
32.	V.	To expose to the circulation of air for purification	*aerate*
33.	Adj.	1. Of, in, or caused by the air 2. Reaching high into the air; lofty	*aerial*
34.	N.	A leader who obtains power by means of impassioned appeals to the emotions and prejudices of the populace	*demagogue*
35.	N.	Schoolteacher; educator	*pedagogue*
36.	N.	The suffering of intense physical or mental pain	*chronic*
37.	Adj.	Of, or pertaining to, consisting of, or belonging to angels	*angelic*
38.	N.	A star-shaped figure (*) used in print to indicate an omission or a reference to a footnote	*asterisk*
39.	N.	1. City of Brotherly Love 2. Large metropolitan city in Pennsylvania	*Philadelphia*
40.	N.	The effort or inclination to increase the well-being of mankind, as by charitable aid or donations	*philanthropy*
41.	Adj.	Occurring at the same time	*synchronous*
42.	N.	The study of the position and aspects of heavenly bodies with a view to predicting their influence on the course of human affairs	*astrology*
43.	Adj.	1. Too small to be seen by the unaided eye 2. Exceedingly small, minute	*microscopic*
44.	N.	A small tube in which patterns of colors are optically produced and viewed for amusement	*kaleidoscope*
45.	Adj.	Pertaining to or dealing with many arts and sciences	*polytechnic*
46.	N.	Beautiful handwriting	*calligraphy*
47.	Adj.	Of or pertaining to, or having the nature of sound, especially speech sound	*vocal*
48.	Adj.	1. Common to the whole world 2. At home in all parts of the earth, or in many spheres of interest	*cosmopolitan*
49.	N.	1. A major city 2. A large urban center of culture, trade, or other activity	*Philadelphia*

Joined at the Roots 9–9

This word sort is a very effective extension of students' exploration of Latin and Greek roots. It is appropriate for individuals, partners, or small groups.

Materials

Word sort board; word cards; word study notebook.

Procedures

1. The teacher begins by modeling how to place words with appropriate roots under a particular category, for example, "speaking and writing," "building/construction," "thinking and feeling," and "movement." The teacher then involves the students in the categorization.
2. Once students have grasped how this categorization scheme works, they can work in small groups or in pairs. Each group or pair will take a different category and sort words whose roots justify their membership in that category.
3. Lists can be written down in word study notebooks and brought back to the larger group to share and discuss. (Note: Several of the words to be sorted may be placed under different categories.) Following are some examples of categories and a few illustrative words.

Word List

Building/Construction	Thinking and Feeling	Movement	Travel
technology	philanthropy	synchrony	astronaut
construct	philosophy	fracture	exodus
tractor	attraction		

Government	Speaking and Writing
economy	autobiography
demagogue	photograph
politics	catalogue
	emphasis

Root Webbing 9–10

This activity also extends students' understanding of how Greek word roots function within words. It facilitates students' awareness of the etymology of particular words.

Materials

Vocabulary notebooks, dictionaries.

Procedures

1. The teacher chooses a set of common roots, such as *photo, geo, aqua,* and *astro.*
2. While the teacher creates one on an overhead, in their vocabulary notebooks students create webs of words in which the root can be found (see Figure 9-5).
3. The students brainstorm related words and figure out root meaning.
4. Students use dictionaries to locate root, verify meaning, find origin, and search for related words.

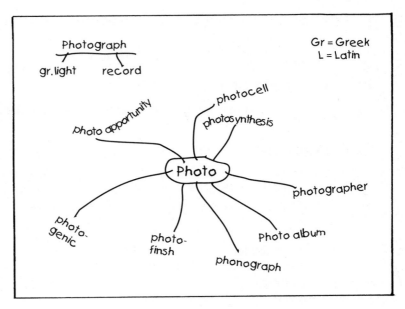

FIGURE 9-5   "Root Web" in Student's Vocabulary Notebook

5. As a group, the students eliminate words that do not fit the meaning of the root. The teacher should honor all suggestions and lead students to examine parts and meaning.

This activity works best after students have been introduced to a number of word roots and examined how they "work" in words. The teacher should precede this activity with a walk-through for Latin and Greek elements (Tables 9-3 and 9-4). Students, alone or in small groups, may sort words by root, using words that contain the most frequently occurring roots.

Materials

File folders with Greek and Latin elements listed at top of inside flap; word cards to be sorted.

Procedures

Have students sort three or four roots at a time. Write each root on a card with its origin and meaning on the back. Words can be sorted by following these directions:

1. Sort the words, matching them with the Greek or Latin word part they contain.
2. Say the words; students should use general knowledge about the meanings to guess what the Greek or Latin word part means. Ask these questions:
   - What do all of the words have in common?
   - How are they related?
3. Students should check the back of the word card to see if their guess about the meaning is correct. What part of the meaning stays constant among the related words?
4. Record the words, by word part, in word study notebooks.

Possible roots are *vor* from Table 9-3 and *astr, bio, chlor, eco, hydr, hypo,* and *photo* from Table 9-4.

Variations

After the students automatically respond to the meaning of about a dozen Greek and Latin word parts, they may work cooperatively as a group to sort words according to their roots. Then, they may categorize the words according to the area of science in which they might be used: for example, plant words, animal words, environment words, or space words.

Is It *able* or *ible?* 9–11

This word sort may be done as a class activity from the board or in a small group.*

Procedures

The features to be examined must be controlled. Students in the middle derivational phase need only examine the first three or four concepts. Students in the late derivational phase may explore the less frequent patterns.

1. Sort words that end in *able* into one group and those that end in *ible* into the other group.

dependable	credible
expendable	audible
passable	edible
profitable	plausible
breakable	visible
agreeable	feasible
predictable	compatible
perishable	terrible
acceptable	horrible
remarkable	possible
readable	indelible
laughable	legible
profitable	
punishable	

Do you see a generalization that tells you when you spell the suffix *able* and when you spell it *ible?* If the suffix is attached to a **base word** (*depend*), it is spelled *able*; if it is attached to a **word root** (*cred*) it is spelled *ible*.

2. Sort the words that drop the *e* before adding *able* into one group. Sort those that keep the *e* when *able* is added into the other group.

presumable	noticeable
pleasurable	peaceable
desirable	marriageable
dispensable	bridgeable
blamable	manageable
usable	changeable
excusable	serviceable
lovable	
deplorable	
comparable	

Can you come up with a generalization that tells you when to drop the *e* and when to keep it? If a word ends with a soft-g or soft-c sound (as in *gem* or *cite*), it cannot precede an *a*. So, to keep the soft sound, words ending in *ce* or *ge* keep the *e* before adding *able*.

---

*Thanks to Neva Viise for this activity.

3. Sort the words into two categories: Those that end with *ible* or with *able.*

negligible	applicable
invincible	navigable
eligible	amicable
intelligible	despicable
legible	impeccable
crucible	
tangible	

There is a generalization for spelling the words in the first column with *ible.* Soft-c or soft-g endings without silent-e must, for the same reason as in sort 2, go to *ible.* There is also a generalization for spelling the words in the second column with *able.* The suffix follows a hard-g or hard-c sound and must therefore take *able.*

4. Sort the words according to suffix *ible* or *able.*

convincible	applicable
inducible	navigable
reducible	amicable
forcible	despicable
producible	impeccable

Notice that a few words ending in silent-e do not retain the *e,* and therefore they also must go to *ible* to maintain the soft-c sound.

    Because *able/ible* is a very complex issue, it is possible to find exceptions or low-frequency patterns. It is interesting to compare and contrast these words and discover or hypothesize reasons for these findings. Since very few students (or adults) will ever totally conquer the mysteries of *ible/able,* it is useful to point out that, if you've tried the different generalizations for adding the suffix and you're still not sure how to spell it, go with *able.* This is because more words end in *able* than in *ible.*

5. Related words: Many base words that are verbs become nouns by adding some form of *ion.* If the *ion* form of the word ends in *ation,* the suffix will be *able.* This is a very helpful rule since *ation* endings all include the long-a sound.

irritate	irritation	irritable
demonstrate	demonstration	demonstrable
estimate	estimation	estimable
tolerate	toleration	tolerable
separate	separation	separable
commend	commendation	commendable
inflame	inflammation	inflammable
vegetate	vegetation	vegetable
educate	education	educable
navigate	navigation	navigable
admire	admiration	admirable
observe	observation	observable
reclaim	reclamation	reclaimable
apply	application	applicable

6. In the same way, if the *ion* form derived from the verb root does not include *ation,* the *ble* form will be *ible.*

collect	collection	collectible
access	accession	accessible

contract	contraction	contractible
suppress	suppression	suppressible
repress	repression	repressible
exhaust	exhaustion	exhaustible
reduce	reduction	reducible
produce	production	producible
express	expression	expressible

This "rule" overrides the simpler idea that base words go to *able*. There are, however, exceptions to this rule involving base words that end in *ct* (*correct* to *correctable; detect* to *detectable; predict* to *predictable*). The *ct* endings must, therefore, be noted and memorized.

7. When a root ends in *ss* or *ns,* the ending is *ible.* Often the root actually ends in *t* (*permit*) or *d* (*comprehend*) and follows the same pattern as the movement to the *ion* or *ive* endings.

permit	permission	permissible
admit	admission	admissible
dismiss	dismissal	dismissible
transmit	transmission	transmissible
comprehend	comprehension	comprehensible

Which Suffix? 9–12

This activity is an excellent follow-up to previous work with base words, roots, and suffixes. It is appropriate for individuals, partners, or small groups. The suffixes included are: *ible/able* (use words in previous activity), *tion/sion, ence/ance,* and *ary/ery/ory* (see lists in the appendix).

Materials

Word cards, pencils and paper. Each card has the base word written on one side and same word with allowable suffixes on the other side.

Procedures

1. The teacher chooses how many suffixes to place at the top of the word sort. (*Note:* Several of the words to be sorted may be placed under different suffixes, for example, *permit: permissible, permission.*)
2. The teacher mixes up the word cards and places the deck with base words faceup. The children in turns choose the top card and decide which suffix category it belongs in.
3. After all the cards are placed, the students record on their papers what they think the correct spelling of the word is.
4. After recording all the words, the children turn the cards over to self-check the correct spelling.

Variation

Students can work in pairs to explore a particular suffix team (for example, *tion* and *sion*) to see what generalization(s) may underlie the use of a suffix.

Defiance or Patience 9–13

Defiance (if using the *ant/ance/ancy* family) or Patience (if using the *ent/ence/ency* family) is simply a version of Go Fish for three to five players. The object of the game is to make as many groups of two, three, or four cards of the same derivation and to be the first to run out of cards.*

Materials

Two decks of 52 blank playing cards. Use words from the lists in the appendix, as well as roots when applicable. To prepare for the game, select words from the list of your choice in groups of two, three, and four until you have a total of 52 words. Do not split any groupings, as this may be misleading. Write each word across the top of a card, and your deck is prepared.

Pregame Warm-Up

Before playing Defiance or Patience, students should engage in a word study activity that addresses both categories of *ant/ance/ancy* and *ent/ence/ency* words. A suggested order follows:

Sort 1: *ent* versus *ant*

Sort 2: Add the related *ence* and *ance* words. Sort *ent/ence* versus *ant/ance.* Then match *ent/ence* pairs and *ant/ance* pairs.

Sort 3: Add the related *ency* and *ancy* words. Sort *ent/ence/ency* versus *ant/ance/ancy.* Then sort *ent/ence/ency* triples, followed by *ant/ance/ancy* triples.

Sort 4: Add those words that do not come in triples, but simply in pairs for both word families.

Sort 5: Add roots to any of the pairs or triplets, sorting first by the *ant* or *ent* category, then by groups of two, three, or four in the same derivational family.

Procedures

1. Each player is dealt five cards from the deck. The player to the left of the dealer begins. The player may first lay down any existing groups of two, three, or four that he has in his hand. Then he may ask any other player for a card of a certain derivation that he holds in his hand: "Matthew, give me all of your *resistance.*" (This could result in gaining *resistance, resistant, resistancy,* or *resist.*)

2. A player who does not have cards with the feature being sought responds, "Be defiant" or "Be patient" depending on which game is being played.

3. At this, the asking player must draw another card from the deck. If the card is of the same family being sought, the player may lay down the match and continue asking other players for cards. However, if the card is not of the correct derivational group, play passes to the person on the left and continues around the circle in the same manner. If the drawn card makes a match in the asking player's hand, but was not that which was being sought, he must hold the pair in hand until his turn comes up again. Of course this means there is a risk of another player taking the pair before the next turn.

4. Play ends when one of the students runs out of cards. The player with the most points wins.

5. Players may play on other players' card groups by laying related cards down in front of themselves.

6. Singles played on other players' matches   1 point
   Pairs   2 points
   Triples   6 points
   Groups of four   10 points
   First player to run out of cards   10 points

---

*Thanks to Elizabeth Harrison White for this activity.

Variations

1. Defy My Patience could be the version that mixes sets of words from both lists to create an *ent/ant* deck.
2. Challenge My Patience or Defy My Challenge: In this version, during scoring before everyone throws down their hand, students should write down on secret slips of paper any additional words for groups they have laid down, which have not been played. Before hands are revealed, these lists should be shared, and an additional point added to every player's score for each related word they wrote. If other players doubt the authenticity of a word claimed by an opponent, someone may challenge the word. The challenger loses a point if the word is valid, or gains a point if it is not. The player, likewise, counts the word if it is valid, or loses a point if the challenger is correct.
3. Students should be encouraged to come up with their own derivational families to be added to this game or another feature to be substituted for the *ant/ent* contrast.

Exploring Assimilated Prefixes: *ad, com,* and *in* 9–14

Materials

1. Chalkboard, word cards, word study notebook. Use Table 9-5 to prepare word cards and prefix cards such as the ones in Figure 9-6.
2. Word cards for individual sorting activity (see list in Table 9-5).
3. Sorting folders with given exemplars for sort.

Procedures

1. Introduce the three prefixes as headers for each category of the sort. Place the exemplars on the board in three columns.
2. Students read each card and place the card in the appropriate column (see Figure 9-6).
3. Discuss any word meanings, if necessary, and how the prefix changes the meaning of the base word. Ask the class if they can think of why the prefix spelling changes in certain words.
4. The students write the words in their word study notebooks under the appropriate exemplar.
5. After all example words have been studied, mix the cards, and have students sort as a small group or individually.
6. Have students go on a word hunt for words with these assimilated prefixes, and add to the word study notebook.

Assimile 9–15

This game can be played by two to six players.*

Materials

Gameboard modeled after Monopoly (see Figure 9-7); dice; game playing pieces; *chance* cards (colored word cards with base words written on each); deck of assimilated prefix base words (only readily apparent base words such as *accompany* or

*Telia Blackard contributed this activity.

TABLE 9-5 Assimilated Prefixes

ad: to, toward
ac accompany, account, accustom, accommodate, accomplish, accumulate, accurate
ad adhere, adhesive, advantage
af affirm, affix, affront, affluent, affect, affiliate, affinity, affluence
ag aggression, aggrieve, aggravate
al allay, allocate, allot, alleviate, allegation, alliteration, allude
an announce, annotate
ap appeal, appendix, appetite, application, apprehend, approximate
ar arrange, arrest, array, arrive, arrogance
as assign, assort, assure, assimilate, assemble, assent, associate, assume
at attend, attune, attain, attempt, attend, attract

sub: under
sub subjugate, subsequent
suc succeed, success
suf suffix, suffuse
sup support, supplant, suppress, suggest, suffix, success

in: not, into
il illiterate, illegal, illuminate, illegitimate
im immature, immigrant, immobile, immortal, immediate
ir irresponsible, irradiate, irregular, irreligious, irrational

ex: out
ef efface, effect, efferent

com: with
col collaborate, colleague, collide, collocate, collect, collapse
con connect, connote
cor correspond, correct, corrupt

ob: against, toward
oc occur, occult, occlusion, occupy
of offend, offer
op oppose, oppress, opportunity, opposite

dis: opposite
dif diffuse, different, diffident

immortal; see list in Table 9-5); sheet of paper and pencil or pen for each player (to use in spelling words).

Procedures

This game is modeled after Monopoly.

1. Place base words *company, mortal* facedown around the board. A particular prefix is chosen to be focused on, and this is placed faceup in the center of the board. *Chance* cards are also placed in the middle. *Chance* cards are a "chance" to think of one's own assimilated prefix word using the base word on the card and any assimilated prefix. *Chance* cards are picked up every time a player passes *go.*
2. Players roll the dice to see who goes first. The player with the highest number rolls again and moves the number of spaces on the board.
3. Upon landing on a particular space, the word card is turned up, and the player has to determine whether this word can be assimilated to the prefix in the center of the

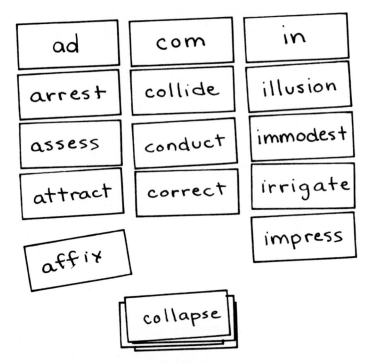

FIGURE 9–6   Exploration of Assimilated Prefixes: *ad, com, in*

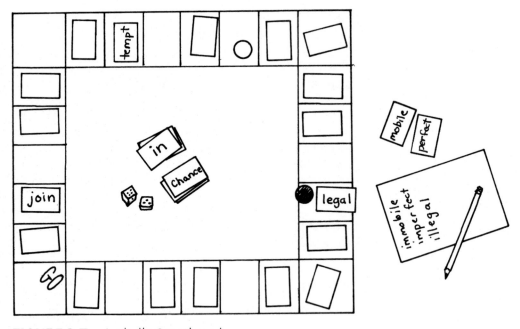

FIGURE 9–7   Assimile Gameboard

board. If the card can be made into a word, the player attempts to both say the word and to correctly spell it. A player who is able to correctly spell the word receives one point and is also allowed another turn. (The word card is actually removed and retained by the player.) If the word cannot be assimilated, it is kept on the board faceup (this word will not be played again). However, if the word can be assimilated, but the player misspells the word, the card is turned back over to be played later in the game.

4. A player who is unable to come up with a word (for whatever reason) forfeits a turn, and play moves to the next player.

5. The game is over when all cards that can be played are played, and the winner is the one with the most correctly spelled words.

Variations

A separate set of *Community Chest* cards using all of the original assimilated prefixes can be placed in the middle of the board, and this can be drawn from after each round of turns. This ensures that all prefixes are studied. (*Community Chest* cards will have the prefixes *ad, in, com, ob, sub, ex, per, dis.*) If this method is played, then word cards that cannot be played with one particular prefix are turned back over until able to be played.

Rolling Prefixes 9–16

Materials

Create a deck of 32 word cards of assimilated prefixes (eight sets of four). Each group of four should consist of a mixed sort from each of the seven sets of assimilated prefixes: *ad, in, com, ob, sub, ex, dis.* One set will have to be a "wild set" (words that have the aforementioned prefixes).* See Table 9-5 for words to use.

Procedures

1. After the initial sorting of assimilated prefixes, each player is dealt eight cards—three cards to each player on the first round, two cards to each player the second round, and three cards to each player the third round.

2. The player on the dealer's left starts the game by putting a card faceup in the center of the table. It doesn't matter what the card is, but the player must read the word and state what the prefix is.

3. The next player to the left and the others that follow, attempt to play a card of the same suit as the first one put on the table ("suit" meaning having the same prefix). Players must read their word and state the prefix.

4. If everybody follows suit, the cards in the center of the table are picked up after all the players have added their cards, and are put to the side. No one scores.

5. The game continues in the same fashion until someone is unable to follow suit. When this occurs, the player can play a wild card, changing the suit for the following players.

6. A player may choose to change suit in this manner at any point in the game. For example, a player may play the word *collide* (prefix *com*), and the next player may either play a *com* prefix word (such as *concoct*) or a word with *com* elsewhere in the word, such as *accommodate*. If the player chooses *accommodate*, the prefix the following player must concentrate on is *ad* or a form of *ad*. Players must be familiar with all types of assimilated prefixes.

7. A player who is unable to follow suit must pick up the center deck of cards. The player who picks up the cards begins the next round. The game continues this way until someone gets rid of all his or her cards. When this happens the game ends.

---

*This was adapted from the game "Rolling Stone" from *Games and Fun with Playing Cards* by J. Leeming. Thanks also to Telia Blackard for her contributions.

This student uses a dictionary in his study of homophones.

Variations

1. At first, players may not wish to state the original prefix of the words.
2. Multiple decks of assimilated prefixes can be made, allowing for variation.
3. Instead of ending the game after one person gets rid of all his or her cards, the game can continue by the winner of the first round receiving one point for each card that the other players hold in their hands at the end of the game.

Words From Greek and Roman Myths and Legends 9–17

Similar to the Jeopardy format but involving more students, this game is intended for advanced students in the intermediate grades and many others in the middle and secondary grades. It is appropriate to use after a number of myths and legends have been read and discussed. The object of the game is to gain the most points by correctly answering the questions.*

Materials

At least 20 word cards with questions representing four categories. In the example game, the categories are *science, arts, timely events,* and *everyday words.* Write the questions on one side of a word card and the assigned points on the other side. As in Jeopardy, the questions progress in difficulty for each category, from 10 to 50. Make a heading card with the name of each category and then attach these heading cards and word cards, with points facing out, into columns of notches made on posterboard.

Procedures

1. Assign students to three teams of four each. Flip a coin to determine who goes first.
2. Select a student to act as emcee, who reads question cards from the chart. All questions begin: "Relating to the category you've selected, *what is a word that comes from* _____?" For example, "Relating to the word you've selected, what is a word that comes from the Cyclops, a monstrous giant with an eye in his forehead?"

---

*Thanks to Lisbeth Kling for this activity.

3. Players take turns responding, but can be helped by any of their coplayers for the answer. Out-of-turn responses result in no points, even if the answer given is correct.
4. Team A's player 1 selects a category and question card (may be any level of points). The student emcee reads the card aloud.
5. Player 1 can answer immediately or discuss with teammates and then answer. Points are awarded if the answer is correct, deducted if the answer is incorrect. (Yes, a team may wind up getting negative scores!)
6. You are the game show judge.
7. The procedure continues until one team wins.

Other words from the list in Table 9-6 can be used in these categories as well. You may select other categories and words, and students may also be involved in suggesting categories and in preparing games for classmates. Use this game format for vocabulary words in other content areas such as math and social studies.

This game format may also be used for *eponyms*, a list of which is given in the appendix.

Sample Game: Categories and Questions

Science

hygiene	Saturn
iris	Neptune
cosmos	cyclone
Pluto	aurora
Jupiter	lunar
Uranus	solar
Mars	
Venus	hydraulics
Mercury	
Earth	

Arts

music
calliope
hymn
museum
orpheum

Timely Events

Easter
dawn
January
March
chronological
the Olympics
nocturnal
June
Valentine's Day

Everyday Words

giant	mnemonic
cosmetics	panacea
ocean	salute
chaos	tantalize
atlas	nectarine

TABLE 9-6   Words From Greek and Roman Myths and Legends

Greek

Chaos: The raw material of the universe—a great, dark, confused mass in which air, earth, and water were all mixed together. *chaos, chaotic, chasm, gas*

Cosmos: The opposite of chaos—things with form and shape; in order, good arrangement. *cosmic, cosmopolitan, cosmetic*

Gaea (JEEuh): Goddess of earth; Greek word for earth. *geography, geology, geometry, geode*

Uranus: God of sky, heaven. *uranium, Uranus (the planet)*

Gigantes: Children of Uranus and Gaea, ferocious beings of tremendous size and power. *giants, gigantic*

Cyclops: Children of Uranus and Gaea; from a Greek word meaning "round-eyed." Monstrous giants with one eye in the forehead. *cyclone*

Titans/Titanesses: Offspring of Uranus and Gaea, these were a race of giants who ruled the world before the Greek gods and goddesses took over. They warred with the gods and lost; their fate was eternal punishment of some sort or another. *Titanic, titanium*

Cronus: Most powerful of Titans; because of the similarity to the Greek word *chronos,* he is often mistakenly referred to as the god of time. *chronological, synchrony, synchronous*

Oceanus (ohSEEuhnus): Oldest of Titans; symbolized water that encircled the land of the world. *ocean, oceanic*

Atlas: One of the Titans, Atlas's punishment was to support the world on his shoulders. A picture of this was often included in the early books of maps, so over time such books came to be called atlases. *atlas, Atlas Mountains* (the god Atlas turned to stone) *Atlantic, Atlanta*

Zeus: Son of Cronus, god of the heavens and the earth. He shared role of the cosmos with Poseidon and Hades.

Poseidon: God of the sea, often portrayed carrying a trident, which he used to cause earthquakes.

Hades: God of the underworld.

Luna: Goddess of the moon. At one time, people believed the moon had the power to drive some people out of their minds—thus, we derive our words *lunacy* and *lunatic* from her. *lunar, lunacy, lunatic*

Fates: Three goddesses who controlled the fate of humans: *Clotho,* who controlled the course of the universe; pictured as spinning all the threads that represent life. *cloth, clothes. Lachesis,* who determined the length of the thread. *Atropes,* who cut the thread.

Hypnos: Greek god of sleep. *hypnosis, hypnotic, hypnotism*

Ares: God of war. Ares has two sons: *Phobos* ("fear," from which we get *phobia*) and *Deimos* ("terror"). Phobos and Deimos are the two moons of Mars (Roman name for Ares).

Mt. Olympus: Where the Greek gods and goddesses lived. *Olympian*

Nox: From Chaos, goddess of darkness of night. *nocturnal, nocturne*

Lethe: Means "forgetfulness." The river in Hades where the spirits of the dead drink and then forget their former life and become listless ghosts. *lethargic, lethal*

Athena: Goddess of knowledge, arts, war, and peace. Daughter of Zeus. *Athens, Athenian*

Eros: Greek god of young love. *erotic*

Pan: God of fields, forests, wild animals, and the patron of shepherds and their flocks. Part man/part goat, he often caused serious trouble. The belief that he was nearby caused people to run in terror. *panic, pandemonium*

Iris: Meaning "rainbow," she was a messenger of the gods. *iris* (flower, part of the eye), *iridescence*

Muses: Zeus's nine daughters. *music, museum*

    1. Calliope: Muse of eloquence. *calliope*

    2. Polyhymnia: Muse of religious music. *hymn, hymnal*

    3. Orpheus: Poet-musician with magic musical powers. *orpheus, orphic*

Mnemosyne: Mother of muses, goddess of memory. *mnemonic, amnesia, amnesty*

Gratiae: The Graces, three sisters who were goddesses of all that is charming in women. *grace, graceful, gracious*

TABLE 9-6 (continued)

Hygeia: Greek goddess of health. *hygiene, hygienic*
Nemesis: God of retribution, justice, or vengeance.
Tantalus: Human son of Zeus. He boasted of his friendship with the gods, so Nemesis followed him and had him punished by a lifetime of standing in water up to his neck with grapes not quite within reach; when he bent to drink, the water receded. *tantalize*
Ambrosia: The food of the gods.
Nectar: The drink of the gods. *nectar, nectarine*
Echo: A mountain nymph, she offended Zeus's wife, Hera, because she talked so much. Hera condemned Echo to haunt the mountainsides, being able only to repeat the last few words of the person speaking. Echo was in love with Narcissus; after he died, she wasted away until nothing was left but her voice.
Dionysus: God of agriculture, most notable for his responsibility for the grape harvest. Also known as *Bacchus,* from which we get *bacchanalia* (extremely festive celebrations). His followers were known as *Maenads;* they would fly into extreme reveries, from which we get the word *mania.*
Narcissus: A young man who fell in love with his own reflection in a pool of water. *narcissism*
Psyche: A maiden who loved Eros. Her name means "soul." *psychology, psychiatrist*
Marathon: A plain located 22 miles from Athens on which a battle was fought between the Greeks and the Persians. A Greek courier ran to Athens to tell the city of the Greek victory and then died. *marathon*
Heracles: The strongest of the Greek heroes; through his Roman name "Hercules" he gave us our word *herculean,* meaning very powerful. We often speak of herculean tasks, which means they are very difficult and trying. Heracles had to perform several seemingly impossible tasks (for example, one was the slaying of a nine-headed monster, the Hydra; when one of its heads was severed, two grew in its place). *herculean*
Hydra: A water serpent that was slain by Heracles. *hydraulics, hydrophobia, hydrant*
Laconia: A part of Greece where the Spartans lived. The Spartans were warlike but not given to boasting. They spoke few words and in few sentences. *laconic*
Odysseus (Roman *Ulysses*): The Greek king whose voyages took him away from home. *odyssey*
Helios: God of the sun. *helium, heliocentric*

Roman

Jupiter or *Jove:* Chief of the Roman gods. *jovial*
Terra: Goddess of the earth. *territory, terrain, terrestrial, terrace, terrarium*
Vulcan: God of fire. *volcano, volcanic, vulcanize*
Sol: God of the sun. *solar, solar system, solarium, parasol*
Morta: Sister of Fate. *mortal, immortal, mortician*
Somnus: God of sleep. *insomnia, somnambulate* (sleepwalk)
Furies: Three sisters who punished those guilty of particularly horrible crimes. *fury, furious*
Ceres: Goddess of grain and the harvest. *cereal*
Venus: Goddess of beauty and love. Her symbol, a looking glass, became the symbol for female. *Venus* (the planet), *venusian, venerate, venerable*
Mars: God of war. His symbols, the shield and the spear, became the universal symbol for male; also means "bloody." *March, Mars* (the red planet), *martial*
Cupid: God of young love.
Faunus: God of animal life. *fauna*
Salus: God of health. *salute, salutation, salutory, salubrious*
Janus: God of doors—entrance and exit. He had two faces. *January, janitor*
Romulus and Remus: Twin brothers who were raised by a she-wolf. *Rome, Roman, Romanic, romance*

furious	ambrosia
clothes	echo
cereal	narcissism
lethargic	clue
panic	labyrinth
pomegranate	

Answers	Questions
	Science
cyclonethe	Cyclops, a monstrous giant with an eye in his forehead?
solar	Sol, the Roman god of the sun?
hydraulics	Hydra, the nine-headed water serpent slain by Heracles?
iris	Iris, the messenger of the gods who used the rainbow as her stairway to Earth?
hygiene	Hygeia, the goddess of health?
	Arts
music	the Muses, Zeus's nine daughters?
calliope	Calliope, the muse of eloquence?
hymn	Polyhymnia, the muse of religious music?
mnemonic	Mnemosyne, the mother of the muses?
	Timely Events
January	Janus, the two-faced god of doors?
nocturnal	Nox, the goddess of darkness of night?
Easter	Eos, the goddess of dawn?
chronological	Chronos, the god of time?
June	Juno, the goddess of love?
	Everyday Words and Idioms
terrarium	Terra, the Roman goddess of earth?
giant	the Gigantes, ferocious beings of tremendous size and power?
ocean	Oceanus, who symbolized the water that encircled the land of the world?
atlas	Atlas, a Titan god who supported the heavens on his shoulders?
clothes	Clotho, who was pictured as spinning all the threads that represent life?

Identifying the Meaning of Word Roots 9–18

Given a series of words that share the same root, students analyze the words to determine the meaning of the root. Each group of three words can be finished with one of the words provided:

introspection   interrupt   distract

1. spectator, inspect, prospector, _____
The root *spect* means _____. (look, count, divide)
2. corrupt, disrupt, eruption, _____
The root *rupt* means _____. (speak, break, fall)
3. tractor, attract, extract, _____
The root *tract* means _____. (place, look, pull)

refract   contradict   audience

1. audible, auditory, audio, _____
The root *aud* means _____. (throw, hear, touch)
2. fraction, fracture, infraction, _____
The root *fract* means _____. (stretch, eat, break)

3. dictate, diction, predict, _____
The root *dict* means _____. (say, touch, fight)

dermatologist   nominative   invaluable

1. nominate, nominal, nominee, _____
The root *nom* means _____. (write, figure, name)
2. value, valor, devalue, _____
The root *val* means _____. (money, to be strong/to be worth, truth)
3. hypodermic, epidermis, dermatology, _____
The root *derm* means _____. (skin, medicine, platform)

Variation

Following this format, groups of students can construct their own exercises and then swap with other groups. Lists of roots in the appendix can be used as a source for additional roots and ideas.

Combining Roots and Affixes 9–19

In the following chart, students indicate with an *x* where words are made by combining the prefix and the root. Then, they write the words below. An engaging variation is to indicate with a question mark where words that do not exist in English—but could! Students may write these words in a special section of their vocabulary notebooks, create a definition for each, and use each in a sentence. When students are uncertain about whether a word is an actual word in English, they may check it in the dictionary.

	duce/duc/duct	port	spect	dict	tract
in/im		x			
trans					
ex					
pre					
		import			

Set up three columns: prefixes, roots, and suffixes. As with the chart activity, students see how many real words they can construct—and how many possible words they can create. Again, follow up with the vocabulary notebooks. Given the number of possibilities, this activity can occur over several days.

re	tract	able/ible
in/im	dict	ion/ation
ex	cred	ic
pre	gress	ibility/ability
trans	port	

The Synonym/Antonym Continuum 9–20

Provide students with a list of words or use prepared word cards. Then, have the students arrange the words along a continuum: At the ends of the continuum will be the antonyms—the words that are most opposite in meaning. Next to each of these words students will decide where to place words that are closest to the meaning of the opposite words—synonyms—and so on until all words have been used.

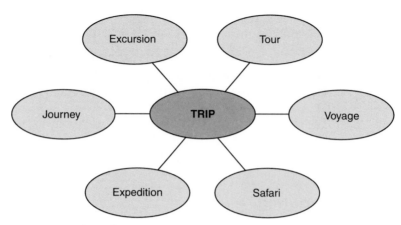

FIGURE 9-8   Semantic Web

For example, the words *balmy, frigid, chilly, boiling, frozen, tepid, hot, cool,* and *warm* could be arranged this way:

frigid   frozen   chilly   cool   tepid   balmy   warm   hot   boiling

First, the students work individually. Then, they compare their continua with one another. They should discuss differences and provide a rationale for why they arranged particular words the way they did. The dictionary will be the final judge of any disagreements.

Semantic Webs 9-21

Semantic webs are graphic aids that may be used (1) to fine-tune students' understanding of words and concepts in the same semantic family; and (2) expand students' vocabulary by presenting new terms. The example in Figure 9-8 elaborates and expands the concepts associated with *trip*. All the words except *excursion* are familiar to the students.

Procedures

1. When first introducing semantic webs, present a completed web. Later, students will help you create them.
2. Have students discuss their understandings of the familiar words (as with the synonym/antonym activity, this discussion requires them to make finer distinctions among the concepts). As they discuss meanings, encourage them to use the words in sentences. As always, the dictionary can resolve uncertainties.
3. Ask students if they have heard or seen the unfamiliar word (*excursion*) before. Discuss its possible meanings. Check the dictionary.
4. Ask students if they can think of any other words that could be added to the web.

Variation

When students are used to this format, involve them in generating a web. Present your core word or concept, and then have the students brainstorm other words that occur to them. You may then add one or two of your own words that will extend the students' vocabulary.

Semantic Feature Analysis 9-22

This analysis (Anders & Bos, 1986) engages students in the examination of words and definitions in relation to each other.

	Cannot Stand Alone	Comes Before a Base Word or Word Root	Usually Comes From Greek or Latin	Can Stand Alone	Comes After a Base Word or Word Root
Prefix	+	+	+	−	−
Base Word	−	−	?	+	−
Affix	+	?	+	−	?
Suffix	+	−	+	−	+
Word Root	+	−	+	−	−

FIGURE 9–9   Semantic Feature Analysis

Following is a description of how the semantic feature analysis is constructed and taught:

- Write the words to be examined down the left-hand margin. Then, write the features of these words across the top. When you first introduce this activity to students, list these features yourself. Later, after students understand how the analysis works, they can be involved in suggesting the features that will be listed.
- Discuss the matrix with the whole class or in small groups. The students will mark each cell with one of the following symbols: a plus sign (+) indicates a definite relationship between the word and a feature; a minus sign (−) indicates the word does not have that feature; and a question mark (?) indicates that the students feel they need more information before responding.
- After students complete the matrix, point out (1) they now really know how much they know about each word; and (2) they also know what they still need to find out (Templeton, 1997).

Figure 9-9 illustrates a semantic feature analysis completed by a group of sixth grade students under the teacher's guidance.

APPENDIX

This appendix contains eight sections. The first section contains the materials you will need for assessments. Most of the appendix consists of pictures, sorts, lists, and materials that you can use to create your own sets of picture and word cards for the basic sorting activities described throughout the book.

ASSESSMENT MATERIALS FOR CHAPTER 3

Elementary Spelling Inventory 1

This is a short spelling inventory to help you learn about your students' orthographic knowledge. The results of the spelling inventories will have implications for reading, writing, vocabulary, and spelling instruction.

Instructions: Let the students know that you are administering this inventory to learn about how they spell. Let them know that this is not a test, but that they will be helping you be a better teacher by doing their best.

Possible script: "I am going to ask you to spell some words. Try to spell them the best you can. Some of the words will be easy to spell; some will be more difficult. When you do not know how to spell a word, spell it the best you can; write down all the sounds you feel and hear."

Say the word once, read the sentence, and then say the word again. Work with groups of five words. You may want to stop testing when students miss three out of five words. See Chapter 3 for further instructions on administration and interpretation.

Have students check their papers for their names and the date.

Set One

1. bed — I hopped out of bed this morning.   *bed*
2. ship — The ship sailed around the island.   *ship*
3. when — When will you come back?   *when*
4. lump — He had a lump on his head after he fell.   *lump*
5. float — I can float on the water with my new raft.   *float*

Set Two

6. train — I rode the train to the next town.   *train*
7. place — I found a new place to put my books.   *place*
8. drive — I learned to drive a car.   *drive*
9. bright — The light is very bright.   *bright*
10. shopping — Mother went shopping at the grocery store.   *shopping*

Set Three

11. spoil — The food will spoil if it is not kept cool.   *spoil*
12. serving — The restaurant is serving dinner tonight.   *serving*
13. chewed — The dog chewed up my favorite sweater yesterday.   *chewed*
14. carries — She carries apples in her basket.   *carries*
15. marched — We marched in the parade.   *marched*

Set Four

16. shower — The shower in the bathroom was very hot.   *shower*
17. cattle — The cowboy rounded up the cattle.   *cattle*
18. favor — He did his brother a favor by taking out the trash.   *favor*
19. ripen — The fruit will ripen over the next few days.   *ripen*
20. cellar — I went down to the cellar for the can of paint.   *cellar*

Set Five

21. pleasure — It was a pleasure to listen to the choir sing.   *pleasure*
22. fortunate — It was fortunate that the driver had snow tires during the snowstorm.   *fortunate*
23. confident — I am confident that we can win the game.   *confident*
24. civilize — They had the idea that they could civilize the forest people.   *civilize*
25. opposition — The coach said the opposition would give us a tough game.   *opposition*

Words Their Way Appendix © 2000 by Prentice-Hall, Inc.

Qualitative Spelling Checklist

Student _____   Observer _____

Use this checklist to help you find what stages of spelling development your students are in. There are three gradations within each stage—early, middle, and late. The words in parentheses refer to spelling words on the first Qualitative Spelling Inventory.

This form can be used to follow students' progress. Check when certain features are observed in students' spelling. When a feature is always present check "Yes." The last place where you check "Often" corresponds to the student's stage of spelling development.

Dates: _____ _____ _____

Emergent Stage

Early
- Does the child scribble on the page?   Yes _____   Often _____   No _____
- Do the scribbles follow the conventional direction?
  (left to right in English)   Yes _____   Often _____   No _____

Middle
- Are there letters and numbers used in pretend writing? (*4BT for ship*)   Yes _____   Often _____   No _____

Late
- Are key sounds used in syllabic writing? *(P for ship)*   Yes _____   Often _____   No _____

Letter Name–Alphabetic

Early
- Are beginning consonants included? *(B for bed, S for ship)*   Yes _____   Often _____   No _____
- Is there a vowel in each word?   Yes _____   Often _____   No _____

Middle
- Are some consonant blends and digraphs spelled correctly?
  (ship, when, float)   Yes _____   Often _____   No _____

Late
- Are short vowels spelled correctly? *(bed, ship, when, lump)*   Yes _____   Often _____   No _____
- Is the *m* included in front of other consonants? *(lump)*   Yes _____   Often _____   No _____

Within Word Pattern

Early
- Are long vowels in single-syllable words "used but confused"?
  (FLOAT for *float*, TRANE for *train*)   Yes _____   Often _____   No _____

Middle
- Are most long vowels in single-syllable words spelled correctly
  but some long vowel spelling and other vowel patterns "used
  but confused"? (SPOLE for *spoil*)   Yes _____   Often _____   No _____
- Are most consonant blends and digraphs spelled correctly?   Yes _____   Often _____   No _____
- Are most other vowel patterns spelled correctly?
  (spoil, chewed, serving)   Yes _____   Often _____   No _____

Syllables and Affixes

Early
- Are inflectional endings added correctly to base vowel
  patterns with short vowel patterns? (*shopping, carries*)   Yes _____   Often _____   No _____
- Are consonant doublets spelled correctly? (*cattle, cellar*)   Yes _____   Often _____   No _____

Middle
- Are inflectional endings added correctly to base words?
  (chewed, marched, shower)   Yes _____   Often _____   No _____

Late
- Are less frequent prefixes and suffixes spelled correctly?
  (confident, favor, ripen, cellar, pleasure)   Yes _____   Often _____   No _____

Derivational Relations

Early
- Are most polysyllabic words spelled correctly? (*fortunate, confident*)   Yes _____   Often _____   No _____

Middle
- Are unaccented vowels in derived words spelled correctly?
  (confident, civilize, opposition)   Yes _____   Often _____   No _____

Late
- Are words from derived forms spelled correctly? (*pleasure, civilize*)   Yes _____   Often _____   No _____

Error Guide for Elementary Spelling Inventory 1

Directions: Circle student's spelling attempts below. If a spelling is not listed, write it in where it belongs on the developmental continuum. Circle the spelling stage that summarizes the student's development.

Student's Name _____ Teacher _____ Grade _____ Date _____

Number spelled correctly: ____ / ____
Number of words attempted:

Features / SPELLING STAGES	Consonants Initial Final — EMERGENT		Short Vowels — LETTER NAME–ALPHABETIC	Digraphs and Blends — LETTER NAME–ALPHABETIC		Long Vowel Patterns — WITHIN WORD PATTERN		Other Vowel Patterns — WITHIN WORD PATTERN	Syllable Junctures, Consonant Doubling, Inflected Endings, Prefixes Suffixes — SYLLABLES & AFFIXES			Bases and Roots — DERIVATIONAL RELATIONS		
	MIDDLE	LATE	EARLY	MIDDLE	LATE	EARLY	MIDDLE	LATE	EARLY	MIDDLE	LATE	EARLY	MIDDLE	LATE
1 bed	b	bd	bad	bed										
2 ship	s sp	shp	sep	shep	ship									
3 when	w yn	wn	wan	whan	when									
4 lump	l lp	lmp	lop	lomp	lump									
5 float	f ft vt	fltt	fot	flot	flott	flowt	floaut flote	float						
6 train	j t	trn	jran	chran tan tran		teran	traen trane	train						
7 place	p ps	pls	pas pas	palac plas	plac	pase	plais place							
8 drive	d j jrv	drf	drv griv	jriv driv		jrive	drieve draive drive							
9 bright	b bt	brt	bit	brit	brit	bite	brite briete	bright						
10 shopping	s sp spg	shp	sapg	sopn shapng	shopn	sopen	sopin shopen shopin	shoping	shopping					
11 spoil					spol	sole sool	spoyle spole	spoal spoil						
12 serving					sefng	srvng srbving	sering serfing surving serveing	serving	serving					
13 chewed						cud cooed cued coyed chued chood	chuwed chud chowd choud chewd	chewed						
14 carries					keres	cares carres	carise carys	cairries	carrys	carries				
15 marched						much	march marchd	marcht	marched	marched				
16 shower					shewr	shour	shower shawer shoer shuor	shower						
17 cattle					catl	cadol	catel	catle cattel	cattle					
18 favor					favr	faver	favir	favor	favor					
19 ripen					ribn	ripn	ripun ripan	ripon		ripen				
20 cellar						salr selr celr	salar seler		seller	sellar celler	cellar			
21 pleasure						plasr	plager plejer pleser	plesour		plesher		pleasure		
22 fortunate						forhnat frehnit foohinit	forchenut			fochininte fortunet		fortunate		
23 confident										confadent confedint confedent		confiednet confodent confodent confident	confident	
24 civilize												sivils sevelies sivilicse cifillazas sivelize	sivalise civalise civilise	civilize
25 opposition												opasion opasishan opozcison opishien oposition	oppasishion opasition opasision	oposision opposition

Adapted from Bear & Barone (1989).

Words Their Way Appendix © 2000 by Prentice-Hall, Inc.

Feature Guide for Elementary Spelling Inventory 1

Student's Name _____ Teacher _____ Grade _____ Date _____ Total Points _____

	EMERGENT LATE	LETTER NAME–ALPHABETIC EARLY MIDDLE LATE				WITHIN WORD PATTERN EARLY MIDDLE LATE		SYLLABLES & AFFIXES EARLY MIDDLE LATE	DERIVATIONAL RELATIONS EARLY		
		Consonants Initial 2	**Final** 6	**Short Vowels** 5	**Digraphs and Blends** 13	**Long Vowel Patterns** 5	**Other Vowel Patterns** 6	**Syllable Junctures, Consonant Doubling, Inflected Endings, Prefixes Suffixes** 24	**Bases and Roots** 5	**Word**	**Points** /66
1 bed		b	d	e						bed	
2 ship			p	i	sh					ship	
3 when			n	e	wh					when	
4 lump		l		u	mp					lump	
5 float			t		fl	oa				float	
6 train			n		tr	ai				train	
7 place					pl	a-e				place	
8 drive			v		dr	i-e				drive	
9 bright					br	igh				bright	
10 shopping				o	sh			pp ing		shopping	
11 spoil					sp		oi			spoil	
12 serving							er	ing		serving	
13 chewed					ch		ew	ed		chewed	
14 carries								rr ies		carries	
15 marched					ch		ar	ed		marched	
16 shower					sh		ow	er		shower	
17 cattle								tt le		cattle	
18 favor								av or		favor	
19 ripen								ip en		ripen	
20 cellar								ll ar		cellar	
21 pleasure								ure	pleas	pleasure	
22 fortunate							or	ate	fortun	fortunate	
23 confident								con ent	fid	confident	
24 civilize								ize	civil	civilize	
25 opposition								op pp tion	pos	opposition	
feature totals											

Elementary Spelling Inventory 2: Qualitative Spelling Inventory

This is a short spelling inventory to help you learn about your students' orthographic knowledge. The results of the spelling inventories will have implications for reading, writing, vocabulary, and spelling instruction.

Instructions: Let the students know that you are administering this inventory to learn about how they spell. Let them know that this is not a test, but that they will be helping you be a better teacher by doing their best.

Possible script: "I am going to ask you to spell some words. Try to spell them the best you can. Some of the words will be easy to spell; some will be more difficult. When you do not know how to spell a word, spell it the best you can; write down all the sounds you feel and hear."

Say the word once, read the sentence, and then say the word again. Work with groups of five words. You may want to stop testing when students miss three out of five words. See Chapter 3 for further instructions on administration and interpretation.

Have students check their papers for their names and the date.

Set One

1.	net	I have a fish in my net.	*net*
2.	trip	My family is going on a trip.	*trip*
3.	crime	The judge said it was a crime to drive so fast.	*crime*
4.	dump	We took our trash to the dump.	*dump*
5.	then	We had lunch, and then we went out to play.	*then*

Set Two

6.	chain	She wore a gold chain around her neck.	*chain*
7.	forest	The forest was full of pine trees.	*forest*
8.	trail	We walked on the trail in the woods.	*trail*
9.	soap	He washed his face with soap.	*soap*
10.	reaches	She reaches for the salt and pepper.	*reaches*

Set Three

11.	preparing	I am preparing for the big game.	*preparing*
12.	popping	We are popping popcorn to eat at the movies.	*popping*
13.	cattle	The cowboy rounded up the cattle.	*cattle*
14.	caught	I caught the ball.	*caught*
15.	inspection	The soldiers polished their shoes for inspection.	*inspection*

Set Four

16.	comparing	We are comparing the cost of the two cars.	*comparing*
17.	topping	He wanted a chocolate topping on his sundae.	*topping*
18.	battle	The soldiers met in battle.	*battle*
19.	fought	The soldiers fought in a war.	*fought*
20.	intention	It was his intention to come back to see his mother.	*intention*

Set Five

21.	rupture	There was a rupture in the sewer line.	*rupture*
22.	stellar	He gave a stellar performance.	*stellar*
23.	treasure	She found the gold and the other treasure.	*treasure*
24.	confident	She is confident in her ability to climb.	*confident*
25.	tempest	He stood calmly in a tempest of disagreement.	*tempest*

Words Their Way Appendix © 2000 by Prentice-Hall, Inc.

Error Guide for Elementary Spelling Inventory 2*

Directions: Circle student's spelling attempts below. If a spelling is not listed, write it in where it belongs on the developmental continuum. Circle the spelling stage that summarizes the student's development.

Student's Name _____ Teacher _____ Grade _____ Date _____

Number spelled correctly: _____
Number of words attempted: _____

Features	Consonants Initial Final — EMERGENT MIDDLE	LATE	Short Vowels — LETTER NAME–ALPHABETIC EARLY	MIDDLE	Digraphs and Blends — LATE	Long Vowel Patterns — WITHIN WORD PATTERN EARLY	MIDDLE	Other Vowel Patterns — LATE	Syllable Junctures, Consonant Doubling, Inflected Endings, Prefixes Suffixes — SYLLABLES AND AFFIXES EARLY	MIDDLE	LATE	Bases and Roots — DERIVATIONAL RELATIONS EARLY	MIDDLE	LATE
1 net	n	nt	nat	<u>net</u>										
2 trip	t	tp chrp	tep trep		<u>trip</u>									
3 crime	c	cr crm	crim			criem	criam <u>crime</u>							
4 dump	d	dp dmp	dop dup	domp	<u>dump</u>									
5 then	t	d th thn	tan than		<u>then</u>									
6 chain	ch	cn chn	can chan	chen		cane chane	<u>chain</u>							
7 forest	f	ft fst	fost	foist frist		forist fourist		<u>forest</u>						
8 trail	t	ch chrl trl	cherl tral	trell		trale trael	<u>trail</u>							
9 soap	s	sp so	sop sap	sap		sope soep	<u>soap</u>							
10 reaches	r	rs	res rechs	reis	rechis	reches reechis		<u>reaches</u>						
11 comparing			cumpering			comepering cumparing		cumparing	<u>comparing</u>					
12 topping								topeen toping	toping	<u>topping</u>				
13 battle							batl badel batel battel	battel		<u>battle</u>				
14 fought				fot		fote faught	<u>fought</u>							
15 intention						inchen intechin	intechin	intenshen intenchin		intenchin	<u>intention</u>			
16 rupture								rupcher ruptur rupchur rupsure			rupsure	<u>rupture</u>		
17 stellar							steler stelar	steler stelar		steler	<u>stellar</u>			
18 treasure						tresur	tresher treaher treasher tresure			treasher tresure				<u>treasure</u>
19 confident							confedent confudent confident			confident				<u>confident</u>
20 tempest							tepist tempes tepist tempist			tempist				<u>tempest</u>

Words Their Way Appendix © 2000 by Prentice-Hall, Inc.

*Thanks to April Wagner for her help in collecting and organizing these errors.

Feature Guide for Elementary Spelling Inventory 2

Student's Name _____ Teacher _____ Grade _____ Date _____ Total Points _____

	EMERGENT LATE	LETTER NAME—ALPHABETIC			WITHIN WORD PATTERN		SYLLABLES AND AFFIXES	DERIVATIONAL RELATIONS EARLY		
		Consonants Initial / Final	Short Vowels	Digraphs and Blends	Long Vowel Patterns	Other Vowel Patterns	Syllable Junctures, Consonant Doubling, Inflected Endings, Prefixes Suffixes	Bases and Roots	Word	Points /20
		3 / 6	6	8	5	3	14	6		
1 net		n / t	e						net	
2 trip		/ p	i	tr					trip	
3 crime		/ m		cr	i-e				crime	
4 dump		d /	u	mp					dump	
5 then		/ n	e	th					then	
6 chain		/ n		ch	ai				chain	
7 forest		f /				or est			forest	
8 trail		/ l		tr	ai				trail	
9 soap					oa				soap	
10 reaches				ch	ea		es		reaches	
11 comparing							com ing		comparing	
12 topping			o				pp ing		topping	
13 battle			a				tt le		battle	
14 fought				ght		ou			fought	
15 intention							in tion	ten	intention	
16 rupture							ure	rupt	rupture	
17 stellar							ar	stell	stellar	
18 treasure							ure	treas	treasure	
19 confident							con ent	fid	confident	
20 tempest								tempest	tempest	
feature totals										

Words Their Way Appendix © 2000 by Prentice-Hall, Inc.

Primary Spelling Inventory

This test will help you to assess the orthographic knowledge elementary students bring to reading and spelling. The results of the spelling inventories will have implications for reading, writing, vocabulary, and spelling instruction. For kindergarten or early first grade you may only need to call out the first five to eight words. For first grade call out at least 15. For second and third grades use the entire primary list. Use the Upper Elementary Spelling Inventory that follows for students who spell most of the words on this list correctly.

    Instructions: Let the students know that you are administering this inventory to learn about how they spell. Let them know that this is not a test, but that they will be helping you be a better teacher by doing their best. Students are not to study these words. That would invalidate the purpose of this inventory which is to find out what they truly know.

    Call the words as you would for any test. Use the words in a sentence to be sure the students know the exact word.

    Possible script: "I am going to ask you to spell some words. Try to spell them the best you can. Some of the words will be easy to spell; some will be more difficult. When you do not know how to spell a word, spell it the best you can; write down all the sounds you feel and hear."

    Say the word once, read the sentence, and then say the word again. Work with groups of five words. You may want to stop testing when students miss three out of five words. See Chapter 3 for further instructions on administration and interpretation.

    Have students check their papers for their names and the date.

Set One

1. fan	I am a baseball fan.	*fan*
2. pet	I have a pet cat.	*pet*
3. dig	He will dig a hole.	*dig*
4. mop	He said he will use a mop to clean up the mess.	*mop*
5. rope	The rope was used to tie the box to the top of the car.	*rope*

Set Two

6. wait	You will need to wait for a letter.	*wait*
7. chunk	A chunk of ice fell off the roof.	*chunk*
8. sled	The dog sled was pulled by huskies.	*sled*
9. stick	I used a stick to poke in the hole.	*stick*
10. shine	He rubbed the coin to make it shine.	*shine*

Set Three

11. dream	Do you ever dream of being an astronaut?	*dream*
12. blade	He bought a new blade for his skates.	*blade*
13. coach	The coach called the team over to the bench.	*coach*
14. fright	She was a fright in her Halloween costume.	*fright*
15. snowing	It would be snowing if it were a little colder.	*snowing*

Set Four

16. talked	They talked all day about their trip.	*talked*
17. camping	Shirley said that her family went camping.	*camping*
18. thorn	The thorn from the rose bush stuck in his finger.	*thorn*
19. shouted	They shouted at the driver as he ran through a red light.	*shouted*
20. spoil	The food will spoil if it sits out too long.	*spoil*

Set Five

21. grow	The plant will grow six inches in the summer.	*grow*
22. chirp	The baby birds will chirp when they are hungry.	*chirp*
23. clapped	The magician clapped her hands twice and the alligator vanished.	*clapped*
24. tries	In basketball, the center tries to block the shot.	*tries*
25. hiking	They started hiking up the mountain this morning.	*hiking*

Feature Guide for Primary Spelling Inventory

Student's Name _____ Teacher _____ Grade _____ Date _____ Total Points _____

	EMERGENT LATE	LETTER NAME–ALPHABETIC — EARLY MIDDLE LATE			WITHIN WORD PATTERN — EARLY MIDDLE LATE		SYLLABLES AND AFFIXES — EARLY MIDDLE LATE	DERIVATIONAL RELATIONS EARLY		
	Consonants Initial 6	Final 6	Short Vowels 7	Digraphs and Blends 21	Long Vowel Patterns 8	Other Vowel Patterns 6	Syllable Junctures, Consonant Doubling, Inflected Endings, Prefixes Suffixes 8	Bases and Roots 0	Word /	Points
1 fan	f	n	a						1 fan	
2 pet	p	t	e						2 pet	
3 dig	d	g	i						3 dig	
4 mop	m	p	o						4 mop	
5 rope	r	p			o-e				5 rope	
6 wait	w	t			ai				6 wait	
7 chunk			u	ch / nk					7 chunk	
8 sled			e	sl					8 sled	
9 stick			i	st / ck					9 stick	
10 shine				sh	i-e				10 shine	
11 dream				dr	ea				11 dream	
12 blade				bl	a-e				12 blade	
13 coach				ch	oa				13 coach	
14 fright				fr / ght					14 fright	
15 snowing				sn		ow	ing		15 snowing	
16 talked				lk			ed		16 talked	
17 camping				mp			ing		17 camping	
18 thorn				th		or			18 thorn	
19 shouted				sh		ou	ed		19 shouted	
20 spoil				sp		oi			20 spoil	
21 grow				gr		ow			21 grow	
22 chirp				ch		ir			22 chirp	
23 clapped				cl			pp / ed		23 clapped	
24 tries				tr			ies		24 tries	
25 hiking							ing		25 hiking	
feature totals										

Upper Elementary Spelling Inventory

This test will help you to assess the orthographic knowledge elementary students bring to reading and spelling. The results of the spelling inventories will have implications for reading, writing, vocabulary, and spelling instruction. For kindergarten or early first grade you may only need to call out the first five to eight words.

Instructions: Let the students know that you are administering this inventory to learn about how they spell. Let them know that this is not a test, but that they will be helping you be a better teacher by doing their best. Students are not to study these words. That would invalidate the purpose of this inventory which is to find out what they truly know.

Call the words as you would for any test. Use the words in a sentence to be sure the students know the exact word.

Possible script: "I am going to ask you to spell some words. Try to spell them the best you can. Some of the words will be easy to spell; some will be more difficult. When you do not know how to spell a word, spell it the best you can; write down all the sounds you feel and hear."

Work with groups of five words. You may want to stop testing when students miss three out of five words. Consider using the Upper Level Spelling Inventory that follows if students spell most of these words correctly. See Chapter 3 for further instructions on administration and interpretation.

Have students check their papers for their names and the date.

Set One

1. speck	There was a speck of mud on his windshield.	*speck*
2. switch	The light switch was turned on.	*switch*
3. throat	The doctor said the baby had a sore throat.	*throat*
4. nurse	The nurse told the patient that her fever was high.	*nurse*
5. scrape	The carpenter will scrape the paint off of the desk.	*scrape*

Set Two

6. charge	What will you charge for this coat?	*charge*
7. phone	Please use the phone to call home.	*phone*
8. smudge	You could see the smudge of chocolate on the paper.	*smudge*
9. point	The point of the knife was sharp.	*point*
10. squirt	The clown had a flower to squirt water.	*squirt*

Set Three

11. drawing	The drawing of the horse was done in charcoal.	*drawing*
12. trapped	The miners were trapped in the tunnel for two days.	*trapped*
13. waving	The crowd was waving to the senator as the train left the station.	*waving*
14. powerful	The jaws are powerful for chewing food.	*powerful*
15. battle	They won the battle but lost the war.	*battle*

Set Four

16. fever	A high fever can be dangerous.	*fever*
17. lesson	The music lesson was last Tuesday.	*lesson*
18. pennies	They danced for pennies at the fair.	*pennies*
19. fraction	One-half is a fraction.	*fraction*
20. sailor	To be a sailor on the high seas was his dream.	*sailor*

Set Five

21. distance	What is the distance from here to there?	*distance*
22. confusion	There was some confusion about who would drive to the movie.	*confusion*
23. discovery	The scientist made a discovery after many hours in the lab.	*discovery*
24. resident	How long have you been a resident of this state?	*resident*
25. visible	The star was visible without a telescope.	*visible*

Feature Guide for Upper Elementary Spelling Inventory

Student's Name _____ Teacher _____ Grade _____ Date _____ Total Points _____

	EMERGENT LATE	LETTER NAME–ALPHABETIC EARLY MIDDLE LATE		WITHIN WORD PATTERN EARLY MIDDLE LATE		SYLLABLES AND AFFIXES EARLY MIDDLE LATE	DERIVATIONAL RELATIONS EARLY		/25
	Consonants Initial / Final	Short Vowels 6	Digraphs and Blends 13	Long Vowel Patterns 4	Other Vowel Patterns 6	Syllable Junctures, Consonant Doubling, Inflected Endings, Prefixes Suffixes 23	Bases and Roots 6	Word	Points
1 speck		e	ck					1 speck	
2 switch		i	sw tch					2 switch	
3 throat			thr	o-a				3 throat	
4 nurse					ur			4 nurse	
5 scrape			scr	a-e				5 scrape	
6 charge			ch		ar			6 charge	
7 phone			ph	o-e				7 phone	
8 smudge		u	sm dge					8 smudge	
9 point			nt		oi			9 point	
10 squirt			squ		ir			10 squirt	
11 drawing			dr		aw	ing		11 drawing	
12 trapped		a				pp ed		12 trapped	
13 waving						ing		13 waving	
14 powerful					ow	er ful		14 powerful	
15 battle		a				tt le		15 battle	
16 fever						ev er		16 fever	
17 lesson						ss on		17 lesson	
18 pennies		e				nn ies		18 pennies	
19 fraction						tion	frac	19 fraction	
20 sailor				ai		or		20 sailor	
21 distance						ance	dis	21 distanced	
22 confusion						con sion	fus	22 confusion	
23 discovery						dis ery	cov	23 discovery	
24 resident						ent	resid	24 resident	
25 visible						ble	visi	25 visible	
feature totals									

Words Their Way Appendix © 2000 by Prentice-Hall, Inc.

McGuffey Qualitative Spelling Inventory

The words on these lists (see table below) have been selected as representative of the words students are expected to master at different grade levels. The features are consistent with the developmental progression established for word knowledge. The directions are as follows:

Step 1. Establish a starting point. Begin by calling out the grade level below the entire class. First grade and kindergarten teachers begin with level 1.

Step 2. Call out the words, use them in a sentence, and then repeat the word. Students write the words in a horizontal column. Kindergarten children and first graders might be given paper with boxes or blank paper rather than lined paper.

Step 3. Collect the papers and check them. Determine a percentage score for each child. Words spelled with reversals are accepted as correct. Make a list of students who scored above 50% and those who scored below 50%.

Step 4. Test again on the next day. Students who scored above 50% should be given the next higher level. Students who scored below 50% should be given the next lower level. In working with upper elementary students, you may find it useful to call out only half the words on a list. When students score greater than 80%, you may want to move to a more advanced list.

Step 5. Again check the papers. Continue to test until every child has scored above or below 50% so that you can establish an instructional level for everyone. The last level at which a student scores between 50% and 90% is his or her instructional level. For example, if Mary scores 30% on level 3 then she is clearly instructional at level 2.

Step 6. Create a class roster by listing scores achieved by each student at all levels. Circle the instructional level scores. This will allow you to form groups for instruction.

Step 7. Examine the spelling errors of students in the groups you form. Errors will give you ideas about the features that students will need to study.

The eight levels are shown in the table below.

McGuffey Qualitative Inventory of Word Knowledge

Level I	Level II	Level III	Level IV	Level V	Level VI	Level VII	Level VIII
bump	batted	find	square	enclosed	absence	illiteracy	meddle
net	such	paint	hockey	piece	civilize	communicate	posture
with	once	crawl	helmet	novel	accomplish	irresponsible	knuckle
trap	chop	dollar	allow	lecture	prohibition	succeed	succumb
chin	milk	knife	skipping	pillar	pledge	patience	newsstand
bell	funny	mouth	ugly	confession	sensibility	confident	permissible
shade	start	fought	hurry	aware	official	analyze	transparent
pig	glasses	comb	bounce	loneliest	inspire	tomatoes	assumption
drum	hugging	useful	lodge	service	permission	necessary	impurities
hid	named	circle	fossil	loyal	irrelevant	beret	pennant
father	pool	early	traced	expansion	conclusion	unbearable	boutique
track	stick	letter	lumber	production	invisible	hasten	wooden
pink	when	weigh	middle	deposited	democratic	aluminum	warrant
drip	easy	real	striped	revenge	responsible	miserable	probable
brave	make	tight	bacon	awaiting	accidental	subscription	respiration
job	went	sock	capture	unskilled	composition	exhibition	reverse
sister	shell	voice	damage	installment	relying	device	olympic
slide	pinned	campfire	nickel	horrible	changeable	regretted	gaseous
box	class	keeper	barber	relate	amusement	arisen	subtle
white	boat	throat	curve	earl	conference	miniature	bookkeeping
	story	waving	statement	uniform	advertise	monopoly	fictional
	plain	carried	collar	rifle	opposition	dissolve	overrate
	smoke	scratch	parading	correction	community	equipped	granular
	size	tripping	sailor	discovering	advantage	solemn	endorse
	sleep	nurse	wrinkle	retirement	cooperation	correspond	insistent
			dinner	salute	spacious	emphasize	snorkel
			medal	treasure	carriage	scoundrel	personality
			tanner	homemade	presumption	cubic	prosperous
			dimmed	conviction	appearance	flexible	
			careful	creature	description	arctic	

Upper Level Qualitative Spelling Inventory

Instructions: Let students know that you are administering this inventory to learn about how they spell. Let them know that this is not a test, but that they will be helping you by doing their best. Some of the words will be easy to spell; some will be more difficult. When they do not know how to spell a word, ask them to spell the best they can.

Possible script: "I am going to ask you to spell some words. Try to spell them the best you can. Some of the words will be easy to spell; some will be more difficult. When you do not know how to spell a word, spell it the best you can; write down all the sounds you feel and hear."

Say the word once, use the word in a sentence, and then say the word a second time. Consider their work on the first eight words before continuing. You may want to stop testing when students miss five out of eight words. See Chapter 3 for further instructions on administration and interpretation.

Have students check their papers for their names and the date.

1. confusion   There was confusion when there was a power failure. *confusion*
2. pleasure   It was our pleasure to have you come over. *pleasure*
3. resident   Mr. Squires has been a resident of this town for over forty years. *resident*
4. puncture   Joan saw the puncture in her bicycle tire. *puncture*
5. confidence   I have confidence in Donna. *confidence*
6. fortunate   We were fortunate to have gotten back safely. *fortunate*
7. decorator   The decorator helped me choose furniture for my living room. *decorator*
8. opposition   The coach said the opposition would give us a tough game. *opposition*

If you wish, stop here, check papers, discontinue, or go to one of the elementary qualitative inventories if a student misspells five out of the first eight words.

9. prosperity   During this period of prosperity, our income increased dramatically. *prosperity*
10. succession   He fired several shots in rapid succession. *succession*
11. emphasize   In conclusion, I want to emphasize the most important points. *emphasize*
12. correspond   The president must correspond with many people each day. *correspond*
13. commotion   The audience heard the commotion backstage. *commotion*
14. propellant   The booster rocket is fueled by a liquid propellant. *propellant*
15. hilarious   John thought the comedian was absolutely hilarious. *hilarious*
16. criticize   The boss will criticize you for your work. *criticize*
17. indictment   The attorney general made the indictment based on the grand jury's findings. *indictment*
18. reversible   Terry wears a reversible coat in the winter. *reversible*
19. category   I will put the bottles in one category and the cans in another. *category*
20. adjourn   The meeting will adjourn at five o'clock. *adjourn*
21. excerpt   I am going to read one excerpt from this chapter. *excerpt*
22. camouflage   The soldier wore camouflage to avoid detection. *camouflage*

Error Guide for the Upper Level Spelling Inventory

Directions: Circle student's spelling attempts below. If a spelling is not listed, write it in where it belongs on the developmental continuum. Circle the spelling stage that summarizes the student's development.

Student's Name _____ Teacher _____ Period _____ Grade _____ Date _____

Number spelled correctly: _____
Number of words attempted: _____

STAGES:

	WITHIN WORD PATTERN		SYLLABLES AND AFFIXES			DERIVATIONAL RELATIONS	
	MIDDLE	LATE	EARLY	MIDDLE	LATE	EARLY	MIDDLE	LATE

1. confusion – confushon confusion confution confussion confusetion confusion confusion
2. pleasure – plasr plager plejer pleser plesher plesour plesure pleasur pleasure
3. resident – resatin reserdent resudent resadent resedint reseadent resident resident
4. puncture – pucshr pungchr puncur puncker punksher punchure puncure punture puncsure puncture
5. confidence – confadents confidense confedense confedance confidense confidense confidence confidence
6. fortunate – forhnat frehnit foohinit forchenut fochininte fortunet fortunate
7. decorator – dector decrater decorator decorater decoratore decorator decorator
8. opposition – opasion opasishan opozcison opasitian oppisition opposition opposition opposition
9. prosperity – proparty properity prosparaty prosperaty prosperity prosperaty prosperity
10. succession – sucksession sucesion sucession sucsession sucession succession succession
11. emphasize – infaside infacize ephacise empasize emfesize emfisize imfasize emphisize emphasize
12. correspond – corspond corispond corespond corrospond corrospond
13. commotion – comoushown comoshion comosion camotion cumotion comocion comossion comotion commotion
14. propellant – porpelent proplent porpelont propelent propelont propellant propellent propellant
15. hilarious – halaris halerace halaryous hollarries halaries hollarous halariuse heleriaus halareous hularious hulairus hilerious helarious hilarious

16. criticize – critise crisize critize critasise critasize critisise criticise criticize criticize
17. indictment – endiment iditment enditement inditment indightment endightment indictment indightment indictment indictment
18. reversible – reversbell reversabul reversobol reversabile reverseabile reverseable revercible reversable revercible reversible reversible
19. category – cadagoure kadacorey cadacory catagery cadigore catagore catigoury catigory catorgory catigorie catagory catgory category category

20. adjourn – ajurn agern ajourn ajorne ajurne adjurn adjorn adjourne adjourn adjourn
21. excerpt – exherpt exhert exherpt exsort exerp ecsert exsert excert exsurpt exsert excerpt excerpt
22. camouflage – camaflag camoflash comoflodge comofloge camaphlauge camaflauge camaflage camaflaug camoflouge camoflodge camoflage camoflauge camouflage camouflage

STAGES:

	WITHIN WORD PATTERN		SYLLABLES AND AFFIXES			DERIVATIONAL RELATIONS	
	MIDDLE	LATE	EARLY	MIDDLE	LATE	EARLY	MIDDLE	LATE

Words Their Way Appendix © 2000 by Prentice-Hall, Inc.

Biology Spelling Inventory*

Instructions: Let students know that you are administering this inventory to learn about their knowledge of terms in biology. Let them know that this is not a test, but that they will be helping you by doing their best. Some of the words will be easy to spell; some will be more difficult. When they do not know how to spell a word, ask them to spell the best they can.

Possible script: "I am going to ask you to spell some words that are related to biology. Try to spell them the best you can. Some of the words will be easy to spell; some will be more difficult. If you do not know how to spell a word, spell it the best you can; write down all the sounds you feel and hear when you say the word."

Say the word clearly once, use the word in a sentence, and then say the word a second time. Make sure that their names, date, and class are at the top of the papers. See Chapter 3 for further instructions on administration and interpretation.

1. allergy	He has an allergy to cat fur.	*allergy*
2. antibiotic	The antibiotic was a cure for his illness.	*antibiotic*
3. antibody	The antibody within his system prevented him from becoming ill.	*antibody*
4. antigen	The antigen destroyed the bacteria.	*antigen*
5. benign	She was glad to hear the oncologist say the tumor was benign.	*benign*
6. cancer	An oncologist studies cancer.	*cancer*
7. carcinogen	Cigarettes have a lethal carcinogen in them that cause cancer.	*carcinogen*
8. immune system	The patient's immune system was strong enough to resist the disease.	*immune system*
9. immunity	The vaccination gave the travelers some immunity to the illness.	*immunity*
10. infection	The child had an ear infection.	*infection*
11. inflammation	The inflammation caused him some pain.	*inflammation*
12. interferon	The interferon protected her from the virus.	*interferon*
13. malignant	The biopsy report reported that the cancer was malignant.	*malignant*
14. toxin	What normally is a toxin has now become an antitoxin and a cure for his illness.	*toxin*
15. tumor	The tumor was enlarged and caused him some pain.	*tumor*
16. vaccine	Pasteur developed a vaccine to protect against anthrax.	*vaccine*

Geometry Spelling Inventory†

Instructions: Let students know that you are administering this inventory to learn about their knowledge of terms in geometry. Let them know that this is not a test, but that they will be helping you by doing their best. Some of the words will be easy to spell; some will be more difficult. When they do not know how to spell a word, ask them to spell the best they can.

Possible script: "I am going to ask you to spell some words that are related to geometry. Try to spell them the best you can. Some of the words will be easy to spell; some will be more difficult. If you do not know how to spell a word, spell it the best you can; write down all the sounds you feel and hear when you say the word."

Say the word clearly once, read the sentence, and then say the word a second time. Make sure that their names, date, and class are at the top of the papers. See Chapter 3 for further instructions on administration and interpretation.

1. perpendicular	One tetherball pole has fallen down, but the other is still perpendicular.	*perpendicular*

---

*Thanks to Lyn Girindo for help developing this list.

†Thanks to Meggin McIntosh, Mark Zimmerman, Connie Merrill, and several Washoe County teachers for help developing this list.

Words Their Way Appendix © 2000 by Prentice-Hall, Inc.

2. adjacent   I'm going to the sporting goods store that is adjacent to the 7-11. *adjacent*
3. equilateral   Equilateral triangles have three identical sides. *equilateral*
4. hypotenuse   Knowing the hypotenuse of a triangle can tell you a lot about the rest of the triangle. *hypotenuse*
5. isosceles   An isosceles triangle is a very even triangle. *isosceles*
6. parallel   The railroad runs parallel to Main Street. *parallel*
7. vertex   Look for the vertex of the last triangle. *vertex*
8. altitude   Tonight, Sirius, the Dog Star, is at an altitude of 18°. *altitude*
9. obtuse   This triangle is obtuse. *obtuse*
10. polygon   A polygon is a complicated shape. *polygon*
11. triangle   Go to where the three paths form a triangle. *triangle*
12. vertical   He's over there, under the tree that leans slightly from the vertical. *vertical*
13. acute   An acute angle is sometimes very small. *acute*
14. bisector   A bisector is a line that cuts an angle in half. *bisector*
15. congruent   Two of these angles are congruent. *congruent*
16. quadrilateral   Which of these two polygons is a quadrilateral? *quadrilateral*
17. scalene   Scalene triangles look somewhat lopsided. *scalene*
18. tangent   On the board you can see that Line B is tangent to circle A. *tangent*
19. trapezoid   A trapezoid is an interesting shape. *trapezoid*
20. collinear   The two lines are not the same length, but they are collinear. *collinear*
21. complementary   Complementary angles fit together to form 90°. *complementary*
22. intersect   The two roads intersect somewhere by the river. *intersect*
23. theorem   A theorem can never be proved absolutely. *theorem*
24. diameter   The diameter is one measure of a circle. *diameter*
25. radius   The radius of a circle depends on the size of the circle. *radius*
26. supplementary   None of these pairs of angles are supplementary. *supplementary*
27. degree   A degree is a very small measure of a circle. *degree*
28. angle   How large is that angle? *angle*
29. geometry   Geometry is the study of shapes. *geometry*
30. cylinder   Most cans are in the shape of a cylinder. *cylinder*

U.S. History Spelling Inventory*

Instructions: Let students know that you are administering this inventory to learn about their knowledge of terms that they will find in the U.S. history textbook. Let them know that this is not a test, but that they will be helping you by doing their best. Some of the words will be easy to spell; some will be more difficult. When they do not know how to spell a word, ask them to spell the best they can.

Possible script: "I am going to ask you to spell some words that are related to U.S. history. Try to spell them the best you can. Some of the words will be easy to spell; some will be more difficult. If you do not know how to spell a word, spell it the best you can; write down all the sounds you feel and hear when you say the word."

Say the word clearly once, read the sentence, and then say the word a second time. Make sure that their names, date, and class are at the top of the papers. See Chapter 3 for further instructions on administration and interpretation.

1. abolition   The abolition movement sought to end slavery. *abolition*
2. political   The main political parties in the United States are the Democratic and the Republican. *political*
3. president   George Washington was the first president of the United States. *president*

*Thanks to Laura Alatorre Parks for developing this list, as well as the error guide.

4. technology	The technology for today's computers improves daily.	*technology*
5. alliance	The United States and Great Britain had a strong alliance during World War II.	*alliance*
6. progressive	In the late 1800s progressive teachers fought for school reform.	*progressive*
7. citizen	To vote in the United States one must be a citizen of this country.	*citizen*
8. communism	The form of government dominating Eastern Europe after World War II was communism.	*communism*
9. frontier	Lewis and Clark explored the western frontier.	*frontier*
10. government	The constitution is the foundation of the U.S. government.	*government*
11. discrimination	Several laws protect people from discrimination.	*discrimination*
12. occupation	Poland suffered under the occupation of Germany.	*occupation*
13. segregation	The civil rights movement sought to end segregation in the 1950s.	*segregation*
14. immigrant	A legal immigrant must maintain current immunizations.	*immigrant*
15. business	The new business in town advertised in the local paper.	*business*
16. racism	Martin Luther King fought against racism.	*racism*
17. foreign	The United States' foreign policies vary from year to year.	*foreign*
18. neutral	The United States tried to avoid involvement in World War II by staying neutral.	*neutral*
19. committee	The committee developed a plan to improve transportation.	*committee*
20. bureau	The Federal Bureau of Investigation, or FBI, investigated President Nixon's involvement in the Watergate scandal.	*bureau*

Words Their Way Appendix © 2000 by Prentice-Hall, Inc.

Error Guide for the U.S. History Spelling Inventory

Student's Name _____ Teacher _____ Period _____ Grade _____ Date _____

Number spelled correctly: _____ /
Number of words attempted: _____

STAGES:

	WITHIN WORD PATTERN		SYLLABLES AND AFFIXES			DERIVATIONAL RELATIONS		
	MIDDLE	LATE	EARLY	MIDDLE	LATE	EARLY	MIDDLE	LATE
1. abolition –	ablishen	abolishone	abolishion	aboliscion	abelition	abolution	**abolition**	
2. political –	pliticl	paliticle	politicial	pelitical	politicle	**political**		
3. president –		parezadent	persendent	prezident	presedent	**president**		
4. technology –	teknlgy	teknowledgy	technlogy	techknology	teknology	**technology**		
5. alliance –	ailus	alyes	allianse	aliance	alliance	**alliance**		
6. progressive –	pragresv	prowgrisve	progressuv	pragrestive	progresive	**progressive**		
7. citizen –	sitisn	sitisen	citison	citizien	**citizen**	**citizen**		
8. communism –	komanm	comunm	comunizome	communisum	comunizm	communism	**communism**	
9. frontier –	frontr	fronter	fronteer	fronteir	**frontier**	**frontier**		
10. government –	gofrmnt	gavernemt	gaverment	goverment	**government**			
11. discrimination –	discriminashion	descriminashion	descrimination	discrimanation	discrimination	**discrimination**		
12. occupation –	okupashn	aqupashon	acupashion	ocupashion	occupashion	ocupation	**occupation**	
13. segregation –	segegayshun	cegretion	segration	segretion	segregation	**segregation**		
14. immigrant –	imagrent	inagrent	imegrent	imagrant	inmigrant	immagrant	**immigrant**	
15. business –		bissness	buissness	busness	**business**	**business**		
16. racism –	raisisn	raceisime	racizum	racizm	raceism	racism	**racism**	
17. foreign –	forigian	foren	forgen	forgien	forien	**foreign**		
18. neutral –	nutruh	netural	nutral	nutral	nuetral	**neutral**		
19. committee –	camity	comity	cummity	commity	committy	committee	commitee	**committee**
20. bureau –	bero	burow	breaugh	beauro	**bureau**	**bureau**		

STAGES:

	WITHIN WORD PATTERN		SYLLABLES AND AFFIXES			DERIVATIONAL RELATIONS		
	MIDDLE	LATE	EARLY	MIDDLE	LATE	EARLY	MIDDLE	LATE

Words Their Way Appendix © 2000 by Prentice-Hall, Inc.

Spelling-by-Stage Classroom Organization Chart

SPELLING STAGES	EMERGENT			LETTER NAME–ALPHABETIC			WITHIN WORD PATTERN			SYLLABLES AND AFFIXES			DERIVATIONAL RELATIONS		
	EARLY	MIDDLE	LATE	EARLY	MIDDLE	LATE	EARLY	MIDDLE	LATE	EARLY	MIDDLE	LATE	EARLY	MIDDLE	LATE

Words Their Way Appendix © 2000 by Prentice-Hall, Inc.

Directions for Using the Classroom Composite for Spelling Inventories

Once you have tested your students and completed a feature guide for each student, you will need to get a sense of your classroom needs as a whole. One way to do this is to use the form on the following page. This form can be used to compile the feature guide results of the following inventories: Elementary Spelling Inventory 1 (page 291), Elementary Spelling Inventory 2 (page 294), Primary Spelling Inventory (page 296), and the Upper Elementary Spelling Inventory (page 298). Follow these steps in using the class composite:

1. Select an inventory on pages 288, 292, 295, or 297. Call the words aloud for your students to spell.

2. Copy a feature guide for each student that corresponds to the list you called aloud (you may want to enlarge this form when you make copies). Check off each feature that was spelled correctly by the student. For example, if *net* is spelled NT, you would make a check beside the *n* and *t* under "Consonants," but not the *e* under "Short Vowels." This will help you determine what each student knows and where instruction is needed. Total the number of correct features in each column and record at the bottom. These numbers will be transferred to the class composite form. Staple the feature guide and test together.

3. Prepare the class composite form by writing in the number of possible points under the headings in the second row for the inventory you used. The number of possible points for the total as well as each feature can be found in the second row of the feature guide for each inventory. For example, Elementary Inventory 1 has a possible total of 66 points. Under "Consonants" it has 2 initials and 6 final consonants. However, if you call less than the total number of words, adjust your totals. For example, a kindergarten teacher may only call out the first 10 words of the Primary Spelling Inventory. That would mean that the total for "Blends and Digraphs" should be adjusted from 21 to 6 and "Long Vowels" from 8 to 3.

4. Now you are ready to transfer each student's feature totals to the class composite form. Use the total scores for each student to rank them from highest to lowest or vice versa. Simply stack the feature guides in rank order. Write the student's name in the left column and their total score in the second column. Then record the score for each feature in the appropriate columns. A sample class composite can be found on page 57.

5. Once all the feature scores have been completed, we recommend that you highlight with a yellow marker cells in which the students make two or more errors on a feature. These students will benefit from instruction on that feature. You should avoid highlighting any student who gets a zero on a feature. That student is probably not ready to study that feature at all unless they are "using but confusing the feature." There are probably earlier features which they need to study first.

6. Use the highlighted cells as a way to get a total picture of your class and to group students for instruction. Remember that earlier features to the left of the table need to be addressed first. For example, students who have not yet mastered long vowel patterns in one-syllable words are not ready to study syllable juncture issues.

Classroom Composite for Feature Guides

Teacher _____ School _____ Grade _____ Date _____

Students' Names	Total Points	EMERGENT LATE — Consonants Initial	Consonants Final	LETTER NAME–ALPHABETIC EARLY — Short Vowels	MIDDLE — Digraphs and Blends	LATE	WITHIN WORD PATTERN EARLY — Long Vowel Patterns	MIDDLE	LATE — Other Vowel Patterns	SYLLABLES AND AFFIXES EARLY MIDDLE LATE — Syllable Junctures, Consonant Doubling, Inflected Endings, Prefixes, Suffixes	DERIVATIONAL RELATIONS EARLY — Bases and Roots
Possible points											
1											
2											
3											
4											
5											
6											
7											
8											
9											
10											
11											
12											
13											
14											
15											
16											
17											
18											
19											
20											
21											
22											
23											
24											
25											
Number who missed two or more											

Words Their Way Appendix © 2000 by Prentice-Hall, Inc.

SOUND BOARDS

Beginning Consonants		
b 🔔 bell		
c 🐱 cat		
d 🐕 dog		
f 🐟 fish		
g 👻 ghost		
h 🖐 hand		

j jug
k key
l lamp
m mouse
n net
p pig
r ring

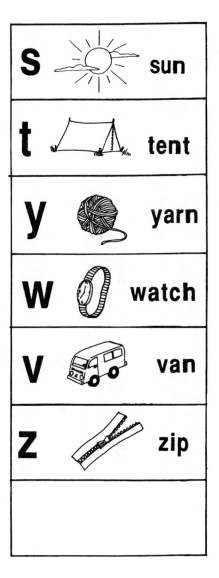

s sun
t tent
y yarn
w watch
v van
z zip

Beginning Blends and Digraphs	**br** broom	**sc** scooter
bl block	**cr** crab	**sk** skate
cl cloud	**dr** drum	**sm** smile
fl flag	**fr** frog	**sn** snail
gl glasses	**gr** grapes	**sp** spider
sl slide	**pr** present	**st** star
pl 2+1=3 plus	**tr** tree	**sw** swing
tw twins	**ch** chair	**th** thumb
qu quilt	**sh** shovel	**wh** wheel

Short Vowels	Long Vowels	
a cat	**a** cake	**a** tray
		a rain
e bed	**e** feet	**e** leaf
i pig	**i** kite	**i** light
o sock	**o** bone	**o** soap
u cup	**u** tube	

PICTURES FOR SORTS AND GAMES

The pictures in Figures A-1 through A-6 can be copied on cardstock or glued to cardstock to create a set of pictures to use for sorting activities. Many teachers find it easiest to create a sheet of pictures which can be cut apart by the students for sorting by using the pictures like clip art. Make copies of the pictures you need (combining two, three, or four sounds) and glue them randomly onto a template such as the one on page 384. Write the letters you will use as headers in the small boxes at the top.

The pictures in Figure A-6 are labeled for long vowels. There are additional long vowel pictures in Figures A-1 through A-3.

Long-a:	gate	game	nail	paint	rake	vase	shave	chair	blade	plane
	plate	scale	skate	train	grapes					
Long-e:	deer	jeep	key	leaf	seal	sheep	dream			
	wheel	sleeve	sleep	sweep	queen	tree				
Long-i:	nine	dice	smile	prize	drive	fire	tie			
	tire	price	cry	fly						
Long-o:	boat	goat	rope	hose	nose	comb	ghost			
	toes	float	globe	yo-yo	snow					

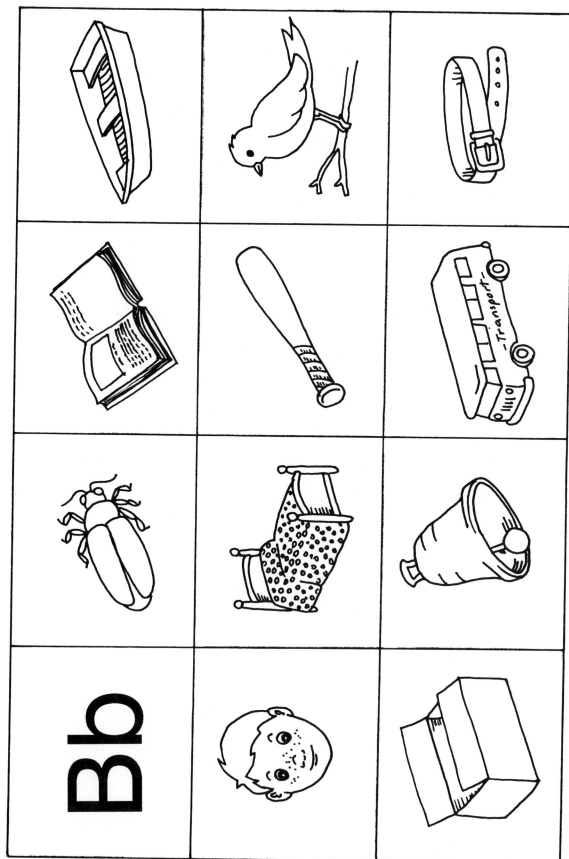

FIGURE A-1 Picture Cards for Initial Consonants

Words Their Way Appendix © 2000 by Prentice-Hall, Inc.

FIGURE A-1 Picture Cards for Initial Consonants (continued)

FIGURE A-1 Picture Cards for Initial Consonants (*continued*)

Words Their Way Appendix © 2000 by Prentice-Hall, Inc.

FIGURE A-1 Picture Cards for Initial Consonants (*continued*)

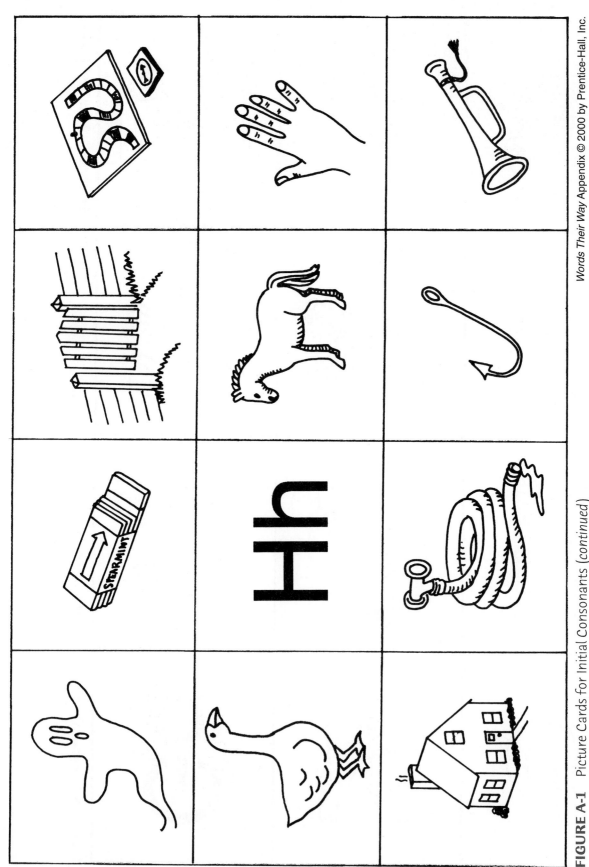

FIGURE A-1 Picture Cards for Initial Consonants (*continued*)

Words Their Way Appendix © 2000 by Prentice-Hall, Inc.

FIGURE A-1 Picture Cards for Initial Consonants (*continued*)

FIGURE A-1 Picture Cards for Initial Consonants *(continued)*

Words Their Way Appendix © 2000 by Prentice-Hall, Inc.

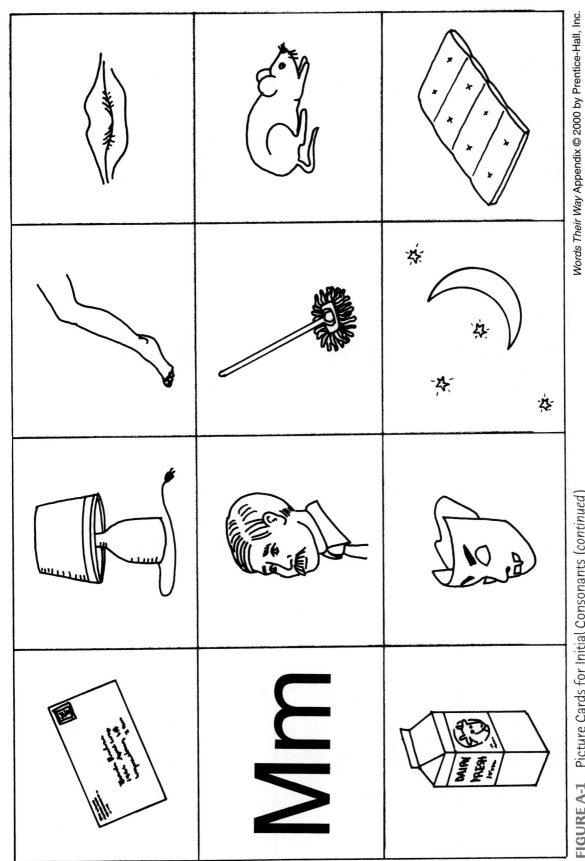

FIGURE A-1 Picture Cards for Initial Consonants (*continued*)

FIGURE A-1 Picture Cards for Initial Consonants (continued)

Words Their Way Appendix © 2000 by Prentice-Hall, Inc.

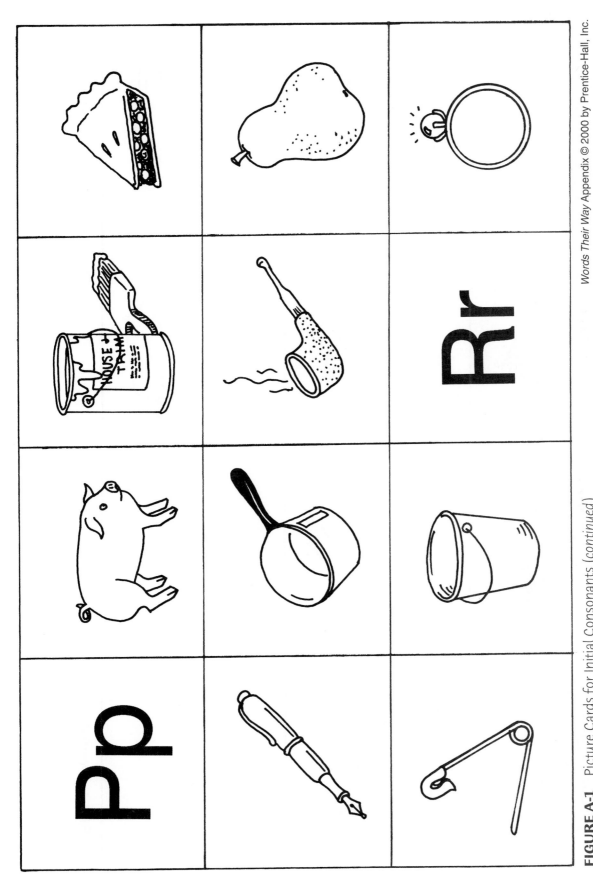

Words Their Way Appendix © 2000 by Prentice-Hall, Inc.

FIGURE A-1 Picture Cards for Initial Consonants (*continued*)

Words Their Way Appendix © 2000 by Prentice-Hall, Inc.

FIGURE A-1 Picture Cards for Initial Consonants (*continued*)

FIGURE A-1   Picture Cards for Initial Consonants (*continued*)

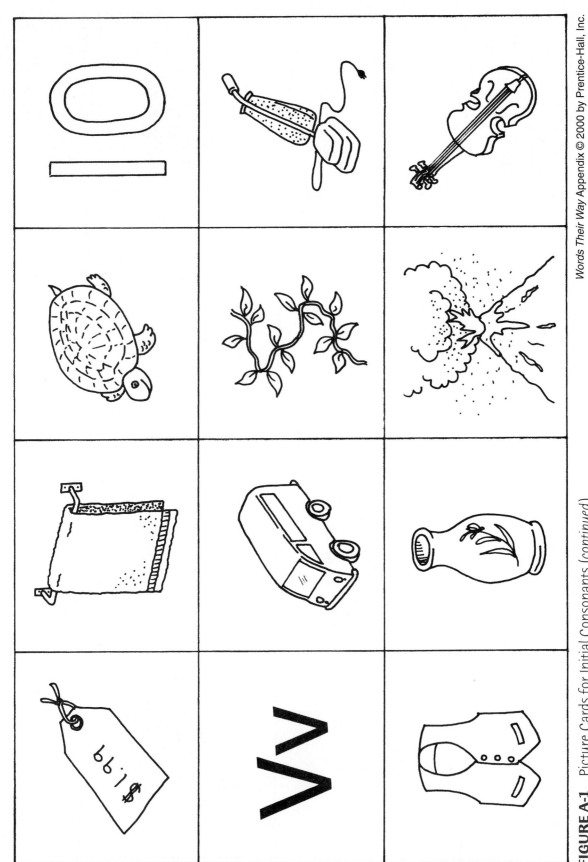

FIGURE A-1 Picture Cards for Initial Consonants (continued)

Words Their Way Appendix © 2000 by Prentice-Hall, Inc.

324

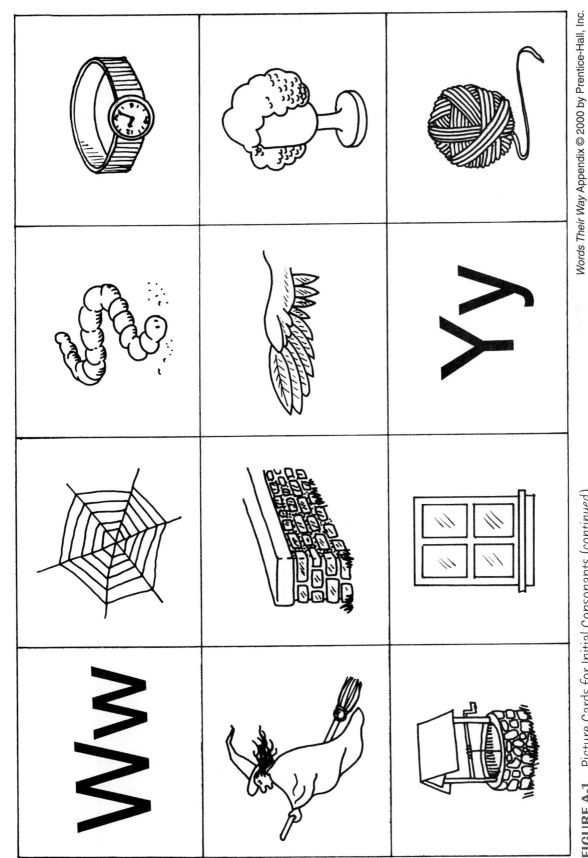

FIGURE A-1   Picture Cards for Initial Consonants (continued)

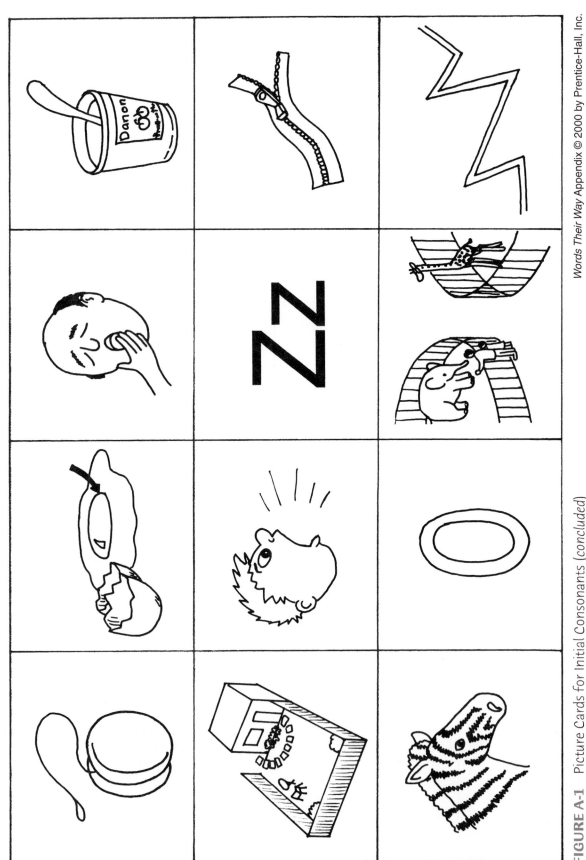

FIGURE A-1 Picture Cards for Initial Consonants (concluded)

Words Their Way Appendix © 2000 by Prentice-Hall, Inc.

FIGURE A-2   Picture Cards for Initial Digraphs

327

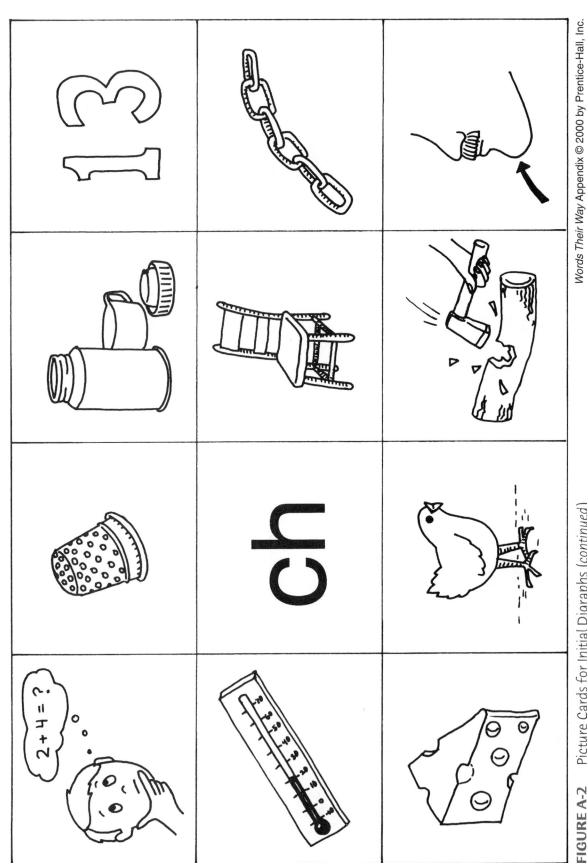

FIGURE A-2 Picture Cards for Initial Digraphs (*continued*)

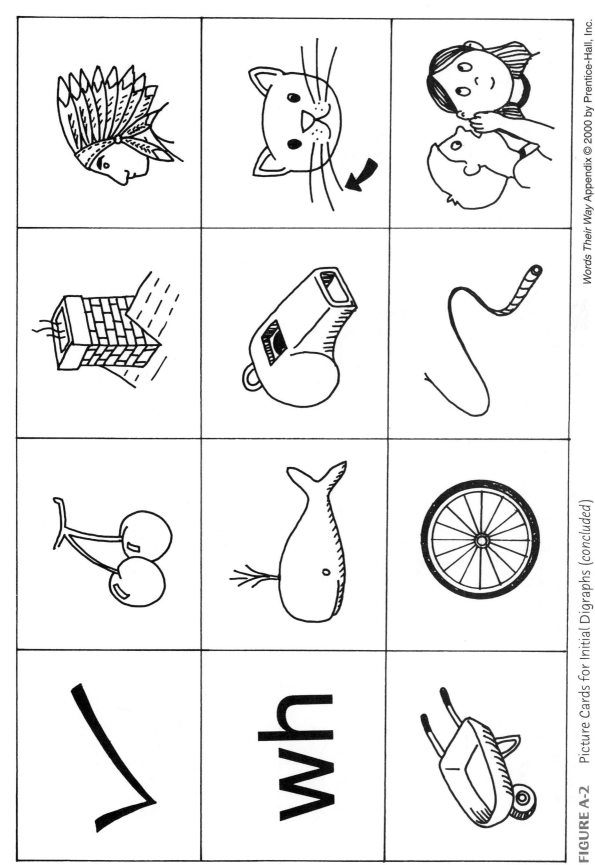

FIGURE A-2 Picture Cards for Initial Digraphs *(concluded)*

Words Their Way Appendix © 2000 by Prentice-Hall, Inc.

FIGURE A-3 Picture Cards for Initial Blends

FIGURE A-3 Picture Cards for Initial Blends *(continued)*

Words Their Way Appendix © 2000 by Prentice-Hall, Inc.

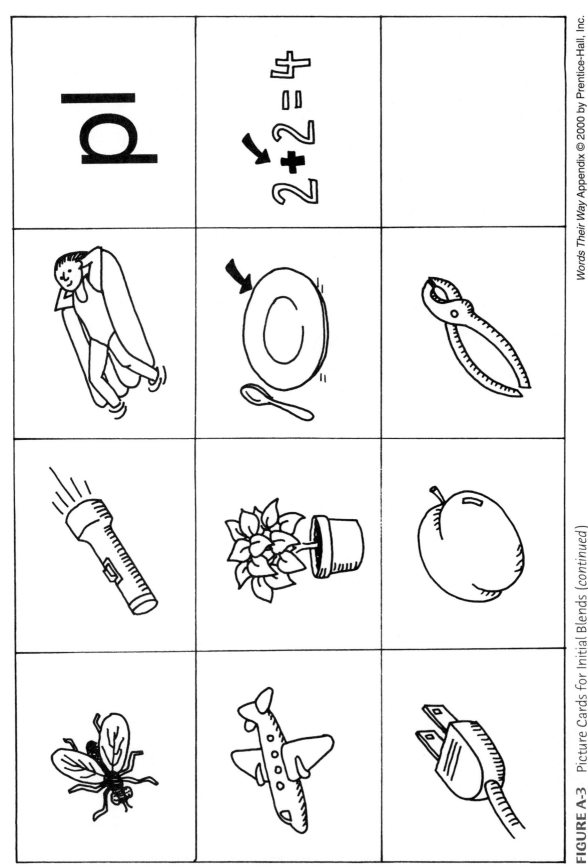

FIGURE A-3 Picture Cards for Initial Blends *(continued)*

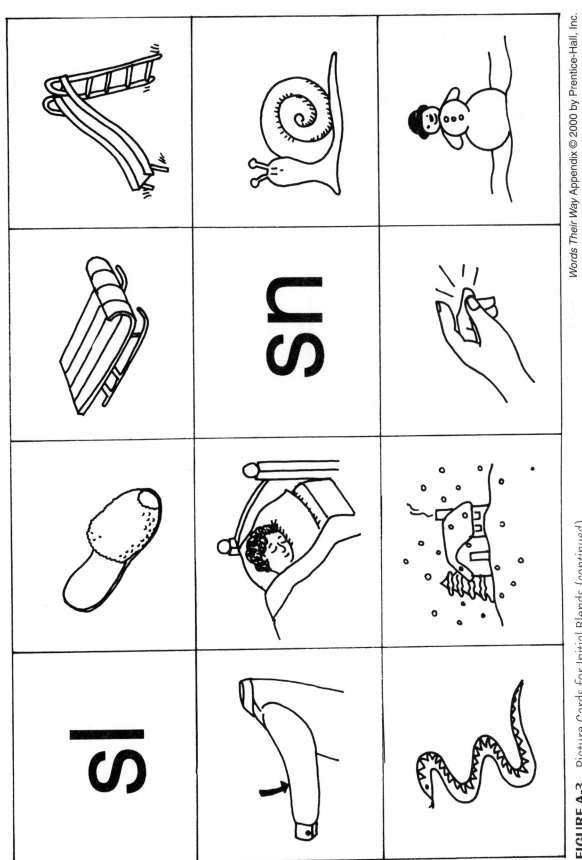

FIGURE A-3 Picture Cards for Initial Blends (*continued*)

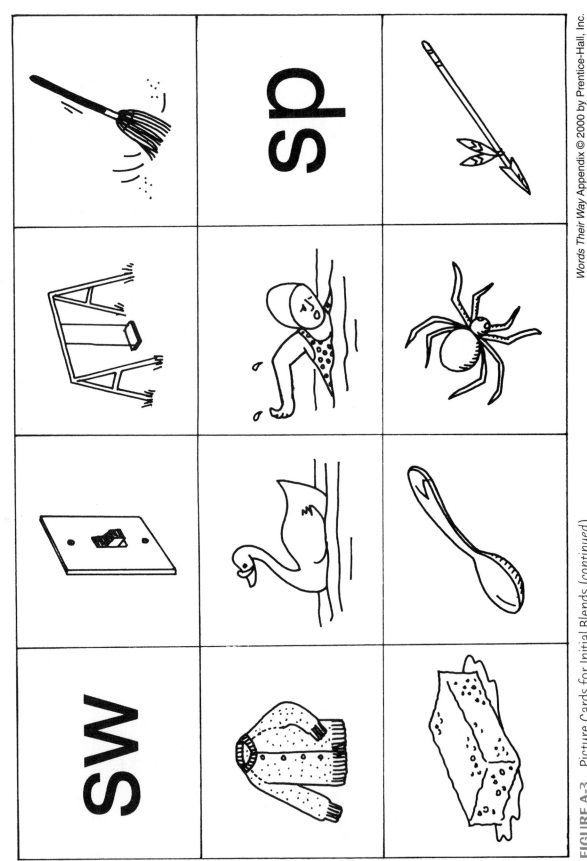

FIGURE A-3 Picture Cards for Initial Blends *(continued)*

Words Their Way Appendix © 2000 by Prentice-Hall, Inc.

Words Their Way Appendix © 2000 by Prentice-Hall, Inc.

FIGURE A-3 Picture Cards for Initial Blends (*continued*)

FIGURE A-3 Picture Cards for Initial Blends (*continued*)

Words Their Way Appendix © 2000 by Prentice-Hall, Inc.

337

FIGURE A-3 Picture Cards for Initial Blends (continued)

FIGURE A-3 Picture Cards for Initial Blends *(continued)*

Words Their Way Appendix © 2000 by Prentice-Hall, Inc.

FIGURE A-3 Picture Cards for Initial Blends (continued)

FIGURE A-3 Picture Cards for Initial Blends (*continued*)

Words Their Way Appendix © 2000 by Prentice-Hall, Inc.

FIGURE A-3 Picture Cards for Initial Blends *(concluded)*

Words Their Way Appendix © 2000 by Prentice-Hall, Inc.

Words Their Way Appendix © 2000 by Prentice-Hall, Inc.

Pictures include: astronaut, ant, ax, alligator, apple, add, egg, Eskimo, etch-a-sketch®, and Ed.

FIGURE A-4 Picture Cards for Initial Short Vowels

Pictures include: itch, ick, igloo, ill, in, ostrich, olive, otter, octopus, and ox.

FIGURE A-4 Picture Cards for Initial Short Vowels (*continued*)

Words Their Way Appendix © 2000 by Prentice-Hall, Inc.

344

Pictures include: umbrella, upside down, under, and up.

FIGURE A-4 Picture Cards for Initial Short Vowels *(concluded)*

FIGURE A-5   Picture Cards for Medial Short Vowels

Words Their Way Appendix © 2000 by Prentice-Hall, Inc.

Words Their Way Appendix © 2000 by Prentice-Hall, Inc.

FIGURE A-5 Picture Cards for Medial Short Vowels (*continued*)

FIGURE A-5 Picture Cards for Medial Short Vowels (*continued*)

Words Their Way Appendix © 2000 by Prentice-Hall, Inc.

Words Their Way Appendix © 2000 by Prentice-Hall, Inc.

FIGURE A-5 Picture Cards for Medial Short Vowels (*continued*)

FIGURE A-5 Picture Cards for Medial Short Vowels (*concluded*)

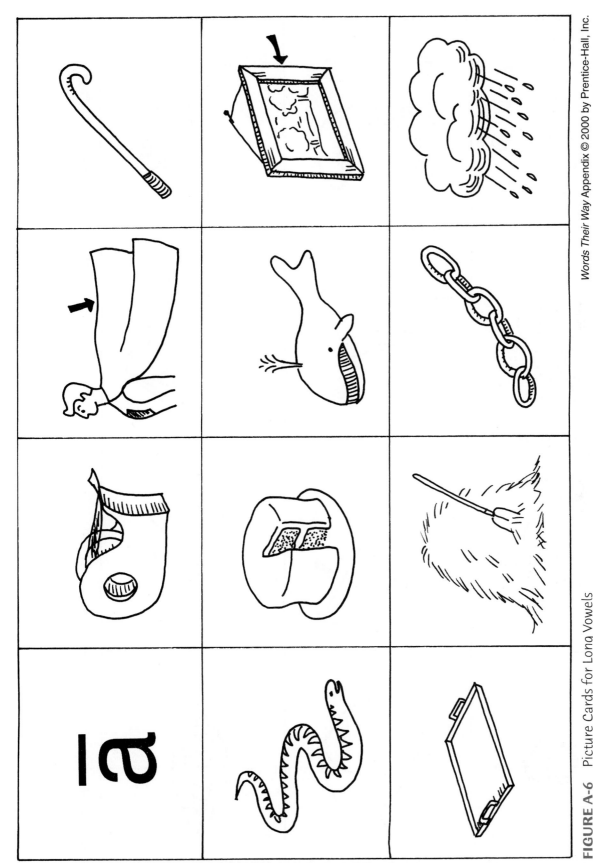

FIGURE A-6 Picture Cards for Long Vowels

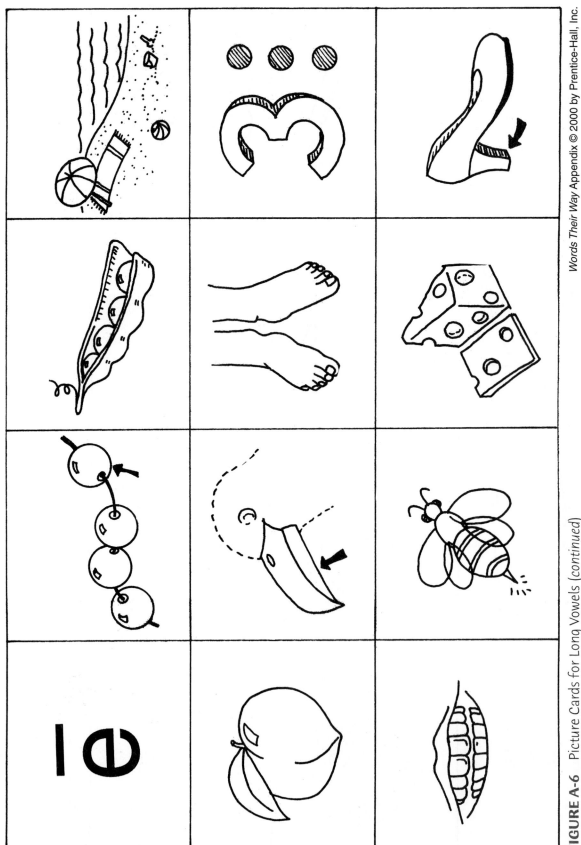

FIGURE A-6 Picture Cards for Long Vowels (*continued*)

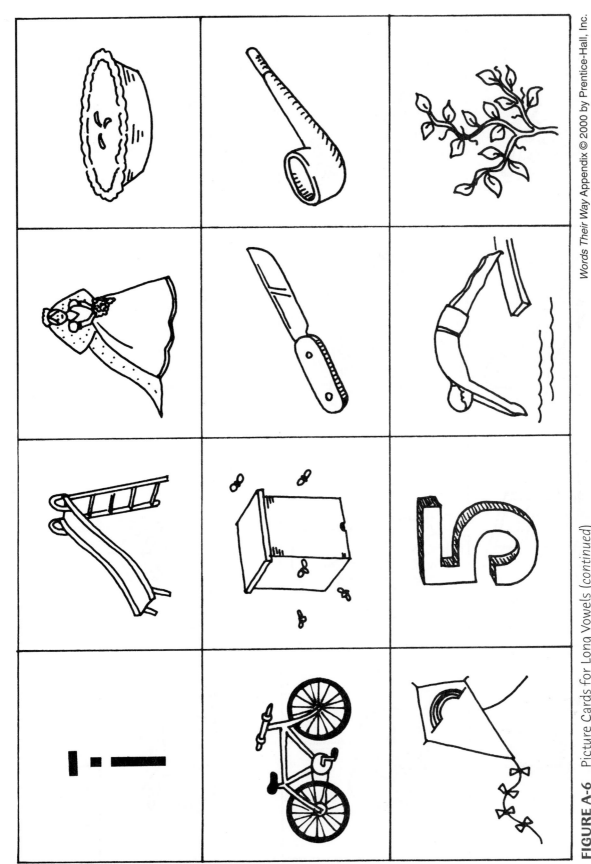

FIGURE A-6 Picture Cards for Long Vowels (continued)

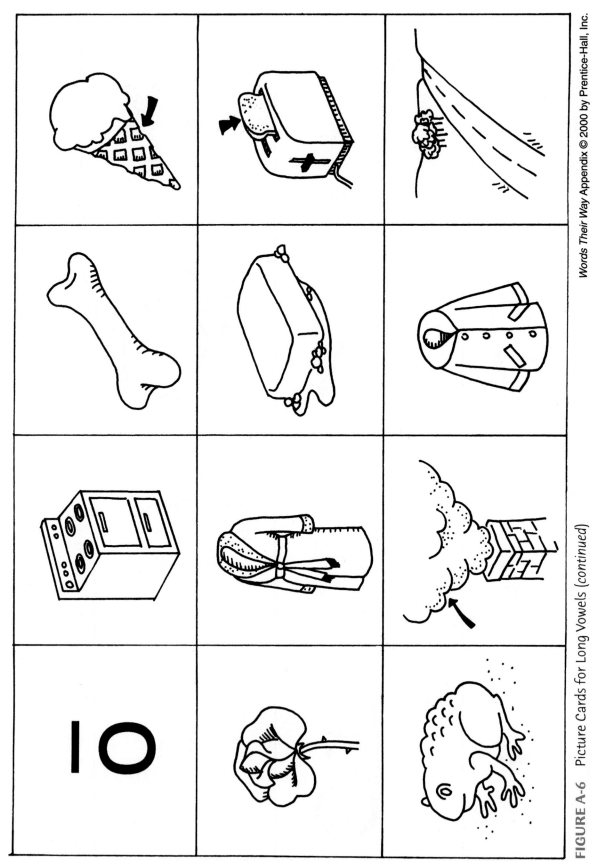

FIGURE A-6 Picture Cards for Long Vowels *(continued)*

Words Their Way Appendix © 2000 by Prentice-Hall, Inc.

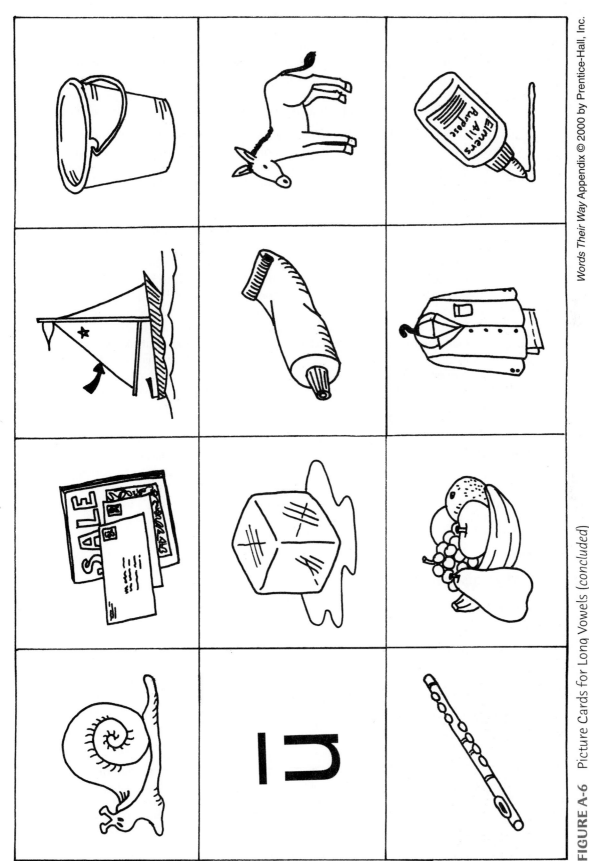

FIGURE A-6 Picture Cards for Long Vowels (concluded)

Words Their Way Appendix © 2000 by Prentice-Hall, Inc.

SAMPLE WORD SORTS BY SPELLING STAGE

The sample word sorts on the following pages are arranged by spelling stage and can be used with many of the activities described in the instructional chapters. Prepare word sorts to use with your own students by copying the words on cards or on a template such as the one on page 385. Be sure to write the words in randomly so students can make their own discoveries as they sort. Several points need to be made considering the use of these sorts.

1. These sorts are not intended to be a sequence for all students. Chapter 3 will help you match your students to the stages of spelling. There are further suggestions in each instructional chapter about the pacing and sequencing of word study for each stage. Choose appropriate sorts from among those presented here.

2. This is not an exhaustive list of sorts, but it does give you a starting point for creating your own. You can adapt these sorts by adding, subtracting, or substituting words that are more appropriate for your students. Words in a sort can be made easier or harder in a number of ways:
   - Common words like *hat* or *store* are easier than uncommon words like *vat* or *boar*. Use words students know from their own reading in the early stages to make sorts easier. This is less important when you get to syllables and affixes and derivational relations where extending a student's vocabulary is important.
   - Add words with blends, digraphs, and complex consonant units like *ce, dge,* or *tch* to make words harder. *Bat* and *blast* are both CVC words but *blast* is harder to spell.
   - Adding more oddballs to a sort makes it harder. Oddballs should never, however, constitute more than about 20% of the words in a sort or students might fail to see the generalizations that govern the majority of words. Don't use oddballs children are not likely to know (like *plaid* in a long-a sort for students early in the within word pattern stage).

3. Due to regional dialects you and your students may pronounce words differently and need to categorize words differently from those indicated in the sorts. These pronunciations should be honored. Substitute words or change categories as needed.

4. Words that look or sound as though they should match the features of a sort, but do not, are included in many of the sorts under an asterisk (*) to mark the oddball category.

Letter Name–Alphabetic Sorts

Same Short Vowel Families, CVC

Words from sorts 1 to 20 can be used in connection with games and activities in Chapter 6.

1. Short-a		**2.** More Short-a's			**3.** Short-i		**4.** More Short-i's			
cat	*man*	*sad*	*cap*	*bag*	*sit*	*big*	*pin*	*pill*	*rip*	*sick*
bat	can	mad	tap	rag	bit	wig	win	will	lip	pick
sat	pan	dad	map	wag	hit	pig	fin	fill	hip	lick
fat	ran	had	nap	tag	fit	dig	thin	hill	zip	kick
mat	fan	pad	lap	flag	kit	fig		mill		tick
rat	van			rap	quit			bill		
hat	tan							kill		

5. Short-o		**6.** More Short-o's			**7.** Short-e				**8.** Short-u				
not	*hop*	*job*	*lock*	*dog*	*pet*	*ten*	*bed*	*bell*	*cut*	*tub*	*bug*	*fun*	*duck*
got	pop	rob	rock	log	net	hen	red	tell	nut	rub	rug	bun	luck
hot	mop	cob	sock	frog	met	pen	fed	well	hut	cub	dug	run	suck
lot	cop		dock	fog	set	men	led	fell	but	club	jug	sun	truck
pot	stop		clock	jog	jet	then	sled	shell	shut		hug	gun	tuck
dot	shop		block		bet	when					tug		
shot					get								

Mixed Short Vowel Families, CVC

9. Short-a, i, u

man	pin	fun
can	win	run
fan	fin	sun
ran	thin	bun
than		gun
plan		

10. Short-a, i, o, u

cat	sit	not	cut
mat	fit	hot	shut
hat	hit	got	nut
that	quit	pot	but
rat	bit	rot	hut

11. Short-a, i, i, e

bag	big	pill	bell
rag	wig	will	sell
wag	pig	hill	tell
flag	jig	fill	well
tag		bill	shell

12. Families With *ck*

back	sick	lock	duck
sack	lick	rock	suck
tack	pick	sock	tuck
jack	tick	dock	truck
pack		clock	

13. Preconsonantal Nasals

camp	jump	band	sink
lamp	dump	hand	pink
ramp	hump	sand	think
stamp	stump	land	wink
damp	lump	stand	drink

14. Families Ending in *sh*

mash	fish	mush
cash	dish	hush
trash	wish	rush
rash		gush

Short Vowels, CVC

15. Short-a and Short-o

cat	not
bag	job
mad	stop
pan	fox
pat	lock
tack	got
lamp	top

16. Short-e and Short-u

pet	nut
bell	sun
red	cup
yes	mud
help	jump
test	hug

17. Short-a, Short-i, and Short-o

hat	dig	pop
fast	lick	rock
sand	lip	spot
tax	did	mom
bath	dish	stop
sack	nip	not

18. All Short Vowels

can	let	hit	rock	hug
that	best	fish	mop	luck
lap	met	fill	dot	run
last	web	six	box	bus
back	nest	this	rob	much
	wet	rich		just

19. Short Vowels With Blends

brat	grab	trip	crab
brick	grin	trap	crib
brag	grass	trot	crash
bring	grand	trick	cram
	grip	truck	
		track	

20. Two-Step Sort

a. Initial consonant and blends

rack	tack	dug	trick	drum
rag	tag	dip	track	drill
rash	tap	duck	trash	drag
rug			trap	drug
rip			trip	drip
			truck	

b. Short vowel sort

tack	tick	truck
tap	trip	drum
trash	drill	dug
drag	dip	rug
rack	rip	duck
rag	trick	drug
rash	drip	
trap		

Within Word Pattern Sorts

Words from sorts 21 to 56 can be used in connection with games and activities in Chapter 7.

Vowel Sorts: Words That Compare Short and Long Vowels, Explore Long Vowel Patterns (CVCe, CVVC, CVV, CV), and R-influenced Words

21. Short/Long-a

hat	name	*
jack	date	was
ask	race	
slap	plane	
fast	cape	
lap	page	
flag	same	
pass	safe	
path	gave	
glad	gate	

22. Short/Long-a

cap	lake	rain	*
last	wave	wait	laugh
plan	late	nail	
sat	tape	gain	
flat	bake	fail	
tax	base	pail	
	shade	plain	
	made	sail	
	maze		
	sale		

23. Long-a Patterns

same	mail	day	*
whale	pain	say	said
flake	train	play	have
grape	paid	may	
stage	brain	pay	
grade	snail	stay	
chase	chain	clay	
shave	tail		
tale	waist		
waste			

24. Less Common Long-a

hay	prey	eight	break
tray	they	weigh	great
stray	obey	vein	steak
pray	hey	veil	
sway		freight	
play		sleigh	
		neigh	

25. *R-influenced a*

car	care	chair	*
star	share	pair	bear
bark	bare	hair	
card	mare	air	
far	rare		
dark	scare		
arm			
start			

26. Short/Long-e

well	week	she
step	peel	he
west	weed	we
men	peek	me
bed	speed	
help	keep	
	peep	

27. Short/Long-e

best	green	mean	*
left	wheel	team	been
neck	sheet	deal	head
bell	street	reach	
bled	bleed	beach	
yet	teeth	steam	
	creep	clean	
	speed	bean	

28. Short/Long-e

mess	head	neat
rest	dead	meal
bell	deaf	speak
kept	breath	meat
nest	death	treat
shell	dread	sneak
vest		heat

29. Less Common Long-e

greed	chief	these	*
speech	field	scene	vein
greet	brief	theme	friend
creek	grief	eve	seize
fleet	shriek		
geese	piece		
cheese	thief		
	niece		

30. *R-influenced e*

her	near	cheer	bear	*
fern	clear	deer	pear	heart
germ	dear	sneer	wear	
jerk	year	queer	swear	
herb	spear	peer		
herd	beard			
perch				

31. Short/Long-i

dish	hike	*
chip	ride	give
king	ripe	live
whip	nice	
twin	white	
miss	dime	
pink	fine	
rich	life	

32. Short/Long-i

clip	mine	try	*
win	price	fly	eye
trick	spine	shy	buy
gift	lime	why	bye
list	wife	sky	
mitt	vine	dry	
thick	five		
swim			

33. Long-i Patterns

kite	might	mind
bride	night	wild
write	right	kind
spice	bright	blind
hide	light	find
wipe	tight	child
mice	sight	mild
		grind

34. *R-blends/R-influenced i*

grin	third	hire
bring	shirt	tire
drip	dirt	fire
grill	bird	wire
trick	skirt	tired
drink	girl	
brick		
crib		

35. Short/Long-o

lock	home	*
doll	slope	love
crop	note	gone
shot	hose	
clock	vote	
shock	joke	
knob	smoke	
slot	hope	
	choke	

36. Long-o Patterns

rope	road	blow	*
woke	boat	grow	now
close	soap	know	cow
stone	soak	slow	
bone	moan	throw	
phone	loaf	snow	
broke	coach		
hole	load		
	toast		

37. Short/Long-o

mock	roll	ghost	*
dock	cold	most	lost
soft	stroll	host	cost
cross	mold	post	
cloth	scold		
lost	fold		
frost	told		
odd	folk		

38. *R-influenced o*

for	more	door	*
born	store	poor	your
short	chore	floor	
porch	tore		
storm	shore		
north	score		
fort	wore		
torch	swore		

39. Short/Long-u

bun	June	blue	*
fuss	cute	glue	truth
luck	rule	clue	
lump	tube	due	
trust	tune	true	
plum	huge		
crust	cube		

40. Long-u Patterns

rude	fruit	new	*
crude	suit	chew	fuel
flute	juice	drew	build
mule	bruise	knew	
fume		stew	
chute		few	
		threw	
		screw	

41. Other Long-u

gloom	dew	who
bloom	grew	to
roost	crew	too
smooth	flew	two
scoop	blew	
school		
mood		
pool		

42. *R-influenced u*

hurt	cure	heard
turn	pure	learn
church	sure	earn
burst	lure	pearl
curl		yearn
purr		earth
purse		search

43. *R-blends/Vowels*

grill	girl
trap	tarp
crush	curl
fry	first
price	purse
track	dark
brag	bark
drip	dirt
frog	fort

44. *R-influenced Vowels*

car	her	for
shark	first	short
farm	bird	corn
hard	burn	horn
card	word	scorn
yard	worm	torn
scar	world	
march	dirt	
	jerk	

45. CVCe Sorts Across Vowels

cave	drive	drove	huge
crane	while	those	fume
change	smile	throne	prune
stage	twice	phone	chute
range	crime	wrote	flute
waste	guide	quote	

46. Sorts Across Long Vowels

day	team	fine	rope	rule
gate	seat	light	post	fruit
mail	free	pie	gold	blue
trade	field	wild	coal	tube
stay	street	time	stone	
eight	she	shy	throw	

47. CVVC Across Vowels

road	team	rain	*
boast	stream	strain	board
coach	sweet	claim	great
groan	queen	waist	
throat	peach	faith	
toast	thief	praise	
roast	peace	strain	
		trail	

Diphthongs and Complex Consonants

48. Diphthongs

toy	*coin*	*town*	*sound*
boy	foil	clown	mouth
joy	boil	brown	scout
	spoil	crown	round
	noise	frown	couch
	point	howl	loud

49. More Diphthongs

salt	*hawk*	*fault*	*
bald	draw	caught	fought
chalk	lawn	cause	ought
stall	raw	taught	
false	crawl	sauce	
small	claw	haul	
	paw		

50. Words Spelled With *w*

watch	*war*	*wrap*
swamp	warn	wreak
swan	warm	write
wand	dwarf	wrist
swat	swarm	wren
wash	wart	wrong

51. Complex Consonants

scram	*straight*	*shrank*	*square*
scrape	strange	shrink	squawk
scratch	stretch	shred	squint
screech	strict	shrunk	squash
screw	string		
	strong		

52. *ck, k, ke*

lick	*leak*	*like*
lack	seek	lake
tack	soak	take
snack	sleek	snake
stuck	weak	stake
stick	week	strike
whack	croak	wake

53. *ch* and *tch*

catch	*reach*	*
witch	coach	rich
patch	peach	such
fetch	roach	
hutch	screech	
itch	beach	
switch	pouch	

54. *ge* and *dge*

badge	*page*
ridge	stage
edge	huge
fudge	rage
bridge	cage
judge	
hedge	

55. Hard and Soft *c* and *g* Across Vowels

cave	*coat*	*cute*	*cent*	*cyst*
camp	coast	cup	cell	gym
cast	cost	cue	cease	
gave	gold	gum	gem	
gain	golf	gush	germ	
gasp	goof			

56. *ce, ge, ve, se*

dance	*charge*	*glove*	*cheese*
chance	large	give	please
prince	wedge	curve	tease
fence	dodge	shove	loose
since	ridge	live	choose
voice	edge	above	
juice	change	have	

Concept Sorts

57. What Lives in Water?

Yes	*No*
frog	toad
fish	lizard
whale	zebra
sea turtle	tortoise
clam	elephant
crab	horse

58. Edible Plants

Grain	*Fruit*	*Vegetable*
wheat	apples	carrots
oats	peaches	beans
rice	berries	lettuce
rye	pears	cucumber
barley	bananas	cabbage
	oranges	beets

59. Animal Attributes

Fish	*Bird*	*Mammal*
scale	feather	hair
eggs	eggs	born alive
gills	lungs	lungs
heart	heart	heart
no legs	two legs	legs
fins	wings	

60. States

East	*West*	*North*	*South*
Virginia	California	Maine	Florida
North Carolina	Nevada	Vermont	Mississippi
Maryland	Utah	New York	Texas
Delaware	Arizona		Alabama

61. Geometry Terms

Shapes	*Lines*	*Measurements*
triangle	ray	perimeter
rhombus	angle	degrees
square	line	diameter
rectangle	right angle	circumference
parallelogram	obtuse angle	area
isosceles triangle		radius

Syllables and Affixes Sorts

Words from sorts 62 to 91 can be used in connection with games and activities in Chapter 8.

Inflected Endings (*ed* and *ing*), Consonant Doubling, and Plurals

62. Sort for Sound of *ed*

trapped	*waited*	*played*
mixed	dotted	mailed
stopped	patted	boiled
chased	treated	raised
cracked	traded	tried
walked	ended	filled
asked	handed	seemed
jumped	needed	yelled

63. Plural Words (*s* and *es*)

cows	*boxes*	*buses*	*dishes*
chicks	mixes	glasses	benches
farms	axes	dresses	watches
fences		passes	lashes
gates		gases	churches
			dishes
			brushes

64. Plurals with *y*

babies	*plays*
carries	monkeys
ponies	boys
bodies	trays
pennies	donkeys
worries	enjoys
daddies	turkeys
trophies	
berries	
parties	

65. Base Words + *ed* and *ing*

jump	*jumped*	*jumping*
reach	reached	reaching
dress	dressed	dressing
wait	waited	waiting
crack	cracked	cracking
pass	passed	passing

66. Adding *ing*

batting	*baking*
shopping	skating
bragging	biting
hopping	hoping
stopping	sliding
begging	waving
skipping	moving
swimming	caring

67. Adding *ing*

trimming	*diving*	*pushing*	*floating*	*
running	riding	jumping	raining	mixing
popping	sliding	finding	sleeping	taxing
dragging	driving	kicking	boating	
wagging	wasting	wanting	waiting	
quitting	whining	munching	cheering	

This sort can be used with Activities 8-5 and 8-6.

68. Past Tense Verbs

kneel	*knelt*	*chase*	*chased*
teach	taught	mix	mixed
bring	brought	walk	walked
deal	dealt	bake	baked
sweep	swept	shop	shopped
send	sent		
think	thought		
lend	lent		
drink	drank		

69. Adding *ed* (Double, Nothing)

slipped	*picked*	*traded*
grabbed	called	baked
stopped	tracked	wasted
wagged	peeled	liked
tripped	watched	stared
knotted	cheered	waved
rubbed	talked	skated
whizzed	dreamed	tasted

70. Adding *ing* to *k* words (*ck*, e-drop, CVVC, VCk)

tacking	*baking*	*leaking*	*asking*
sticking	flaking	speaking	spending
tracking	shaking	croaking	shrinking
plucking	smoking	squeaking	drinking
wrecking	stroking	hooking	marking
clucking	making	looking	working
quacking	raking	cooking	frisking

Use with Double Crazy Eights Activity 8-9.

Syllable Juncture Sorts, Open and Closed Syllables (VCCV, VCV)

71. Compound Words

someone	*downtown*
something	downstairs
somehow	lowdown
someday	downcast
somewhere	downfall

72. VCCV at Juncture (same/different)

button	*market*
sunny	garden
yellow	signal
happy	member
happen	basket
sitting	center
fellow	plastic
matter	tablet

73. Syllable Juncture (VCCV, VCV)

tablet	*baby*
napkin	human
happen	music
winter	fever
foggy	silent
tennis	duty
sudden	writer
fossil	rival

74. VCV Open and Closed

meter	*petal*
human	rapid
secret	punish
paper	magic
lazy	shiver
even	comet
major	river
climate	clever
crater	proper
clover	liquid
bacon	

75. Closed VCCV / Open VCV

funny	*picture*	*pilot*
happen	expert	navy
pretty	until	nature
dollar	forget	music
goggles	napkin	spoken
gossip	canyon	frozen
letter	sister	spider
mattress	army	student

76. Closed/Open With Endings

sadden	*dusting*	*sliding*
chipped	rented	shining
matted	helping	named
scarred	sifted	scaring
winner	faster	rider
biggest	longest	tamest
running	walker	moping

Use with Slap Jack Activity 8-7.

Words Their Way Appendix © 2000 by Prentice-Hall, Inc.

Unaccented Final Syllable Sorts

77. *le* and *el*

fable	*camel*
angle	angel
little	model
rattle	gravel
settle	motel
cattle	bushel
nibble	level
turtle	pretzel
table	travel
	smaller

Use with Activity 8-11.

78. *er, ar, or*

bigger	*burglar*	*doctor*
freezer	grammar	favor
dreamer	collar	author
faster	dollar	editor
blister	lunar	tractor
jogger	solar	motor
speaker		mayor
skater		

79. *er, ar, or*

comparatives	*agents*	*things*
sweeter	worker	cellar
thinner	teacher	meter
smarter	waiter	river
slower	voter	pillar
younger	actor	anchor
gentler	beggar	vapor
steeper	director	trailer
cheaper	barber	

80. /j/ Sound

carriage	*budget*	*magic*
voyage	agent	engine
message	angel	region
postage	gorgeous	fragile
village	danger	margin
storage	legend	logic
sausage	pigeon	
savage	dungeon	
courage	gadget	

81. Changing *y* to *i*

cry	*cries*	*cried*
hurry	hurries	hurried
party	parties	partied
empty	empties	emptied
baby	babies	babied
reply	replies	replied
supply	supplies	supplied
carry	carries	carried
fry	fries	fried

82. *y* Words by Part of Speech

Long-i *verb*	*noun*	Long-e *adjective*	*adverb*
try	celery	happy	happily
certify	candy	pretty	correctly
apply	gypsy	guilty	clearly
occupy	quarry	angry	safely
rely	country	silly	horribly
	cemetery		hourly
	category		certainly
	copy		sensibly

Sorts to Explore Stress

83. Stress in Homographs

re'cord n.	*re cord'* v.
protest n.	protest v.
conduct n.	conduct v.
subject n.	subject v.
extract n.	extract v.
permit n.	permit v.
insert n.	insert v.
desert n.	desert v.
rebel n.	rebel v.
combat n.	combat v.
conflict n.	conflict v.

84. Stress in VCV Words

me'ter	*be cause'*
pilot	away
omen	around
never	below
picture	regard
famous	awake
wagon	again
diner	reward
habit	become
open	delay
vivid	defend

85. Two-Step First-Syllable Stress

a. Sort by closed/open

closed	
VCV	VCCV
radish	*dentist*
decade	nostril
novel	children
atom	chapter
lizard	picnic

b. Pattern

	open
VCCV	VCV
dipper	*bison*
foggy	major
spatter	pirate
sudden	climate
cottage	agent

86. Stress in VCCV Words

per'son	*at tend'*
welcome	perform
offer	support
expert	survive
harvest	escape
fellow	allow
barber	disturb
tender	suppose
common	hello
urgent	raccoon

87. Stress in Three Syllables

cam'er a	*to ge'ther*
yesterday	deliver
victory	important
animal	hamburger
library	department
enemy	tomorrow
carpenter	another
several	however
article	edition
alphabet	remember

88. Long-u in Stressed Syllable

bu'gle	*a muse'*
future	compute
ruby	confuse
rumor	reduce
tulip	perfume
tuna	pollute
tutor	salute
super	excuse
pupil	abuse
ruler	include

Revisiting Patterns in Longer Words

89. Short / Long-a

canvas	*agent*
lantern	basic
package	cradle
tragic	fatal
attic	labor
bandage	vapor
tablet	sacred
cannon	April

90. Patterns for Long-a

debate	*explain*	*layer*
mistake	dainty	dismay
grapefruit	trainer	payment
parade	complain	crayons
engage	acquaint	hooray
bracelet	raisin	decay
estate	refrain	betray

91. Sort by Number of Syllables

hazard	*banana*	*motorcycle*	*hippopotamus*
number	alphabet	unusual	inspirational
helmet	hospital	supermarket	refrigerator
lumber	decimal	intersection	
machine	important	information	
sister	yesterday	transportation	

92. Diphthongs in Two Syllables

coin	moisture	joyful
spoil	appoint	boycott
broil	poison	royal
void	turquoise	soybean
coil	moisten	oyster
poise	pointless	voyage
noise	broiler	annoy
join	embroider	enjoy
point	rejoice	destroy
moist		employ

Use for Oygo, Activity 8-15.

93. More Dipthongs in Two Syllables

county	flower
council	allow
lousy	brownie
fountain	vowel
mountain	shower
scoundrel	towel
counter	tower
around	chowder
bounty	coward
foundry	drowsy
mouthful	powder
	rowdy
	prowler
	power

94. *or, ar, er,* and Parts of Speech

noun	adjective	comparative adjective
doctor	circular	thinner
conductor	rectangular	cleaner
agitator	lunar	smarter
inspector	solar	happier
refrigerator	similar	sorrier
instigator	particular	dirtier
incubator	spectacular	sleepier
employer	peculiar	slower

95. Spelling the /er/ Sound in Stressed and Unstressed Syllables

cer' tain	re verse'	sur prise'	lan'tern
person	observe	perhaps	concert
thirsty	alert	survive	modern
service	prefer	surround	western
hurry	emerge		govern
turkey			

96. Words With *ure* **and** *er (ture, sure, cher)*

capture	measure	archer	*
creature	treasure	butcher	injure
fracture	pleasure	preacher	failure
mixture	closure	stretcher	manicure
pasture	leisure	teacher	procedure
texture		rancher	
future			
nature			

97. Advanced Homophones

Stressed Syllable		Unstressed Syllable	
aloud	allowed	patience	patients
cinder	sender	accept	except
morning	mourning	alter	altar
berry	bury	miner	minor
roomer	rumor	council	counsel
kernel	colonel	hanger	hangar
holy	wholly	profit	prophet
oral	aural	mussel	muscle
vary	very	lesson	lessen
censor	sensor	presence	presents
awful	offal	canvas	canvass
incite	insight	baron	barren

98. Prefixes

unfair	retell	disagree
unable	replay	disappear
uncover	retrain	disgrace
unkind	return	disarm
undress	reuse	disorder
unplug	research	disobey
		disable

99. More Prefixes

preschool	explode	triangle	subway
preview	exceed	tricycle	submarine
prevent	expose	triad	subsoil
preheat	explore	tripod	subtract
prefix	exile	trio	subset
prepare			
predict			

Derivational Relations Sorts

Words from sorts 100 to 117 can be used in connection with games and activities in Chapter 9.

Adding Suffixes

100. Adding *ion*

ct + ion		ss + ion	
affect	affection	express	expression
distinct	distinction	impress	impression
select	selection	process	procession
extinct	extinction	depress	depression
predict	prediction	success	succession
subtract	subtraction	profess	profession
contract	contraction	discuss	discussion

101. E-drop + *ion*

te + ion		ce + ion		se + ion	
educate	education	induce	induction	expulse	expulsion
congratulate	congratulation	introduce	introduction	convulse	convulsion
create	creation	produce	production	repulse	repulsion
decorate	decoration	deduce	deduction		
generate	generation	reproduce	reproduction		
imitate	imitation	reduce	reduction		

102. *sion* and Spelling Changes

t to s + sion		*E-drop, then d to s, + ion*	
commit	*commission*	*explode*	*explosion*
transmit	transmission	collide	collision
permit	permission	conclude	conclusion
emit	emission	persuade	persuasion
omit	omission	erode	erosion
regret	regression	delude	delusion
remit	remission	include	inclusion

103. E-drop + *ation* or *ition*

E-drop + ation		*E-drop + ition*	
admire	*admiration*	*compose*	*composition*
determine	determination	define	definition
explore	exploration	dispose	disposition
combine	combination	oppose	opposition
declare	declaration	expose	exposition
inspire	inspiration	decompose	decomposition
organize	organization		
examine	examination		
perspire	perspiration		

104. *ible* and *able*

base + able	*root + ible*
dependable	audible
expendable	edible
breakable	visible
agreeable	feasible
predictable	terrible
remarkable	possible
readable	legible
profitable	plausible
perishable	horrible
punishable	tangible
laughable	

105. *ible* and *able* after *e*

e-drop	*soft ce/ge*	*hard c/g*
presumable	changeable	navigable
desirable	manageable	amicable
usable	peaceable	despicable
lovable	serviceable	impeccable
deplorable	noticeable	applicable
comparable		
excusable		
eligible		
intelligible		
legible		

106. Related Words + *able* and *ible*

ation to able		*sion or tion to ible*	
toleration	tolerable	collection	collectible
separation	separable	contraction	contractible
education	educable	reduction	reducible
vegetation	vegetable	exhaustion	exhaustible
application	applicable	repression	repressible
observation	observable	expression	expressible
navigation	navigable	production	producible

107. *tion*, from Verbs to Nouns

Use this sort with "Is it sion or tion?" Making the Spelling-Meaning Connection, Activity 9-2.

separate		*separation*		*convulse*	*convulsion*
fascinate	extinct	fascination	extinction	repulse	repulsion
educate	conduct	education	conduction	express	expression
complicate	affect	complication	affection	profess	profession
generate	act	generation	action		
navigate	contract	navigation	contraction		
vegetate		vegetation			

108. Assimilated Prefix Sort

com	*ad*	*in*
contest	allot	illegal
conform	affair	irresponsible
colleague	affront	immature
confront	assemble	irrational
context	affirm	immortal
correlate	arrange	illogical
constrain	acclaim	innumerable

Vowel Alternations

109. Vowel Alternations in Related Pairs

Sort words into two different alternation patterns. Keep partners together.

Long-a to Short-a	Long-a to Schwa
cave/cavity	*major/majority*
humane/humanity	narrate/narrative
nation/national	relate/relative
volcano/volcanic	famous/infamous
grave/gravity	able/ability
nature/natural	native/nativity
insane/insanity	educate/educable

110. Vowel Alternations in Related Pairs

Sort words in two different alternation patterns. Keep partners together.

Long-e to Short-e	Long-e to Schwa
serene/serenity	*compete/competition*
brief/brevity	repeat/repetition
proceed/procession	remedial/remedy
recede/recession	
succeed/succession	
conceive/conception	
receive/reception	

111. Vowel Alternations in Related Pairs

Sort words into two different alternation patterns. Keep partners together.

Long-i to Short-i	Long-i to Schwa
resign/resignation	*invite/invitation*
sign/signal	define/definition
divine/divinity	reside/resident
divide/division	recite/recitation
revise/revision	deprive/deprivation
deride/derision	admire/admiration
	inspire/inspiration

112. Vowel Alternations in Related Pairs

Sort words in two different alternation patterns.

Long-u to Short-u	Long-o to Schwa
induce/induction	*compose/composition*
seduce/seduction	propose/proposition
misconstrue/misconstruction	impose/imposition
conduce/conduction	expose/exposition
reduce/reduction	harmonious/harmony
produce/production	

Sorting by Roots

113. Vowel Alternation Patterns in Related Words

Long to Short	Long to Schwa	Schwa to Short
divine/divinity	*compose/composition*	*metal/metallic*
prescribe/prescription	proclaim/proclamation	brutal/brutality
sage/sagacity	stable/stability	local/locality
profane/profanity	preside/president	spiritual/spirituality
criticize/criticism	adore/adoration	vital/vitality
telescope/telescopic	compete/competition	fatal/fatality
microscope/microscopic	repeat/repetition	total/totality
cone/conic	impose/imposition	normal/normality
flame/flammable		final/finality
arise/arisen		original/originality

114. Greek and Latin Science Vocabulary Sort

See the Greek and Latin Science Vocabulary Sort, Activity 9-4.

astro	astronomer, astronaut, astrology, astrolabe
bio	biology, biome, biosphere, biotic
chlor	chlorophyll, chloroplast, chlorine, chlorella
eco	ecology, economy, ecosystem, ecotype
hydro	hydrophobia, hydrology, hydrogen
hypo	hypodermis, hypodermic, hypothermia, hypotension
photo/phos	phosphorescent, photography, telephoto
vor	voracious, omnivore, carnivore

115. Greek Roots

autograph	*telegram*
automatic	telepathy
autobiography	telegraph
autonomy	televise
automobile	telephone
autonomous	teleconference

116. Latin Roots

Sort words by Latin root.

jud	*tract*	*spec*
judge	contract	spectator
adjudicate	attract	inspect
judgment	intractable	respect
judicial	subtraction	spectacular
prejudice	tractor	inspector
judicious	contraction	spectacles
prejudicial	protractor	disrespect
judiciary	distraction	

117. Latin Roots

See Joined at the Roots, Activity 9-8.

visual	transplant	geology	portable	photo
visionary	transportation	geographic	porter	photogenic
vision	transaction	geometry	opportunity	photosensitive
vista	transfer	geologist	portfolio	photographer
	transparent	geography	export	photosynthesis
		geometric	import	

WORD LISTS

The following lists of words are organized by features starting with the word families and then vowel sounds and patterns for each vowel. Under each feature the words are sometimes grouped by frequency and complexity. For example, under short-a, the early part of the list contains words most likely encountered by first graders (*am, ran, that*). The latter part of the list contains words which may be obscure in meaning and spelled with blends or digraphs (*yam, brass, tramp*).

These words can be transferred to a word sheet to create your own customized lessons. Many people have found it easy to create the word sheets you have seen throughout the book by making a table in a word processing program. Set the margins all around at zero, and create a table that is three columns by six to eight rows. Select a large font and save it as a template that you use each time before you fill it in. After creating each sort by typing in the words you want, simply save it using a name that defines the features such as "Short Vowels: a, o, e."

Here are three reminders and tips about creating word sorts:

1. Create sorts which will help your students form their own generalizations about how words work. Use a collection of 15 to 25 words so that there are plenty of examples to consider.

2. Contrast at least two and up to four features in a sort. There are many sample sorts here in the appendix to give you ideas about how to do this. You can contrast sounds, spelling patterns, word endings, prefixes, root words, and so on.

Examples of sound sorts:

Contrast short-o and long-o.

Contrast the sound of *ear* in *learn* and in *hear*.

Contrast the sound of *g* in *guest* and *gym*.

Examples of pattern sorts:

Contrast long-o spelled with *oa*, *o-e*, and *ow*.

Contrast words that end with *or*, *er*, and *ar*.

Contrast words that double before *ing* with those that don't.

Examples of meaning sorts:

Contrast words derived from *spect* and *port*.

Contrast words with prefixes *sub*, *un*, and *trans*.

The most elegant sorts are those that combine a sound sort with a pattern sort. For example, a long-o and short-o sort can begin with a picture sort and then proceed to a sort by patterns—CVVC and CVCe.

3. In most sorts, include up to three words that have the same sound or pattern but are not consistent with the generalization that governs the other words. Sometimes the oddballs you include will be true exceptions such as *said* but other times the oddballs may represent a less common spelling pattern such as *ey* representing long-a in *prey* and *grey*.

The following lists include possible exceptions that can be included. For example, in a long-o sort, with words sorted by the *oa*, *o-e*, and *ow* patterns, the exceptions might include the words *now* and *love* since they are high-frequency words which look like they would have the long-o sound but do not.

A Families

at	*ad*	*ag*	*an*	*ap*	*ab*	*am*	*all*
cat	bad	bag	can	cap	cab	dam	ball
bat	dad	rag	fan	lap	dab	ham	call
fat	had	sag	man	map	jab	ram	fall
hat	mad	wag	pan	nap	nab	jam	hall
mat	pad	nag	ran	rap	lab	clam	mall
pat	sad	flag	tan	yap	tab	slam	tall
rat	rad	brag	van	tap	blab	cram	wall
sat	glad	drag	plan	zap	crab	wham	small
that	lad	shag	than	clap	scab	swam	stall
flat		snag	clan	flap	stab	yam	
brat		lag	scan	slap	grab	gram	
chat		tag		trap	slab	cram	
				chap		wham	
				snap			
				wrap			
				strap			

ar	*art*	*and*	*ash*	*ang*	*ack*	*ank*
bar	cart	band	bash	bang	back	bank
car	dart	hand	cash	fang	pack	sank
far	mart	land	dash	hang	jack	tank
jar	part	sand	gash	sang	rack	yank
par	tart	brand	hash	rang	lack	blank
star	start	grand	mash	clang	sack	plank
	chart	stand	rash		tack	crank
	smart	strand	sash		black	drank
			flash		quack	prank
			trash		crack	spank
			crash		track	thank
			smash		shack	
			slash		snack	
			clash		stack	

E Families

et	*en*	*ed*	*ell*	*eg*	*eck*	*est*
bet	den	bed	bell	beg	deck	best
get	hen	fed	cell	peg	neck	nest
let	men	led	fell	leg	peck	pest
met	ten	red	jell	keg	wreck	rest
net	pen	wed	sell		speck	test
pet	then	bled	tell		check	vest
set	when	fled	well			west
wet	wren	sled	shell			
vet		shed	smell			
fret		shred	spell			
jet			swell			
yet			dwell			

I Families

it	*ig*	*in*	*ill*	*ip*	*ick*	*ink*	*ing*
bit	big	bin	bill	dip	lick	link	king
kit	dig	fin	dill	hip	kick	mink	ping
fit	fig	pin	fill	lip	pick	pink	sing
hit	pig	tin	kill	nip	sick	sink	ring
lit	rig	win	mill	rip	tick	rink	wing
pit	wig	grin	pill	sip	slick	wink	sling
sit	zig	thin	will	tip	quick	blink	bring
quit		twin	drill	zip	trick	drink	sting
skit		chin	grill	whip	chick	stink	swing
spit		shin	chill	clip	flick	think	thing
		skin	skill	flip	brick	clink	spring
		spin	spill	slip	stick	shrink	string
			still	skip	thick		cling
				drip			fling
				trip			wring
				chip			
				ship			

O Families

ot	*ob*	*og*	*op*	*ock*	*ong*	*oss*
cot	cob	dog	cop	dock	bong	boss
dot	job	bog	hop	lock	gong	toss
got	rob	fog	pop	rock	long	moss
hot	gob	hog	mop	sock	song	gloss
jot	mob	jog	top	tock	strong	loss
lot	sob	log	slop	block	throng	cross
not	snob	clog	flop	clock		
pot	blob	frog	drop	flock		
blot	glob		shop	smock		
slot			stop	shock		
plot						
shot						
spot						

Words Their Way Appendix © 2000 by Prentice-Hall, Inc.

U Families

ut	*ub*	*ug*	*um*	*un*	*uck*	*ump*	*ung*
but	cub	bug	bum	bun	buck	bump	sung
cut	hub	dug	gum	fun	duck	jump	rung
gut	rub	hug	hum	gun	luck	dump	hung
hut	tub	jug	drum	run	suck	hump	lung
nut	club	mug	plum	sun	tuck	lump	swung
rut	grub	rug	slum	spun	yuck	pump	clung
shut	snub	tug	scum	stun	pluck	rump	strung
	stub	slug	chum		cluck	plump	slung
		plug			truck	stump	sprung
		drug			stuck	thump	wrung
		snug					

up	*uff*
cup	buff
pup	cuff
	huff
	muff
	puff
	fluff

Short-a Words *(See also word family lists.)*

CVC	CVCC				
crab	lamp	batch	mass	draft	past
wax	last	glass	mast	shaft	patch
gnat	match	grass	raft	branch	path
pal	math	calf	staff	camp	ranch
stab	scratch	graph	vast	catch	shall
tax	snatch	plant	bask	fact	brass
ant	stamp	grasp	brand	half	grand
ask	task	bath	cash	mask	grant
fast	class	lash	clash	pant	hatch
last	tramp	latch	cramp	pass	lamb
gap					

Short-e *(See also word family lists.)*

CVC	CVCC				
step	next	nest	knelt	bless	Exceptions:
them	best	rest	guess	clench	went
yes	bend	send	less	crest	weft
stem	chest	sent	mend	elm	wept
web	desk	slept	peck	elder	debt
hem	dress	stretch	pest	flesh	drench
gem	egg	tent	rent	lend	etch
	help	test	self	lens	jest
	held	west	shelf	lest	lent
	kept	bent	swept	scent	pelt
	left	cent	tend	sketch	pes
	melt	check	tenth	speck	stress
	neck	fetch	fresh	vest	tempt
					wretch

Short-i *(See also word family lists.)*

CVC		CVCC				
if	did	fish	kill	film	gill	disc
in	lid	hill	kiss	fist	hitch	tilt
is	rid	miss	lick	gift	inn	frisk
it	slid	pick	lift	hint	limb	glint
did	slit	stick	milk	ill	mill	grill
fix	strip	still	print	inch	mint	hint
hid	trim	trick	quick	limp	risk	nick
him	din	which	quilt	mitt	shift	prick
his	grim	will	rich	pill	shrimp	quill
mix	jig	wind	sick	pinch	twist	switch
six	skid	wish	spill	pitch	squint	sift
swim	skim	sixth	till	sill	stiff	skill
this	twig	bill	brick	brisk	swift	still
brim	whiz	chick	chill	ditch	swish	thrill
crib	wit	click	cliff	drill	thick	
		dish	crisp	flick	witch	
		hiss	drift	frill	chimp	
		kick	fifth		dill	

Short-o *(See also word family lists.)*

CVC		CVCC			
bob	ox	cock	notch	frost	Exceptions:
box	prop	doll	romp	gloss	from
fox	sod	lock	frog	loft	of
mom	throb	fond	lost	moss	son
knot	con	odd	off	moth	front
trot	pox	bond	boss	broth	won
crop	prod	gosh	cloth	golf	
god	bog	prompt	cost	loss	
plod	hog	stock	cross	long	
plop	on	stomp	soft	lost	
rod	log	blond	toss	bong	
knob	fog	mock			

Short-u *(See also word family lists.)*

CVC	CVCC				
bus	duck	crunch	skunk	gush	*ul*
mud	jump	crush	bluff	husk	bulge
shut	just	dull	blush	plumb	bulk
bud	lunch	dumb	brusk	ruff	gulf
uh	much	dusk	butt	scuff	gulp
huh	must	fuss	clump	shucks	sulk
lug	bunk	gruff	crumb	slump	pulse
plus	brush	hush	crust	snuff	
shrub	bump	lump	grunt	stunt	
strut	bunch	munch	gust		
stud	dust	mush	hump	Exceptions:	
sum	fuzz	must	hunch	push	
thud	hunt	pump	mutt	put	
thus	rush	punch	numb	bush	
jut	stuff	rust	plump	truth	
nub	such	stump	suck		
smug	thumb	struck	tuft		
strum	thump	trust	tusk		

Words Their Way Appendix © **2000 by Prentice-Hall, Inc.**

Long-a Lists

CVCe

a-e

ate	state	cane
bake	strange	crate
cake	tape	date
came	taste	daze
cave	wake	drape
face	wave	fade
gave	ache	flake
lake	bathe	gape
made	blame	grave
make	blaze	graze
place	brake	jade
same	cape	lame
care	crane	mane
take	fake	rate
age	fame	sake
base	flame	slate
cage	gaze	slave
change	grace	stale
chase	grape	drake
gate	lace	fate
grade	lane	grate
hate	male	haste
late	mate	haze
page	pace	pane
paste	pale	phase
plane	rage	quake
plate	range	vane
race	scale	vase
safe	tale	
sale	tame	Exceptions:
save	trace	have
shade	trade	dance
shake	wade	chance
shape	waste	prance
skate	whale	
space	ape	
stage	babe	

CVVC

ai

paint
rain
tail
train
mail
main
nail
pail
rail
sail
aid
bait
braid
brain
fail
grain
maid
pain
waist
wait
claim
gain
praise
straight
strait
vain
aide
ail
faith
quaint
stain

Exceptions:
said
aisle
plaid

ea

break
great
steak

ei

eight
neigh
rein
weigh
weight
eighth
freight
reign
veil
sleigh
weigh
beige

CVV

ay

day
jay
may
play
say
stay
way
clay
gray
pray
tray
slay

ey

prey
grey
they
hey

Long-e Lists

CVVC

ea

bean	reach	peace	cease	green	seek
clean	read	peach	crease	deep	seem
each	scream	peak	ease	need	sheet
eat	sneak	plead	feat	see	teeth
leave	stream	seal	grease	seed	weed
mean	tea	squeak	plea	seen	week
real	team	steal	seam	sheep	wheel
sea	bead	steam		sleep	beep
seat	beak	treat	Exceptions:	street	bleed
teach	beam	weak	great	three	cheek
beach	beast	weave	break	tree	creek
beat	cream	flea	steak	breeze	creep
breathe	creak	heal		cheese	greed
dream	deal	knead	*ee*	deep	greet
east	feast	league	bee	free	heel
lead	heap	leak	beet	geese	peel
lean	least	leash	feed	knee	reed
meat	meal	squeal	feel	meet	speech
pea	neat	bleat	feet	queen	speed

Long-e Lists (continued)
CVVC

steel	reef	Exception:	piece	Exceptions:
steep	sleek	been	thief	friend
sweep	thee		belief	fierce
sleeve	wee		grief	pier
sneeze	breed	*e*	brief	edge
beef	fee	he	shriek	else
deed	flee	be		seize
eel	freeze	me		vein
fleet	keen	she	*e-e*	they
glee	reel	we	eve	hey
kneel	seep		scene	weird
peep		*ie*	theme	brief
preen		chief	these	
		field		

Long-i Lists
CVCe

				CV		iCC	
i-e				*ie*	*y/ye*	*igh*	find
bike	quite	whine		lie	cry	high	kind
bite	prize	wipe		pie	fly	light	child
dime	shine	crime		tie	my	might	climb
fine	size	fife		die	sky	night	mind
hide	slide	file			try	right	wild
kite	strike	lice		Exceptions:	why	bright	blind
like	stripe	mite		buy	by	fight	grind
line	vine	prime		guy	dry	sigh	hind
live	wide	spike			shy	tight	sign
nice	wife	spite			sly	flight	bind
ride	wise	stride			bye	fright	wind
side	write	chime			dye	sight	
smile	glide	lime			lye	slight	
time	guide	scribes			rye	thigh	
while	hike	site					
white	hive	spice					
dive	knife	thrive					
drive	pine						
five	price	Exceptions:					
ice	pride	live					
life	ripe	bridge					
mice	rise	give					
mile	slice	prince					
mine	spine	since					
nine	tide	hinge					
pile	tribe	ridge					
pipe	twice	fringe					

Long-o Lists

CVCe

o-e

close	wove	joke
drove	doze	lone
hole	froze	stove
lone	globe	whole
nose	lone	woke
note	robe	wrote
rope	role	
stone	slope	Exceptions:
those	sole	come
broke	cove	gone
chose	dome	love
clothe	lope	move
choke	pose	some
code	quote	done
cone	rove	lose
home	yoke	none
mole	zone	one
owe	phone	once
poke	pole	prove
shone	ode	dove
stole	smoke	glove
stroke	spoke	whose
throne	hope	shove
tone	hose	
vote		

CVVC

oa

boat	oat
coat	roam
float	roast
goat	soak
moan	throat
road	cloak
soap	goal
toad	loaf
toast	loaves
coach	whoa
coal	boast
coast	coax
croak	loan
groan	
foam	Exceptions:
load	broad
moat	sew
oak	

CV

o

go
no
so
ho
yo-yo

CVV

ow

grow
know
show
slow
snow
blow
bowl
crow
grown
low
own
throw
blown
flow
flown
glow
sow
tow

VCC

oCC

cold
gold
hold
most
old
told
both
fold
roll
scold
bolt
folk
ghost
post
sold
bold
colt
host
mold
stroll
volt
jolt
poll
scroll

Other *a* Patterns

al	*au*	*aw*	*o*	*w + a*
tall	caught	draw	dog	watch
wall	fault	saw	frog	want
small	pause	crawl	lost	wash
talk	sauce	paw	off	wand
walk	taught	straw	on	wasp
salt	haunt	claw	cost	watt
calm	launch	dawn	boss	swap
chalk		drawn	cloth	swat
halt	Exceptions:	law	cross	
palm	aunt	lawn	log	
stalk	laugh	shawl	long	
stall		squawk	soft	
bald		yawn	toss	
		awe	fog	
		bawl	frost	
		hawk	gloss	
		raw	honk	
		caw	bog	
		fawn	hog	
		gnaw	loft	
		sprawl	moss	
		thaw	moth	
			bong	
			broth	
			golf	
			loss	
			throng	

Other Words With *o*

ow	*oo*	*oo=u*	*ou*	*ough*	*oi*
brown	book	food	could	thought	coin
clown	cook	room	would	ought	join
cow	good	school	should	bought	oil
down	look	soon		brought	point
how	took	too	*ou*	trough	soil
now	wood	zoo	cloud	cough	boil
town	brook	bloom	found	fought	coil
bow	foot	boot	ground		foil
growl	shook	cool	out		joint
howl	stood	fool	pound		hoist
owl	wool	moo	shout		moist
crowd	crook	moon	proud		toil
crown	hood	noon	round		broil
drown	hook	pool	sound		
frown	hoof	roof	count		*oi-e*
gown	soot	roost	mount		voice
plow		root	loud		noise
sow		shoot	mount		choice
wow		smooth	bound		
bow		spoon	hound		*oy*
prowl		tool	wound		boy
scowl		zoom	couch		toy
fowl		boom	crouch		joy
vow		gloom	doubt		enjoy
		loom	mound		

/u/	/u/ o-e	loop	ouch
from	come	mood	pouch
of	love	pooh	scout
does	some	proof	snout
son	done	scoop	sprout
front	none	spook	stout
rough	once	tooth	drought
ton	one	stool	foul
touch	glove	troop	mouth
won	dove	whoop	
young	shove	goof	
tough		brood	

Exceptions:
poor
blood

Long-u Lists

u-e		*ue*	*ui*	*ew*
dune	prune	blue	fruit	new
flute	cute	sue	suit	grew
rude	use	clue	bruise	chew
rule	huge	glue	cruise	drew
tube	June	due	juice	few
tune	cube	flue		flew
chute	mule	hue	Exceptions:	knew
dude	fume	true	build	threw
duke	muse		built	crew
nude	mute	Exceptions:	guide	grew
crude		cruel		stew
plume	Exception:	fuel		dew
prude	truth			screw
				brew
				shrewd
				strewn
				whew

Words Their Way Appendix © 2000 by Prentice-Hall, Inc.

R-influenced Vowels

ar		*are*	*air*	*er*
bark	yard	care	chair	her
car	scarf	bare	hair	fern
dark	shark	scare	pair	herd
far	yarn	share	stair	jerk
part	arch	stare	flair	perch
star	dart	dare	lair	clerk
start	hard	flare		germ
arm	lark	glare	Exceptions:	herb
art	mar	mare	are	per
bar	scar	rare	bear	perk
card	snarl	square	wear	stern
cart	barb	snare	swear	term
charm	harp	blare	pear	
harm		fare	where	
jar		hare	there	
arch			their	
sharp			heart	

ar + e	*ear*	*eer*	*ir*	*ire*	*or*		*ore*	*our*	*oar*	*w + ar*
carve	near	cheer	bird	fire	for	nor	more	your	roar	warm
large	clear	deer	first	tire	born	chord	store	course	hoarse	war
starve	dear	peer	girl	wire	corn	ford	shore	four	soar	ward
barge	fear	steer	chirp	hire	forth	fort	bore	pour	boar	wharf
	tear	queer	dirt	sire	horn	lord	chore	court	coarse	quart
	year	jeer	shirt		north	pork	score	fourth		
ur	beard	sneer	third	*ure*	porch	torch	sore	mourn		
burn	gear	steer	birth	cure	short	scorn	wore	source	*w + or*	
hurt	spear		firm	pure	storm	force	tore	gourd	word	
turn		/ur/*ear*	stir		worn	horse	swore		work	
curl	Exceptions:	heard	swirl		cord	forge		Exceptions:	world	
purr	bear	earth	thirst		cork	gorge	*oor*	our	worm	
burst	heart	learn	whirl				door	flour	worth	
church	wear	earn	squirt				poor	hour	worse	
churn	pear	search	twirl				floor	scour		
curb	swear	pearl	fir					sour		
hurl		yearn					ōor			
burr							lure			
blurt		/ur/*er-e*					sure			
lurch		nerve								
lurk		verse								
spur		swerve								
surf										

Complex Consonants

ch	Cch	tch	ge	Hard-g	Soft-g	y-words	
teach	lunch	catch	stage	dog	huge	/i/	/e/
reach	watch	patch	rage	get	magic	try	funny
beach	bench	stretch	huge	good	orange	cry	county
peach	branch	clutch	page	go	page	fly	family
coach	bunch	fetch		gave	stage		party
screech	march	hatch		pig	age	spy	story
couch	porch	match	dge	gone	cage	fry	baby
crouch	stretch	pitch	edge	tiger	giant	pry	berry
pouch	birch	witch	ledge	frog	village	terrify	body
	church	scratch	bridge	got	strange	identify	carry
	munch	batch	judge	girl	gym	rely	copy
	perch	ditch	budge	game	danger	classify	marry
	pinch	clutch	dodge	bug	gem	reply	study
	punch	latch	hedge	gain	gentle	supply	worry
	search	sketch	lodge	dragon	engine	July	pony
	clench	stitch	nudge	egg	giraffe		puppy
	hunch	switch	ridge	gate	legend		twenty
	torch	twitch	trudge	gear	general		army
	haunch		wedge	geese	pigeon		hobby
	drench		smudge	ghost	rage		ferry
	lurch		bulge	goat	germ		entry
	gulch			gold	dungeon		trophy
	starch		Cge	guilt	gesture		injury
	drench		charge	gulp	geology		envy
	arch		change	guess	ginger		gravity
			strange	drug	oxygen		glory
			range	gust	angel		pantry
			barge	gum	genuine		city
			forge	gun	genius		
			surge	golf			
			gorge	guy			
			large	goof			
				gag			
				gas			
				gift			
				rug			
				gill			
				sugar			
				giggle			
				gorilla			
				angle			

Words Their Way Appendix © 2000 by Prentice-Hall, Inc.

Homophones*

be/bee
blue/blew
I/eye/aye
no/know
here/hear
to/too/two
hi/high
new/knew/gnu
see/sea
there/they're/their
bear/bare
by/buy/bye
deer/dear
ate/eight
for/four/fore
our/hour
red/read
lead/led
meat/meet
plane/plain
rode/road/rowed
sail/sale
stare/stair
we'd/weed
we'll/wheel
hole/whole
wear/ware/where
one/won
flower/flour
right/write
your/you're
lye/lie
its/it's
not/knot
gate/gait
jeans/genes
time/thyme
son/sun
boy/buoy

hey/hay
made/maid
male/mail
nay/neigh
oh/owe
pail/pale
pair/pear/pare
peek/peak/pique
reed/read/Reid
so/sew/sow
root/route
shone/shown
aid/aide
add/ad
break/brake
cent/sent/scent
flee/flea
creak/creek
die/dye
fair/fare
hair/hare
heard/herd
night/knight
steel/steal
tail/tale
thrown/throne
fir/fur
waist/waste
week/weak
we've/weave
way/weigh
wait/weight
threw/through
Vail/veil/vale
aisle/I'll/isle
ball/bawl
beat/beet
bolder/boulder
course/coarse

serial/cereal
cheap/cheep
days/daze
dew/do/due
doe/dough
gray/Grey
heel/heal
horse/hoarse
ho/hoe
in/inn
need/kneed/knead
lone/loan
we/wee
ring/wring
peddle/petal/pedal
straight/strait
pole/poll
earn/urn
past/passed
sweet/suite
ore/or
rain/reign/rein
role/roll
sole/soul
seller/cellar
shoo/shoe
soar/sore
steak/stake
some/sum
tow/toe
vein/vane/vain
medal/metal/meddle
wrote/rote
forth/fourth
tea/tee
been/bin

sox/socks
board/bored

Mary/mary/merry
great/grate
plane/plain
seem/seam
knew/new
stair/stare
hour/our
rough/ruff
lie/lye
poor/pour
haul/hall
piece/peace
ant/aunt
flair/flare
mist/missed
mane/main
wail/whale/wale
died/dyed
manor/manner
pier/peer
Ann/an
tacks/tax
cash/cache
rap/wrap
maze/maize
air/heir
bail/bale
ail/ale
prays/praise
base/bass
faint/feint
wade/weighed
wave/waive
knave/nave
whet/wet
sell/cell
bell/belle
bowled/bold
bough/bow

bred/bread
tred/tread
guessed/guest
rest/wrest
beech/beach
real/reel
peel/peal
team/teem
leak/leek
sees/seas
sheer/shear
feet/feat
hymn/him
whit/wit
scents/cents/sense
tents/tense
gilt/guile
knit/nit
tic/tick
sight/site/cite
rye/wry
style/stile
might/mite
climb/clime
fined/find
side/sighed
tide/tied
vice/vise
awl/all
paws/pause
born/borne
chord/cord
foul/fowl
mall/maul
mourn/morn
rot/wrought
bomb/balm
bald/balled
browse/brows

*Use these homophones to play Homophone Rummy, Activity 7-21.

Plurals and Changes from *y* to *i*

Plurals With *es*

arches	crashes	kisses
beaches	crosses	lunches
bonuses	dishes	notches
bosses	flashes	passes
boxes	foxes	peaches
bushes	gases	pushes
brushes	guesses	
classes	inches	

Change *y* to *i*

babies	fries
berries	guppies
bodies	ladies
bunnies	parties
cities	pennies
copies	ponies
counties	supplies
fairies	trophies
flies	

Verbs for Inflected Ending Sorts

VCC		VVC	VCe E-drop		CVC Words That Double		Miscellaneous Verbs
help	chirp	need	lie				see/saw
jump	curl	wait	time	snare	stop	drip	fall/fell
want	dash	boat	live	adore	pat	fan	feel/felt
will	dust	shout	name	babble	sun	flop	find/found
ask	farm	cook	bake	bruise	top	grin	grow/grew
back	fold	head	care	cease	hop	grip	know/knew
talk	growl	meet	close	cruise	plan	mop	sing/sang
call	hunt	peek	love	fume	pot	plod	sleep/slept
thank	kick	bloom	move	grease	shop	rob	tell/told
last	land	cool	smile	grieve	trip	shrug	draw/drew
laugh	learn	cheer	use	pose	bet	sip	drink/drank
trick	nest	clear	hate	quote	cap	skin	feed/fed
park	lick	dream	hope	smoke	clap	skip	hear/heard
pick	lock	float	ice	rove	slip	slam	hold/held
plant	mark	flood	joke		snap	slap	keep/kept
rock	melt	fool	paste		spot	snip	stand/stood
start	scold	oil	phone	**Two-Syllable**	tag	sob	blow/blew
bark	patch	join	prove		thin	strip	break/broke
work	point	lean	race	arrive	trap	wrap	bring/brought
walk	print	mail	scare	escape	trot	zip	build/built
yell	quack	nail	share	excuse	tug	brag	buy/bought
wish	reach	moan	skate	nibble	wag	char	lay/laid
fill	rest	scream	stare	rattle	drop	chug	pay/paid
watch	touch	pour	taste	refuse	drum	hem	send/sent
guess	wash	sail	wave	amuse	fit	jog	speak/spoke
turn	wink	trail	blame	ignore	flap	mob	wear/wore
stand		zoom	bounce	retire	flip	plot	
smell			carve		grab	prop	
track			dance		hug	scar	
push			glance		jam	skim	
miss			hike		kid	slug	
pound			hire		log	stab	
paint			serve		map	throb	
act			score		nap	whiz	
add			solve		nod	blot	
bang			sneeze		pin	chat	
crash			trace		pop	scan	
belong			trade		bob	slop	
crack			vote		rub	strum	
block			drape		beg	swap	
bowl			fade		blur	swat	
count			graze		bud		
brush			praise		chip	Exceptions:	
bump			rhyme		chop	box	
burn			scrape		crop	fix	
climb			seize		dim	wax	
camp			shave		dip	row	
			shove			chew	

Words Their Way Appendix © 2000 by Prentice-Hall, Inc.

VCCV, VCCV Doublet, C/VC, CV/C, VCCCV, VV

VCCV			VCCV Doublet	C/VC	CV/C	CV/C	VCCCV
First Syllable Accent	pilgrim	*Second Syllable Accent*	*First Syllable Accent*	*First Syllable Accent*	*First Syllable Accent*	*Second Syllable Accent*	constant
after	picture	absorb	attic	baby	cabin	around	dolphin
artist	plastic	admire	better	hoping	planet	because	laughter
border	powder	admit	blizzard	writer	finish	before	pilgrim
carpet	problem	although	blossom	basic	robin	believe	instant
chapter	public	complete	button	even	magic	beyond	complain
chimney	pumpkin	compose	cabbage	waving	limit	decide	hundred
dentist	reptile	confess	copper	bacon	cousin	demand	monster
elbow	rescue	confuse	cottage	chosen	prison	event	orchard
current	seldom	contain	dipper	moment	habit	hotel	orphan
canyon	sentence	disturb	fellow	raking	punish	prepare	public
harvest	signal	enjoy	foggy	human	cover	pretend	purchase
barber	sister	forget	follow	pilot	manage	prevent	
basket	subject	ignore	common	silent	medal	remain	**VV**
cactus	Sunday		funny	season	promise	repair	
canyon	temper		happen	navy	closet	resist	create
capture	thunder		mammal	music	camel	return	riot
carpet	trumpet		message	female	cavern	select	liar
center	turkey		office	stolen	comet		fuel
chapter	twenty		pattern	robot	dozen		poem
children	umpire		sudden	crater	finish		diary
chimney	under		tennis	climate	habit		area
compass	walnut		traffic	duty	honest		trial
contest	welcome		tunnel	famous	level		radio
costume	whimper		valley	female	lever		cruel
dentist	window		village	fever	lizard		diet
dolphin	winter		hollow	final	modern		variety
doctor	wonder			flavor	never		neon
fabric	plastic		*Second Syllable Accent*	humid	oven		video
garden	organ		attack	labor	palace		meteor
harvest	lumber		balloon	legal	panel		champion
hammer	carpet		dessert	local	panic		violin
helmet	perfect			music	rapid		annual
husband	master			pirate	robin		casual
injure	thirty			private	shovel		
insect	fellow			program	solid		
lumber	enter			recent	stomach		
market	harvest			rumor	timid		
master	index			siren	topic		
monster	insect			solar	travel		
morning	problem			spiral	vanish		
napkin	rescue			vacant	visit		
number	seldom				volume		
orbit	sentence				wagon		
order	signal				weather		
pardon	thunder						
pencil	turkey						
person	velvet						
picnic	welcome						

Final Unstressed Syllables

al	il/ile	el	le		er		ar
central	April	angel	able	hurdle	banner	manner	beggar
crystal	civil	barrel	ample	hustle	barber	peddler	burglar
cymbal	council	bagel	angle	juggle	bigger	plumber	cellar
dental	evil	bushel	ankle	jungle	blister	poster	cedar
fatal	fossil	camel	apple	kettle	border	printer	cheddar
feudal	gerbil	cancel	battle	knuckle	cancer	quicker	collar
final	lentil	channel	beagle	little	cheaper	racer	cougar
focal	nostril	chapel	beetle	maple	cider	ranger	dollar
formal	pencil	diesel	bottle	middle	cleaner	shower	grammar
global	peril	flannel	bramble	needle	clover	shopper	hangar
journal	pupil	funnel	bridle	noodle	cluster	skater	lunar
legal	stencil	gravel	bubble	noble	crater	soldier	molar
mammal	tonsil	hazel	buckle	paddle	dreamer	speaker	mortar
medal	docile	jewel	bundle	pebble	fiber	timber	pillar
mental	facile	kennel	bugle	people	farther	toaster	scholar
metal	fertile	kernel	candle	pickle	founder	trooper	sugar
nasal	fragile	label	castle	purple	freezer	trouser	calendar
naval	futile	level	cattle	puzzle	gentler	usher	circular
neutral	hostile	model	cable	riddle	grocer	voter	muscular
normal	missile	morsel	chuckle	saddle	jogger	younger	peculiar
oval	mobile	nickel	circle	sample	ledger	composer	
pedal	sterile	novel	cradle	scribble	liter	consumer	
petal		panel	cripple	settle	litter	employer	
plural		parcel	cuddle	single	lumber	officer	
rascal		quarrel	cycle	steeple		cylinder	
rival		ravel	dimple	struggle		disaster	
royal		satchel	doodle	stumble			
rural		sequel	double	tackle			
sandal		shovel	eagle	tickle			
scandal		shrivel	fable	title			
signal		squirrel	fiddle	triple			
spiral		swivel	freckle	trouble			
tidal		tinsel	fumble	twinkle			
total		towel	gamble	turtle			
vandal		travel	gargle	waffle			
vital		tunnel	gentle	whistle			
vocal		vessel	grumble	wrinkle			
		vowel	handle				

or		ure	cher	et		it
actor	error	motor	capture	archer	basket	magnet	audit
anchor	equator	neighbor	creature	bleacher	blanket	midget	bandit
author	favor	razor	culture	butcher	bucket	planet	credit
armor	governor	rumor	feature	catcher	budget	poet	digit
color	honor	sailor	fracture	pitcher	carpet	puppet	edit
cursor	horror	scissors	juncture	preacher	closet	racket	exit
director	juror	senior	lecture	rancher	comet	scarlet	habit
doctor	humor	splendor	mixture	stretcher	cricket	secret	hermit
donor	mayor	sponsor	moisture	teacher	faucet	skillet	limit
editor	meteor	tailor	nature		fidget	sonnet	merit
	mirror	terror	pasture		gadget	tablet	orbit
		tractor	picture		hatchet	target	profit
		traitor	posture		helmet	thicket	rabbit
		tremor	puncture		hornet	toilet	spirit
		tutor	texture		jacket	trumpet	summit
		vapor	torture		locket	velvet	unit
		visitor				wallet	visit
							vomit

Words Their Way Appendix © 2000 by Prentice-Hall, Inc.

Spelling the /er/ Sound in Stressed and Unstressed Syllables

First Syllable Accent

				Second Syllable Accent	First Syllable Accent	Second Syllable Accent
certain	birdbath	burglar	jury	alert	northern	surprise
merchant	birthday	bursting	plural	emerge	western	perhaps
mermaid	circle	curly	purchase	exert	eastern	surround
nervous	chirping	cursor	purpose	prefer	southern	pursue
person	dirty	curtain	sturdy	reverse	expert	survive
serpent	firmly	turtle	surface	reserve	lantern	
service	girlfriend	during	surgeon	observe	concert	
version	thirsty	purple	Thursday		modern	
	whirlwind	further	turkey		govern	
		burrow	current			
		furnace	hurry			
		furnish	purring			
		gurgle	burro			
		hurdle				

Unaccented Final /n/ Syllables

ain	*an*	*en*	*in*	*on*
captain	human	frighten	basin	apron
certain	organ	garden	cabin	button
curtain	orphan	kitten	cousin	cannon
fountain	slogan	often	margin	common
mountain	urban	sharpen	pumpkin	dragon
	woman	shorten	raisin	gallon
		spoken	robin	pardon
		sweeten		person
		thicken		reason
		widen		season
				salmon
				wagon

ure   Use these lists in You're Up/Password, Activity 8-10 .

/ch r/		/shoor/	/j r/	/yoor/	/zh r/	/cher/ (for contrast)
culture	nurture	assure	conjure	endure	leisure	archer
capture	rapture	ensure	injure	failure	measure	butcher
creature	sculpture	insure	procedure	obscure	closure	catcher
denture	stature	pressure		secure	pleasure	marcher
feature	stricture	fissure		manicure	treasure	poacher
fixture	texture	brochure		insecure		preacher
fracture	tincture	enclosure				rancher
future	torture	exposure				scorcher
gesture	venture	reassure				stretcher
juncture	adventure	composure				teacher
lecture	departure	disclosure				
mature	furniture					
mixture	indenture					
moisture	premature					
picture	signature					
pasture	immature					
posture	miniature					
puncture	overture					
nature	aperture					

Prefixes and Suffixes

mis	*pre*	*re*	*un*	*dis*
misbehave	precook	rebound	unable	disable
misconduct	predate	recall	unafraid	disagreeable
miscount	prefix	recapture	unarmed	disappear
misdeed	pregame	recharge	unbeaten	disarm
misfit	preheat	reclaim	unbroken	discharge
misgivings	prejudge	recopy	uncertain	disclose
misguide	premature	recount	unclean	discolor
misjudge	prepay	recycle	unclear	discomfort
mislay	preschool	reelect	uncommon	discontent
mislead	preset	refill	uncover	discover
mismatch	preteen	refinish	undone	dishonest
misplace	pretest	reform	unequal	disinfect
misprint	preview	refresh	unfair	dislike
misspell	prewash	relearn	unkind	disloyal
mistake		remind	unlike	disobey
mistreat		remodel	unlock	disorder
mistrust		renew	unpack	
misuse		reorder	displace	disregard
misspell		repay	unreal	disrespect
misjudge		reprint	unripe	distaste
		research	unselfish	distrust
		restore	unstable	
		retrace	unsteady	
		return	untangle	
		review	untie	
		rewrite	unwrap	

ly	*y*	*er/est*	*less*	*ful*
badly	breezy	blacker/blackest	ageless	careful
barely	bumpy	bigger/biggest	breathless	cheerful
bravely	chilly	bolder/boldest	careless	colorful
closely	choppy	braver/bravest	ceaseless	fearful
coarsely	cloudy	calmer/calmest	endless	graceful
constantly	dirty	closer/closest	helpless	harmful
costly	dusty	cheaper/cheapest	homeless	hopeful
cowardly	easy	cleaner/cleanest	lawless	lawful
cruelly	floppy	cooler/coolest	painless	peaceful
deadly	frosty	colder/coldest	powerless	playful
directly	gloomy	dirtier/dirtiest	priceless	powerful
eagerly	greasy	easier/easiest	reckless	tasteful
finally	grouchy	fewer/fewest	spotless	thoughtful
frequently	injury	finer/finest	tasteless	truthful
loudly	noisy	funnier/funniest		useful
loyally	rainy	harder/hardest		wasteful
proudly	sandy	hotter/hottest		wonderful
really	soapy	juicier/juiciest		youthful
smoothly	snowy	lazier/laziest		beautiful
angrily	stormy	lighter/lightest		
busily	sweaty	louder/loudest		
easily	thirsty	larger/largest		
happily	windy	meaner/meanest		
		nearer/nearest		
		newer/newest		
		noisier/noisiest		
		prettier/prettiest		
		quicker/quickest		
		sadder/saddest		
		smaller/smallest		
		thinner/thinnest		

Words Their Way Appendix © 2000 by Prentice-Hall, Inc.

Word List of Accented Syllables

This list is used in Stressbusters, a board game on page 243, Activity 8-19.

First Syllable	Second Syllable	Third Syllable
anything	December	constitution
somebody	November	population
beautiful	October	planetarium
families	September	Sacramento
grandfather	uncommon	Tallahassee
January	unusual	understand
libraries	unwanted	imitation
Wednesday	protection	regulation
wonderful	reduction	California
populate	romantic	definition
acrobat	unable	diagnosis
amateur	providing	hippopotamus
aptitude	vacation	irrigation
architect	whoever	Mississippi
artery	accountant	declaration
avalanche	agility	exclamation
calculator	amphibian	
cantaloupe	apprentice	
comedy	asparagus	
customer	attorney	
engineer	computer	
evidence	election	
forestry	endurance	
generator	executive	
improvise	erosion	
iodine	ignition	
meteorite	judicial	
navigator	mechanic	
average	banana	
camera	department	
carpenter	important	
everything	deliver	
colorful	remember	
gasoline	whenever	
everywhere	tomorrow	
hamburger	abilities	
	apartment	
	companion	
	condition	

ence and *ance*

These lists can be used to play Defiance or Patience, Activity 9-13.

ent	*ence*	*ency*	other
patient	patience		
silent	silence		
impatient	impatience		
present	presence		
evident	evidence		
iridescent	iridescence		
incident	incidence		
adolescent	adolescence		
diligent	diligence		
prominent	prominence		
florescent	florescence		
absent	absence		
innocent	innocence		
turbulent	turbulence	turbulency	
belligerent	belligerence	belligerency	
translucent	translucence	translucency	
confident	confidence		confide
obedient	obedience		obey
different	difference		differ
magnificent	magnificence		magnify
violent	violence		violate
coincident	coincidence		coincide
phosphorescent	phosphorescence		phosphorous
reverent	reverence		revere
subsequent	subsequence		sequel
competent	competence	competency	compete
excellent	excellence	excellency	excel
independent	independence	independency	depend
dependent	dependence	dependency	depend
convenient	convenience	conveniency	convene
persistent	persistence	persistency	persist
correspondent	correspondence	correspondency	correspond
resident	residence	residency	reside
equivalent	equivalence	equivalency	equal

ant	*ance*	*ancy*	other
constant		constancy	
tenant		tenancy	
vagrant		vagrancy	
dormant		dormancy	
distant	distance		
grievant	grievance		grief
instant	instance		
fragrant	fragrance	fragrancy	
valiant	valiance	valiancy	
brilliant	brilliance	brilliancy	
buoyant	buoyance	buoyancy	buoy
vibrant	vibrance	vibrancy	vibrate
vacant		vacancy	vacate

Words Their Way Appendix © 2000 by Prentice-Hall, Inc.

Three and Four Syllables

attendant	attendance		attend
assistant	assistance		assist
important	importance		import
defiant	defiance		defy
arrogant	arrogance		arrogate
dominant	dominance		dominate
ambulant	ambulance		ambulate/tory
ignorant	ignorance		ignore
vigilant	vigilance		vigil
significant	significance		signify
elegant	elegance	elegancy	
hesitant	hesitance	hesitancy	hesitate
reluctant	reluctance	reluctancy	reluct
expectant	expectance	expectancy	expect
radiant	radiance	radiancy	radiate
abundant	abundance	abundancy	abound
resistant	resistance	resistancy	resist

ary, ery, and ory

These lists can be used to play Which Suffix?, Activity 9-12.

ary	*ary*	*ory*
customary	anniversary	allegory
fragmentary	boundary	auditory
extraordinary	documentary	category
hereditary	elementary	dormitory
imaginary	glossary	explanatory
legendary	salary	inventory
literary	summary	observatory
military		territory
missionary	*ery*	
necessary	artery	
ordinary	bribery	
revolutionary	celery	
secretary	discovery	
solitary	gallery	
stationary	grocery	
temporary	imagery	
vocabulary	machinery	
	mystery	
ery	nursery	
cemetery	scenery	
stationery	surgery	

ory
compulsory
cursory
directory
memory
satisfactory
theory
victory

Sample Word Sorts

Word Family Sort for *et* and *en*

pet	wet	jet
ten	pen	net
hen	men	vet
(image)	(image)	(image)
(image)	(image)	(image)
(image)	(image)	(image)

Within Word Pattern Sort 1

Short-e CVC
Long-e CVC EE
Long-e CVC EA
1 pair of homophones

(web image)	(mouth image)	see
feel	fell	tree
meat	fed	read
leak	bee	sled
seen	leap	free
sea	jeep	neck
bleed	seat	mess
treat	feet	sweet
help	team	

brick	panic	picnic
music	limerick	flick
cowlick	trick	basic
homesick	arctic	attic
quick	classic	chopstick
comic	fabric	drastic
fantastic	yardstick	garlic
gimmick	magic	Pacific

Words Their Way Appendix © 2000 by Prentice-Hall, Inc.

Within Word Pattern Sort 2		Long-a CVVC *ai* Long-a CVV *ay* L-controlled *al* 1 oddball
rain	may	call
small	pail	pain
play	say	mail
tail	hay	said
wall	clay	gray
day	tall	talk
walk	stay	sail
fall	snail	train

GAMEBOARDS

Figures A-7 through A-13 are gameboard templates that can be used to create some of the games described throughout the book. Note that there are two sides for each gameboard. When the two sides are placed together they form a continuous track or path. These games can be adapted for many different features and for many different levels. Here are some general tips on creating the games.

1. The gameboards can be photocopied and mounted on manila file folders (colored ones are nice), making them easy to create and store. All the materials needed for the game, such as spinners, word cards, or game markers, can be put in plastic bags or envelopes labeled with the name of the game and stored in the folder. You might mark the flip side of word cards in some way so that lost cards can be returned to the correct game. Rubber stamp figures work well.

2. When mounting a gameboard in a folder be sure to leave a slight gap (about an eighth of an inch) between the two sides so that the folder will still fold. If you do not leave this gap the paper will buckle. Trim the gameboards to line up neatly or cut out the entire path.

3. A variety of things can be used for game markers or pawns that the children will move around the board such as buttons, plastic discs, coins, and bottle caps. Flat objects store best in the folders or you may just want to put a collection of game markers, dice, and spinners in a box. This box can be stored near the games, and students can take what they need.

4. Add pizazz to the games with pictures cut from magazines or old workbooks, stickers, comic characters, clip art, and so on. Rubber stamps, your drawings, or children's drawings can be used to add interest and color. Create catchy themes such as Rabbit Race, Lost in Space, Through the Woods, Mouse Maze, Rainforest Adventure, and so forth.

5. Include directions and correct answers (when appropriate) with the game. They might be stored inside along with playing pieces or glued to the game itself.

6. Label the spaces around the path or track according to the feature you want to reinforce, and laminate for durability. If you want to create open-ended games that can be adapted to a variety of features, laminate the path before you label the spaces. Then you can write in letters or words with a washable overhead pen and change them as needed. Permanent marker can also be used and removed with hairspray or fingernail polish remover.

7. Add interest to the game by labeling some spaces with special directions (if you are using a numbered die or spinner) or add cards with special directions to the deck of words. Directions might offer the students a bonus in the form of an extra turn or there might be a penalty such as lose a turn. These bonus or penalty directions can tie in with your themes. For example, in the Rainforest Adventure the player might forget a lunch and be asked to go back to the starting space. Keep the reading ability of your children in mind as you create these special directions.

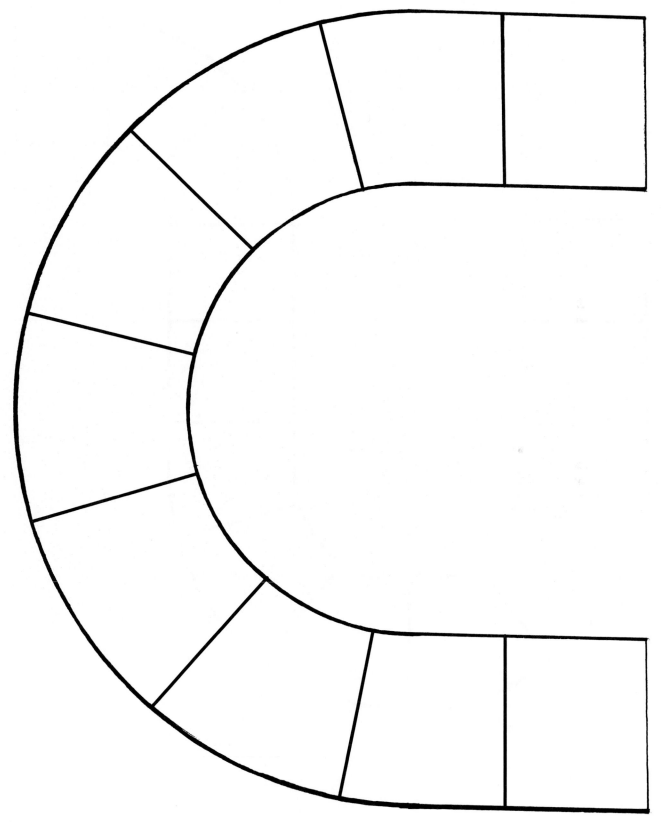

FIGURE A-7 Racetrack Gameboard (left and right)

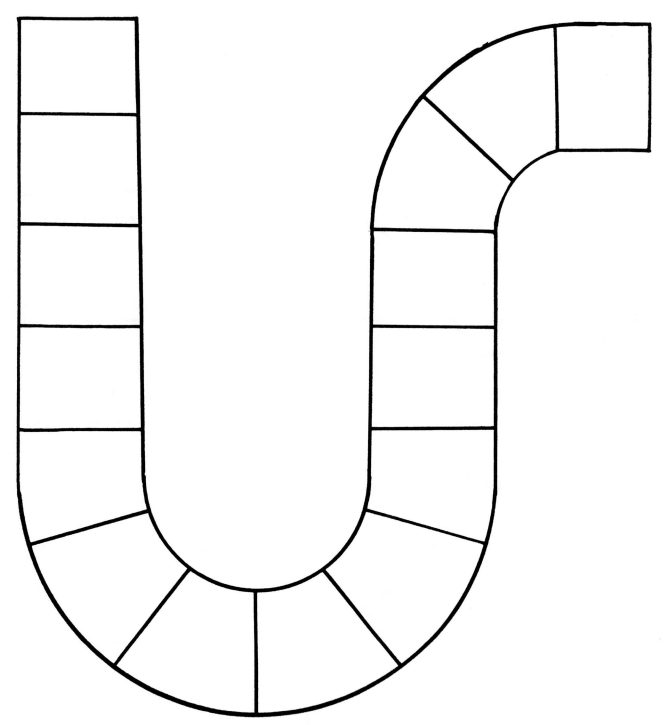

FIGURE A-8   U-gameboard (left)

Words Their Way Appendix © 2000 by Prentice-Hall, Inc.

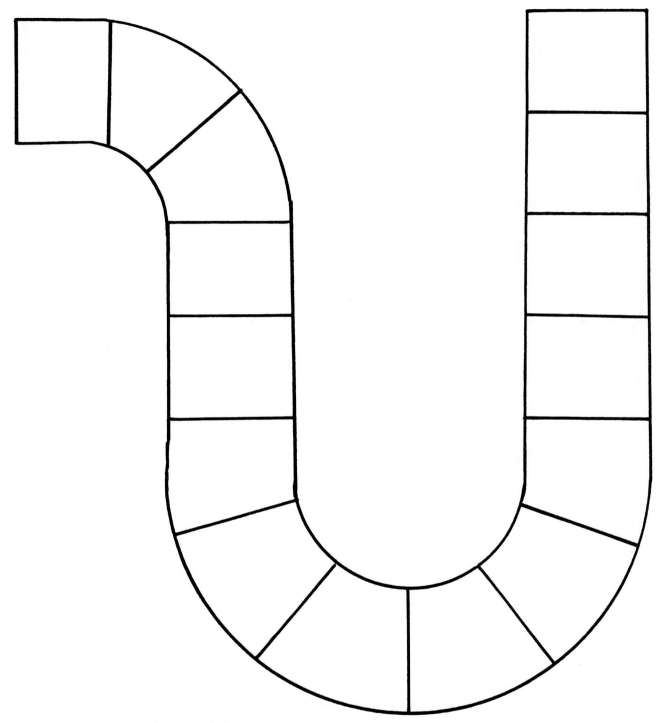

FIGURE A-9   U-gameboard (right)

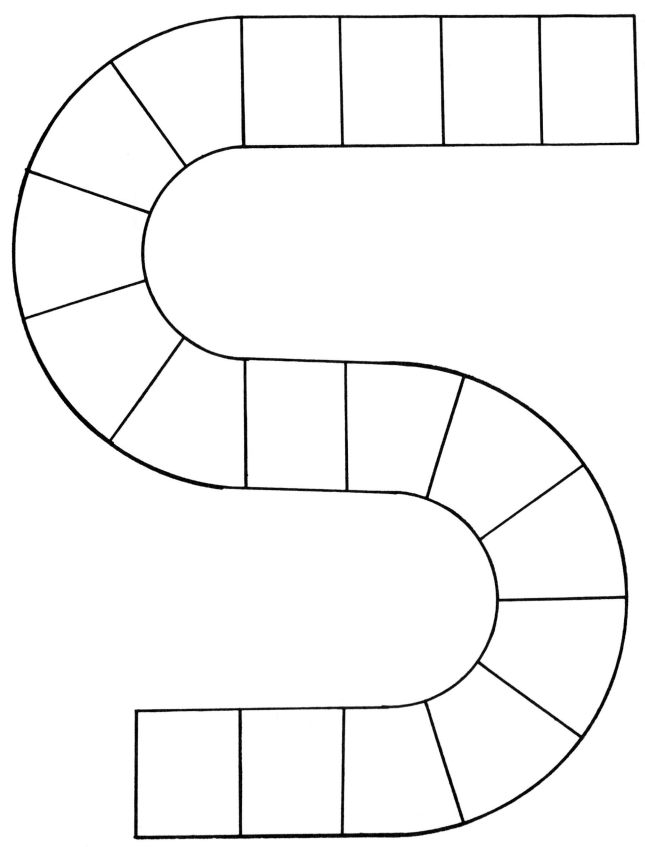

FIGURE A-10 S-gameboard (left)

Words Their Way Appendix © 2000 by Prentice-Hall, Inc.

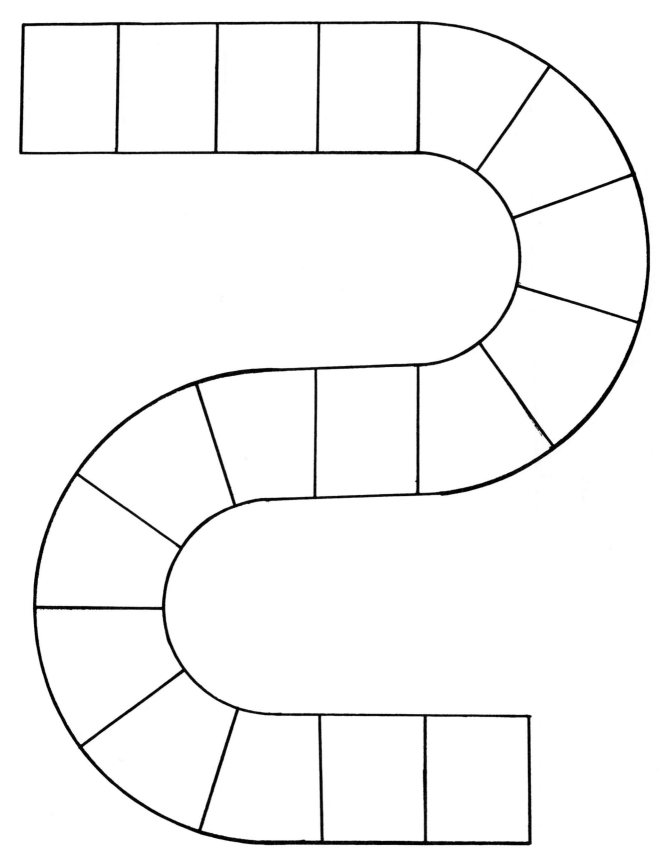

FIGURE A-11   S-gameboard (right)

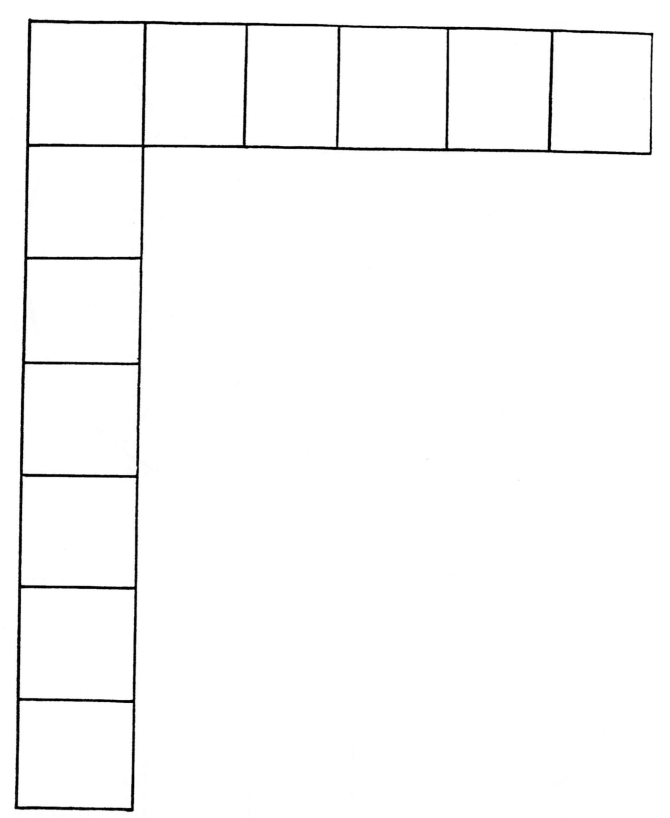

FIGURE A-12 Rectangle Gameboard (left)

Words Their Way Appendix © 2000 by Prentice-Hall, Inc.

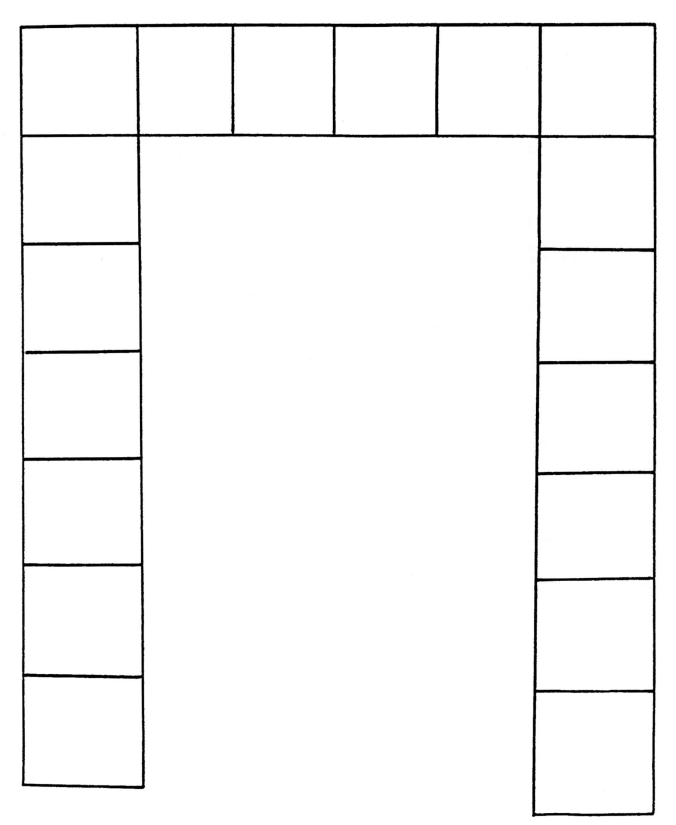

FIGURE A-13 Rectangle Gameboard (right)

Spinners

Many of the word study games described in this book use a game spinner. Figure A-14 provides simple directions for making a spinner.

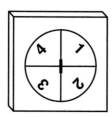

1. Glue a **circle** (patterns or cutouts below) onto **heavy cardboard** that is no smaller than 4" x 4".

2. Cut a narrow slot in the center with the point of a sharp pair of scissors or a razor blade.

pointer
pattern

3. Cut the pointer from **soft plastic** (such as a milk jug) and make a clean round hole with a **hole punch**.

4. A **washer,** either a metal one from the hardware store or one cut from cardboard, helps the pointer move freely.

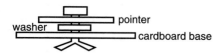

washer
pointer
cardboard base

5. Push a **paper fastener** through the pointer hole, the washer, and the slot in the spinner base. Flatten the legs, leaving space for the pointer to spin easily.

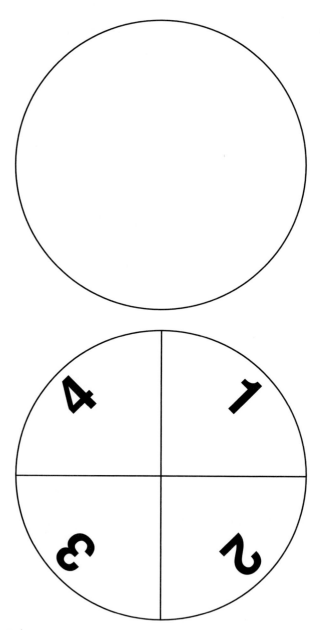

FIGURE A-14   Directions for Making a Game Spinner

RESOURCES

Children's Literature*

Asimov, I. (1960). *Words from the myths*. Boston: Houghton Mifflin.

Barchas, S. E. (1975). *I was walking down the road.* Illustrated by Jack Kent. New York: Scholastic.

Bauer, M. D. (1986). *On my honor.* New York: Clarion.

Carle, E. (1974). *My very first book of shapes.* New York: HarperCollins.

Dahl, R. (1982). *The BFG.* New York: Trumpet Club.

D'Aulaire, I., & D'Aulaire, E. (1980). *D'Aulaires' book of Greek myths.* Doubleday.

Fisher, L. (1984). *The Olympians: Great gods and goddesses of ancient Greece.* Holiday.

Galdone, P. (1973). *The three billy goats gruff.* New York: Clarion Books.

Gates, D. (1974). *Two queens of heaven: Aphrodite and Demeter.* Viking.

Heller, R. (1993). *Chickens aren't the only ones.* New York: Putnam.

Hoban, T. (1978). *Is it red? Is it yellow? Is it blue?* New York: Greenwillow Books.

Hoffman, P. (1990). *We play.* Illustrated by Sara Wilson. New York: Scholastic.

Langstaff, J. (1974). *Oh, a hunting we will go.* New York: Atheneum.

Lionni, L. (1969). *Alexander and the wind-up mouse.* New York: Pantheon.

Martin, B. (1983). *Brown bear, brown bear, what do you see?* New York: Henry Holt.

Martin, B., & Archambault, J. (1989). *Chicka chicka boom boom.* Illustrated by Lois Ehlert. New York: Simon & Schuster.

McLenighan, V. (1982). *Stop-go, fast-slow.* Chicago: Children's Press.

O'Dell, S. (1989). *Black star, bright dawn.* Boston: Houghton Mifflin.

Parish, P. (1981). *Amelia Bedelia.* New York: Avon.

Raffi (1976). *Singable songs for the very young.* Universal City, CA: Troubadour Records.

Raffi (1985). *One light, one sun.* Universal City, CA: Troubadour Records.

Seuss, Dr. (1974). *There's a wocket in my pocket.* New York: Random House.

Sharmat, M. *Gregory the terrible eater.* New York: Four Winds Press.

Shaw, N. (1986). *Sheep in a jeep.* Boston: Houghton Mifflin.

Shaw, N. (1992). *Sheep on a ship.* Boston: Houghton Mifflin.

Slepian, J., & Seidler, A. (1967). *The hungry thing.* Illustrated by Richard E. Martin. New York: Follet.

Slepian, J., & Seidler, A. (1987). *The cat who wore a pot on her head.* New York: Scholastic.

Slepian, J., & Seidler, A. (1990). *The hungry thing returns.* New York: Scholastic.

Steig, W. (1978). *Amos and Boris.* New York: Farrar, Straus and Giroux.

Straus, B., & Friedman, H. (1987). *See you later alligator: A first book of rhyming word play.* New York: Trumpet Club.

Taylor, T. (1993). *Timothy of the cay.* San Diego, CA: Harcourt Brace.

Wallner, J. (1987a). *City mouse–country mouse.* New York: Scholastic.

Wallner, J. (1987b). *The country mouse and the city mouse and two more mouse tales from Aesop.* New York: Scholastic.

Wells, N. (1980). *Noisy Nora.* New York: Dial Press.

White, E. B. (1945). *Stuart Little.* New York: Harper Row.

Bibliography of Word Study Books

Allen, M. S., & Cunningham, M. (1999). *Webster's new world rhyming dictionary.* New York: Simon & Schuster.

Almond, J. (1995). *Dictionary of word origins: A history of the words, expressions, and cliches we use.* New Jersey: Carol Publishing Group.

Asimov, I. (1959). *Words of science, and the history behind them.* Boston: Houghton Mifflin.

Asimov, I. (1961). *Words from the myths.* Boston: Houghton Mifflin.

Asimov, I. (1962). *Words on the map.* Boston: Houghton Mifflin.

Ayers, D. M. (1986). *English words from Latin and Greek elements* (2nd ed.). Tucson: University of Arizona.

Ayto, J. (1990). *Dictionary of word origins.* New York: Arcade Publishing.

Black, D. C. (1988). *Spoonerisms, sycophants and sops: A celebration of fascinating facts about words.* New York: Harper & Row.

Byson, B. (1990). *The mother tongue: English and how it got that way.* New York: Morrow.

Byson, B. (1994). *Made in America: An informal history of the English language in the United States.* New York: Morrow.

Ciardi, J. (1980). *A browser's dictionary: A compendium of curious expressions and intriguing facts.* New York: Harper & Row.

Collis, H. (1981). *Colloquial English.* New York: Regents Pub.

Collis, H. (1986). *American English idioms.* Illinois: Passport Books.

Cummings, D. W. (1988). *American English spelling.* Baltimore: Johns Hopkins University Press.

Folsom, M. (1985). *Easy as pie: A guessing game of sayings.* New York: Clarion.

Franlyn, J. (1987). *Which is witch?* New York: Dorset Press.

Funk, C. E. (1948). *A hog on ice and other curious expressions.* New York: Harper & Row.

---

*See Chapter 5 for rhyme and ABC books.

Funk, C. E. (1955). *Heavens to Betsy and other curious sayings.* New York: Harper & Row.

Funk, W. (1954). *Word origins and their romantic stories.* New York: Grosset and Dunlap.

Gwynne, F. (1970). *The kind who rained* (homophones). New York: Simon & Schuster.

Gwynne, F. (1976). *A chocolate moose for dinner* (homophones). New York: Simon & Schuster.

Gwynne, F. (1980). *A sixteen hand horse* (homophones). New York: Simon & Schuster.

Gwynne, F. (1988). *A little pigeon toad* (homophones). New York: Simon & Schuster.

Harrison, J. S. (1987). *Confusion reigns.* New York: St. Martin's Press.

Heacock, P. (1989). *Which word when?* New York: Dell Pub.

Heller, R. (1987). *A cache of jewels and other collective nouns.* New York: Grosset & Dunlap.

Heller, R. (1988). *Kites sail high.* New York: Grosset & Dunlap.

Heller, R. (1989). *Many luscious lollipops: A book about adjectives.* New York: Grosset & Dunlap.

Heller, R. (1990). *Merry-go-round: A book about nouns.* New York: Grosset & Dunlap.

Heller, R. (1991). *Up, up and away: A book about adverbs.* New York: Grosset & Dunlap.

Heller, R. (1995). *Behind the mask: A book about prepositions.* New York: Grosset & Dunlap.

Hoad, T. F. (1986.) *The concise Oxford dictionary of English etymology.* New York: Oxford University Press.

Kennedy, J. (1996). *Word stems.* New York: Soho Press.

Kingsley, C. (1980). *The heroes.* Mayflower.

Lewis, N. (1983). *Dictionary of correct spelling.* New York: Harper & Row.

Maestro, G. (1983). *Riddle romp.* New York: Clarion.

Maestro, G. (1984). *What's a frank frank? Easy homograph riddles.* New York: Clarion.

Maestro, G. (1985). *Razzle-dazzle riddles.* New York: Clarion.

Maestro, G. (1986). *What's mite might? Homophone riddles to boost your word power.* New York: Clarion.

Maestro, G. (1989). *Riddle roundup: A wild bunch to beef up your word power.* New York: Clarion.

Partridge, E. (1984). *Origins: A short etymological dictionary of modern English.* New York: Greenwich House.

Pei, M. (1965). *The story of language.* Philadelphia: Lippincott and Company.

Presspon, L. (1997). *A dictionary of homophones.* New York: Barrons.

Randall, B. (1992). *When is a pig a hog? A guide to confoundingly related English words.* New York: Prentice Hall.

Room, A. (1992). *A NTC's dictionary of word origins.* Lincolnwood, IL: National Textbook.

Safire, W. (1984). *I stand corrected: More on language.* New York: Avon.

Sarnoff, J., & Ruffins, R. (1981). *Words: A book about word origins of everyday words and phrases.* New York: Charles Scribner's Sons.

Schleifer, R. (1995). *Grow your own vocabulary: By learning the roots of English words.* New York: Random House.

Scragg, D. G. (1974). *A history of English spelling.* Manchester, England: Manchester University Press.

Shipley, J. T. (1967). *Dictionary of word origins.* MD: Rowman & Littlefield.

Shipley, J. (1984). *The origins of English words.* Baltimore: Johns Hopkins University Press.

The Oxford English Dictionary on CD-Rom (1994). Oxford: Oxford University Press.

The American heritage book of English usage: A practical and authoritative guide to contemporary English. (1996). Boston: Houghton Mifflin.

The Scholastic dictionary of synonyms, antonyms, homonyms. (1965). New York: Scholastic.

The Scholastic rhyming dictionary. (1994). New York: Scholastic.

Terban, M. (1982). *Eight ate: A feast of homonym riddles.* New York: Clarion.

Terban, M. (1983). *In a pickle and other funny idioms.* New York: Clarion.

Terban, M. (1984). *I think I thought and other tricky verbs.* New York: Clarion.

Terban, M. (1986). *Your foot's on my feet! and other tricky nouns.* New York: Clarion.

Terban, M. (1987). *Mad as a wet hen! and other funny idioms.* New York: Clarion.

Terban, M. (1988). *The dove dove: Funny homograph riddles.* New York: Clarion.

Terban, M. (1988). *Guppies in tuxedoes: Funny eponyms.* New York: Clarion.

Terban, M. (1988). *Too hot to hoot: Funny palindrome riddles.* New York: Clarion.

Terban, M. (1991). *Hey, hay! A wagonful of funny homonym riddles.* New York: Clarion.

Terban, M. (1992). *Funny you should ask: How to make up jokes and riddles with wordplay.* New York: Clarion.

Venezky, R. L. (1999). *The American way of spelling: The structure and origins of American English Orthography.* New York: Guilford Press.

Webster's dictionary of word origins. (1992). New York: Smithmark.

Weiner, S. (1981). *Handy book of commonly used American idioms.* New York: Regents Pub.

GLOSSARY

advanced readers   Highly skilled readers and writers capable of reading different genres of texts for different purposes with speed, accuracy, and comprehension. Advanced readers acquire an advanced Greek- and Latin-derived vocabulary particular to specific fields of study. See also *specialized readers* or *derivational relations spelling stage.*

affix   Most commonly a suffix or prefix attached to a base word, stem, or root.

affixation   The process of attaching a word part, such as a prefix or suffix, to a base word, stem, or root.

affricate   A speech sound produced when the breath stream is stopped and released at the point of articulation, usually where the tip of the tongue rubs against the roof of the mouth just behind the teeth when pronouncing the final sound in the word *clutch* or the beginning sound in the word *trip.*

alliteration   The occurrence in a phrase or line of speech of two or more words having the same beginning sound.

alphabetic   A writing system containing characters or symbols representing sounds.

alphabetic layer of instruction   The first layer of word study instruction focusing on letters and letter-sound correspondences.

alternation patterns   The regular pattern of change in moving from one form of a word to another. *Admire/admiration, perspire/perspiration,* and *declare/declaration* form a consistent pattern of change in moving from one form of the word to another.

articulation   How sounds are shaped in the mouth during speech. The ways sounds are articulated guides some invented spellings. Some confusions are made in spelling based on similarities in articulation (e.g., *tr* for *dr*).

assimilated/absorbed prefixes   The spelling and sound of the consonant in a prefix has been assimilated into the same spelling and sound at the beginning of the base or root to which the prefix is affixed (e.g., *ad + tract = attract*).

base word   A word to which prefixes and/or suffixes are added. For example, the base word of *unwholesome* is *whole.*

beginning period of literacy development   A period of literacy development that begins when students have a concept of word and can make sound-symbol correspondences. This period is noted for disfluent reading and writing, and letter name–alphabetic spelling.

blends   An orthographic term referring to consonant blends. Consonant blends are made of two- or three-letter sequences that are blended together. There are l-blends (*bl, cl, fl, gl, pl, sl*), r-blends (*br, cr, dr, fr, gr, pr, tr*), and s-blends (*sc, scr, sk, sp, st, squ, sw*). Although the letter-sounds are blended together quickly, each one is pronounced. A two-letter blend represents two sounds; a three-letter blend represents three sounds. Consonant blends occurring at the beginning of words are *onsets,* and as such, are treated orthographically as a unit. See *onset.*

buddy sorts   A picture or word sort done with a partner.

center time/center work   Work completed independently in prepared areas within a classroom.

checklist   A form, available in the appendix, used for conducting feature analyses of spelling samples. See *feature analysis.*

choral reading   Oral reading done in unison with another person or persons.

circle time   See *circle work.*

circle work   Group work conducted under the teacher's direction.

classroom composite   A classroom profile that organizes children into instructional groups by spelling stage and by features to be taught within each stage.

closed sorts   Word sorts that classify words into predetermined categories.

closed syllable   A closed syllable ends with or is "closed" by a consonant sound. In polysyllabic words, a closed syllable contains a short vowel sound that is closed by two consonants (*rabbit, racket*). See *open syllable.*

cloze An activity in which children supply a single missing word in the middle or end of a sentence, as in, "the cat sat on the _____." Usually the omitted word can be predicted by the recurring rhyming pattern and/or by supplying the initial consonant sound, as in, "the cat sat on the m_____."

complex consonant patterns Consonant units occurring at the end of words that correspond to the vowel sound in the middle of the word. Final *tch* corresponds to the short vowel sound in the middle of *fetch* and *scotch*, while final *ch* corresponds to the long vowel sound in the middle of *peach* and *coach*. Other complex consonant patterns include final *ck* (*pack* vs. *peak*) and final *dge* (*badge* vs. *cage*).

compound words Words made up of two or more smaller words. A compound word may or may not be hyphenated, depending on its part of speech.

concept of word The ability to match spoken words to printed words as demonstrated by the ability to point to the words of a memorized text while reading. This demonstration must include one or more two-syllable words.

concept sorts A categorization task in which pictures, objects, or words are grouped together by shared attributes or meanings. A concept and vocabulary development activity.

connotation/connotative The associative meaning of words—what words suggest to an individual and how they make an individual feel. For example, the word *sick* to a particular individual may suggest extreme discomfort and depression; to another, the word may suggest bad taste, as in a "sick" joke. See *denotation/denotative*.

consonant alternation The process in which the pronunciation of consonants changes in the base or root of derivationally related words, while the spelling does not change. For example, the silent-to-sounded pattern in the words *sign* and *signal*; the /k/ to /sh/ pattern in the words *music* and *musician*.

consonants Students often learn what consonants are by what they are not: they are not vowels (*a, e, i, o,* and *u*). Where vowel sounds are thought of as musical with resonance, consonant sounds are known for their noise and the way in which air is constricted as it is stopped and released or forced through the vocal tract, mouth, teeth, and lips.

continuant sound A consonant sound, such as /s/ or /m/, that can be prolonged as long as the breath lasts without distorting the sound quality.

cut and paste activities A variation of picture sorting in which students cut out pictures from magazines or catalogs and paste them into categories.

CVC A spelling pattern referring to a sequence of letters in a consonant-vowel-consonant order. The CVC pattern is associated with the short vowel sound.

denotation/denotative The literal meaning of words; what words refer to. For example, the word *sick* refers to or denotes the condition of not being well. See *connotation/connotative*.

derivational relations spelling stage The last stage of spelling development in which spellers learn about derivational relationships preserved in the spelling of words. *Derivational* refers to (a) the process by which new words are created from existing words, chiefly through affixation; and (b) the development of a word from its historical origin. *Derivational constancy* refers to spelling patterns that remain the same despite changes in pronunciation across derived forms. *Bomb* retains the *b* from *bombard* because of its historical evolution.

developmental classroom profiles A class roster arranged by developmental spelling stages. These profiles are used to plan small-group word study activities.

developmental level One of five stages of spelling development: emergent, letter name–alphabetic, within word pattern, syllables and affixes, or derivational relations.

digraph Two letters that represent one sound. There are consonant digraphs and vowel digraphs, though the term most commonly refers to consonant digraphs. Common consonant digraphs include *sh, ch, th,* and *wh*. Consonant digraphs at the beginning of words are *onsets*.

diphthong A complex speech sound beginning with one vowel sound and moving to another within the same syllable. The *oy* in *boy* is a diphthong as is the *oi* in *noise*.

directed reading-thinking activities (DRTAs) A strategy for developing comprehension processes during reading. The strategy is a variation of a predict-read-prove routine.

directionality The left-to-right direction used for reading and writing English.

draw and label activities A variation of picture sorting in which students draw pictures of things that begin with the sounds under study. The pictures are drawn in the appropriate categories and labeled with the letter(s) corresponding to that sound.

echo reading Oral reading in which the student echoes or imitates the reading of the teacher or buddy. Echo reading is used with very beginning readers as a form of support and as a default option when the text is too hard. Echo reading can also be used to model fluent reading.

emergent A period of literacy development ranging from birth to beginning reading. This period precedes the letter name–alphabetic stage of spelling development.

eponyms Places, things, and actions that are named after an individual.

error guide A sample of spelling errors arranged by spelling stages that enables teachers to place children in instructional groups.

etymology The study of the origin and historical development of words.

familiarity The degree to which a student already knows something about a text to be read. Familiarity comes from prior experience with the text, or with an event described in the text. Familiarity is also defined by the closeness of match between the language of the text and the language of the child.

feature analysis   More than scoring for just right and wrong, feature analyses provide a way of interpreting children's spelling errors by taking into account their knowledge of specific orthographic features such as consonant blends or short vowels. Feature analyses inform teachers what spelling features to teach to whom.

fingerpoint reading   Refers to the kind of reading that emergent and beginning readers do, using a finger to point to each word as it is spoken.

frustration level   A dysfunctional level of instruction where there is a mismatch between instruction and what an individual is able to grasp. This mismatch precludes learning and often results in frustration.

generative   An approach to word study that emphasizes processes that apply to many words, as opposed to an approach that focuses on one word at a time.

homographs   Words that are spelled alike, but have different pronunciations and different meanings, e.g., "*tear* a piece of paper" and "to shed a *tear*"; "*lead* someone along" and "the element *lead*."

homonyms/homophones   Words that sound alike, are spelled differently, and have different meanings, e.g., *bear* and *bare, pane* and *pain,* and *forth* and *fourth.*

independent level   That level of academic engagement in which an individual works independently, without need of instructional support. Independent-level behaviors demonstrate a high degree of accuracy, speed, ease, and fluency.

instructional level   A level of academic engagement in which instruction is comfortably matched to what an individual is able to grasp.

intermediate readers   Intermediate readers are fluent readers and writers whose word recognition of one- and two-syllable words is automatic. Intermediate readers are grappling with a more advanced vocabulary involving meaning units such as prefixes and suffixes. Intermediate readers negotiate unfamiliar genres and expository texts typical of the upper elementary and middle grades. Intermediate readers are spellers learning about syllables and affixes.

invariance   Spelling features which do not vary, but remain constant.

juncture   Syllable juncture refers to the transition from one syllable to the next. Frequently this transition involves a spelling change such as consonant doubling or dropping the final-e before adding *ing.*

key pictures   Pictures placed at the top of each category in a picture sort. Key pictures act as headers for each column and can be used for analogy.

key words   Words placed at the top of each category in a word sort. Key words act as headers for each column and can be used for analogy.

language experience   An approach to the teaching of reading in which students read about their own experiences recorded in their own language. Experience stories are dictated by the student to a teacher who writes them down. Dictated accounts are reread in unison, in echo fashion, and independently. Known words are lifted out of context and grouped by various phonic elements.

lax   Lax vowels are commonly known as the short vowel sound.

letter name–alphabetic spelling stage   The second stage of spelling development in which students represent beginning, middle, and ending sounds of words with phonetically accurate letter choices. Often the selections are based on the sound of the letter name itself, rather than abstract letter-sound associations. The letter name *h* (aitch), for example, produces the /ch/ sound, and is often selected to represent that sound rather than the abstract /huh/.

liquids   The consonant sounds for /r/ and /l/ are referred to as liquids because, unlike other consonant sounds, they do not obstruct air in the mouth. The sounds for /r/ and /l/ are more vowel-like in that they do not involve direct contact between the lips, tongue, and the roof of the mouth as other consonants do. Instead, they sort of roll around in the mouth, as if liquid.

long vowels   Every vowel (a, e, i, o, and u) has two sounds, commonly referred to as "long" and "short." The long vowel sound "says its letter name." The vocal chords are tense when producing the long vowel sound. Because of this, the linguistic term for the long vowel sound is *tense.*

meaning layer of information   The third layer of English orthography including meaning units such as prefixes, suffixes, and word roots. These word elements were acquired primarily during the Renaissance when English was overlaid with many words of Greek and Latin derivation.

memory reading   An accurate recitation of text accompanied by fingerpoint reading. See *fingerpoint reading.*

metaphor   A word or phrase that means one thing is used, through implication, to refer to something else. For example, "His remark created a blizzard of controversy." See *simile.*

mock linear   Writing characteristic of the emergent stage of spelling development in which the linear arrangement of written English is mimicked in long rows of letter-like shapes and squiggles.

morphemic   Refers to morphemes, or meaning units in the spelling of words, such as the suffix *ed* which signals past tense, or the root *graph* in the words *autograph* or *graphite.*

nasals   A sound produced when the air is blocked in the oral cavity but escapes through the nose. The first consonants in the words *mom* and *no* represent nasal sounds.

oddballs   Exception words that do not fit the targeted letter-sound or pattern feature.

onset   The onset of a single syllable or word is the initial consonant(s) sound. The onset of the word *sun* is /s/. The onset of the word *slide* is /sl/.

open sorts   A type of picture or word sort in which the categories for sorting are left open. Students sort pictures or words into groups according to the students' own judgment. Open sorts are useful for determining what word features are salient for students.

open syllable   An open syllable ends with a long vowel sound (*labor, reason*). See *closed syllable.*

orthography/orthographic   Orthography refers to the writing system of a language, specifically, the correct sequence of letters, characters, or symbols.

pattern   Letter sequences that function as a unit and are related to a consistent category of sound. Frequently these patterns form rhyming families, as in the *ain* of *Spain, rain,* and *drain.*

pattern layer of information   The second layer or tier of English orthography in which patterns of letter sequences, rather than individual letters themselves, represent vowel sounds. This layer of information was acquired during the period of English history following the Norman Invasion. Many of the vowel patterns of English are of French derivation.

pattern sort   A word sort in which students categorize words according to similar spelling patterns.

personal readers   Individual books of reading materials that beginning readers can read with good accuracy. Group experience charts, dictations, and rhymes comprise the majority of the reading material.

phoneme   The smallest unit of speech that distinguishes one word from another. For example, the *t* of *tug* and the *r* of *rug* are two English phonemes.

phonemic awareness   Refers to the ability to consciously separate individual phonemes in a spoken language. Phonemic awareness is often assessed by the ability to tap or push a penny forward for every sound heard in a word like *cat:* /c/ /a/ /t/.

phonics   The systematic relationship between letters and sounds.

phonics readers   Beginning reading books that are leveled in difficulty and contain recurring phonics elements.

phonograms   Often called *word families,* phonograms end in high-frequency rimes that require only a beginning consonant sound to make a word. For example, *ack, ight, aw,* and *all* are all high-frequency phonograms.

phonological awareness   An awareness of various speech sounds such as syllables, rhyme, and individual phonemes.

picture sort   A categorization task in which pictures are sorted into categories of similarity and difference. Pictures may be sorted by sound or by meaning. Pictures cannot be sorted by pattern.

picture-sorting activities   Various categorization games and routines using picture cards. Picture-sorting activities are all variations on the process of compare and contrast.

preconsonantal nasals   Nasals that occur before consonants, as in the words *bump* or *sink.* The vowel is nasalized as part of the air escapes through the nose during pronunciation. See *nasals.*

prefix   An affix attached at the beginning of a base word or word root.

pretend reading   A paraphrase or spontaneous retelling told by children as they turn the pages of a familiar storybook.

prosody/prosodic   The musical qualities of language, including intonation, expression, stress, and rhythm.

rimes   A rime unit is composed of the vowel and any following consonants within a syllable. For example, the rime unit in the word *tag* would be *ag.*

r-influenced vowels   In English, when an *r* colors the way the preceding vowel is pronounced. For example, compare the pronunciation of the vowels in *bar* and *bad.* The vowel in *bar* is influenced by the *r.*

root word/roots   Root word is most often used as a synonym for *base word. Roots* also refer to Greek roots or word parts of Greek origin that are often combined with other roots to form words such as *telephone* (*tele* and *phone*).

scaffold   A form of support. The familiar structures of oral language offer a form of support for beginning readers.

schwa   A vowel sound ə in English that often occurs in an unstressed syllable, such as the /uh/ sound in the first syllable of the word *above.*

seat work   School work that is completed independently at the student's own desk. Students are already familiar with whatever seat work is assigned. Seat work is usually on a student's independent level and is usually assigned for practice. See *independent level.*

short-term word banks   Word banks are collections of known words recognized immediately out of context. Short-term word banks are words that are not consistently recognized out of context. Words in the short-term word bank are promoted to word bank status when consistently recognized out of context or, conversely, are discarded if they remain problematic.

short vowels   Every vowel (a, e, i, o, and u) has two sounds, commonly referred to as "long" and "short." The vocal chords are more relaxed when producing the short vowel sound, as opposed to the long vowel sound. See *long vowels.* Because of this, short vowel sounds are often referred to as *lax.* The short vowel sound for a is the same sound you hear at the beginning of *apple.* The short vowel sound for e is the same sound you hear at the beginning of *Ed.* The short vowel sound for i is the same sound you hear at the beginning of *igloo.* The short vowel sound for o is the same sound you hear at the beginning of *octopus.* The short vowel sound for u is the same sound you hear at the beginning of *umbrella.*

sight words   Words recognized and pronounced immediately "at first sight." The term *sight words* does not necessarily mean high-frequency words, phonetically irregular words, or lists of words. A sight word is simply any *known* word, regardless of its frequency or phonetic regularity.

simile Two unlike things are explicitly compared, usually with the words *like* or *as*. For example, "Her tousled hair was like an explosion in a spaghetti factory." See *metaphor*.

sound See *sound sort*.

sound board Charts used by letter name–alphabetic spellers that contain pictures and letters for the basic sound-symbol correspondences (e.g., the letter *b*, a picture of a bell, and the word *bell*). Individual copies of sound boards are given to students for easy reference, and sound board charts are posted so students can refer to them as they write. Sound boards are provided in the appendix.

sound sort Sorts that ask students to categorize pictures or words by sound as opposed to visual patterns.

specialized readers Proficient readers whose reading speeds exceed 250 to 300 words per minute and vary thereafter according to interest and background knowledge. Specialized readers encounter derivational vocabulary of Greek and Latin origin. Vocabulary growth begins to specialize according to academic discipline, personal interest, or profession.

spectrograph An acoustic record of sound levels present in speech. We can see how speech is organized in contours through a spectrograph.

speed sorts Pictures or words that are sorted under a timed condition. Students try to beat their own time.

spelling-by-stage classroom organization chart Another form of a classroom composite sheet that places children in a developmental spelling stage.

spelling-meaning connections Words that are related in meaning often share the same spelling despite changes in pronunciation from one form of the word to the next. The word *sign*, for example, retains the *g* from *signal* even though it is not pronounced, thus "signaling" the meaning connection through the spelling.

stems Word parts, usually of Latin origin, that cannot stand alone, but are used in combination with other word parts in words related in meaning. Latin stems carry consistent though abstract meanings and can appear in various positions in words. For example, the Latin stem *spect* means roughly "to look at" or "to watch" and occurs at the beginning of the word *spectator,* the end of the word *inspect*, and the middle of the word *respectable.*

suffix An affix attached at the end of a base word or word root.

syllable patterns The alternating patterns of consonants (C) and vowels (V) at the point where syllables meet. For example, the word *rabbit* follows a VCCV syllable pattern at the point where the syllables meet.

syllables Units of spoken language that consist of a vowel that may be preceded and/or followed by several consonants. Syllables are units of sound and can often be detected by paying attention to movements of the mouth. Syllabic divisions indicated in the dictionary are not always correct since the dictionary will always separate meaning units regardless of how the word is pronounced. For example, the proper syllable division for the word *naming* is *na-ming.* However, the dictionary divides this word as *nam-ing* in order to separate the *ing.*

syllables and affixes stage The fourth stage of spelling development which coincides with intermediate reading. Syllables and affixes spellers learn about the spelling changes which often take place at the point of transition from one syllable to the next. Frequently this transition involves consonant doubling or dropping the final-e before adding *ing.* See *juncture.*

synchrony Occurring at the same time. In this book, stages of spelling development are described in the context of reading and writing behaviors occurring at the same time.

tense A tense vowel sound is commonly known as the long vowel sound. Long vowel sounds are produced by tensing the vocal chords.

tracking The ability to fingerpoint read a text, demonstrating concept of word.

transitional stage of literacy development A period of literacy development when learners are becoming fluent in reading easy materials. Silent reading becomes the preferred mode of reading. There is some expression in oral reading. This stage is between the beginning and intermediate stages of literacy development. The transitional period corresponds to the within word pattern stage of spelling development.

unaccented Unstressed syllables. The final unstressed syllable in words such as *label* and *doctor*, have no distinct vowel sound.

unvoiced A sound that, when produced, does not necessitate the vibration of the vocal chords. See *vibrate.*

voiced A sound that, when produced, vibrates the vocal chords. The letter-sound *d*, for example, vibrates the vocal chords in a way that the letter-sound *t* does not. See *unvoiced.*

vowel A speech sound produced by the easy passage of air through a relatively open vocal tract. Vowels form the most central sound of a syllable. In English, vowel sounds are represented by the following letters: *a, e, i, o, u,* and sometimes *y.* See *consonants.*

vowel alternation The process in which the pronunciation of vowels changes in the base or root of derivationally related words, while the spelling does not change. For example, the long-to-short vowel change in the related words *crime* and *criminal*; the long-to-schwa vowel change in the related words *impose* and *imposition.*

vowel digraphs See *digraph.*

vowel marker A silent letter used to indicate the sound of the vowel. In English, silent letters are used to form patterns associated with specific vowel sounds. Vowel markers are usually vowels themselves, as the *i* in *drain* or the *a* in *treat,* but they can also be consonants, as the *l* in *told.*

within word pattern spelling stage   The third stage of spelling development that coincides with the transitional period of literacy development. Within word pattern spellers have mastered the basic letter-sound correspondences of written English, and they grapple with letter sequences which function as a unit, especially long vowel patterns. Some of the letters in the unit may have no sound themselves. These silent letters, such as the silent-e in *snake* or the silent-i in *drain,* serve as important markers in the pattern.

word   A unit of meaning. A word may be a single syllable or a combination of syllables. A word may contain smaller units of meaning within it. In print, a word is separated by white space. In speech, several words may be strung together in a breath group. For this reason, it takes a while for young children to develop a clear concept of word. See *concept of word.*

word bank   A collection of known words harvested from frequently read texts such as little leveled books, dictated stories, basal preprimers, and primers. Word bank words are *sight words.*

word cards   Known words are written on 2-by-1-inch pieces of cardstock. Words students can recognize with ease are used in word study games and word sorts.

word hunts   A word study activity in which students are sent back to texts they have previously read to hunt for other words that follow the same spelling features examined during the word or picture sort.

word root   A Greek or Latin element to which affixes are attached, for example, *cred, dict, fract, phon.* A word root usually cannot stand alone as a word. See *stems.*

word sort   A basic word study routine in which students group words into categories. Word sorting involves comparing and contrasting within and across categories. Word sorts are often cued by key words placed at the top of each category. See *key words.*

word study   Word study is a learner-centered, conceptual approach to instruction in phonics, spelling, word recognition, and vocabulary.

word study notebooks   Notebooks in which students write their word sorts into columns and add other words that follow similar spelling patterns throughout the week. Word study notebooks are organized around the orthographic features students are studying. Within word pattern students have sections of their notebooks dedicated to long vowel sounds and patterns. Students in the syllables and affixes stage have sections dedicated to lists of different prefixes and suffixes (e.g., *es* words and *tion* words). Derivational relations students collect words by their common meanings (e.g., words that have *ter* in them: *terrain, terrestrial*).

writing sorts   A writing sort often follows a word sort. Students write key words as headings of columns. Word cards are jumbled up and called out. Students write the words they hear under the appropriate key word and column. See *key words.*

zone of proximal development (ZPD)   A term coined by the Russian psychologist Vygotsky referring to the ripe conditions for learning something new. A person's ZPD is that zone which is neither too hard nor too easy. The term is similar to the concept of *instructional level.*

REFERENCES

Adams, M.J. (1990). *Beginning to read: Thinking and learning about print.* Cambridge, MA: MIT Press.

Anders, P., & Bos, C. (1986). Semantic feature analysis: An interactive strategy for vocabulary development and text comprehension. *Journal of Reading, 29,* 610–616.

Ashton-Warner, S. (1963). *Teacher.* New York: Simon & Schuster.

Ayers, D.W. (1986). *English words from Latin and Greek elements* (2nd ed.). Tucson: University of Arizona Press.

Ball, E.W., & Blachman, B.A. (1988). Phoneme segmentation training: Effect on reading readiness. *Annals of Dyslexia, 38,* 208–225.

Baretta-Lorton, M.L. (1968). *Math their way.* Reading, MA: Addison-Wesley.

Barnes, G.W. (1989). Word sorting: The cultivation of rules for spelling in English. *Reading Psychology, 10,* 293–307.

Barone, D. (1989). Young children's written responses to literature: The relationship between written response and orthographic knowledge. In S. McCormick & J. Zutell (Eds.), *Cognitive and social perspectives for literacy research and instruction* (pp. 371–380). Chicago: National Reading Conference.

Barone, D. (1990). The written responses of young children: Beyond comprehension to story understanding. *The New Advocate, 3*(1), 49–56.

Bear, D. (1982). *Patterns of oral reading across stages of word knowledge.* Unpublished manuscript, University of Virginia, Charlottesville.

Bear, D. (1988). *"On the hurricane deck of a mule": Teaching adults to read using language-experience and oral history techniques.* A manual distributed by the Nevada Literacy Coalition & University of Nevada-Reno. (ERIC Document Reproduction Service No. ED 294-155)

Bear, D. (1991a). Copying fluency and orthographic development. *Visible Language, 25*(1), 40–53.

Bear, D. (1991b). "Learning to fasten the seat of my union suit without looking around": The synchrony of literacy development. *Theory Into Practice, 30*(3), 149–157.

Bear, D. (1992). The prosody of oral reading and stage of word knowledge. In S. Templeton & D. Bear (Eds.), *Development of orthographic knowledge and the foundations of literacy: A memorial Festschrift for Edmund H. Henderson* (pp. 137–186). Hillsdale, NJ: Lawrence Erlbaum.

Bear, D., & Barone, D. (1989). Using children's spellings to group for word study and directed reading in the primary classroom. *Reading Psychology, 10*(3), 275–292.

Bear, D., & Cathey, S. (1989, November). *Reading fluency in beginning readers and expression in practiced oral reading: Links with word knowledge.* Paper presented at National Reading Conference, Austin, TX.

Bear, D., & McIntosh, M. (1990). Directed reading-thinking activities to promote reading and study habits in social studies. *Social Education, 54*(6), 385–388.

Bear, D., Templeton, S., & Warner, M. (1991). The development of a qualitative inventory of higher levels of orthographic knowledge. In J. Zutell & S. McCormick (Eds.), *Learner factors/teacher factors: Issues in literacy research and instruction: Fortieth yearbook of the National Reading Conference* (pp. 105–110). Chicago: NRC.

Bear, D., Truex, P., & Barone, D. (1989). In search of meaningful diagnoses: Spelling-by-stage assessment of literacy proficiency. *Adult Literacy and Basic Education, 13*(3), 165–185.

Bear, D.R., & Barone, D. (1998). *Developing literacy: An integrated approach to assessment and instruction.* Boston: Houghton Mifflin.

Bear, D.R., & Templeton, S. (1998). Explorations in developmental spelling: Foundations for learning and teaching phonics, spelling, and vocabulary. *The Reading Teacher, 52,* 222–242.

Beck, I.L., & McKeown, M. (1991). Conditions of vocabulary acquisition. In R. Barr, M.L. Kamil, P. Mosenthal, & P.D. Pearson (Eds.), *Handbook of reading research* (Vol. 2, pp. 789–814). White Plains, NY: Longman.

Beers, J.W., & Henderson, E. (1977). A study of developing orthographic concepts among first graders. *Research in the Teaching of English, 11,* 133–148.

Blachman, B.A. (1994). What we have learned from longitudinal studies of phonological processing and reading, and some unanswered questions: A response to Torgeson, Wagner, and Rashotte. *Journal of Learning Disabilities, 27,* 287–291.

Button, K., Johnson, M.J., & Furgerson, P. (1996). Interactive writing in a primary classroom. *The Reading Teacher, 49,* 446–454.

Carle, E. (1987). *Have you seen my cat?* Picture Books LTD.

Cathey, S.S. (1991). *Emerging concept of word: Exploring young children's abilities to read rhythmic text.* Doctoral dissertation, University of Nevada. Reno, UMI #9220355.

Chall, J.S. (1983). *Stages of reading development.* New York: McGraw-Hill.

Chomsky, C. (1970). Reading, writing, and phonology. *Harvard Educational Review, 40*(2), 287–309.

Chomsky, C. (1971). Write first, read later. *Childhood Education, 47,* 296–299.

Chomsky, N., & Halle, M. (1968). *The sound patterns of English.* New York: Harper & Row.

Christelow, E. (1989). *Five little monkeys jumping on the bed.* Clarion Books.

Clarke, L.K. (1988). Invented versus traditional spelling in first graders' writing: Effects on learning to spell and read. *Research in the Teaching of English, 22,* 281–309.

Clay, M. (1975). *What did I write?* Exeter, NH: Heinemann.

Clay, M.M. (1991). Introducing a new storybook to young readers. *The Reading Teacher, 45,* 264–273.

Cole, M., & Scribner, S. (1978). *Mind in society.* Cambridge, MA: Harvard University Press.

Crystal, D. (1987). *The Cambridge encyclopedia of language.* New York: Cambridge University Press.

Cummings, D. (1988). *American English spelling.* Baltimore: Johns Hopkins University Press.

Cunningham, P. (1988). Names—A natural for early reading and writing. *Reading Horizons, 28,* 114–122.

Cunningham, P. (1995). *Phonics they use: Words for reading and writing.* Boston: Allyn & Bacon.

Cutler, A., Mehler, J., Norris, D., & Segui, J. (1987). Phoneme identification and the lexicon. *Cognitive Psychology, 19,* 141–177.

Dahl, R. (1988). *Fantastic Mr. Fox.* Puffin Books.

Dale, D., O'Rourke, J., & Bamman, H. (1971). *Techniques of teaching vocabulary.* Palo Alto, CA: Field Educational Enterprises.

Delpit, L.D. (1988). The silenced dialogue: Power and pedagogy in educating other people's children. *Harvard Educational Review, 58,* 280–298.

Ehri, L. (1992). Review and commentary: Stages of spelling development. In S. Templeton & D. Bear (Eds.), *Development of orthographic knowledge and the foundations of literacy: A memorial Festschrift for Edmund H. Henderson* (pp. 307–332). Hillsdale, NJ: Lawrence Erlbaum.

Ehri, L.C. (1993). How English orthography influences phonological knowledge as children learn to read and spell. In R.J. Scales (Ed.), *Literacy and language analysis* (pp. 21–43). Hillsdale, NJ: Lawrence Erlbaum.

Ehri, L.C. (1997). Learning to read and learning to spell are one and the same, almost. In C.A. Perfetti, L. Rieban, & M. Fayol (Eds.), *Learning to spell—Research, theory, and practice across languages* (pp. 237–269). Mahwah, NJ: Lawrence Erlbaum.

Ehri, L.C., & Wilce, L.S. (1980). Do beginning readers learn to read function words better in sentences or lists? *Reading Research Quarterly, 15,* 675–685.

Elkonin, D.B. (1973). U.S.S.R. In J. Downing (Ed.), *Comparative reading.* New York: Macmillan.

Estes, T. (1998). *Spanish spelling inventory.* htpp/:curry.edschool.Virginia.EDU/curry/centers/ciera/p4.html.

Ferreiro, E., & Teberosky, A. (1982). *Literacy before schooling.* Portsmouth, NH: Heinemann.

Frith, U. (1985). Beneath the surface of developmental dyslexia. In K. Patterson, J. Marshall, & M. Coltheart (Eds.), *Surface dyslexia: Neuropsychological and cognitive studies of phonological reading* (pp. 301–330). London: Lawrence Erlbaum.

Fromkin, V., & Rodman, R. (1993). *An introduction to language* (5th ed.). Fort Worth, TX: Harcourt Brace Jovanovich College Publishers.

Ganske, K. (1994). Developmental spelling analysis: A diagnostic measure for instruction and research (University of Virginia). *Dissertation Abstracts International, 55*(05), 1230A.

Gelb, I.J. (1963). *A study of writing* (2nd ed.). Chicago: University of Chicago Press.

Gibson, E.J. (1965). Learning to read. *Science, 148,* 1006–1072.

Gibson, J.J., & Yonas, P.M. (1968). A new theory of scribbling and drawing in children. In *The analysis of reading skill: A program of basic and applied research* (Final Report, Project No. 5-1213, Cornell University and the U.S. Office of Education, pp. 335–370). Ithaca, NY: Cornell University.

Gill, C. (1980). An analysis of spelling errors in French (Doctoral dissertation, University of Virginia, 1980). *Dissertation Abstracts International, 41*(09), 3924A. (University Microfilms No. 79-16, 258)

Gill, J., & Bear, D. (1988). No book, whole book, and chapter DR-TAs: Three study techniques. *Journal of Reading, 31*(5), 444–449.

Gill, J., & Bear, D. (1989). *Directions for upper level word study.* Unpublished paper.

Gill, J.T. (1992). Focus on research: Development of word knowledge as it relates to reading, spelling, and instruction. *Language Arts, 69*(6), 444–453.

Gillet, J., & Kita, M.J. (1978). Words, kids, and categories. *The Reading Teacher, 32,* 538–542.

Goswami, U. (1990). A special link between rhyming skill and the use of orthographic analogies by beginning readers. *Journal of Child Psychiatry, 31,* 301–311.

Goswami, U., & Bryant, P. (1990). *Phonological skills and learning to read.* E. Sussex, UK: Lawrence Erlbaum Associates, LTD.

Gough, P.B., & Hillenger, M.L. (1980). Learning to read: An unnatural act. *Bulletin of the Orton Society, 20,* 179–196.

Hall, M. (1980). *Teaching reading as a language experience.* Columbus, OH: Merrill.

Henderson, E. (1981). *Learning to read and spell: The child's knowledge of words.* DeKalb: Northern Illinois Press.

Henderson, E. (1990). *Teaching spelling* (2nd ed.). Boston: Houghton Mifflin.

Henderson, E. (1992). The interface of lexical competence and knowledge of written words. In S. Templeton & D. Bear (Eds.), *Development of orthographic knowledge and the foundations of literacy: A memorial Festschrift for Edmund H. Henderson* (pp. 1–30). Hillsdale, NJ: Lawrence Erlbaum.

Henderson, E., & Beers, J. (1980). *Developmental and cognitive aspects of learning to spell.* Newark, DE: International Reading Association.

Henderson, E., Estes, T., & Stonecash, S. (1972). An exploratory study of word acquisition among first graders at midyear in a language experience approach. *Journal of Reading Behavior, 4,* 21–30.

Henderson, E.H., & Templeton, S. (1986). The development of spelling ability through alphabet, pattern, and meaning. *Elementary School Journal, 86,* 305–316.

Horn, E. (1954). *Teaching spelling.* Washington, DC: National Education Association.

Invernizzi, M. (1985). *A cross-sectional analysis of children's recognition and recall of word elements.* Unpublished manuscript, University of Virginia, Charlottesville.

Invernizzi, M. (1992). The vowel and what follows: A phonological frame of orthographic analysis. In S. Templeton & D. Bear (Eds.), *Development of orthographic knowledge and the foundations of literacy: A memorial Festschrift for Edmund H. Henderson* (pp. 106–136). Hillsdale, NJ: Lawrence Erlbaum.

Invernizzi, M. (1993, April). *Orthographic development within the emergent reading stage.* Paper presented at the Early Childhood Association annual conference, Charlottesville, VA.

Invernizzi, M., Abouzeid, M., & Gill, T. (1994). Using students' invented spelling as a guide for spelling instruction that emphasizes word study. *Elementary School Journal, 95*(2), 155–167.

Invernizzi, M., Meier, J., Swank, L., & Juel, C. (1998). *Phonological awareness literacy screening: Teacher's manual.* Charlottesville, VA: University of Virginia Printing Services.

Invernizzi, M.A. (1992). The vowel and what follows: A phonological frame of orthographic analysis. In S. Templeton & D. Bear (Eds.), *Development of orthographic knowledge and the foundations of literacy: A memorial Festschrift for Edmund H. Henderson* (pp. 105–136). Hillsdale, NJ: Lawrence Erlbaum.

Jacobson, M. (1974, Spring). Predicting reading difficulty from spelling. *The Spelling Progress Bulletin,* 8–10.

James, W. (1958). *Talks to teachers on psychology and to students on some of life's ideals.* New York: Norton. (Original work published 1899)

Johnson, D., & Pearson, P.D. (1984). *Teaching vocabulary* (2nd ed.). New York: Holt, Rinehart, & Winston.

Johnston, F.R. (1998). The reader, the text, and the task: Learning words in first grade. *The Reading Teacher, 51,* 666–675.

Johnston, F.R., Invernizzi, M., & Juel, C. (1998). *Bookbuddies: Guidelines for volunteer tutors of emergent and beginning readers.* New York: Guilford Press.

Juel, C. (1991). Beginning reading. In R. Barr, M. Kamil, P. Mosenthal, & P.D. Pearson (Eds.), *Handbook of reading research* (Vol. II, pp. 759–788). New York: Longman Press.

Juel, C., & Roper/Schneider, D. (1985). The influence of basal readers on first grade reading. *Reading Research Quarterly, 18,* 306–327.

Just, M., & Carpenter, P. (1987). *The psychology of reading and language comprehension.* Boston: Allyn & Bacon.

Kamhi, A.G., & Catts, H.W. (1991). Language and reading: Convergences, divergences, and development. In A.G. Kamhi & H.W. Catts (Eds.), *Reading disabilities: A developmental language perspective* (pp. 1–34). Boston: Allyn & Bacon.

Koch, K. (1970). *Wishes, lies, and dreams: Teaching children to write poetry.* New York: Harper and Row.

Lenneberg, E. (1967). *Biological foundations of language.* New York: Wiley.

Liberman, I., & Shankweiler, D. (1991). Phonology and beginning reading: A tutorial. In L. Rieben & C. Perfetti (Eds.), *Learning to read: Basic research and its implication.* Hillsdale, NJ: Lawrence Erlbaum.

Lieberman, P. (1991). *Uniquely human.* Cambridge, MA: Harvard University Press.

Lundberg, I., Frost, J., & Peterson, O. (1988). Effects of an extensive program for stimulating phonological awareness in preschool children. *Reading Research Quarterly, 23,* 267–284.

Malinowski, B. (1952). The problem of meaning in primitive languages. In C.K. Ogden & I.A. Richards (Eds.), *The meaning of meaning* (10th ed.). New York: Harcourt.

McIntosh, M., & Bear, D. (1993, December). *The development of content-specific orthographic knowledge: A look at vocabulary in geometry.* Paper presented at the 43rd Annual National Reading Conference, Charleston, SC.

McKenzie, M.G. (1985). Shared writing: Apprenticeship in writing. *Language Matters, 1–2.* 1–5.

Morais, J., Cary, L., Alegria, J., & Bertelson, P. (1979). Does awareness of speech as a sequence of phonemes arise spontaneously? *Cognition, 7,* 323–331.

Morris, D. (1980). Beginning readers' concept of word. In E. Henderson & J. Beers (Eds.), *Developmental and cognitive aspects of learning to spell* (pp. 97–111). Newark, DE: International Reading Association.

Morris, D. (1981). Concept of word: A developmental phenomenon in the beginning reading and writing process. *Language Arts, 58*(6), 659–668.

Morris, D. (1982). "Word sort": A categorization strategy for improving word recognition ability. *Reading Psychology, 3,* 247–259.

Morris, D. (1992a). *Case studies in teaching beginning readers: The Howard Street tutoring manual.* Boone, NC: Stream Publications.

Morris, D. (1992b). Concept of word: A pivotal understanding in the learning to read process. In S. Templeton & D. Bear (Eds.), *Development of orthographic knowledge and the foundations of literacy: A memorial Festschrift for Edmund H. Henderson* (pp. 53–77). Hillsdale, NJ: Lawrence Erlbaum.

Morris, D. (1993). Concept of word and phoneme awareness in the beginning reader. *Research in the Teaching of English, 17,* 359–373.

Morris, D., & Perney, J. (1984). Developmental spelling as a predictor of first-grade reading achievement. *The Elementary School Journal, 84,* 441–457.

Morris, D., Blanton, L., Blanton, W., & Perney, J. (1995). Spelling instruction and achievement in six elementary classrooms. *The Elementary School Journal, 96,* 145–162.

Morris, D., Nelson, L., & Perney, J. (1986). Exploring the concept of "spelling instructional level" through the analysis of error-types. *Elementary School Journal, 87,* 181–200.

Nessel, D., & Jones, M. (1981). *The language-experience approach to reading.* New York: Teachers College Press.

Read, C. (1971). Pre-school children's knowledge of English phonology. *Harvard Educational Review, 41*(1), 1–34.

Read, C. (1975). *Children's categorization of speech sounds in English.* Urbana, IL: NCTE Research Report No. 17.

Read, C., & Hodges, R. (1982). Spelling. In H. Mitzel (Ed.), *Encyclopedia of educational research* (5th ed.). New York: Macmillan.

Read, C., Zhang, Y., Nile, H., & Ding, B. (1986). The ability to manipulate speech sounds depends on knowing alphabetic reading. *Cognition, 24,* 31–44.

Richgels, D. (1995). Invented spelling ability and printed word learning in kindergarten. *Reading Research Quarterly, 30*(1), 96–109.

Roberts, B.S. (1992). The evolution of the young child's concept of word as a unit of spoken and written language. *Reading Research Quarterly, 27*(2), 125–138.

Sawyer, D.J., Lipa-Wade, S., Kim, J., Ritenour, D., & Knight, D.F. (1997). *Spelling errors as a window on dyslexia.* Paper presented at the 1997 annual convention of the American Educational Research Association, Chicago.

Schlagal, R. (1992). Patterns of orthographic development into the intermediate grades. In S. Templeton & D. Bear (Eds.), *Development of orthographic knowledge and the foundations of literacy: A memorial Festschrift for Edmund H. Henderson* (pp. 31–52). Hillsdale, NJ: Lawrence Erlbaum.

Scragg, D. (1974). *A history of English spelling.* New York: Barnes & Noble Books, Manchester.

Shen, H.H. (1996). Spelling errors and the development of orthographic knowledge among Chinese-speaking elementary students (University of Nevada, Reno). *Dissertation Abstracts International, 57*(12), 5101A.

Smith, S.B., Simmons, D.C., & Kame'enui, E.J. (1995). *Synthesis of research on phonological awareness: Principles and implications for reading acquisition* (Tech. Rep. No. 21). National Center to Improve the Tools of Educators, University of Oregon, Eugene.

Snow, C.E. (1983). Literacy and language: Relationships during the preschool years. *Harvard Educational Review, 53*(2), 165–189.

Snow, C.E., Burns, M.S., & Griffin, P. (1998). *Preventing reading difficulties in young children.* Washington, DC: National Academy Press.

Southworth, F., & Chander, D. (1974). *Foundations of literacy.* New York: The Free Press/Macmillan.

Spenser, B. (1989). *The development of the young child's concept of word: A longitudinal study* [Monograph]. Newark, DE: International Reading Association.

Stanovich, K. (1986). Matthew effects in reading: Some consequences of individual differences in the acquisition of literacy. *Reading Research Quarterly, 21,* 360–406.

Stauffer, R. (1980). *The language-experience approach to the teaching of reading* (2nd ed.). New York: Harper and Row.

Stever, E. (1980). Dialect and spelling. In E.H. Henderson & J.W. Beers (Eds.), *Cognitive and developmental aspects of learning to spell English* (pp. 46–51). Newark, DE: International Reading Association.

Stever, E.F. (1981). Dialect in spelling. In E. Henderson & J. Beers (Eds.), *Developmental and cognitive aspects of learning to spell* (pp. 46–51). Newark, DE: International Reading Association.

Strickland, D., & Morrow, L. (1989). Environments rich in print promote literacy behavior during play. *Reading Teacher, 43,* 178–179.

Sulzby, E. (1986). Writing and reading organization. In W.H. Teale & E. Sulzby (Eds.), *Emergent literacy: Writing and reading* (pp. 50–89). Norwood, NJ: Abex.

Taft, M. (1991). Reading and the mental lexicon. London: Lawrence Erlbaum Associates.

Temple, C. (1978). *An analysis of spelling errors in Spanish.* Doctoral dissertation, University of Virginia, Charlottesville.

Templeton, S. (1976, December). *The spelling of young children in relation to the logic of alphabetic orthography.* Paper presented at the 26th annual convention of the National Reading Conference, Atlanta, GA.

Templeton, S. (1983). Using the spelling/meaning connection to develop word knowledge in older students. *Journal of Reading, 27*(1), 8–14.

Templeton, S. (1989). Tacit and explicit knowledge of derivational morphology: Foundations for a unified approach to spelling and vocabulary development in the intermediate grades and beyond. *Reading Psychology, 10,* 233–253.

Templeton, S. (1991a). Teaching and learning, the English spelling system: Reconceptualizing method and purpose. *Elementary School Journal, 92,* 185–201.

Templeton, S. (1991b). *Teaching the integrated language arts.* Boston: Houghton Mifflin.

Templeton, S. (1992). Theory, nature, and pedagogy of higher-order orthographic development in older children. In S. Templeton & D. Bear (Eds.), *Development of orthographic knowledge and the foundations of literacy: A memorial Festschrift for Edmund H. Henderson* (pp. 253–278). Hillsdale, NJ: Lawrence Erlbaum.

Templeton, S. (1997). *Teaching the integrated language arts* (2nd ed.). Boston: Houghton Mifflin.

Templeton, S., & Bear, D. (Eds.). (1992a). *Development of orthographic knowledge and the foundations of literacy: A memorial Festschrift for Edmund H. Henderson.* Hillsdale, NJ: Lawrence Erlbaum.

Templeton, S., & Bear, D. (1992b). Teaching the lexicon to read and spell. In S. Templeton & D. Bear (Eds.), *Development of orthographic knowledge and the foundations of literacy: A memorial Festschrift for Edmund H. Henderson.* (pp. 333–352). Hillsdale, NJ: Lawrence Erlbaum.

Templeton, S., & Morris, D. (1999). Questions teachers ask about spelling. *Reading Research Quarterly, 34,* 102–112.

Templeton, S., & Spivey, E.M. (1980). The concept of "word" in young children as a function of level of cognitive development. *Research in the Teaching of English, 14*(3), 265–278.

Treiman, R. (1985). Onsets and rimes as units of spoken syllables: Evidence from children. *Journal of Educational Psychology, 77*(4), 417–427.

Treiman, R. (1991). The role of intrasyllabic units in learning to read. In L. Rieben & C.A. Perfetti (Eds.), *Learning to read: Basic research and its implications* (pp. 149–160). Hillsdale, NJ: Lawrence Erlbaum.

Tunmer, W.E. (1991). Phonological awareness and literacy acquisition. In L. Rieben & C.A. Perfetti (Eds.), *Learning to read: Basic research and its implications* (pp. 105–120). Hillsdale, NJ: Lawrence Erlbaum.

Venesky, R. (1970). *The structure of English orthography.* The Hague: Mouton.

Viise, N. (1996). A study of the spelling development of adult literacy learners compared with that of classroom children. *Journal of Literacy Research, 28*(4), 561–587.

Viise, N. (1992). A comparison of child and adult spelling development (University of Virginia). *Dissertation Abstracts International, 54*(05), 1745A.

Vygotsky, L.S. (1962). *Thought and language.* Cambridge, MA: MIT Press.

White, T.G., Power, M.A., & White, S. (1989). Morphological analysis: Implications for teaching and understanding vocabulary growth. *Reading Research Quarterly, 24*(3), 283–304.

Wilde, S. (1991). *You kan red this!* Portsmouth, NH: Heinemann.

Wildsmith, B. (1982). *The cat on the mat.* New York: Oxford Press.

Worthy, J., & Viise, N. (1993). *Can we know what we know about children in teaching adults to read?* Unpublished paper.

Worthy, M.J., & Invernizzi, M. (1989). Spelling errors of normal and disabled students on achievement levels one through four: Instructional implications. *Bulletin of the Orton Society, 40,* 138–149.

Wylie, R.E., & Durrell, D.D. (1970). Teaching vowels through phonograms. *Elementary English, 47,* 787–791.

Wysocki, K., & Jenkins, J.R. (1987). Deriving word meanings through morphological generalization. *Reading Research Quarterly, 22,* 66–81.

Zutell, J. (1994). Spelling *instruction.* In A.C. Purves, L. Papa, & S. Jordan (Eds.), *Encyclopedia of English studies and language arts* (Vol. 2, pp. 1098–1100). New York: Scholastic.

Zutell, J., & Rasinski, T. (1989). Reading and spelling connections in third and fourth grade students. *Reading Psychology, 10,* 137–156.

INDEX